CRISIS MANAGEMENT AND THE SUPER-POWERS IN THE MIDDLE EAST

The Adelphi Library

Crisis Management and the Super-powers in the Middle East

ADELPHI LIBRARY 5

edited by

GREGORY TREVERTON

Assistant Director, IISS

Published for

THE INTERNATIONAL INSTITUTE FOR STRATEGIC STUDIES

by

Gower and ALLANHELD, OSMUN

Published by

Gower Publishing Company Limited, Westmead, Farnborough, Hampshire, England

and

Allanheld, Osmun & Co. Publishers, Inc. 6 South Fullerton Avenue, Montclair, New Jersey 07042, USA

British Library Cataloguing in Publication Data

Treverton, G.

   Crisis management and the super-powers in the Middle East — (Adelphi Library; 5)

   1. Near East — Politics and government — 1945—
   I. Title   II. Series
   956'.04   DS63.1
   ISBN 0-566-00347-3

Library of Congress Cataloging in Publication Data

Main entry under title:

Crisis management and the super-powers in the Middle East
   (The Adelphi Library; 5)
   Includes index

   1. Near East—Politics and government—1945—
   —Addresses, essays, lectures. 2. Jewish—Arab
   relations—1973— —Addresses, essays, lectures.

   I. Treverton, Gregory F. II. International Institute
   for Strategic Studies. III. Series: Adelphi Library; 5

   DS63.1.C74   327'.0956   80-67837
   ISBN 0-916672-73-5

Printed and bound in Great Britain

0 566 00347 3 (UK)
0-916672-73-5 (US)

CONTENTS

INTRODUCTION

Throughout the post-war period, the Middle East has been the world's most prominent area of crisis. The region has exemplified in a stark form the complicated tangle of interests and relationships that run through international politics: regional conflict and the continuing struggle for self-determination, the competition between the two superpowers, and increasing awareness of the West's dependence on imported resources, especially petroleum from the Middle East and the Persian Gulf. The 1973 Arab-Israeli War and the ensuing Arab oil embargo drove home that combination of factors. In 1978 another conjunction of events brought forward the old elements in a new form, and underscored the importance of a resolution to the problem that had been beneath the surface of the conflict for a long time—that of the Palestinians.

The elements of the Middle East crisis have gone through a number of combinations since the first Arab-Israeli war of 1948. What seemed at first a regional confrontation became increasingly in the 1950s a superpower issue, as the Soviet Union gained footholds in the Arab world, especially in Egypt. That phase culminated in the June War of 1967. The results of that war suggested that Soviet military assistance to the Arabs could not produce victory but could deny Israel the political fruits of her own military victory. The mix of superpower jockeying and regional conflict continued during the so-called 'Canal War' or 'War of Attrition' for the next six years, through a number of American-sponsored efforts to reach a political solution to the Arab-Israeli conflict.

The October War of 1973 marked the failure of those political efforts, and ushered in a new phase to the conflict. The 1973 War brought the United States and the Soviet Union closer to the brink of direct conflict than ever before. It also dented Israel's image of unquestioned military superiority. More important, it brought the Arab-Israeli conflict to the Persian Gulf, involving the moderate, pro-Western Arab states that had previously struggled to remain aloof. The oil embargo also demonstrated how dependent the Western world was on those Arab states. For the confrontation states, Egypt in particular, the war's outcome drove home the lesson that continued reliance on the Soviet Union would not achieve their political objectives, resulting in President Sadat's decision to curtail the Soviet presence in Egypt and turn increasingly to the United States.

The 1973 War underlined the Western interest in resolving the Arab-Israeli conflict, and provided impetus to American Secretary of State Kissinger's shuttle diplomacy between Cairo and Tel Aviv. That effort produced some results in the Sinai disengagement agreements, but at high cost: it revealed how difficult yet how necessary it was for the United States to put pressure on Israel to move towards accommodation with her Arab foes.

1

1978 saw yet another conjunction of events which reshaped the Middle East conflict. In frustration at the failure of American diplomacy and concern over the possibility of a renewed Soviet role, President Sadat made his historic visit to Israel in 1977. The process he began resulted in the Egyptian-Israeli accords signed at Camp David in late 1978. However, the ink on that agreement was scarcely dry before new events in the region called its future into question.

The revolution in Iran, culminating in the Shah's departure in January 1979, drove home again the instability and fragility of the region. With the Shah's downfall, the moderate Arab states, Saudi Arabia in particular, were all the more exposed to pressure because of the continuing conflict between Israel and the Arabs. As the peace process between Cairo and Tel Aviv moved forward, the tension shifted to the question of the Palestinians. Unless the bilateral peace agreement could be translated into a comprehensive framework that would provide a solution to the Palestinian problem, the moderate Arab states could not embrace it and would remain under increasing pressure, the Soviet Union would be provided with new opportunities, and the prospect of another use of the oil weapon would be real.

The selections in this volume provide a broad historical background to and assessment of the major issues in the Middle Eastern conflict and the connections between them. "The Middle East and the International System: The Impact of the 1973 War" analyses, from a number of perspectives, the immediate effects of the October War—on the region, on relations between the superpowers, on future Arab options and on the specific conflict between Israel and the Arabs. A following chapter "The Arab-Israeli Dispute: Great Power Behaviour", focuses on the role of the superpowers in three phases: during the June War of 1967, during the continuing skirmishes and diplomatic efforts that characterize the

period between 1967 and 1973, and during and after the October War of 1973. Yet another chapter, "The Soviet Record in the Middle East", provides a general assessment of Soviet relations to the region. It sets out the Soviet advantages and liabilities in dealing with the Arab world, and it assesses early Soviet gains, later Soviet setbacks, and Moscow's possibilities for the future.

"Revolution in Iran" chronicles the fall of the Shah and its effects on the region. That assessment is taken one step further by "Repercussions of the Crisis in Iran", which draws the implications for Iran herself, for the region, including the Arab-Israeli conflict, and for the American and Soviet policies. Another excerpt, "Shifts in the Arab World", outlines the changing pattern of relations in the Arab world occasioned by the revolution in Iran and by the Arab-Israeli peace process. It focuses particularly on the increasing exposure of Egypt. "Egypt and Israel: the Search for Peace" provides a record of the peace process between Cairo and Tel Aviv, culminating in the Camp David accords of 1978.

With the Camp David accords, the Palestinian problem became the central issue. "A Homeland for the Palestinians?", written before President Sadat's visit to Jerusalem, points out the centrality of the Palestinian problem, and argues that any solution to the problem will comprise a large measure of autonomy for the Palestinians. Finally, "The Soviet Union and the PLO" describes the changing pattern of relations between the two and Moscow's ambiguous position with respect to the PLO—seeking to use political support for it as an instrument of leverage in Arab politics while remaining aloof from full identification with PLO objectives.

In thirty years the Middle East has been transformed from a major regional conflict into a major global issue. The specific conflict between the Arab states and Israel cannot be separated from superpower relations or from access to oil resources. On the prospects for the solution to the Palestinian problem hang not only the success of the

2

Camp David accords but also to a significant extent, the stability of moderate regimes in the Persian Gulf. That brings in train issues of Western resource dependence. The Middle East is also the clearest test of whether the common interests of America and the Soviet Union in avoiding direct conflict runs beyond that, into joint support for measures which dampen regional conflict, instead of enhancing it. On this as in other issues in the Middle East the verdict is not yet in.

Gregory Treverton

1 THE MIDDLE EAST AND THE INTERNATIONAL SYSTEM:
The impact of the 1973 War

The Impact of the Middle East Crisis on Super-power Relations

MALCOLM MACKINTOSH

The subject of this presentation – the impact of the Middle East crisis on the super-powers' relations – may perhaps be dealt with under two broad headings. The first is the way in which the crisis has affected relations between the Soviet Union and the United States in the Middle East itself; and the second is the effect of this relationship on the attitudes of the super-powers towards each other and on the international scene as a whole. In order to place both parts of this study in perspective, it may be worthwhile recalling briefly the situation and attitudes of the two super-powers before the recent Middle East crisis broke out, so that we can make some valid comparisons when we come to look at the relationship as it now stands.

The super-powers in perspective

Acknowledging the element of over-simplification in this analysis, the United States may be described as the long-established super-power, which is strong economically and technologically, has a wide range of military capabilities, and has been used to exercising its authority as a super-power for several decades, but particularly since the foundation of NATO in 1949. Yet the broad aim of the United States in recent years has been to hold the line in international affairs. The United States has 'levelled off' her active involvement in different parts of the world, accepting the Soviet Union as a super-power (though behind the United States in economic and technological achievement), and

The author gratefully acknowledges assistance in preparing this article from A. Chadwick at Stanford University, California.

also accepting China, Japan and perhaps Western Europe as potential super-powers. While the United States has been anxious to strengthen and develop her influence and commercial dealings with the rest of the world, her philosophy has been to consolidate, to conserve, to make situations safe and, in some cases, to withdraw from exposed positions – especially those which led to doubts, heart-searching and unrest at home. There is, of course, plenty of dynamism in American foreign policy, but it is, in general, directed towards securing the best for the United States and her friends within the *status quo*, minimizing the risks of instability and the effects of what she sees as excessive ambition in others.

The outlook and philosophy of the Soviet Union is radically different. The Soviet view of history is dominated by a concept according to which great nations in the past have risen and fallen in a kind of cyclical pattern. The Soviet Union believes that she and her allies, however, are in a position to break this pattern by maintaining the impetus of their advance indefinitely. According to this view, the Soviet advance towards world power has been brought about by developing and controlling political forces capable of organizing the military, economic and human resources of the Soviet Union along 'scientifically and ideologically correct' lines. This is how its present leaders see the efforts of the Communist Party of the Soviet Union in bringing their country forward from great-power to super-power status. Having achieved super-power status, these leaders ask themselves: how can this status be used and exploited to improve the security and influence of the Soviet

Union in a fundamentally hostile world? Among other things, they believe that it should be exploited to build an advantageous relationship with the United States, to acquire Western know-how and tap Western economic achievements; to weaken Western political and economic alliances and to undermine Western societies; and to lay the foundations of a future Soviet sphere of influence in Europe as a whole (the traditional area of Soviet foreign policy), in the Middle East and in other areas of the world. The main target is the acquisition of real political influence in countries regarded as important by the Soviet Union. Soviet military power serves to impress these countries with Soviet strength, while Soviet foreign policy seeks to build up the right environment for the development of the Soviet Union's current foreign policy.

Policy and interests in the Middle East
Over-simplification is, of course, unavoidable in drawing such broad sketches of super-power aims and outlooks. But it seems likely that the forces at work in the formulation of each country's foreign policy can be observed in their policies in the Middle East. For almost twenty years the United States and the Soviet Union have been actively involved there. For the United States the issues had become clear-cut by the early 1950s: to provide the financial and military aid that would enable Israel to defend herself within her chosen territory and to build up her military strength and skills to the point where the Israeli armed forces could deal with all foreseeable combinations of Arab military power. Later she also tried to limit the expansion of Soviet influence in the area and to support friendly Middle Eastern states – Saudi Arabia, Jordan, Iran and the members of NATO and the Central Treaty Organization (CENTO) in the area – especially those providing the greater part of the West's oil supplies. The United States' influence with the other Arab countries – Egypt, Syria and Iraq – waned after the 1967 Middle East war. However, her aim in the Arab–Israeli conflict was to work for an agreed political settlement broadly within the *status quo* – that is, reached via a change of heart by the Arab states involved about the acceptance of a State of Israel within frontiers which recognized some of Israel's views of her security needs, and via a change of heart in Israel about the justice of the

moderate Arab case. The United States' main hope thus lay in promoting a gradual change in the climate of opinion in Cairo, Damascus and Amman. In formulating her policy she took great account of the accepted view of Israeli military superiority, which led her, and most other countries, to assume that a major Arab attack on Israeli forces was very unlikely and would not succeed if it was launched.

In the period from 1955 to 1973 the Soviet Union had a different view of the Middle East. She had long regarded it as a neighbouring area important to her security in strategic terms, over which it would be desirable to extend some form of influence or (if possible) even control. As early as 1945–46 she had tried to set up a puppet state in northern Iran and to annex territory from Turkey. In the 1950s and 1960s she came to see the Middle East also as an area of emerging nationalism, where the West (especially the former colonial or mandate powers) would be vulnerable to the results of skilful Soviet diplomacy and the encouragement of local nationalist ambitions against the West. The pattern of Soviet policy towards the Middle East included programmes of much-needed and valuable Soviet economic aid to a number of countries, a firm Soviet political and propaganda commitment to the Arab cause in the Arab–Israeli dispute, and military aid to Egypt, Syria and Iraq – and later to Sudan, South Yemen and Somalia. At the height of Soviet military involvement in the Middle East Soviet air-defence troops were stationed along the Suez Canal, and Soviet naval air squadrons deployed at Cairo and Aswan to carry out air surveillance of the Mediterranean; in 1970, in fact, Egyptian soil had been made available to the Soviet Union for purely anti-NATO activities. At the same time Soviet political penetration of the Arab Socialist Union was already under way. Indeed, it looked, by late 1970, as though the growth of Soviet political and military influence in Egypt, Syria and Iraq was, as the Soviet Union proclaimed it to be, irreversible. At that point, President Nasser died.

Although at first little seemed to change in the Soviet Union's involvement in the Middle East, Egypt under her new President, Sadat, showed that she was ready to make decisions in foreign policy which forced her main benefactor, the Soviet Union, on to the defensive. In April 1971

5

Sadat halted Soviet penetration of the Arab Socialist Union by arresting the leading pro-Soviet group of Egyptian politicians under Ali Sabry, and just over a year later expelled almost all Soviet military personnel in Egypt, including those deployed in combat units at Cairo and Aswan airfields. Yet, in spite of her treatment of the Soviet Union, Egypt continued to press for more and improved arms supplies, exploiting the leverage provided by Moscow's need to retain as much of its threatened position in Cairo as possible. President Sadat in fact made the most of the growing Soviet dilemma in the Middle East. For the supply of arms was the only way open to the Soviet Union to retain her position in Egypt; yet even the arms failed to produce the political influence she wanted. The United States stood by, somewhat incredulous that Nasser's relatively unknown successor should have proved himself so artful a practitioner of power politics towards his country's main benefactor and ally. There was, however, one other factor which affected Egypt's relations with both super-powers. The Soviet–American summit meetings of 1972–73 began to arouse President Sadat's suspicions about the possibilities of super-power deals at Egypt's expense and made the Egyptians look warily at the developing relationship between Moscow and Washington.

This seemed to be the essence of the super-power relationship in the Middle East at the time the leaders of Egypt and Syria undertook their most momentous initiative: the decision to launch a major combined attack on Israeli positions on the Suez Canal and the Golan Heights. However, before looking at this decision, I would like to define two of the terms which I wish to use in this Paper. We often find the word *détente* used to describe a number of aspects of the current relationship between East and West, but I want to restrict it (quite arbitrarily) to the general atmosphere of relaxation which has developed in East–West relations in recent years. For the bilateral relationship which has grown up between the United States and the Soviet Union, particularly since 1969, I propose (equally arbitrarily) to use the phrase 'the special relationship'.

To return to the Middle East, which erupted into war in October 1973, opinion is still divided over Soviet responsibility or foreknowledge of the Syrian–Egyptian decision. On the whole, however, it seems likely that the Soviet Union, while obviously aware that something unusual was afoot, was not privy to the decision to go to war and did not know of the date of the attack beforehand.

Lessons of the war

The course of the fighting is well known, as are the major decisions taken by the super-powers in reaction to it and to each other's policies during the crisis. For our purposes the most important factor to note is that both super-powers, in hurrying to the practical support of their friends (the Soviet airlift of arms to Egypt and Syria began on 10 October, the American airlift to Israel on 13 October), were reacting to events, rather than controlling them. The pattern of the war was established by the initial achievements of the Arab armies and then changed by Israel's success in recovering the military initiative which led her forces across the Suez Canal and, against Syria, to within 22 miles of Damascus; it was not established by American or Soviet policies. The decision of the Soviet Union to turn to the United States for a joint crisis-control action through the United Nations was largely because of Israel's military successes. The apparent Soviet readiness unilaterally to despatch troops to Egypt, which escalated the conflict to a direct American–Soviet confrontation for the space of a few hours on 24–25 October, originated in the movement of events outside Soviet control. The American response – a world-wide alert of American strategic forces – was accepted and acted upon in Moscow as a warning not to proceed with the Soviet plan. But both were hurried decisions arising out of circumstances over which neither the United States nor the Soviet Union had effective control. The speed with which the crisis escalated to a direct American–Soviet confrontation probably contributed to the pressure which both powers brought to bear on their friends (especially that which the United States exerted on Israel, whose forces were on the road to a resounding victory) in order to ensure acceptance of the final United Nations resolutions.

The first impact of the October crisis on the relations between the super-powers in the Middle

East itself must therefore be contained in the lessons they both learned from the crisis. First and foremost both learned that they were dealing with smaller countries capable of taking their own decisions on peace and war, overriding considerations of escalation, affecting the super-powers who supported them and supplied them with arms. This, together with the success of the Arab countries in concealing their intentions from their patrons, should weigh in favour of some kind of improved collaboration between Moscow and Washington on crisis control.

The second lesson perhaps concerns the super-powers' interpretation of their summit agreements. It is part of the American case that the American–Soviet summit agreements of 1972 and 1973 contained an understanding that each side should inform the other if it obtained prior information about a dangerous crisis likely to lead to war. Even if the Soviet Union, which still had a military presence in Syria and some influence in Egypt, had known about Arab intentions only a few days beforehand, she should, according to the American point of view, have contacted the United States – which she did not do. A feeling therefore grew in the United States that the Soviet Union cannot expect to reap the benefits of crisis-control collaboration with the United States while avoiding her responsibilities. The United States, while recognizing the need for collaboration with the Soviet Union in similar circumstances, may well insist that the latter should in future observe the ground rules, as the United States understands them, more effectively than in October 1973. The Soviet Union, of course, challenges this interpretation of her behaviour, but may well have learnt the lesson that she cannot wholly disregard this aspect of American thinking in the future.

Perhaps the most striking lesson of the events of October 1973 on super-power relations was the Soviet and American reaction to the brief direct confrontation between their two countries on 24–25 October. The Soviet Union had alerted a number of her airborne divisions early in October, presumably as a potential intervention force along with troops from the United States (echoing Marshal Bulganin's offer to President Eisenhower at the end of the Suez crisis of 1956). Clearly, she would only consider potentially dangerous *unilateral* action if: (a) she believed that a vital interest of hers was at stake; (b) she reckoned she should 'get away with' the uni-lateral return of Soviet combat troops to Egypt at a time when the United Nations seemed to be paralysed and the United States hesitant about using troops abroad after her experience in Vietnam; or (c) she believed that by making such a military threat (perhaps largely a bluff) she could somehow regain some of the initiative in the crisis diplomatically. What little evidence there is suggests that, while some elements of all these considerations may have been present, the main Soviet fear *at that moment* was an Israeli military demonstration against Cairo. The Soviet Union may have calculated that such a move by Israel could have led to a collapse of the Egyptian regime and a total loss of Soviet prestige, in-fluence or power in that important country. The Soviet leaders may not have believed American assertions that the United States was urging restraint on Israel. In any event, the American declaration of a world-wide alert of her strategic nuclear forces put an end to the confrontation immediately; but the impact of those few hours is bound to affect the development of their future relationship.

In the first place, the United States became aware as a result of this Soviet reaction that, in fundamental terms, the present Soviet leadership was prepared to put the special relationship with the United States ahead of what might be called 'targets of opportunity', specifically in the Middle East. At the same time, the United States acquired further practical evidence that the Soviet leaders see no contradiction between on the one hand, *détente* and the special relationship with the United States, and on the other, at least the threat of unilateral military action to defend important Soviet interests in areas far from Soviet borders. The United States therefore has to consider the most effective way of dealing with such deviations from the spirit of the relationship, if and when they arise. In the case of this Middle East crisis she learned that the most effective way to warn the Soviet leaders off such a course is still the despatch of a direct politico–military signal to Moscow. I realize at this point that many Western observers believe that the American response in alerting the strategic nuclear forces was an over-reaction to the Soviet threat – in whatever form the threat was in fact presented – but from the point of view of this study I want to stress that, over-reaction or not, the American initiative achieved an immediate result.

The overall effect of these factors must be to inject further elements of caution into the American assessment of Moscow's view of the meaning of *détente* and of the special relationship. The confrontation also gave the United States a practical demonstration of the present Soviet leaders' behaviour when acting under stress on a critical issue. But it may also strengthen the belief that, in the last resort, the Soviet Union can still be deflected from risky policies by an indication that the United States has the will-power to use her military strength in this way (which presupposes that American strength and will-power is retained undiminished by the present and succeeding administrations).

To the Soviet Union these few hours of direct confrontation probably suggested that the United States' view of the special relationship with Moscow is based, in the last resort, on reliance upon American military and political power to achieve United States' goals in a crisis. When the tide of military success began to run against Egypt and Syria, the Soviet Union, realizing that the United States has a stake in the Middle East, because of Israel and the energy problem, was anxious to act in concert with her, and within the framework of the United Nations, in bringing the war to an end. If such collaboration could include the re-introduction of Soviet troops into Egypt, so much the better. Then she became aware that the kind of collaboration which she had in mind – including the despatch of a joint Soviet and American force to the Middle East – did not form part of American thinking. However, she continued to press for such action during the bilateral exchanges with the United States and was rebuffed. The most likely Soviet reaction to this would be to assume that the United States is still not prepared to countenance one-sided gains in the Middle East under cover, as it were, of *détente* and the special relationship. The Soviet Union probably realizes that if she tries to adopt such tactics in the future she will be challenged by the United States, using traditional methods of power politics. This interpretation of American actions may, in fact, colour Soviet attitudes to forthcoming negotiations on the Middle East and to the next crisis in which the two super-powers are involved.

Diplomacy and goals

So much for the impact of the war itself. Of equal importance to our subject is the effect on the super-power relationship of Soviet and American diplomacy carried on since the end of the war. The original intention of the powers involved was to hold multilateral talks in Geneva to settle the problem, but, as it turned out, it fell to the United States to mediate directly – first between Egypt and Israel and then between Israel and Syria – and to conduct negotiations which led to successful disengagement agreements on the two main fronts. At first the Soviet Union was content to stand aside from this mediation – probably believing that it would not succeed, and not wishing to be associated with a potentially serious diplomatic failure – but when Dr Kissinger brought about the Egyptian–Israeli disengagement she hurried to get in on the act. Wherever the American Secretary of State went, Mr Gromyko followed, accompanied by calls from Moscow for a transfer of the negotiations to the Geneva Conference. The pattern which emerged from this process was of a dynamic and successful American policy of negotiations with the warring countries, all of whom accepted American mediation, while no one – not even the Syrians – seemed anxious to involve the Soviet Union in their diplomacy or to seek Soviet support. It was hardly surprising in the circumstances that in this period of apparent rejection Soviet diplomacy concentrated its attention again on Iraq, and also turned to the Palestinians in the search for some participant in the crisis who would appreciate Soviet support.

In fact, the widespread acceptability of the United States to Egypt and Syria, as well as to the traditionally pro-western states of Jordan and Saudi Arabia, despite her record of support for Israel, was the main unpredictable element in the situation. Of course there were good practical reasons for it: the United States could bring some pressure to bear in Israel while the Soviet Union could not; Dr Kissinger, was believed in Arab capitals, to be the man most likely to move Israel from her long-standing positions; and he also represented a country anxious to put an end to the recurring crises in the Middle East on terms acceptable to the Arab states as well as to Israel. But what was unpredictable – and seemed so unfair to the Soviet leaders – was the evident enthusiasm with which President Sadat greeted and supported the American conduct of the negotiations, and the readiness of the Syrian President ultimately to play his part in their success.

There can be no doubt that American diplomacy in the Middle East in the twelve months since the October war raised the prestige and reputation of the United States in the area to a high level, and there might well have been some temptation (the Soviet Union would fear) to exploit this advantage to squeeze the Soviet Union out of the Middle East, at least in terms of diplomacy. But this has not happened. It has been American policy, while welcoming the warmth of the new Arab attitudes to the United States, to try to bring the Soviet Union along with her as American diplomacy has evolved: this was again stressed at the Moscow summit in July 1974. No doubt the United States does not want to carry the burden of a Middle East settlement alone, especially as the problems become more intractable: the risk of a new war if further Israeli withdrawals are not carried out soon; the future of Jerusalem and the claims of the Palestinians. No doubt there are shrewd American calculations on more than one possible *quid pro quo* to be sought in the American–Soviet bilateral relationship, but the United States *does* appear to want to involve the Soviet Union in the next stages of the Middle East negotiations. She is therefore reluctant to 'score' a total 'victory' in the Middle East. Such a policy would have a number of potential disadvantages for her. It would mean that interim or permanent peace settlements in the area would not have Soviet support, and might perhaps lead the Soviet Union at a later stage to work against them. It would also create and intensify Soviet resentments against the United States and make future efforts at crisis control more difficult. The American decision not to go all out for 'victory' over the Soviet Union (even if this were feasible) is a practical recognition of the more permanent elements in the special relationship.

What, then, do the two super-powers hope for the Middle East? Without underestimating the enormous difficulties ahead, it seems likely that the United States cautiously believes that a breakthrough has occurred in Arab–Israeli relations, and that with patient negotiation a long-term solution will be found which would involve Arab acceptance of the State of Israel within agreed borders, uninterrupted oil supplies for the United States, and a Soviet presence in the area which would be limited to activities unlikely to place the United States' political, economic or strategic interests in danger.

The Soviet Union, on the other hand, is faced with what might be called the 'tactics of recovery'. Since the death of President Nasser Soviet influence has been on the wane in Egypt, and to a lesser extent in Syria. The Soviet Union has probably learnt all sorts of hard lessons about the uncertain role of military and economic aid and the presence of combat forces as purveyors of reliable political influence. She should have learnt some lessons about the unacceptability to most of her client states of Soviet methods of operation, such as excessive secretiveness and suspicion of the clients' motives. However, it is not in the nature of the Soviet Union to give up when she believes that her setbacks are temporary. She is convinced that her achievements in the Middle East are more impressive and long-lasting than her setbacks, and she must go on building on the former to protect and justify her enormous investments in the area.

It is at this point that the Soviet leaders must consider how far their 'tactics of recovery' can develop, and what practical results may be achieved by pursuit of their main aims in the Middle East. Their maximum goal is likely to be to promote, by political action and economic and military aid, a return to pro-Soviet policies by the Egyptian government, with the consequent weakening and, hopefully, elimination of American and Western influence in Cairo and the rest of the Arab world. This goal probably also includes the exploitation against the West of the energy factor, the political isolation of Israel, and the achievement of Arab goals in the Arab–Israeli dispute under Soviet auspices. The Soviet Union would also hope for the return of Soviet anti-NATO forces to an Arab country in the Mediterranean area, and the emergence of a unified Palestinian organization responsive to Soviet wishes and policy recommendations. And all this should, ideally, take place alongside the reopening of the Suez Canal, and the break-up or serious disruption of NATO in the eastern Mediterranean as a result of the Cyprus crisis.

At the very least, the present Soviet leadership would hope to hold on to existing Soviet gains

9

in the Middle East and to protect vested interests – political, economic and military – in the area. It would hope to hold Soviet influence in Egypt, Syria and Iraq at its present level in the short term, while seizing any opportunities which might appear to improve it – perhaps through further supplies of advanced weapons, especially to Egypt. The Soviet Union would also demand maximum involvement in bargaining on the future of the Middle East. Her minimum goals would also probably include exploitation, where possible, of the West's vulnerability to the effects of the rising cost of energy; and, when the Suez Canal has been reopened, development of the strategic advantages for Soviet military power of the restored link between the Mediterranean and the Indian Ocean – to which the 1974 Soviet–Somali treaty has particular relevance.

What is particularly hard to envisage is any kind of readiness on the part of the Soviet Union to cut her losses in the Middle East and embark upon a pragmatic policy of collaboration with the United States designed to put an end to tension in the area. Even her minimum aims contain too strong an element of political competition and confrontation with the West for that to be a realistic hope.

In fact, the Soviet Union will probably adopt policies which fall between her maximum and minimum aims. She is unlikely to want a final settlement of the Arab–Israeli dispute, which, in her view, would probably lead to the elimination of her influence altogether; nor does she want, in the foreseeable future, another major round of hostilities, with its unpredictability of outcome. She would also like to lessen the possibilities of Middle East countries displaying further independence in decision-making. It seems that her best hope lies in continuing economic and military aid to Arab countries on a selective basis demonstrating support for the Arab cause (including even more specific support for the Palestinians) and at the same time trying to improve collaboration with the United States in the field of crisis control in the area, so that it leads to more favourable results for the Soviet Union. This would, of course, commit her in American eyes to the broad concept of a final political settlement in the Middle East agreeable to the Arab states, Israel and the United States. The Soviet Union accepts that this would be the American interpretation. But it would not weaken her conviction that Soviet diplomacy is likely to find opportunities to work towards some of her maximum goals in the difficult period ahead. Taking into consideration possible further crises in the West's energy supplies, the problems facing President Ford's administration, and the possibility of favourable governmental changes in Middle Eastern countries, the Soviet Union no doubt hopes that she will be able to pursue effective 'tactics of recovery' and restore a significant measure of Soviet influence in the key capitals of the Middle East.

Super-power relations and the war
Moving now from the Middle East itself to the wider impact of the crisis on Soviet–American relations, probably the most important conclusion we can draw is to re-emphasize that, despite strains, difficulties and a momentary confrontation, the special relationship between the two super-powers in the atmosphere of *détente* survived, and was used to solve the crisis. As Dr Kissinger said, when reviewing the crisis on 21 November 1973, 'very frequent, very confidential exchanges' took place between President Nixon and Mr Brezhnev. Security Council resolutions 338, 339 and 340 were sponsored jointly by the Soviet Union and the United States, and consultation has taken place at Geneva and elsewhere to keep the two governments in close touch. It has long been a Soviet aim to get the relationship with the United States institutionalized, irreversible and operative particularly in areas of the world regarded as important by the Soviet Union, such as Europe, the Middle East and East Asia. To some extent the fact that the machinery of the special relationship functioned – however imperfectly – in the Middle East crisis, taken together with the Moscow summit of July 1974, may have gone some way to improve the chances of the institutionalization which the Soviet Union wants.

The crisis also taught each super-power how the relationship tends to work under stress, and at what points it might break down. When a really critical situation developed for the Soviet Union, such as the apparent and imminent collapse of part of the Egyptian Army, or when she appeared to threaten unilateral military intervention, for a few hours confrontation took the place of the special relationship. Undoubtedly, both sides have taken this lesson to heart. The special relationship may be on the road to institutionalization, but it still has its limitations and is not yet approaching irreversibility.

This leads to a consideration of the factors which come into play when the special relationship does begin to waver, and these must include, first and foremost, the two powers' military strength and capabilities. The brief super-power confrontation could suggest two courses of action, neither of which excludes the other. It could lead to an awareness in Moscow and Washington of the need to make more rapid progress in SALT II, which appeared to have been the subject of Dr Kissinger's visit to Moscow in October 1974. At the same time it could lead both governments independently to ensure that work is speeded up on weapons systems now under development or projected, so that they can be included in the list of 'established' systems if a freeze on offensive strategic weapons, for example, is eventually agreed in a delayed SALT II treaty. Neither side would accept the risk of needing to call on its military strength in any future crisis in which the special relationship broke down – even momentarily – only to find that the forces to which it was appealing were inferior to those of its adversary. On the whole, it seems likely that both trains of thought will be discussed in Moscow and Washington and both policies may be put into effect by the two governments.

But perhaps the most intriguing, and possibly the most important, impact of the crisis on super-power relations for the future is the evidence it provided to each country of the other's view of the role and limitations of the relationship between them. While anxious to improve American influence in various parts of the world by diplomacy, economic aid and alliances, the United States believes that each crisis contains elements that would support its satisfactory resolution without basic alterations in the political, social and ideological alignment or convictions of all the important participants in the crisis. This does not mean to say that the United States would not welcome or work for a change in outlook, or in the balance of power in crisis areas where the current alignment is anti-American or anti-Western. But she does not regard such a change as historically inevitable, nor does she see it as her duty, before

history or political truth, to work unremittingly towards it using all methods short of war.

It seems likely that this is precisely the framework within which the Soviet Union views her relationship with the United States. Since the Soviet Union achieved super-power status her leaders have followed active and confident policies abroad, and even when Soviet policy has suffered setbacks, as in the Middle East crisis, the fundamental resilience of her foreign policy is still much in evidence.

Whatever the basis for this (real or misguided) sense of Soviet confidence, recent Soviet foreign-policy experience still seems to allow the Soviet Union to present her understanding of the special relationship to the United States in something like the following terms: 'we welcome *détente* and a special relationship with you, and we want them to cover a wide variety of international activities, and to become institutionalized and irreversible. We also want you to accept our definitions of parity in military strength. But we believe that our policies and outlook are scientifically based and historically correct; that if we seek a change in the balance of power in our favour and a move in individual countries towards regimes favourable to us, we are justified in doing so before history and our political beliefs. Our successes will turn out in the long run to be the irreversible ones: we shall never give up our attempts to change the political alignments of countries we regard as important. If you think that *détente* or our new relationship will lessen the intensity of the ideological (i.e., political) struggle between us, you are making a great mistake.'

Soviet statesmen have, of course, been proclaiming this doctrine to the faithful for many years, and its importance in Soviet thinking should not be minimized in the West simply because it is described as 'ideological' in Soviet material. We should recognize that one of the fundamental differences between the Soviet and American concepts of the special relationship and *détente* is precisely their views on the role these two factors have to play in the future development of the East–West balance of power. I believe that the experience of the two super-powers in the Middle East crisis of 1973 underlined this basic difference and indeed spelled it out: crisis control with stability for the United States; opportunities for carefully controlled changes in the balance of power for the Soviet Union. Perhaps recognition by the super-powers of this aspect of their relationship may lead to increasing difficulties in developing their contacts in the future. Perhaps, on the other hand, the more realistic assessment it involves can help the relationship and *détente* to move forward, encumbered by fewer illusions and assisted by more attention to practical possibilities.

The Arab-Israeli Conflict: The Next Phase

HISHAM SHARABI

The kind of formula proposed for the settlement of the Arab–Israeli conflict at the Geneva Conference seems inadequate and unattractive to all involved. Yet all the parties seem to have given up hope of a more perfect formula and accepted this one as the only possible way out. This attitude may have deeper roots than mere practicality or despair over the current situation. Freud illustrates this attitude, in an essay entitled 'Wit and its Relation to the Unconscious', by the following anecdote:

A suitor objects [to the marriage broker] because the bride has a short leg and therefore limps. The [broker] contradicts him.
'You are wrong,' he says. 'Suppose you marry a woman whose legs are sound and straight. What do you gain by it? You are not sure from day to day that she will not fall down, break a leg, and then be lame for the rest of her life. Just consider the pain, the excitement, and the doctor's bill. But if you marry this one, nothing can happen. Here you have a finished job.'

War in the Middle East appears only a theoretical possibility from these peaceful shores, but in the Middle East it confronts us daily as a pressing and imminent reality. I live in Beirut, along the Corniche in a sixth-floor apartment overlooking Beirut bay. Almost every day I see, high in the sky, the vapour streak of one, sometimes two Israeli jets. Sometimes they just turn westward and disappear; often, however, they fly over Beirut and break the sound barrier over the centre of the city. Their sonic booms remind us daily of the war that may break out any day.

The October war, although one of the shortest of the twentieth century, had consequences that extended far beyond its relatively limited duration and scale. While it is still too early to predict its final effects, it has already brought about a transformation of the region's internal alignment of forces and its relationship with the rest of the world.

Consequences in the region

Although the war had a great impact upon all participants, probably the most immediate consequences affected Israel, whose position seemed to be weakened in three major respects. On the military level the widely-held international image of Israel as an autonomous hegemonic power suffered heavily. Her initial losses in the air and setbacks in Sinai underlined Israeli military vulnerability, while the need for a massive arms transfusion in the course of the war revealed the extent to which she was dependent on United States support. Serious revision of opinion as to the degree of Israeli military superiority resulted, especially in the United States, where many official conceptions about the strategic role that Israel was capable of playing in the Middle East were changed.

As a result of the October war Israel's former policies towards the Arab world also came under close international scrutiny, resulting in a diplomatic isolation that indicated the danger of overestimating her power. Even the United States, Israel's principal supporter and ally, seemed to be taking up the opportunity offered by the war to re-establish her position in the Arab world and to assume a more 'even-handed' role as mediator and peace-maker.

Within Israel the impact of the war was reflected psychologically in erosion of confidence in the political leadership and criticism of the army. Israeli commentators spoke of the war as an 'earthquake' which shook the country to her foundations and forced her to seek new ways out

13

of a difficult situation. Dissatisfaction with government policies increased on both the Right and the Left; the right-wing parties were strengthened, while in some left-wing circles even the viability of Zionism itself was questioned. Polls taken shortly after the war showed that an increasing number of young Israelis were disillusioned with life in Israel and were willing to emigrate if given the opportunity. In the daily press, echoes of the Massada complex were revived.

For the Arab world the immediate consequences of the October war were in some respects equally dramatic, but they reinforced the existing regimes and their policies, rather than weakened them. For most Arabs the Arab image had been transformed; at long last they had shown that they could fight bravely, use advanced weapons effectively and unite in a common front. Above all, they could employ their most potent resource, oil, as a weapon of remarkable effectiveness; it was the success of the embargo that was perhaps the major turning-point in the war. The enormous power the Arabs possessed was now demonstrated, along with their determination to use it, both to the Arabs themselves and to the rest of the world.

Thus on the international level the Arabs gained new stature as their economic and political power became explicit. But on the internal plane, too, the October war had radical effects in serving to bring about a new balance of forces in the Arab world that replaced the one which had prevailed under Nasser. The newly emergent hegemony derived from the alignment of the conservative and moderate states, particularly Saudi Arabia and Egypt, which came to form the new axis of power in the Arab world. The 'radical' states, with Egypt no longer in their ranks, were no longer on the offensive; they either formed part of the new equilibrium or kept to the side, as did Iraq and Libya. The ideas of Arab unity and revolution, the motive forces of the Nasser era, were replaced by empirical co-existence and co-operation by the Arab states. The new coalition expressed itself in practical arrangements organized within a flexible and pragmatic alliance which included as its core Egypt, Saudi Arabia, Syria and Algeria. This alliance was now willing to work towards a political solution of the Palestine problem which explicitly accepted recognition of Israel, a policy

only barely conceivable for the Arab establishments that suffered the shame of the June defeat but one which was now realistic in the aftermath of the effective performance of the Arab regimes in October 1973.

In an Arab world where the position and prestige of the conservative oil-producing states had been dramatically enhanced during the war, along with that of Egypt and Syria, the position of the radical and militant forces in the Arab world was now undercut. The foremost party to suffer from the new balance of forces, both militarily and politically, was the Palestinian resistance movement, whose rise had been in great part the produce of the failure and disgrace of 1967 which the Arab regimes redeemed in October 1973. The movement had become the catalyst of Arab nationalism and revolution that Nasser had been until 1967, basing itself upon Nasserist aspirations of Arab nationalism and unity (which it regarded as preconditions for an all-Arab – not merely Palestinian – revolutionary movement that would liberate Palestine). Now, as the influence of the radicals waned for the time being, the Palestinian guerrillas found themselves in a position of isolation from the key Arab states reminiscent of that which they experienced before the June war.

The Palestinians were now confronted with the Arab states' acceptance of the very conditions which they and the Nasserist movement had rejected for nearly a quarter of a century. The October war so eroded the Palestinian position that they seemed forced to choose one of two alternatives: either to accept the Arab states' commitment to political settlement based on the recognition of Israel, or to reject any settlement and risk opposition to the Arab states and the new *status quo* they formed. Yet paradoxically, although the Palestinians were no longer prime movers in the Arab world, it had never previously been so widely recognized that a firm and lasting solution of the Middle East crisis would be difficult to achieve without them. Whether the Palestinian movement would now compromise and enter talks for a settlement with Israel was recognized as one of the most, perhaps *the* most crucial issue in the conflict.

The role of the Palestinians
Some Palestinian guerrilla organizations, particularly the Popular Front for the Liberation of

Palestine, have remained firmly opposed to the idea of negotiations with Israel. Their opposition is based not only on ideological but also on practical grounds, because the Palestinian movement will clearly be entering any negotiations from a position of weakness. None of its strategic goals have been achieved: thus, the stage of people's war has not been reached, organized popular resistance has not been fully developed in the occupied territories, and no Palestinian territory has been liberated by armed struggle. That this weakness has been due to the repression of Arab governments and not to defeat by the enemy does not alter the situation. The Palestinian position in any negotiations will, moreover, be restricted by the self-limiting commitment of the Arab states to Security Council resolution 242. Unless the framework of the Geneva Conference is somehow adjusted, the Palestinians can participate only as refugees, not as a people with national rights, something which they have strongly resisted.

What, then, would be the bargaining power of the Palestinians in any future negotiations? What could they hope to achieve?

There is one source of Palestinian strength deriving from the general realization that a lasting settlement in the Middle East will have to include the Palestinians. This bestows on them considerable political power in the Arab world as well as internationally.

As for the other question, what the Palestinians may expect to achieve under present circumstances will probably depend on two factors: on the extent to which Egypt and Syria are willing to commit themselves to Palestinian claims, and on the extent to which the two super-powers (particularly the United States) are willing to accommodate these claims. The combined force of these two factors would make it difficult for the Israeli government to prevent independent Palestinian representation in some form in support of demands for 'Palestinian rights'.

What, precisely, is meant by references to these rights? Palestinian demands may be summarized in three points:

1. The right to repatriation or compensation.
2. Civil and political rights.
3. The right to self-determination.

The first addresses itself to the right to choose between going back to their homes or being re-settled elsewhere and receiving compensation; the second applies to the Palestinians living in Israel who demand equal rights and the abrogation of discriminatory laws against them; while the third deals with the right of the Palestinians to exercise national sovereignty and self-rule in Palestine.

Given the international situation and the framework of the Geneva Conference which of these demands could be realized, and in what fashion?

The pragmatists (the 'moderates') among the Palestinians concede that on the first demand little can be achieved in the forseeable future beyond the repatriation of a few thousand Palestinians. Compensation for property taken by the Israelis may become a central issue. As for the political and civil rights of the Palestinians living in Israel, the most that one could achieve is to focus attention on the plight of the 'Israeli' Palestinians, and to obtain some improvement in their juridical, educational and economic lot.

It is the third demand which is the principal one, namely, the right to self-determination and the exercise of national sovereignty; hence the crucial significance of the idea of a Palestinian 'national authority' in the West Bank and Gaza Strip. A pragmatic Palestinian position has evolved which calls for a separate and independent Palestinian state in these areas as a basic condition for any political settlement. In this conception, complex questions dealing with demilitarization, inspection, international guarantees, etc., will have to be settled, but without compromising the principle of Palestinian sovereignty over Palestinian territory (an intricate problem which presents many difficulties). As for the alternative to such a state, the idea of a Palestinian state confederated with Jordan seems unacceptable to the majority of Palestinians. Equally unlikely would be the establishment of a Palestinian state divorced from the Palestinian resistance movement (the Palestine Liberation Organization) and the power and authority which it wields among Palestinians. Confederation with Israel, another theoretical alternative, has no support whatsoever.

Although the idea of a Palestinian state in the West Bank may with time gain increasing support among Palestinians, there is a prime stumbling block, for implicit in the notion of a Palestinian state is the recognition of Israel within clearly specified boundaries. It is precisely this recognition, implying as it does renunciation by the Palestinian people of their rights in most of a land which they once possessed in its entirety, that makes most Palestinians balk at the price of a Palestinian state. The 'Rejection Front' headed by the Popular Front for the Liberation of Palestine enjoys wide sympathy among the Palestinian public because of its refusal to abdicate precisely these rights.

The difficulty concerning the problem of recognition of Israel may well prove insurmountable for the pragmatists. In June 1974 the National Council, the Palestinian parliament-in-exile, failed to adopt a resolution in favour of participation in the Geneva Conference pushed through by the moderate elements. The Council stipulated that participation is possible only within a framework which acknowledges the right of the Palestinians as a people and not merely as refugees, and, significantly, voted to present the Executive Committee of the Palestine Liberation Organization from taking any decision on the question of participation without prior approval by the Council.

The possibility thus arises of Palestinian absence from the Geneva talks simply by default, by failure to decide, should the resolution of the problem of recognition prove impossible. The Palestinians may be by-passed, not because they turned down an offer, but because they failed to agree on a policy.

Among the moderate elements, however, there seems to be growing willingness to reconsider the question of recognition. These elements hold that Israel cannot be destroyed by war and that refusal to achieve settlement now will inevitably lead to Israel's *de facto* absorption of the West Bank and Gaza with the resultant obliteration of their Palestinian Arab character within a decade or so. Peace, on the other hand, may eventually bring about the de-Zionization of Israel, i.e., the abandonment of expansionist policies and goals, and of the idea of an exclusively Jewish state from which most Palestinians are automatically excluded on ethnic grounds. This in turn raises the possibility of genuine Palestinian–Israeli coexistence including federation or a bi-national state comprising all of Palestine – something similar to what the Palestinian liberation movement has all along

envisaged as its goal of a 'secular, democratic Palestine'. This possibility, the moderates contend, is not based on wishful thinking or merely on the hope that reason and goodwill will one day prevail. It rests on the certainty that economic necessity and sound political sense in the face of an overwhelmingly powerful Arab world will force the Israelis in the direction of reconciliation, once their militance has been softened by a period of peace.

So far the mainstream of Palestinians remains opposed to this line of thought. As articulated by the left and the militants, rejection of a compromise solution maintains that to accept settlement based on surrender of fundamental rights after fifty years of struggle constitutes an irreversible defeat, not only of the Palestinians but also of the movement of liberation throughout the Arab world. Now that the Arabs have entered into a new era of economic and political power, it is argued, compromise of fundamental rights is unwarranted. Were there to be a rebuff to the current moves of Arab governments towards peace, this stance could become extremely potent in the Arab world.

The American breakthrough

In the context of the international system, the most significant event for the Middle East during the last year has been the dramatic breakthrough of American diplomacy after the October war, which has brought about the beginning of a new balance of power in the eastern Mediterranean and the Gulf. Although the emerging power-structure has not fully formed, the American position in it has consolidated sufficiently to allow for a number of tentative observations.

American policy in the area seems motivated by three main objectives: first, to secure relations of peace and stability in the region; second, to assure a continuous flow of oil at an adequate level of production and at an acceptable price; and third, to contain (but not altogether to eliminate) Soviet influence and to maintain a position of strength in the area.

The American strategy for achieving these aims seems fully predicated on close relations with the two core countries of the Arab world, Egypt and Saudi Arabia, without abandoning its commitment to Israel's existence. One the richest, the other the most populous and strategically centred of the Arab states, they are the potential mainstays of peace and stability in the region. Between them they have the power to contain or at least offer an effective counterweight to radical forces within it. The importance of Egypt, as the lynch-pin in the Arab side of the confrontation with Israel, is such that she alone among the Arab countries can act as the key to war or peace in the Israeli–Arab conflict. From the point of view of stability in the area, if Egypt is removed from the conflict the other Arab states will be incapable of waging war against Israel on their own; a conflagration can thus be delayed for a long time. Likewise, should Egypt decide upon an overall political settlement between the Arab states and Israel along the lines of Security Council resolution 242, it will be difficult for the other Arab confrontation states not to follow suit.

Saudi Arabia plays an equally significant role in the vital Gulf area, and, indirectly, an important one in the Arab–Israeli confrontation. Stability in Arab–Iranian relations and the preservation of peace in the Gulf depends to a large extent on the Saudi position. As the recipient of the largest portion of oil revenue in the Middle East, Saudi Arabia's economic power will be crucial in determining the social stability and political development of the Arab countries in the next decade. The use of the oil weapon in October 1973 gave credibility to all future Saudi threats to use the oil weapon again, which has further enhanced the influence and prestige of King Feisal both in the Middle East and abroad. His single-minded determination to wrest Arab Jerusalem and the Muslim Holy Places from Israeli control represents, in the present context, an instance in which an individual's will becomes a major historical factor determining the outcome of events. Through its increasing capacity for large-scale development in the Arab world and the poorer African and Asian countries and for affecting the world balance of trade, Saudi Arabian power in economic as well as political terms is bound to grow.

The military and economic agreements concluded between Saudi Arabia and the United States have brought the United States to the position of strongest ally and most influential power in Saudi Arabia. Equally, the new economic and political ties with Egypt have placed the United States in a position perhaps even stronger than that occupied by the Soviet Union during the Nasser regime. It can be said that so long as the Egyptian–Saudi axis is maintained, an American-dominated system of stability in both the Arab–Israeli conflict and the Gulf will probably prevail.

It has been maintained that as a result of the American breakthrough, the Soviet Union has been displeased by the form taken by progress towards peace in the area, and that this raises doubts about its willingness to assist in the peace-making process. Yet the Soviet Union, despite obvious grievances and reservations, may not be too dissatisfied to step back a little in the face of the changed situation. So long as she is recognized as the other great Middle Eastern power and so long as she maintains strong ties with countries such as Syria and Iraq, she will probably find it quite tolerable to coexist for the time being in the new American-dominated system. The emerging regional *status quo* may be seen as less of a setback to the Soviet Union than appears at first glance, especially if it contributes to strengthening *détente*. One is tempted to think that, with Egypt no longer a Soviet responsibility but an American one, the Soviet leaders may temporarily be satisfied with waiting and seeing. After all, their perspective is a long-term one which allows for positive aspects in situations which on the surface appear not altogether to their advantage.

Prospects of peace and stability

The disengagement of forces on the Syrian and Egyptian fronts with Israel following the October war introduced a totally new element into the conflict. Not only did the disengagement agreements render more difficult the resumption of hostilities; they locked the Arabs and Israel into a diplomacy actively oriented towards peaceful settlement for the first time in twenty-five years.

The disengagement agreements achieved through American mediation were not only a triumph for Dr Kissinger but also for President Sadat. President Sadat's policy has been based on the de-emphasis of the military option in favour of a sustained American-sponsored peace initiative, the result of which would be to induce an Israeli withdrawal from the Arab territories occupied in 1967. Egyptian agreement to disengagement on the Canal front before Israel committed herself to total withdrawal from Sinai – the original Egyptian condition for such an agreement – marked the initiation of a policy based on faith in the United States for its ultimate fulfilment. The manner in which Egypt accepted disengagement simultaneously demonstrated her power to make her policy effective in the Arab world. By confronting Syria with a *fait accompli* on the Canal front, Sadat made it difficult for Syria to continue fighting alone and thus easier for it to negotiate a disengagement agreement.

Can a final settlement of the conflict result from the peace process that has been initiated? President Sadat has gambled on American influence upon Israel to bring about a settlement. The one which he envisages would probably comprise an Israeli withdrawal to essentially the pre-1967 war borders and the creation of a Palestinian state or a political entity confederated with Jordan, in exchange for which Israel would receive Arab recognition, demilitarization of parts of the occupied territories and guarantees against future Arab attacks. An Arab compromise on the issue of the full return of the occupied territories is extremely improbable; the prospects of a peaceful settlement depend on the leverage of the United States *vis-à-vis* Israel, and her willingness to use such leverage.

It is difficult at this stage to assess final Israeli intentions. Israeli policy after the October war fell under the influence of three fundamental but not completely compatible determinants. In the first place, Israeli government thinking has been forced in the direction of settlement based on substantial territorial and political concessions, although a wide gap still remains between the Israeli and Arab positions. Secondly, Israel's military and economic dependence on the United States has now reached its highest point. But, thirdly, the Rabin government which succeeded the government of Mrs Meir was based on a fragile coalition seriously limiting its flexibility.

There seems to be general agreement, at least within the ranks of the moderates, that another war, even if it results in an Israeli victory, is likely to be politically even more sterile than the 1967 war. Thus the only realistic option is to comply with the imperatives of the situation and steer a course of action leading to a position that the moderates hope would enable Israel to make the least concessions territorially and to realize the maximum gains politically, while retaining the support of the United States.

By the behaviour and pronouncements of the Rabin government the Israeli view as how best to achieve these objectives seems to be along these lines: by insisting on state-to-state exchanges that exclude recognition of the Palestinians as an equal and independent entity; by rejecting the idea of a Palestinian state in the West Bank and Gaza and the unacceptable territorial concessions that this would entail; and by convincing the United States of the viability of Israel's position on these and other major issues in terms of the future stability of the region.

It seems that the Israeli leadership is convinced that if Egypt can be drawn to further agreement (on further withdrawal from Sinai, etc.) Israel's negotiating position would be greatly strengthened. The government's refusal to talk about Jerusalem or about definite boundary lines reflects not merely hesitations and disagreements, but probably also the determination not to tackle the central issues before further steps have been taken and the final alignment of forces in the negotiations becomes clear.

The problem of securing public support for the government in the event of any important concessions remains to be solved. The Israeli leadership may well see in Egypt's new relationship with the United States the grounds for new possibilities of agreement. But the pressure from the right to reject out of hand any significant territorial or political concessions may limit the Israeli government's capacity to explore these fully.

Of the three factors determining Israeli policy options, however, the one likely to be felt most strongly as the Geneva Conference approaches is the pressure of the United States. The October war re-emphasized that Israel cannot risk isolation from the United States and this may well be the most decisive factor in the current situation. Clearly, the seriousness of the United States' call on Israel to adhere to a policy of withdrawal and peaceful settlement (basically the policy enunciated by former Secretary of State William Rogers) precluded the kind of response Israel gave to the Jarring mission, causing its collapse in February 1971. Failure to move sufficiently and convincingly in the direction of resolution 242 would in a way represent an American failure. Sadat's position, predicated on the ability of the United States to 'deliver' would be seriously undermined by such a 'failure'.

Such American moves as there have been in the last year have started out in the direction of securing a settlement acceptable to Egypt. As Dr Kissinger, in an interview published shortly after the October war with Mohammad Hassanein Heikal, former editor of *al-Ahram*, said: 'The USSR can give you (Egypt) arms, but what the United States can give you is a just solution.' Yet the gap in the negotiating positions between Israel and the Arab states remains so wide, that it is impossible to predict with any certainty that peace can come about. What, then, are the alternatives?

Put schematically, no solution would be forthcoming if (1) a breakdown takes place before the Geneva Conference is reconvened, or, if reconvened, it is terminated or indefinitely postponed; (2) inconclusive negotiations drag on in the manner of the SALT and Paris talks; and (3) agreement is concluded which is found inadequate, i.e., unacceptable to the mainstream of Palestinian and Arab opinion.

In the unlikely event that an agreement was reached between the Arab states and Israel and rejected by the Palestinians, the suppression of the guerrilla organizations and coercive measures against all Palestinians would sooner or later have to follow as necessary consequences.

In certain countries such a move is likely to have far-reaching political repercussions. It may be recalled that the Palestinian problem has always been a pan-Arab problem. For the Arab nationalists, for the forces of the left, for the intellectuals as well as for the young army officers, the Palestine problem has always been a central nationalist and ideological concern.

For its part the Palestinian leadership has a fair assessment of the political leverage the Palestinians have in various Arab countries. The resistance movement is quite aware of its power in influencing mass attitudes. The final reaction to attempts at Palestinian suppression would probably be acts of violence in those regimes that had accepted political settlement. I estimate that there are 60,000 to 70,000 Palestinians under arms (including the Palestine Liberation Army,

the guerrilla units, and camp militias) and perhaps several thousand others trained in the use of firearms. There are large caches of weapons and ammunition available to the Palestinians in many Arab countries, and the guerrilla organizations are known to have access to large sums of money. Should they go underground and engage in large-scale terrorism in the Arab world, they could conceivably undermine the stability of the newly established *status quo* in the Arab world and thus set new political forces in motion, just as happened following the 1948 armistice agreements between Israel and the Arab states.

But matters may take a different course. The failure of peace diplomacy, either as a result of inflexible attitudes on both sides or of too much dragging of feet or as a result of the outright breakdown of talks, could lead to the resumption of hostilities between Israel and the Arab countries. One can see changes taking place within certain regimes, and, under such conditions, sliding into a fifth Arab–Israeli war. In such an event the oil weapon may be used again.

Finally, a situation could come about as the result of neither comprehensive solution nor total deadlock, but one of only partial solution in which each party obtained something and felt that to accept it would not constitute a defeat. This is probably the kind of settlement that Dr Kissinger's diplomacy might be well satisfied in achieving. The narrow focus of any such agreements, however, contains obvious dangers.

Indeed, conflict theory makes it clear that while disputes over *pragmatic* and *instrumental* values are more or less easily resolved, disputes over *fundamentals* raise a different kind of difficulty. The disengagement of forces on the Egyptian and Syrian fronts represents the resolution of a dispute concerning peripheral rather than central issues. The core of the Arab–Israeli conflict has been left untouched in the course of negotiations this far. Whether settlement of non-fundamental issues can lead to settlement of fundamental issues remains an open question. But it seems obvious that the vaguer the definition of the territorial withdrawal demanded of Israel and of the meaning of Palestinian rights, which are at the centre of the conflict, the more difficult the resolution of these issues becomes.

The success of Dr Kissinger's approach so far may be attributed largely to his fine sense for the distinction between the various sets of problems constituting the dispute and to his remarkable ability to keep them separate in the conduct of negotiations. Yet one feels that the kind of diplomacy he has been pursuing may be better suited to achieving the peripheral goals than to resolving the central issues. He is, that is to say, more at home with facts than with rights, and even in the realm of power politics this is not always advantageous. For while it is perhaps naive to think in terms of justice in dealing with international conflict, it is less hard-headed than it seems to think that conflicts can be resolved outside their proper historical context.

Conclusion: The Middle East conflict and the international system

It is perhaps proper to conclude this Paper by attempting to consider likely developments in the Middle East in the context of the international system.

Whether peace or war materializes it will have a direct impact on a global scale. For the near future it is the prospects of peace that look increasingly discouraging. The negotiating positions of both Arabs and Israelis have hardened, and the gap between them – always very large – has progressively widened. While it is of course to be expected that with the approaching peace conference each side will try to jockey for a better position, accompanying these manoeuvres there have been ominous signs of mounting tension.

Both Israel and Syria – and to a lesser extent Egypt and Jordan – have now rebuilt their military forces. Syria and Israel – and possibly the others – are now certainly better equipped than they were at the beginning of the October war and in the fighting preceding the disengagement agreement. The new Syrian acquisitions include T-62 tanks, the most advanced in Soviet service, which now constitute almost the entire Syrian tank force; new sophisticated aircraft and equipment, including the most advanced versions of the MiG-21 and probably the MiG-23 and MiG-25; a large number of mobile surface-to-air missile launchers; and, reportedly, Scud surface-to-surface missiles with a range of 320km.

On the other side of the build-up, the Israeli Army has been fully re-equipped by the United States. The air force has been strengthened by the acquisition of F-4E Phantom jets and new A-4N

type Skyhawk;[1] it has been given an advanced version of the laser-guided 'smart' bombs and new equipment for electronic counter-measures specially designed to foil radar-guided surface-to-air missiles; it has also been provided with the Chaparal surface-to-air missile system along with the radar-guided Vulcan anti-aircraft gun system. Israel's mobilization system has meanwhile been streamlined and greatly strengthened, and she feels confident of her ability in another war to inflict a heavy defeat on the Arabs.

Disengagement of forces and the presence of UN troops do not rule out the military option for either the Arab or Israeli side. War will probably be rendered less likely in the next few weeks if the two sides successfully enter into negotiations at Geneva. However, bringing the various parties to the negotiating table is not in itself sufficient to dispel the possibility of renewed conflict, and the breakdown of talks could provide the occasion for a fifth Arab–Israeli war.

In the present military balance in which Israel may still have the upper hand, it is unlikely that either Syria or Egypt will strike the first blow. If war breaks out, however, Israel can expect to achieve certain military, political and psychological advantages. She could deal a hard blow to the Syrian armed forces, thereby demonstrating her military superiority and strengthening her bargaining power in subsequent negotiation. On the other hand, a strike by Israel against Syria (or Egypt or both) will have to take into account two factors (which may prove sufficiently inhibitive to dissuade Israel from such a strike): the reimposition of the Arab oil embargo and the reaction of the Soviet Union and the United States.

Both super-powers are today more deeply involved in the Middle East than at any time in the past. Their wish to strengthen détente is reflected in their desire for a peaceful settlement of the conflict. But their regional allies still retain considerable scope for independent initiative, and, should a situation of conflict be opened, both super-powers will be drawn in as principal arms suppliers and supporters of one side or the other. In recent months the Soviet Union has reaffirmed her obligations to Syria and intensified

---

[1] An Israeli request for the new F-14 fighter is still under consideration in Washington.

relations with the Palestine Liberation Organization, while the United States has maintained her obligations to Israel, and neither commitment will be ignored in the event of war.

Although the great powers have hitherto prevented the Middle East conflict from extending to disrupt *détente*, their tacit collaboration is still highly vulnerable. If the Middle East conflict is allowed to continue in the short term, *détente* will never be secure.

It is noteworthy that, in spite of super-power involvement in the area, the local parties have escaped the formal alliances with super-powers that have divided Europe and parts of Asia. Whatever the relatively minor treaties between the Soviet Union and Egypt and Iraq, or the special relationship between the United States and Israel, the future complexion of the region in the international balance of power is unlikely to be determined by one or other of the super-powers. Indeed the emergence of the Arab world as a cohesive power bloc has become much more probable as a consequence of the recent shift in importance in the international economic and political order from economic access to *markets* to access to *resources*. The world power-structure has begun to change in favour of the resource-rich countries of the world, and the central resource of the Middle East, oil, on which world dependence is expected to continue to increase for the next ten to fifteen years, is largely an Arab resource within the Middle East.[2]

Economic dislocations caused by the drastic rises in oil prices have demonstrated that the oil-producing countries can directly influence the international economic system without fear of effective intervention by the great industrial powers; and that Arab capacity to determine the structure of the world monetary system will be crucial to the future stability of the system.[3]

It is to be expected that as the Arabs' part in overhauling the international economic system becomes more active Arab political influence will increase commensurately. And as the Arab bloc becomes internally more closely integrated and better adapted to dealing with the outside world it will demand increasing participation in the vital decisions concerning the structure and functions of the international system.

In the next few years the Arab world is bound to develop new kinds of relations with both the industrialized countries of the First World and the resource-poor countries of the Third World.

In dealing with the advanced countries the Arabs have until recently relied on bilateral relations. Since the October war and the successful use of oil as a political weapon, the collective approach has been more and more emphasized. Recently the league of Arab States and the EEC have agreed on a framework of collective dealing between the European nine and the Arab twenty, taking the first step in the direction of Arab-European cooperation on a massive scale.[4]

Continued instability in the area will probably generate increasing demand for arms. And a fifth Arab-Israeli war will almost certainly bring about severe cut-backs in production, if not an embargo on oil. Conditions of peace and stability, on the other hand, are likely to induce the Arab oil-rich countries to develop collective measures to help significantly in the development of poor Third World countries and to channel increasing amounts of their income into productive projects in the Arab world and elsewhere.

Regarding the international political impact of any future war, I would like, by way of conclusion, to put forward two central questions which Mr François Duchêne raised with me before this conference. His questions are as follows: 'What is the real stability of any advantage the United States may have gained in Middle East diplomacy subsequent to the October war? If there were to be major difficulties in following up the disengagement agreements leading to the renewed use of the oil weapon and possibly a shift in Saudi-Egyptian policies towards the United States, might we not see new reversals of the situation?

It is very difficult to give precise answers to these questions. One can probably deal with them indirectly. Dialectically, any advantage the United States may have gained since the October

---

[2] Arab production in 1974 reached a little over 18 million barrels per day.

[3] According to a recent estimate, OPEC reserves could reach $250 billion by 1980, the major proportion being Arab reserves.

[4] This does not of course exclude bilateral agreements between the states. Indeed, in seeking to obtain technological resources and arms from the advanced countries of Europe and North America the Arab oil-producing countries have shown a distinct preference for the bilateral approach.

war will be stabilized as the new *status quo* in the Middle East is stabilized; that is to say, American diplomacy will consolidate its gains to the extent to which it succeeds in bringing about progress towards the solution of the Arab–Israeli conflict. But there is a basic constraint on American diplomacy, and this is the time-frame in which it is forced to function. The disengagement agreements represent a breakthrough only in that they create a new modality for pursuing negotiations on substantive issues. Thus clearly the stability of the advantages gained by American diplomacy depends directly on achieving further gains within a delimited time-frame. The element of time is decisive for two reasons: first, because the disengagement agreements can prevent war only as long as there are expectations for further progress towards settlement; and, secondly, because opposition to settlement gains strength with time as hardline positions in both camps solidify and become more prevalent.

The problem can be seen from another point of view. Assuming the failure of the present peace initiative, one can follow a scenario in which Israel deals a pre-emptive strike against Syria. If the war continues beyond a few days Egypt (and perhaps Jordan) will probably be drawn in, and Saudi Arabia and the other Arab oil-producing countries will be forced to reimpose the oil embargo. A chain reaction will thus follow which will reactivate the Middle East crisis on all levels and bring about a more intense and dangerous crisis than the one we have been living with. This is a situation in which developments in the Middle East will have direct impact on the international system. Thus the advantages gained by American diplomacy subsequent to the October war and the stability of the Egyptian–Saudi alliance will probably continue to be threatened unless palpable progress is demonstrated soon at Geneva or elsewhere.

Future Arab Options

HANNS MAULL

With its application of the oil weapon and its initial military successes against Israel, the Arab world has finally left the era of post-colonial struggle against the economic and political remnants of Western control over the Middle East. An underlying theme of Arab politics during this period has been nationalism directed against Western influence (symbolized, above all, in the superiority of Israel and the international oil companies).

Now things seem to be changing. The sudden enhanced riches of the Arab oil producers together with Egypt's declared intention to turn inwards (and westwards) and to solve her vast economic and social problems have introduced an additional theme which may well characterize the next decade: the theme of economic and social development, which now seems to have top priority among Arab decision-makers.

This shift in emphasis is not least the consequence of vastly increased financial resources, and 'the great leap forward' now seems a distinct possibility. Expectations in the Arab world are rising, and the hopes pinned on oil money are high. Emphasis on development therefore appears to be fundamental to the survival of present regimes, but, on the other hand, development poses difficult problems of managing and controlling economic and social change without endangering these regimes. There is a contradiction between modernization and political stability, between mobilizing human resources essential for development and excluding (or restricting) new groups from participation in the decision-making processes. However, it now appears virtually impossible for any Arab regime to pursue political stabilization by the sort of isolationism practised by Saudi Arabia and North Yemen well into the last decade. Social and economic progress can, therefore, be postulated as the main objective of Arab policies in the next decade.

Whether this objective can be achieved in the years ahead will depend on the prevailing patterns of co-operation or, alternatively, confrontation. Confrontation, involving instability, would seriously disturb social and economic development, especially since strong linkages exist between the international, regional and internal levels of politics. Social and economic development needs co-operation and consensus, implying compromises and the pursuit of limited (as opposed to extreme) objectives. Success will therefore depend on how far elements of confrontation can be eliminated and the proponents of extreme objectives isolated. If successful, modernization could lead to greater stability on all levels – and moderate policies could have a self-perpetuating effect.

The Israeli–Arab conflict

The Israeli–Arab conflict is the main remnant of the period of nationalism and the main disturbing factor from the point of view of social and economic development. The strong linkages between the Israeli–Arab conflict, inter-Arab politics and the internal position of a regime require a settlement sufficiently beneficial for the Arabs to defuse the conflict's potential for disrupting both domestic and inter-Arab politics.

This explains Saudi Arabia's active stand. Though the ultimate aim of the 'moderates' is a settlement of the conflict, they had to trigger off an escalation of that conflict to break the political stalemate, for the linkage between the Israeli–Arab conflict, inter-Arab politics and domestic politics did not allow countries like Egypt and Saudi Arabia to accept the pre-

23

October *status quo*. To illustrate this, let us look at possible Saudi motivations and political objectives in applying the oil weapon (an analysis of Egyptian objectives in launching the October war would follow similar lines):

1. If Saudi Arabia had not applied the oil weapon, confrontation between 'progressive' and 'conservative' regimes would have followed. Egypt would probably have turned towards Libya, which would have raised the prospect of increasing radicalization.
2. Such a confrontation would have posed a serious threat to the stability of conservative regimes in the Persian Gulf, alienating large sectors of politically important groups (such as the officer corps and the bureaucracy) and creating a definite danger of a *coup d'état*. Refusal to support the front-line states with the oil weapon would have incensed public opinion, leading to a high risk of violence, strikes, and subversive action against oil installations, directed from outside with the help of the large Palestinian community in the Gulf.
3. On the other hand, the swing towards the mainstream of Arab public opinion and towards Egypt allowed King Feisal to point out that he backed pan-Arab aspirations more effectively than radical regimes like Libya and Iraq: Saudi prestige was thus greatly enhanced at home and throughout the Arab world.
4. Co-operation with Egypt, once Saudi Arabia's most dangerous adversary, dramatically weakened the forces opposed to the Saudi regime and isolated them from the mainstream of Arab politics.
5. The lead taken in applying the oil weapon, together with the influence which financial support can enlist, have greatly strengthened Saudi Arabia's control over the Arab environment and for the time being practically eliminated domestic opposition and outside threats to Feisal's regime.

The Arab states achieved a high (though essentially negative) degree of solidarity in the last Israeli–Arab war. Such solidarity can be expected again if negotiations on the Israeli–Arab conflict break down, and would almost certainly result in renewed hostilities and the unsheathing of the oil weapon.

As long as the negotiation process continues, however, Arab motivations will most likely differ. Essentially, there are three different groups on the Arab side of the conflict:

1. States with a direct but limited stake in the conflict and/or a strong interest in a settlement to reduce the risks and costs of continued hostility.
2. States with no direct interest in the conflict, involved essentially through pursuit of internal or inter-Arab objectives. These states can afford radical attitudes.
3. The Palestinians, whose attitude to Israel differs fundamentally from that of the Arab states. Israeli and Palestinian interests are difficult to reconcile, and the Palestinians are still in the phase of national assertion and organization. At the moment, they depend heavily on Arab states and outside support, but they possess a considerable potential for undermining the stability of the region and of individual regimes.

The negotiation process now under way makes it necessary to formulate common principles and then translate them into concrete and realistic political objectives. In both phases, splits appear quickly in the Arab ranks. In the first phase, for example, the principles laid down by the front-line states and the oil producers under Saudi Arabian leadership (return of all occupied territories, restoration of Palestinian rights) have not been accepted by Libya and Iraq, and in the second phase the plan for a Palestinian state on the West Bank of the Jordan and the Gaza Strip still meets with stiff resistance from large parts of the Palestine Liberation Organization. If the threat of a shifting balance between moderates and radicals cannot be eliminated, the moderates will probably be forced to retreat. The 'parameters of acceptance' for each phase of the negotiations can therefore be summed up thus: there must be a sufficient majority supporting the moderate line, both within the Arab world and among the Palestinians; and dissenters must be isolated sufficiently to eliminate the risk of large-scale instability.

A drawn-out negotiating process with small but continuous progress might serve stability best, the hope being that during this process Arab preoccupation with Israel could be

24

eliminated to the extent that a final settlement would find sufficient support to open the way to some degree of stability and concentrate on internal development. The key is, of course, the Palestinians: can they be sufficiently isolated to make a political settlement possible?

The great powers

It is possible to draw some conclusions about future Arab objectives in their relations with the great powers on the basis of the arguments developed so far. The group of countries concerned with internal development, thus having a strong interest in an Israeli–Arab settlement, will essentially steer a pro-Western course. They need the United States and the leverage *vis-à-vis* Israel to maintain the momentum of the negotiation process, and they need the assistance of Western countries (including Japan) in order effectively to translate oil wealth into economic and social progress. At the same time, the Soviet Union is still needed as a counterweight to provide the Arabs with additional bargaining strength, and above all Soviet arms are necessary to make the threat of renewed hostilities credible. Even the group of countries favouring a political settlement will therefore maintain relations with the Soviet Union – if Moscow finds that in its own interest.

The groups and countries opposed to a settlement will rely heavily on the Soviet Union. As long as negotiations are under way, the Soviet dilemma between maintaining *détente* with the United States (which implies some support for a Middle East settlement) and regaining and expanding influence in the area (which requires support for the Arab dissenters) can be bridged by advocating and supporting additional Arab demands.

This conclusion can be extrapolated and expanded. The interests of the Arab states (as well as of the great powers themselves) will indicate a continued great-power presence in the Middle East. This is basically because Arab power is still very fragile and limited – resting mainly on vast financial resources, on the power to withhold oil supplies to the consumer nations, and the capacity to provoke military conflict in the area. However, the Arabs still depend for military muscle on arms supplies and training from the great powers. Their oil power has probably already passed its peak, and in any case

political power derived from a trade relationship is an exceptional and evanescent phenomenon. In order to translate oil power into other forms of power the co-operation and assistance of great powers is needed. Europe and Japan will be restricted essentially to an economic role: neither in the Israeli–Arab zone nor in the Persian Gulf do they possess any significant political leverage.

Confrontation between the Arab world and the industrialized countries could be caused by either side. The oil consumers might attempt to force the price of oil down and change the terms of trade adversely for the Arab states, while the latter could try to link the Israeli–Arab conflict to their economic relations with Europe and Japan – for example, by attempting to induce the countries to break political and economic contacts with Israel. This would probably lead to tension, since Europe would be caught between the United States and the Arab world. The Arab countries might also use the oil weapon again to secure their political objectives. At present this could only be done by using Europe and Japan as hostages to exert pressure on the United States (most likely in a breakdown of negotiations on the Israeli–Arab conflict). Assuming that the United States now assumes the role of neutral mediator between the Arabs and Israelis and exerts fully the leverage she has on Israel, a further dramatic alteration in American policies over the Israeli–Arab conflict appears much less likely than prolonged producer–consumer confrontation. But such a confrontation would also go against Arab interests, since it would interrupt the process of transforming oil power into progress in development. Nevertheless it could come about if the complex patterns of foreign policy objectives (Arab objectives resulting from internal and regional requirements and restraints, and American objectives born of alignments with both parties to the conflict: Israel/the Arab countries, Iran/Saudi Arabia) simply do not overlap, and there is no freedom of manoeuvre.

Since Europe and Japan cannot be expected to play an influential role in meeting Arab political demands, and since, alternatively, a producer–consumer confrontation would hurt the Arabs, it would seem advisable for the Arab countries to concentrate American–Arab relations on the political aspects, and Arab–European and Japanese relations on the economic apsects.

This does not exclude some measure of diplomatic support from Europe and Japan for Arab political demands, but it would exclude blunt pressure for political reasons.

The Soviet Union offers only a limited alternative to the West in economic terms: she has no comparable economic potential and insufficient markets for Arab oil. Politically, however, she provides an alternative source of support for a regime and its objectives, represents an additional bargaining card, and is also a supplier of arms. One can therefore expect continued Soviet influence not only because of the Israeli–Arab conflict, but also because of inter-Arab rivalries (e.g., that ranging Saudi Arabia and Iran against Iraq) and because the great-power relationships of the Arab states are functionally diversified (Egypt might try to use the Soviet Union for supplying arms and the United States for projects of economic co-operation and mediating in the Israeli–Arab negotiations; Iraq could rely for political support on the Soviet Union, and for economic development on Europe and Japan).

The Third World
The Arab failure to establish a two-tier oil-price system or set up large-scale multilateral funds to help the Third World overcome the impact of quadrupled oil prices indicates that the Arab oil producers will essentially follow a bilateral approach in relations with the Third World. From their point of view, such an approach has distinct advantages.

Politically, it allows strong leverage to be applied to the recipient country. Concessionary terms for oil supplies (those granted to India by Iraq and Iran, for example, or to Pakistan by Iran) can be withdrawn, and credits and investment can be made conditional upon political prerequisites. One political demand could be the breaking of diplomatic relations with Israel. There could even be competition between suppliers of Third World countries to offset each other's influence (as has apparently happened between Libya and Saudi Arabia in some African countries).

Economically, an analysis of bilateral deals concluded with Third World countries seems to indicate that producer investment in Third World areas aims not only at profitable capital exports with high returns but also aims to solve the manpower problem in some producer

countries (by importing foreign skilled labour for joint ventures, such as the two car-assembly plants to be set up by Arab Gulf states with Pakistani assistance) and to secure the supply of raw materials and other goods. Developments might head towards a new division of labour within the Third World.

It therefore looks as if Arab objectives in the Third World are to establish bilateral influence and co-operation, sometimes by means of multilateral projects involving several Arab states (e.g., plans to set up a Guinean aluminium industry using Egyptian know-how and man-power, and Arab Gulf capital). On the whole, Arab economic aid has fallen far short of off-setting the damage caused to the Third World by oil price increases. It has also been spread unequally, according to the political and economic interests of the donors rather than the needs of the recipients. The Arab states seem to be following the unfortunate example of the industrialized countries.

The Persian Gulf
The Gulf is simultaneously the theatre of inter-Arab rivalries and of potential confrontation with a strong non-Arab power, Iran. This confrontation could well assume features similar to the Israeli–Arab conflict – super-power involvement on opposing sides, and a common stand by the Arab world against an outsider. It could dominate the politics of the Middle East in the next decade.

Iran can be considered the initiator of the present arms race in the Gulf, and her policies will largely determine the state of Arab–Iranian relations. In recent years she has established herself as the dominant power in the Gulf, and is now about to expand her influence into the Indian Ocean, partly in order to secure her trade routes in the Gulf and beyond, and partly in order to become a regional super-power (the 'Japan of the Middle East') in political as well as economic terms.

Iran's foreign policy aims at maintaining the *status quo* in the Gulf and expanding Iranian influence within this framework. This includes containment and isolation of radical forces in the Gulf (Iraq, South Yemen, the Popular Front for the Liberation of Oman and the Arab Gulf) and attempts to weaken them (support for the Sultan of Oman, the Kurdish rebels and North

Yemen). Since the radical threat is perceived as a Soviet-inspired 'encirclement', alignment with the United States can be considered a stable feature of Iranian foreign policy.

Political stability in the region is a precondition for opening the region to Iranian goods and securing raw material supplies – in short, for economic penetration, which can in turn serve political stability. Iran's remarkable diplomatic and economic offensive in the Arab world, which has led to major agreements with, for example, Egypt and Syria, can be interpreted as an attempt to pre-empt an Iranian–Arab confrontation.

The possibility of open reversal of this *status quo* policy appears to exist in three cases: Iran might seize a chance to overthrow the regime in Baghdad; she could try to gain control of the other shore of the Gulf after internal changes in one or several small sheikhdoms or in Saudi Arabia; or internal weaknesses and opposition to the Shah's regime might induce him to resort to blunt imposition of Iranian hegemony over the whole Gulf. All three cases could lead to an Arab–Iranian confrontation.

Both Iraq and Saudi Arabia resent Iranian hegemony in the Gulf, and both have reacted to Iran's vast arms purchases with attempts to build up their own military strength. However, the two countries have different and even contradictory objectives.

Iraq's present regime has a middle-class leadership of army and Baathist party members with a revolutionary and socialist ideology dedicated to radical and rapid social and economic change. The country is in desperate need and has vast potential for a decisive development effort, but her capabilities and resources are heavily strained by internal instability, the past policies of the various military-party regimes, and the Kurdish revolt. There is a real danger of constant frustration of internal expectations.

Iraq traditionally claims a leading position in the Arab world and the regime probably feels that its virtual isolation in Arab affairs unjustly deprives it of the position it deserves. Competition for Arab leadership, as well as the revolutionary ideology of the regime, has led to Iraqi support for Arab dissenters (Popular Front for the Liberation of Palestine) and a pledge to reverse the *status quo* both in the Persian Gulf

and the Israeli–Arab conflict. In the Persian Gulf, where Iraq's support for policies against the *status quo* is founded on a series of concrete problems such as on- and offshore border demarcations, her main opponents are Saudi Arabia and Iran. While Iran and Iraq are in direct confrontation over a common border and various other issues, Iraqi–Saudi rivalry revolves around Kuwait and Yemen.

Given Iraq's opposition to these two allies of the United States, alliance with the Soviet Union is politically essential to the present regime. For various reasons this might be a restraining influence: Moscow might not be willing to accept a large-scale confrontation between Iraq and Iran.

Saudi Arabia will continue to play an important part in inter-Arab affairs in order to control the external environment and appease the nationalistic aspirations of her people and of relevant political groups, such as officers and administrators. In the Persian Gulf her interests and those of Iran thus largely coincide over stabilizing the political *status quo* and containing radical forces. However, it is unlikely that the new Saudi posture in the Arab world could be reconciled with blunt attempts by Iran to impose her hegemony on the Gulf.

Should the present Saudi regime be unable to manage the process of modernization, a military coup seems a distinct possibility. If a strong new order emerges a radical regime in Saudi Arabia would change the pattern of Gulf politics into a tripolar relationship. Internal instability resulting from a coup, on the other hand, would tempt both Iran and Iraq (and possibly also other Arab countries) to intervene, and this could lead to Iranian–Arab or inter-Arab confrontation. A strong Saudi Arabia under a radical regime would probably seek to increase her influence in the Gulf with a different, imperial, attitude towards the smaller sheikhdoms. The balance between Arab moderates and radicals would probably swing with the change in Saudi leadership, and one could expect mounting tensions and confrontation.

Conclusions

Even if the mainstream of Arab policies in the next decade is dominated by a desire to achieve social and economic progress and, as a pre-

27

condition, to foster stability in the Middle East, there are still ample possibilities for instability and upheaval. The key appears to be the regional setting, especially the Israeli–Arab conflict and the Persian Gulf, since these zones provide a focus for Arab solidarity and also underline the need to develop realistic objectives if this solidarity is not to be endangered.

The outside world will be drawn into the Middle East both to develop the Arab world (and its capabilities and power) and to assist in the political process of eliminating the regional sources of tension. But again, there is a risk of relationships with outside countries being enmeshed in the dilemmas of regional and inter-Arab rivalries and conflicts.

We have focused so far on regionally-produced sources of instability, assuming that successful and speedy social and economic transformation is possible. There is, however, a distinct chance of this process breaking down. The result would be growing frustration and mounting inequality between the successful few and the multitude of poor. This could lead to large-scale instability, originating inside the Arab countries but spilling over on to the regional and international level.

Military Lessons of the October War

GÉNÉRAL A. MERGLEN

Two fundamental military facts emerged from the fourth Arab–Israeli war in October 1973: first, the unexpected efficiency of anti-tank and anti-aircraft missiles; second, the incredibly successful launching of a surprise general offensive. These two factors were the main causes of the amazing destruction of material in so short a time. They are likely to alter significantly the balance of forces in the Middle East and in Europe, as well as in other possible theatres of military operations, notably China.

Missiles and the war

Anti-tank and anti-aircraft missiles were known before the October war and had been integrated in military organizations, just as the machine-gun had been taken into account before the First World War. The machine-gun immediately turned out to be the key weapon in land battles in the summer of 1914. The missiles' destructive capacity, when used in large numbers, was spectacular in the October war of 1973.

Of course, anti-aircraft missiles had already proved their worth in the skies of North Vietnam, providing a very testing time for the morale, tactics and technology of the American Air Force. But the impact of anti-aircraft missiles still had to be shown in land battles. This experience was provided by the October war with astonishing effect.

Within the space of two weeks, Israel lost half her armoured force (a major part to missiles) and a quarter of her air force (mainly through missiles) – facts and figures which underline the crucial importance of both anti-tank and anti-aircraft missiles and surprise.

The lesson to be learned about missiles can be summed up as follows: anti-tank and anti-aircraft missiles can be used *en masse* and have a decisive effect in land battles, in both offensive and defensive operations. Compared with tanks and armoured vehicles of all types and with ground attack, tactical bombing and reconnaissance aircraft, as well as helicopters, missiles are easy to carry and to train people to use, and simple and reliable to operate – characteristics which add up to formidable effectiveness against an opponent superior in tanks and aircraft. Above all, this can be achieved at relatively lower cost: about sixteen missile launchers and eighty missiles can be bought for the present price of a single tank.

This lesson from recent events, relating to conventional-type battles, could be cautiously extrapolated to apply to other types of armed conflict. In a war covering large areas, of a subversive or counter-insurgent nature, anti-tank missiles could be used accurately to destroy command posts, communication centres, material depots, stationary or parked vehicles and industrial areas. Small teams equipped with such missiles could infiltrate rear zones and score direct hits by guiding their missiles, with minimum risk to themselves due to the long firing range.

Again, when a battle is fought in depth and formations are widely spread and highly mobile, anti-tank missile units would find useful targets to hit accurately, whose destruction would otherwise require concentrated artillery fire or a considerable or impossible number of aircraft missions. Against airplanes or helicopters, light anti-aircraft missiles could, in the same circumstances, produce results that were not fully anticipated before the October war.

On the whole, the conclusion seems to be that in warfare between regular forces, the new missilry looks like reinforcing in many ways the potential of the defence more than that of the attack; but that in irregular, insurgent operations it tends to strengthen the concealed rebel against the authorities who have more to lose and protect.

If the new weapons may, other things being equal, strengthen the defender in a conventional battle, nevertheless the lesson to be derived from the October war is in line with many historical examples (France 1940, Russia and Hawaii 1941, Korea 1950, Czechoslovakia 1968). Even today there is no assurance of success against a sudden general offensive by an enemy well prepared beforehand. The wealth and complexity of the clues to his hidden intentions, the difficulties of interpreting them, the effects of diplomatic and psychological manoeuvres, the economic constraints in reacting to every potential threat, and sheer errors in reasoning, all combine to produce such an impenetrable opacity that a surprise of the kind which overtook the Israeli and American Intelligence Services and governments must always be considered a possibility.

A new military imbalance

In the Middle East these two essential military lessons (missilry, surprise) will work to Israel's net disadvantage and in favour of war initiatives by the Arabs. Missiles reduce the advantages of the Israeli Defence Force's trump cards, i.e. its armour and aircraft. Because of their demographic superiority, the Arabs can muster and employ a large number of missile-equipped combatants, and this will seriously restrict the power of action of the better quality crews of the Israeli tanks and aircraft. The Arab armies are able to acquire an impressive number of missiles and to train personnel quickly. In the fairly near future, they may even be able to manufacture these weapons, since they are technologically fairly simple, and easy to store and carry. There are limits still to their offensive usefulness: missiles alone are no substitute for a mix of tanks and missiles in the attack. None the less their power in static warfare makes it possible to impose a war of attrition which basically favours the Arabs with their superior numbers.

The value of this tactical counter to traditional Israeli superiority is increased by the permanent possibility of strategic and tactical surprise, since the Arabs, unlike the Israelis, have a political freedom of movement which makes it far easier for them to launch an attack. Until all occupied Arab lands are completely liberated and, beyond that, until the Palestinian problem has found a suitable solution, the Arab governments involved possess a strong legal case and psychological excuse for recourse to such action. The presence of United Nations troops or observers will prove no impediment; it may even be used as camouflage. The strength of the Arab oil-related economic arguments will tend to soften any European, Japanese, and even perhaps American reactions, so long as Israel's very existence is not at stake.

Israel, however, seems no longer in a political position to take a similar military initiative. She lacks the motives or justification of the Arab countries, and the almost complete diplomatic support which their actions have. Israel is therefore very dependent on the support, and subject to the restraints, which the United States may apply.

The October war has disturbed the balance of forces in the Middle East, not so much the numerical balance of the armies and their equipment as their relative worth and the options and actions open to the two adversaries.

This observation takes on new meaning if, as is probable after the successes of light missiles, there is the possibility of medium missiles being used. These are not anti-tank and anti-aircraft, but 'ground-to-ground' missiles, such as the American *Honest John*, *Sergeant* and *Pershing*, or the Soviet *Frog* and *Scud*. They are used to destroy large human or material targets and are capable of firing large high-explosive or nuclear warheads over hundreds of miles. Israel's geographical position, with its small and densely populated areas, surrounded on all sides by large Arab countries whose vital targets are widely distributed, is a grave handicap to Israel and an advantage to her enemies. True, for Egypt, the medium-range missile is to a considerable extent a deterrent to prevent the Israeli air force from striking Cairo or Alexandria, which are not covered by anti-aircraft missiles like the Suez Canal zone. Nevertheless, in the last resort, the considerable demographic superiority of the Arabs would enable them to bear much larger losses in human lives than Israel.

The use of missiles would also make it easier to stop all navigation both in the Tiran Straits, at the entrance of the Gulf of Aqaba, and the Bab-el-Mandeb Straits, at the southern outlet of the Red Sea. If the east bank and Gaza were to be made into a Palestine state, they would become launching bases inserted into Israel, placing all her vital zones, without exception, within direct reach of medium missiles. This military consideration, arising from the October war, is one of the reasons for Israel's refusal to accept the creation of such a state until her own existence is guaranteed on a secure and permanent basis.

These observations lead to the conclusion that the Arab countries will probably try to equip themselves with a strong 'ground-to-ground' missile force, while Israel is already in possession of such an arsenal. The next step, that of nuclear armament, must also be considered. India has shown that a country, once possessing nuclear reactors, can manufacture nuclear devices. It is conceivable that Israel already has nuclear weapons; and though it would certainly require a fairly long time before Egypt could also acquire them, the possibility cannot ultimately be excluded, since both Israel and Egypt are peculiarly vulnerable to nuclear attack. Here, however, the element of mutual deterrence would presumably be uppermost.

If development follows along these lines it is difficult to assess how the two super-powers, each supporting one party to the quarrel will seek to influence or intervene. One of the secondary military lessons of the October war – a local conventional conflict supported by the United States and the Soviet Union – is that the small powers, certainly the Arabs, still retain more freedom of manoeuvre than their patrons would wish. It does seem that Egypt and Syria decided on a general offensive against the wishes of their Soviet ally. On the other hand, once the battle was joined, both camps had an over-riding need of their patrons' material help. The very high destruction rates on the battlefield, the need for new supplies of weapons and ammunition, and, more important still, of new equipment and arms to counter the enemy's technological innovations, are forcing the Middle East countries to base their military effort on the support of the great industrial nations. It should not be thought, for all that, that a simple ban on this external help would compel these countries to refrain from all war activities. Local manufacture of arms and ammunition, and the large stocks already accumulated, would enable hostilities to continue on a lesser scale. It would be a less modern war, as regards heavy armament, but would probably be just as violent, and even more destructive in view of the large number of fighting men involved. Israel would hold a technical advantage, because of her more modern armament industries, but the Arabs could throw into battle much larger numbers of fanatical peasant soldiers. One of the secondary lessons of the October war is that the worth of the Arab field soldiers and officers has considerably improved, both in morale and capacity to use complex weapons. That being said, recent experience shows that the super-powers are able to send adequate supplies to small nations engaged in active land and air operations. In spite of the limited battle zones, the heavy losses incurred in modern and intensive warfare should be emphasized. In eighteen days, some 100,000 soldiers of both camps were killed or wounded, 9,000 were taken prisoner and 2,000 tanks and 500 aircraft were destroyed.

Overall, the Arab countries have sharply shifted the balance in the Middle East and restored Arab military honour. Their leaders will certainly, now, assess carefully the causes of their shortcomings and failures during the war, and draw their own conclusions. Both Syria's heavy frontal attack on the Golan on 6 October 1973, and Egypt's cautious immobility east of the Suez Canal, up to 14 October will be reappraised. The occupied territories might have been recovered had there been a more imaginative and lively High Command, greater mobility in the major units, a more rapid and flexible deployment of anti-aircraft missiles, and a more adroit use of the anti-tank missile cover against Israeli counter-attacks.

Both camps must be expected to draw the strategic and tactical lessons of the October war. But the Arabs are more likely to benefit by it. The Israelis have already brought their armed forces to a very high pitch of military efficiency. The Arabs, whose people have been morally encouraged by this first achievement, who possess ten times as many soldiers as the enemy, who are using the Soviet technical advance in simplifying missiles and electronic warfare, have more scope for improving their general military performance.

31

Lessons for Europe

For Europe, the military lesson to be learned from the October war is that if there were to be a conventional war in the near future it would go against the Atlantic Alliance. The two essential factors, surprise and missiles, are a positive element in favour of the Warsaw Pact countries. It is unthinkable, in the present political and psychological context, and in view of its military organization and existing material means, that the West would take the initiative of a surprise attack against the East. The reverse is possible, however, due to the Eastern bloc's centralization, its military infrastructure, logistic standardization and armed forces, which are moreover being steadily enlarged and improved. The possibility of a surprise general offensive should be taken seriously. To rely on a five- to ten-day warning period to deploy large formations, to call up reservists, to take civil-defence measures, and to receive reinforcements from neighbouring countries or from across the Atlantic, seems excessively optimistic if not self-deluding, due to laziness of mind or unwillingness or inability to act. This is particularly the case as NATO cannot rely on an 'Israeli-type reaction', i.e., a response by a single, quick-moving government, a single High Command ready for action at a moment's notice, reservists trained over thirty months of military service and one- to two-month annual refresher courses, operating over a small territory and on internal lines of communication better than those of the enemy.

Today, if there were a surprise attack, the main Western counter, beyond static and mobile defence, would be based on armoured units and ground-attack aircraft. The large number and high quality of the Warsaw Pact forces' anti-tank and anti-aircraft missiles might well nip in the bud such armoured and air counters. Because of the high rate of human and material destruction in battle, the initial advantages held by the aggressor who would have, in any case, more than double the number of tanks, planes, helicopters, artillery and air defences, would be of capital importance and probably decisive. Reinforcements and reserve forces would arrive more quickly and massively by land from the Soviet Union than be sea and air from the United States. The efficiency of the American air bridge to the Middle East should not hide the fact that the size of the supplies carried – 23,000 tons in fifteen days – would be relatively minute for theatres of operations larger than the 180km of the Suez Canal or the 75km of the Golan, in which several army groups were involved, or if the air bridge were submitted to air or missile attacks by a powerful enemy.

A surprise general conventional attack from East to West could, in present conditions, hope to achieve its objectives in such a short time as to exclude political intervention and to render any nuclear threat doubtful or inoperative. If the West does not wish to stake its independence and existence on the single card of general nuclear war, the only remaining effective means of resistance, the lessons of the October war should induce it to modify its defensive forces by giving priority to light, anti-tank and anti-aircraft missiles. Their small cost, compared with that of tanks and aircraft, and their ease of handling, would make it possible to equip a large number of men who, spread in depth over large territories, would be able to pin down the enemy's motorized advance without themselves constituting suitable nuclear targets. Of course, the soldiers would have to have the will to fight as had both the Arabs and the Israelis in the October war. The new weapons could ultimately improve the relative potential for defence of NATO but only if there were sufficient conventional forces, which is not the case today.

For a huge country like China, with its immeasurable population and its industries disseminated throughout the provinces, the proof of the efficiency of light anti-tank and anti-aircraft missiles offers an important lesson. Faced with a highly industrialized potential enemy, armed with sophisticated tanks and planes, its best counter might seem to be the use of a large mass of fighters equipped with machine-guns and missiles, rather than expensive armoured divisions and air assault squadrons, which take time to form, age quickly and offer ideal nuclear targets. The Soviet motorized forces, limited in number, would risk being submerged by the Chinese masses who would be transformed by their simple but efficient weaponry combined with a superior national and fighting faith into untamable opponents in a conventional war, and a large number of whom would survive any nuclear conflagration.

The light anti-tank and anti-aircraft missiles which proved themselves in the October war, as the machine-gun did in the summer of 1914, may also prove to be decisive weapons in subversive activities and revolutionary conflict in which, in the past, tanks and planes have been formidable weapons against isolated insurgents fighting in rural or mountain areas and against rebellious urban concentrations. Light or medium missiles could impede navigation in the Hormuz Straits, at the entrance of the Persian Gulf, or stop any movement by law-and-order forces in some African or South American countries.

Recent experience is likely to encourage the military leaders of rebels in Kurdistan, the Dho-far, Eritrea, Angola and Mozambique to try and acquire by any means, financial or political, the anti-tank and anti-aircraft missiles which enable a rustic fighter, hidden in the landscape to destroy from a distance, without much risk, a tank, a plane, a helicopter, a lorry, a small fort, a group of enemy soldiers, as well as petrol installations and other industrial sites.

These are potentially portentous develop-ments, even if it is very difficult, and risky, at this early stage to draw all the possible military lessons that there may be to learn from the fourth Arab–Israeli war.

The Military Build-Up: Arms Control or Arms Trade?

GEOFFREY KEMP

Over the past twelve months the quantities of military equipment transferred to the Middle East or negotiated for future transfer has reached what can only be described as staggering proportions. The estimated value of transfers and orders has been put at about $13 billion. Of this total by far the largest proportions have resulted from American aid and sales to Israel, Iran and Saudi Arabia (about $8·5 billion) and Soviet transfers to Egypt and Syria (about $4 billion).

The magnitude of these transactions can be explained by two separate phenomena: first, the October 1973 war between Israel, Egypt and Syria which drastically depleted weapons inventories and required major American and Soviet replenishment programmes; second, the decision by the oil-producing nations, especially Iran, Saudi Arabia and Kuwait to embark upon major rearmament programmes designed, in part, to bolster their security in a region beset with political and military conflict. In terms of defence expenditure, the proposed outlays for 1974 by the Gulf states now equal, if not exceed, the proposed outlays for those countries most directly involved in the Arab–Israel dispute. Iran now ranks ninth in the world defence expenditure league. In 1966 she ranked twenty-ninth.

The quality of the weapons ordered or requested by the major consumers parallels the quantitative aspects of the build-up. Iran has ordered the very latest generation of American air-superiority fighters (80 F-14 *Tom Cat* and the *Phoenix* missile system at the time of writing). The Iranian Air Force already has in service or on order over 150 F-4 *Phantom*, and 250 F-5 as well as 6 707-320 Boeing air tankers and many of the latest American avionic systems. Soon Iran will have one of the world's largest inven-

tories of modern tanks (800 *Chieftain* are on order from Britain) and helicopters (over 550 American helicopters are on order, including 200 *Sea Cobra* gunships). In terms of naval forces, the Shah will soon possess the world's largest hovercraft fleet (supplied by Britain), as well as two of the very latest British SAAM-class frigates.

The proposed Saudi Arabian and Kuwaiti programmes, although less spectacular, are replete with extremely modern weapons, including the American F-5E fighter, French *Mirage III*, and possibly American F-4 *Phantom*. The Soviet Union is reported to have made available the MiG-25 to Kuwait, and would almost certainly sell such weapons to the Shah if he wanted them. Israel has reached an agreement in principle for the most advanced American air systems, including the F-14 *Tom Cat* and more F-4 *Phantom*, plus dozens of sophisticated armaments and support systems, including air- and surface-launched precision guided munitions and electronic counter-measures aircraft. However, unlike the oil-rich countries, Israel and her immediate Arab adversaries – Egypt, Syria and Jordan, and Lebanon – cannot afford to be choosy about their suppliers, since none of them has the foreign exchange to buy on the open market. The United States has now tentatively approved the sale to Israel of very advanced weapon systems, including the *Lance* surface-to-surface missile and the F-15 air-superiority fighter. The Soviet Union has reportedly transferred some Tu-22 to Iraq and has transferred but retained control over the *Scud* surface-to-surface missiles believed to be in Egypt and Syria.

Thus, while the quantitative and qualitative dimensions of build-up are impressive through-

34

out the Middle East, there is an important difference between those recipients who are operating in what can only be described as a 'buyers' market', and those, like Israel and Egypt, who are becoming more and more dependent upon their friends and allies to provide them with weapons at highly subsidized rates.

In addition to the build-up of advanced conventional arms, Egypt, Iran and Israel have all recently negotiated for the sale of American and French nuclear power plants. Such negotiations suggest a potentially ominous linkage between the growing availability of nuclear fuel and the conventional arms race, which includes weapons easily adapted to nuclear delivery systems such as the American F-4 and F-14 and the Soviet Tu-16 and MiG-23.

As suggested, these weapons are being sent to a geographical area replete with sources for military conflict. The potential for interstate war remains high between Israel and her Arab neighbours, between Iran and Iraq, Iraq and Kuwait, and between the countries surrounding or adjacent to the southern Arabian peninsula and the Horn of Africa. Serious intra-state military conflict continues in Ethiopia, and especially Iraq and Oman. If peripheral regional conflicts such as those between India and Pakistan, and Greece and Turkey and Cyprus are taken into account, it can be appreciated that the scope for violence in a region of crucial importance to the West is probably on the ascendency rather than on the decline. Though it is the view of many that the propensity for violence is increased by the transfer of advanced arms this still remains an open question.

Strategic issues and perspectives
What are the most important strategic implications of the military build-up? Are the major supplier nations engaged in competitive policies which are feeding the fires of existing conflict – as in the case of American and Soviet transfers to those countries directly involved in the Arab–Israeli conflict – and also paving the way for future conflict – as in the case of American, British, and French arms sales to the oil-rich countries of the Gulf? Is this behaviour likely, in the long run, to increase the risks of war and the disruption of oil supplies, or are the supplier countries acting rationally given the uncertainties

of political trends in such a highly volatile area? If the former proposition is believed, what steps should the supplier countries in general, and the NATO countries in particular, take to defuse or moderate the dangers of the military build-up? Should not Britain, France and the United States explore either among themselves or, preferably, with the Soviet Union the possibility of more stringent regulations on the transfer of arms?

Alternatively, if it is believed that current supplier policies reflect the realities of power in the region, should *unrestricted* arms transfers be further encouraged, or should some informal limits be placed upon the issue of export licences or upon credit for sales? For instance, should the United States sell the Shah of Iran *any* non-nuclear weapons he wants, including such possibilities as *Lance* surface-to-surface missiles, or should some attempt be made to impose qualitative constraints on his growing arsenal?

In searching for answers to these questions, it should be remembered that our understanding of the political and strategic dynamics and consequences of regional, non-nuclear arms races is exceedingly primitive despite a growing literature on the statistics and mechanisms of the international transfer of arms. The Western strategic and arms-control communities have devoted far more study to the analysis of the American–Soviet nuclear balance than to the nuances of the Arab–Israel or Iran–Iraq–Saudi Arabia military equation. Why? First, in spite of its undoubted complexities, the parameters of the bipolar nuclear arms race are easier to define and, therefore, easier to analyse, than the parameters of multipolar conventional arms races. Second, there has been much more government sponsorship and private funding of arms-control research directly relating to nuclear issues. Third, the initial impetus for studying the control of nuclear weapons came from Western scientists, predominantly American, who had personally been involved in the Manhattan Project during World War II. This community, which still enjoys great prestige in international circles, has not, by and large, had the same personal stake or interest in the basic practical questions relating to the control and regulation of conventional conflict. For this reason, a great many of the general strategic propositions put forward to explain the role of arms in the Middle East and other conflict regions are highly subjective and are rarely based on empirical analysis.

For the sake of simplicity, the most frequently used arguments can be presented within the framework of two opposing propositions. The first proposition advocates what might be called the arms-control perspective. It holds that a continuance of the *status quo* or 'free market' in arms transfers is not likely to serve the long-run interests of either the suppliers or the recipients.[1] In contrast, the second proposition argues that the present 'free market' is the only viable alternative and that arms-control measures are likely to be either useless, discriminatory, dangerous, or all three, and, for that reason, are not likely to be supported by suppliers and recipients of arms. The key arguments in both propositions can be summarized as follows:

Proposition 1: the case for arms control

1. If massive American and Soviet military aid to Israel and the Arab countries continues, and if a 'free market' for arms sales persists in the Persian Gulf area, the numerous sources for political conflict between the many recipients will be intensified as a result of the escalating arms race and fears concerning a change in the balance of power. This, in turn, can only increase the long-run risks of military conflict. Military conflict anywhere in the Middle East cannot be in the interests of the major arms suppliers and is unlikely to be in the long-run interests of the major recipients. However, disruptive military conflict *is* in the interests of the revolutionary forces who believe they can only benefit from growing international chaos.

2. Recent wars in the Middle East (and elsewhere) have demonstrated the importance of deception, speed, surprise and advanced technology in achieving successful military victories. Such stratagems require good planning and modern weapons. In particular, those weapons

systems that emphasize mobility and rapid accurate fire-power are essential. Given the international political environment in which all Middle East conflicts take place, there are strong incentives on the part of the local powers to use blitzkrieg tactics to ensure quick success. However, the political dangers of such tactics are high, and, if military success is not forthcoming within a very short time-frame, the prospects for international intervention and a possible escalation of the conflict will increase.

3. If unrestricted transfers of very advanced long-range weapons, such as the F-14 *Tom Cat*, the F-4 *Phantom*, the MiG-23/25 and modern destroyers, were to continue, the strategic implications would soon spread beyond traditional regional boundaries. For instance, India could not remain indifferent to major procurement programmes in Iran, especially if they were accompanied by large-scale construction for new air, land, and naval bases such as the facility Iran is developing on the Gulf of Oman at Chah Bahar. The combined Iranian and Pakistani defence programmes could eventually pose a serious threat to India's western front and western maritime approaches. Likewise, Israel will eventually have to include the military potential of Saudi Arabia, Kuwait and Libya, and even Sudan, Somalia and North and South Yemen in her calculations of the Arab–Israeli balance of power. This would be particularly relevant if the major Arab nations were ever to standardize their weapons programmes and agree to confront Israel by blockading her oil supplies at strategic choke points far away from Israel's borders, such as the Bab-el-Mandeb Straits at the southern entrance to the Red Sea.

4. An unrestricted arms build-up throughout the Middle East, although initially limited to 'conventional' weapons, albeit of a highly sophisticated variety, might soon whet the appetites of some of the major recipients, especially those with a lot of money, for the most prestigious of all instruments of military power – nuclear weapons. Appetites could also be stimulated by the example of India's nuclear programme and the renaissance of nuclear proliferation as an important international issue. It is highly unlikely that the introduction of nuclear weapons into the Middle East would be paralleled by the emergence of politically stable regimes. Aside from Israel – which may have the bomb al-

---

[1] I use the term 'free market' to describe the situation in which arms consumers with adequate funding can shop around among the various supplier nations and buy from whom they like. The term should not be confused with the free market which exists in a situation of perfect competition. That is to say it is *not* assumed that the major arms manufacturers in the private sector can sell to consumers free of government control since this is, most certainly, not the case.

ready – and Lebanon, political leadership in the Arab countries and Iran is based upon the rule of individuals such as Sadat or the Shah, conservative dynasties such as those headed by King Feisal, and volatile political elites such as the Baathist parties in Iraq and Syria. Leadership changes in many of these countries are frequent and men such as the Shah, Feisal and Hussein, who have shown a remarkable proclivity to survive, could be victims of *coups d'état*. For example, the type of person who ousted the Shah would have serious implications for the West and the Soviet Union. This would be especially so if he were replaced by a Gaddafi-type radical or, alternatively, a right-wing but nationalist anti-Western junta.

5. The transfer of large quantities of advanced technology into undeveloped countries will have major effects upon the social system. While in the long run such changes may lead to a general improvement in living standards, in the short run the emergence of a technocratic class may prove disruptive and add to the already long agenda of sources for domestic conflict in many Middle East countries.

6. For those who support Israel, a continuance of current arms-supply policies can only work in favour of the Arabs. They have more money, more manpower and more friends. Their performance in October 1973 suggests that their capacity to co-ordinate joint military operations has improved. Over time, they could establish an effective high command and even a 'common market' for arms procurement. This could lead them to develop a capability that would almost certainly ensure that any future war with Israel would be as protracted and as bloody as the October 1973 encounter. Although Israel might still 'win' the war, her military and civilian casualties would be high, perhaps higher than in 1973, and the domestic political and psychological repercussions would be traumatic, to say the least.

7. Those who argue that the flow of arms cannot be controlled or regulated, given the conflicting goals of the suppliers and recipients, ignore the experience of the past and prefer, instead, to adopt excessively pessimistic and negative postures. Between 1950 and 1954 Britain, France and the United States were successful in regulating the flow of arms through the machinery of the Near East Arms Co-ordinating Committee which was set up as a result of the 1950 Tripartite Declaration. This policy only began to fail when the Soviet Union, which was not a party to the Declaration, decided it was in her interests to supply Egypt and Syria with modern weapons. Clearly, any new proposed regulations would have to include Soviet participation, but this is not out of the question, especially if Soviet co-operation on this matter were linked to the broader issues of *détente* diplomacy. If the big four arms suppliers reached accord to impose greater restrictions, starting, perhaps, with long-range surface-to-surface missiles, no other country or group of countries would be able to replace them in terms of credit and equipment, certainly not the other major arms producers such as China, Germany, Poland, Czechoslovakia, Italy and Sweden. Furthermore, Secretary Kissinger's recent diplomacy has shown that limited forms of arms control can be implemented on the battlefield as witnessed by the Sinai and Golan cease-fire arrangements between Egypt, Israel and Syria. There is no reason why these arrangements could not be augmented and improved to cover expanded geographical areas, more specific types of force structures, and changes in political–military doctrines. Furthermore if, as some experts argue, the new military technologies such as precision-guided munitions are more likely to benefit the defence of territory rather than traditional offensive operations, it might be possible for Israel to withdraw nearly to her 1967 borders and still retain a strong security position.

Proposition 2: the case for a 'free market' in arms
1. The demand for arms by Middle East countries is based upon genuine security requirements. To suggest that the external powers can either determine or dictate these requirements to less powerful sovereign states has overtones of patronage and colonialism that are all too familiar to the population of the region. For this reason, arms-control proposals will certainly not be greeted with enthusiasm by the local powers, and will probably be regarded with amusement or hostility, depending upon how serious they are. If any Middle East arms-control agreement were to be negotiable, it would probably have to be restricted to weapons systems which had either not yet been transferred (e.g., aircraft carriers) or those weapons already in the area

whose utility was low (e.g., sub-sonic, low payload interceptors). Hence the most 'controllable' weapons would probably not cover those which are currently regarded as essential for national security (air-superiority weapons, deep interdiction aircraft, armoured fighting vehicles, helicopters, and small warships and their associated systems). Furthermore, all this assumes that it would be possible to delineate the boundaries for a regional arms-control agreement. Which countries would participate? Turkey and Algeria, as well as Egypt and Israel? Pakistan and India, as well as Iran and Iraq? Once the linkages between the strategic balance in different specific areas are taken into account, it becomes exceedingly difficult to foresee a workable, acceptable regional agreement that has teeth.

2. If, however, the external powers, acting alone, could agree upon *effective* arms control measures to certain countries (e.g., major limitations on the supply of Mach 2·0 aircraft and heavy armour), it is doubtful whether they could be fair to all recipients. The fundamental geographical, demographic and cultural differences among the local states in terms of their preferred military–political doctrines would seem to ensure that a universally-agreed standard of the requirements for a military balance would be impossible to achieve. For example, how would one trade off Israel's technical skills for her small population? A suppliers' agreement to place *qualitative* restrictions on armaments would have more disadvantages for Israel since her ability to defeat the Arabs in the last four wars has depended upon the possession of modern armaments, as well as upon the skills of her armed forces. *Reductio ad absurdum*, an arms control agreement limiting everybody to small arms would ensure eventual Arab victory in battle. Consequently, a suppliers' agreement that was regarded as unfair by one or more of the recipients would undoubtedly lead to strong counter-reactions. Ultimately it might encourage preventive war and the expansion of local armament-production, or, equally serious, it might encourage the development of indigenous nuclear weapons, which, in turn, might lead to preventive war. Thus, it is not at all clear that well-meaning but discriminatory regulations on arms transfers would serve the three usually-stated goals of arms control – to reduce the

risks of war; to reduce the level and intensity of war, should it occur; to reduce the costs of military programmes.

3. Therefore, greater controls on the flow of arms to the Middle East might not be in the interests of the external suppliers, let alone the recipients. While it might be possible for all parties to reach accord on the *principles* of conventional arms control, and also agree to keep nuclear weapons out of the area, any *serious* proposals to control non-nuclear weapons would require as careful study as the problems of strategic nuclear arms limitation and mutual and balanced force reduction (MBFR) in the European theatre. Both the strategic arms limitation and MBFR negotiations have shown that the process is painfully slow and complex even when there are strong incentives to reach accord.

4. Those who point to the 1950 Tripartite Declaration as a model for possible suppliers' agreements ignore the most important lessons from that period. The restrictions on arms supplies did not eliminate or significantly reduce tensions within the Middle East. Egypt and Iraq continued to vie for leadership of the Arab world; Israel and the Arab countries continued to engage in low-level hostilities culminating in the raids and counter-raids across the Sinai and Gaza in 1955–56. Furthermore, the Western arms regulations made it possible for the Soviet Union to enter the Middle East in the guise of providing arms to Egypt. A quadripartite agreement might pave the way for Chinese or even Indian arms transfers. Although neither of these countries could match the quality of arms and the amounts of credit which the major suppliers can provide, they could obstruct the attempts to limit armaments to certain levels. Thus, at the margin, other maverick suppliers could well torpedo efforts designed to promote mutual and balanced force levels. Similarly, those who point to the early 1974 Kissinger cease-fire agreements between Egypt, Israel and Syria base their optimism on the most spurious of evidence. The sources for conflict between the Arabs and Israel have not been significantly reduced. A new war is a distinct possibility, and, for this reason, neither the Arabs nor the Israelis are going to accept willingly externally imposed restrictions on their military capabilities.

5. In terms of the oil-rich countries, it is beyond

the bounds of credibility to think that Britain, France, the United States, or even the Soviet Union would turn down multi-million and even billion dollar arms deals which guaranteed future oil supplies. Not only does it make good business sense to sell arms, since Iran, Saudi Arabia, and Kuwait have huge shopping lists for commercial products, ranging from supersonic airliners to soft drink factories, but it is also a political necessity, and, in the case of Europe, an economic necessity. Without large export orders to reduce unit costs, the viability of an independent Western European arms industry and advanced research and development base would be in jeopardy. The economic power of the Organization of Petroleum Exporting Countries (OPEC) is such that they can get what they want, at least for the next five years. Furthermore, the largest of them can buy significant shares in the industries of the advanced world, including conceivably, Western armaments industries. The Shah of Iran's recent acquisition of about 25 per cent of the Krupp empire may be a sign of things to come.

Strategic realities

How does one weigh the arguments presented in these two conflicting perspectives? As suggested, the issues are complex, and, precisely because there are so many uncertainties in the Middle East situation, elements of both arguments have merit. My own inclination is to avoid dogmatic judgments as to what will or will not happen as a result of the continuing military build-up. Nevertheless, there are certain strategic issues which, it can be argued, transcend the extreme positions portrayed in the two propositions, and are more likely to influence the nature of conflict in the Middle East.

The first reality is that the prospects for armed conflict between Israel and her neighbours, between the countries of the South Arabian peninsula, and among the countries on the littoral of the Persian Gulf remain high, *irrespective* of the magnitude and nature of the arms flow. This suggests that the effect upon propensities for violence of arms transfers or arms control measures by themselves will be marginal. In some cases these effects could make all the difference between peace and war; on other occasions they might have no discernible effects.

The second reality is that the October war of 1973 has dramatically changed the overall balance of power in the Middle East. Although, from a military perspective, Israel won that war in a very impressive way, the economic and political effects of the oil embargo have isolated Israel and have made her totally dependent for the time being upon the United States for her military survival. Thus the United States is more directly involved in the Arab–Israeli conflict than at any time in the past twenty-five years. This, in turn, suggests that the United States has much more control of the relationship between arms and conflict in the context of the Arab–Israel dispute than in the Persian Gulf.

The third reality is that, apart from Iran, the oil-rich states presently have very small, poorly-educated populations. There will be severe constraints over at least the next decade upon their capacity to absorb and effectively operate the endless supply of advanced arms which they seem to want to buy. Thus it can be expected that the current boom in sales will soon peak, and thereafter the annual value of transfers will decline.

The fourth reality is that although the transfer of advanced arms may not exacerbate conflict – and in some circumstances may even help to deter it if, for whatever reasons, conflict occurs – the existence of large, modern inventories of weapons will most certainly influence the nature, scope and intensity of the war. It is difficult to see how F-14 *Tom Cat* and *Chieftain* tanks can protect highly vulnerable installations such as oil fields, oil refineries, and loading piers if war breaks out. It is very easy to see how they could destroy them. This suggests that the stakes in Middle East conflicts – as distinct from the risks of those conflicts occurring – are growing commensurate with the magnitude of the military programmes. It is also becoming more difficult to insulate conflict in, say, the Horn of Africa or the Persian Gulf from the wider strategic environment in the Eastern Mediterranean and the Indian Ocean.

The fifth reality is that new trends in highly effective, small, non-nuclear weapons technology may alter some of the basic tactics and doctrine of non-nuclear warfare. First, although there is no agreement as to the implications of new non-nuclear technology for general military strategy and tactics, it can be argued that in certain

39

environments small, accurate, easily operated and relatively cheap anti-tank and anti-aircraft missiles may make sustained offensive operations against a well-prepared defence less effective. If this is correct, then it places greater premium than ever upon deception, speed and surprise as the crucial elements in any offensive military operation.

Second, at least for the next few years, the delicate infrastructure of modern industrial societies will become more vulnerable to attack by man-portable weapons which will soon be readily available on the arms market to any buyer with money. Facilities for oil extraction, production and distribution are among the most vulnerable targets. A radical government or irregular forces equipped with modern weapons could attack oil facilities on the Gulf and perhaps close the Bab-el-Mandeb Straits for periods of time. Provided they possessed heavy firepower weapons, they might even be able to interfere with sea traffic through the Straits of Hormuz. In the latter case, the ability to close those Straits would have catastrophic implications, especially for Japan and Western Europe. It is Iran's policy to prevent this possibility by using whatever military force is required, and it was for precisely this reason that the islands of Greater and Lesser Tumb and Abu Musa were annexed in 1971. In the absence of any Western initiatives for managing the sources of conflict in the Gulf, Iranian policy has clear political attractions despite the risks involved. However, it does presume that Iran will eventually play the role of a regional super-power and will require the necessary weapons to be one. To this extent, the destiny of the Gulf, and, for the next ten years, of the West may be in the hands of the Shah, a man who has numerous enemies.

In contrast, the destiny of the countries in the Arab–Israel conflict lies in the hands of the United States, the Soviet Union, and King Feisal. In other words, external powers have much greater control over events along the Arab–Israel border than they do along the shores of the Persian Gulf. In the former case, the United States and the Soviet Union could dictate a settlement including far-reaching arms-control proposals. They and the other industrial powers are far less able to influence the trends in the Gulf. The fact that neither the Soviet Union nor the United States could easily justify intervention in the Gulf may, in a perverse way, increase the risks that a war might continue long enough to interfere physically with the oil supplies. Despite all the talk of Iran's growing military power, her forces are untested in major battle.

The sixth reality is that we do not know what to do about the military build-up. We do not know whether the arms-control approach or the free market approach, or what combination of the two, will best serve the long-term interests of an extremely heterogeneous group of local and external nations. We assume that major military conflict in the Middle East is not in the general Western, Iranian, Israeli, Arab or even Soviet interest because it could lead to nuclear war and the disruption of oil supplies. For this reason, it is in the interests of the strategic community to treat the problem of military power and regional conflict in the Middle East with the analytical precision it has so far reserved for studies of the bipolar American–Soviet arms race.

Committee Discussions on the Impact of the 1973 War

Report to the Conference

LESLIE ASPIN

Discussions on the 'Military Lessons of the October War' came back again and again to the missiles (anti-air, anti-tank) which so dominated the newspaper-reporting in that war. Général Merglen in his paper thought the introduction of missiles an extremely significant development in the history of warfare. Others were not so sure.

Those emphasizing the importance of missiles pointed to what the Egyptians were able to do on the east side of the Canal under the cover of missiles only. Others emphasized that Israeli tanks did much better against anti-tank missiles when they were part of a balanced force, and Israeli planes did much better against anti-air missiles when they were using proper electronic counter-measures (ECM).

What may be true is that missiles, while certainly not making the tank and the aircraft obsolete, change their roles somewhat. Tanks, in addition to their more conventional role as an anti-tank weapon, may now be called upon more and more to attack the enemy's infrastructure after breakthroughs (communication centres, anti-air units, and especially ammunition stockpiles, which, in the light of recent experience of ammunition expenditures will probably be very large and very near the front). Aircraft may also be better used after a breakthrough and may lose their close air-support role to missile artillery or at least perform that role differently via air-to-ground standoff missiles with TV guidance.

Beyond the missile dispute there was general agreement that the war offered a combination of new lessons learned (the importance of ECM) and old lessons relearned (the importance of the balance of forces, e.g., Israel early in the war; and the importance of flexibility, e.g., the Arabs after crossing the Canal).

It is not easy projecting the effect that further development of these weapons will have either on the structure of the peace or on the war should it happen again. Particularly there was concern about surface-to-surface missiles (*Honest John*, *Sergeant* and *Pershing* of the United States or the Soviet's *FROG* and *Scud*).

Depending upon the further development of these kinds of weapons the balance may tilt against Israel with its more concentrated population and smaller territory. Such missiles may also make pre-emptive attack a possibility again. By 1973 the Arabs had made pre-emptive attack by the Israelis much more difficult as the result of having aircraft shelters with gun and missile defence, and runway repair facilities. Newer and better surface-to-surface missiles may overcome these obstacles and make pre-emptive attacks possible again.

All of the above depends upon further improvements in surface-to-surface missiles. Currently these missiles are a more expensive way of delivering ordnance than say F-4 aircraft. It also depends heavily and importantly on what kind of electronic counter-measures each side develops.

The military lessons of the October war for NATO are not simple because of terrain, visibility and other differences. One point of significance is Israeli progressive mobilization – tanks going into battle early without balance of mechanized infantry units and thus most vulnerable to missiles.

Another lesson for NATO, or anyone else for

41

that matter, concerns surprise and warning. This is an old subject which has been given renewed emphasis. As an old subject many of the old problems remain. Mechanical devices are still vulnerable to human error. The decision to mobilize is a political decision which brings in a lot of other factors (e.g., economic cost) and in any case takes time. There are many ways to lull the enemy's political leadership (many practice manoeuvres, frequent false alarms, etc.).

Geoffrey Kemp in his Paper gave a number of reasons why limiting arms sales in the Middle East would be very difficult. The discussions on the paper immediately added more to the list. Economic advantages of arms sales for the seller countries (balance of payments, lowering the unit cost of weapons) was emphasized. The importance of linkages to other regions was also stressed as were such reasons as the utility war still has for achieving political ends in the Middle East.

Controlling arms sales in general, not only for the Middle East, has, of course, been discussed for many years. But there are factors today which are in many ways different from those that have prevailed in the past. Today there are many arms *sales* whereas before it was mainly aid. Seller governments are pushing the arms trade much more than before. And the weapons sold are no longer of a previous generation; now they are the latest models.

There are two approaches to reducing the arms trade which are not always distinguished. One would achieve reductions through agreement by the recipient nations, the other through agreement by the seller nations. The problems are very different in each case.

Reduction in the arms trade through agreement by the recipient nations has all the problems of arms reduction in Europe and then some. Certain pre-conditions must exist. There should already be a political settlement. There ought to be a recognition of the costs of waging war by the two sides and some kind of a desire to avoid incurring those costs. A certain level of security should exist. What it all means is that reducing the arms trade through agreement by recipient nations if at all possible is nevertheless a long way off.

But several factors may in the long-run help recipient nations agree to such a reduction.

Severe financial limitations of the immediate combat countries (Israel, Egypt and Syria) is one. The problem of absorbing large quantities of sophisticated weapons is another. Technically-trained people are a scarce resource and economic development competes with the military for their talents. The vast attrition rate coupled with high unit costs of these weapons also imposes some kind of limitation. Thus while arms-control *agreement* among recipient nations may be a long way off, some kinds of limitations may eventually be possible.

The second approach of limiting arms trade via agreement by the seller nations has its difficulties too. Not the least of these are the economic pressures as well as internal and external political pressures.

Looking at complete controls is, however, not the only way of considering the problem. Perhaps some kind of action short of total agreement might be possible. Maybe some informal agreement of some limited restraints rather than a carefully worked out formal agreement is possible. Is there any possibility of concentrating on certain *kinds* of weapons rather than all weapons? Is there any possibility of starting with regional agreements?

An aspect of the problem which many of those in the discussion thought should receive a good deal more attention was the effect that arms sales had on the economy and social conditions within the Arab states. Potentially of great importance is the effect the development of a technically trained younger military group might have on the system. It could be both internally and externally destabilizing.

A much discussed point following Hanns Maull's Paper 'Future Arab Options' is the extent to which the Arab states might be interested in shifting from external aggression to internal economic development. There is still no settlement. There is still big power influence. There is still rivalry between states and within states.

There are many reasons why a Middle East settlement is so difficult, so factors that will encourage a settlement should be noted. One is fear of destruction in Israel, particularly after Arab successes in the last war. Second is the pressure for economic development in the Arab states. Third is the limits on Soviet actions if the Soviet Union wants to maintain *détente*.

The main problem is of course the Palestinians. In any future course of action the Arabs will need to press for a settlement which satisfies the largest number of Palestinians. The Palestinian question may however prove to be a two-edged sword – useful to the Arabs in settlement discussions now, but following a settlement there may be problems with internal subversion. The discussion produced no new or ideal solutions to the Palestinians land question.

Sprinkled throughout all the discussions were thoughts and speculation about the kinds of changes that will be taking place in Arab societies. There is no precedent for the kind of shift in economic power which has occurred. The internal repercussions could be very great – wealth in few hands, more military weapons and a military elite to operate them. Some countries have gained enormously from the economic shift, others not at all. Some regimes have taken some steps in the direction of social change, while others have achieved only very little progress.

2 THE ARAB-ISRAELI DISPUTE:
Great power behaviour
LAWRENCE L. WHETTEN

INTRODUCTION

For a quarter of a century the consequences of the Arab–Israeli conflict have been felt in virtually every nation in the world. Yet the interests and policies of the two great powers have been characterized by ambivalence, partiality and only marginal success in resolving the central issues of the dispute.

The purpose of this brief study is to examine the policies of the United States and the Soviet Union in the Arab–Israeli conflict since the June War of 1967, to determine what trends in interactions have emerged, whether any lasting commonality of interests has been mutually recognized, and what lessons seem to have been learned. In the initial period from about 1955 to 1965, Soviet and American policies were characterized, in general, by assertion and containment. This was an era of confrontation in which the conventional action–reaction syndrome often dictated choices. By the mid-1960s, however, significant changes in the two great powers' relations had altered their behaviour patterns from expansive expectations and antagonistic reactions to include a broader range of interactions. Yet from 1967 to 1976 limits on the expectations of both powers developed that permitted operational rules of conduct to emerge, though they were subsequently violated by both sides. Overall behaviour during this period may best be seen when broken down into its components:

1 trends in great-power national interests in the region;
2 the extent to which common interests have emerged;
3 the patterns and nature of interactions;
4 characteristics of great-power/small-power state relations;
5 the correlation between military balance and political adjustment.

In order to facilitate the analysis of these different aspects, this study sets out a historical reconstruction, starting with a brief look at behaviour before and during the 1967 war. Four lines of enquiry are pursued:

1 the extent to which there is a correlation between the military prowess of the smaller states and their willingness to negotiate a political settlement;
2 the degree to which security requirements enhanced the desire of smaller states to reach some form of political normalization;
3 the effect that the interests of smaller states had on great-power behaviour;
4 the influence that mutual perceptions, constraints, warnings and deceptions had on great-power interactions over the last decade of the conflict.

I. INTERACTIONS DURING THE JUNE WAR

The nature of great-power relations underwent significant change between the 1956 Suez and the 1967 June Wars. After the Cuban missile crisis in 1962 great-power confrontation declined in intensity, despite the Soviet decision to launch a programme for achieving nuclear strategic parity with the United States. Both great powers showed interest in cultivating a special relationship in a narrow field of technical arms-control issues. When China publicly abandoned her policy of active challenge to the Soviet Union and withdrew into the Sinocentric Cultural Revolution the Soviet leadership made five major decisions:

1 to reopen an activist European policy, with the call in April 1966 for a European Security Conference;
2 to accelerate its United Action campaign supporting North Vietnam;
3 to increase investment in strategic nuclear forces, with new ICBM procurements beginning in 1967;
4 to confine interests in the Third World to immediately adjacent regions while conventional military forces were being constructed;
5 to assume a positive role in organizing the 'progressive' Arab forces in the Middle East into an 'anti-imperialist' instrument.

Non-intervention and Under-involvement
Pressure in the Arab world for the resumption of hostilities mounted over the Israeli diversion of waters from the Sea of Galilee to the Negev, which the Arabs regarded as an act of aggression, but opinions were divided about what would be appropriate actions to counter the 'growing Zionist threat'. Syria had been effectively isolated since she broke up the federation with Egypt, while the Palestinian refugees were the virtual dependants of host governments and were subject to various degrees of political control, especially in Egypt. But the Syrians and Palestinians formed the core of a growing militant wing of the Arab world. As a tactical concession and a manoeuvre to block the resumption of hostilities, President Nasser of Egypt agreed to convene the first Arab summit conference in 1964, which recognized the Palestinian Liberation Organization (PLO) and accepted the Right-Ba'athist regime in Syria but also adopted a ban on all activities that might trigger Israeli military reprisals.

Nasser remained adamantly against the use of force.[1] But Syria and Al-Fatah (the military wing of the PLO) believed that the Arab unity necessary for the resumption of regular warfare could best be achieved through irregular operations that would invite Israeli retaliation. Accordingly, Syria launched her own water-diversion programme, which Israel destroyed by air attacks. Syria responded by shelling Israeli villages, and in January 1965 Fatah restarted terrorism. On 27 May Israel likewise resumed her strategy of reprisals with a major raid against Jordan which, in turn, led to estrangement between Amman and the other Arab capitals over the issue of terrorism. The question of militancy had again divided, rather than unified, the Arab world.[2] The foundation for a viable Arab military coalition emerged after the Left-Ba'athist coup in Syria in February 1966. Soviet Prime Minister Kosygin stressed this point during his official visit to Cairo in May, when he urged the 'progressive' Arab states to unite into a single anti-imperialist front. At the same time there was a sharp increase in Soviet propaganda warning of an imminent Israeli attack against Syria. One plausible reason for this artificially induced war scare is that after the Arab rupture in relations with Jordan, over guerrilla operations, Syria became the most likely alternative target for Israeli reprisals, and the Soviet Union sought to deter these until greater Arab cohesion could be achieved.[3] A further reason may have been to create an atmosphere that might convince the various Arab factions of the dangers inherent in their militant but independent actions and to induce Egypt to end her isolation of Syria.

The enticement of increased military and economic aid to both countries was apparently sufficiently reassuring for Egypt to drop her reservations and resume diplomatic relations with Syria in November 1966, consummating

[1] In 1964 he stated 'We will tell you the truth . . . that we cannot use force today, our circumstances do not allow us; be patient with us . . . For I would lead you to disaster if I were to proclaim that I would fight at a time when I was unable to do so. I would not lead my country to disaster and would not gamble with its destiny'. Quoted in David Kimche and Dan Bawly, *The Sandstorm* (New York: Stein and Day, 1968), p. 25.

[2] Nasser answered his Syrian critics and warned that terrorism defied the formal position of the Arab League when he stated, 'They say "Drive out the UNEF". Suppose that we do, is it not essential that we have a plan? If Israeli aggression takes place against Syria shall I attack Israel? It takes a tractor or two to force me to move. Then Israel is the one which determines the battle for me . . . Is it conceivable that I should attack Israel while there are 50,000 Egyptian troops in the Yemen?' (*Al Ahram*, 31 May 1965).

[3] *Izvestia*, 7 May 1966, claimed that one-third of Israel's army had been deployed to the Syrian border. See also *Pravda*, 21 May, and an official protest lodged with the Israeli ambassador, Tass, 27 May 1967.

the link with a Mutual Defence Treaty.[4] Another reason for Egyptian acceptance of the alliance may have been Nasser's growing awareness of the need to ensure greater influence and control over Syria and Fatah, which was now completely dominated by the Syrian Intelligence Service. The treaty, which provided for a United Arab Command, was probably the best mechanism for bringing the two states and Fatah into closer co-ordination.

There were also important strategic grounds for alliance. Egypt reasoned that the Golan Heights could be so well defended that Israeli reprisals would require concentration massive enough to verge on all-out war. From this favourable position Syria and Fatah no doubt calculated that they could use terror and border tension to trigger war, and thereby cement Arab unity. But Egypt held that any concentration of the Israel Defence Force (IDF) in the north would leave Israel exposed in the south, and after the IDF reprisal against Tawafiq in Syria argued that the deployment of four Egyptian divisions in the Sinai in 1960 deterred Israel from launching even more devastating raids. The IDF's heavy attack against the Jordanian village of Es Samu on 13 November 1966 seemed to confirm the soundness of this reasoning; Israel had been effectively deterred from attacking Syria, the prime target, because of the new two-front alliance. But when Israel deliberately escalated reprisals against Syria in April 1967 this logic was questioned. Egypt answered, however, that deterrence had failed because her best units were deployed in the Yemen and because of the presence of the United Nations Emergency Force (UNEF). Both defects had to be corrected to restore deterrence.

In March 1967 the Soviet Foreign Minister, Mr Gromyko, made an unannounced visit to Cairo that was clouded in secrecy. Yugoslavia claimed that the purpose of the visit was to discuss the future of the UN peacekeeping force in the Sinai, to which she had assigned a contingent.[5] If true, this would indicate that Moscow and Cairo had assessed the implications of ousting UNEF two months later as necessary to offset long-standing Syrian charges that Egypt was hiding behind the UN forces. Both

Moscow and Cairo may also have considered that removing UN forces might prevent the military centre of gravity shifting northwards, which neither desired, without necessarily pushing the crisis into a dangerous phase. Tension grew sharply in the aftermath of an aerial incident on 7 April when Israel shot down six MiG-21s – a quarter of the Syrian air force. This deliberate escalation was accompanied by a severe Israeli warning.

While the Soviet Union had appeared to manage the gradual escalation of the crisis up to this point in a calculated manner, her ultimate objectives remained unclear. On the one hand, she successfully blocked any American initiative towards a negotiated solution. After a terrorist raid on Jerusalem in October 1966 the United States persuaded Israel to forgo the customary reprisals and to take the entire issue to the Security Council, where she hoped to solicit Soviet co-operation; but the Soviet Union refused and continued to veto any resolution favouring Israel. After this experience, even the optimistic Israelis became convinced that they were so overwhelmingly outnumbered in the United Nations that the organization's usefulness in defending Israeli national interests should be ignored in the future. On the other hand, the dominant opinion in Washington was that the Soviet Union did not want another Middle East war and would use her influence to control the radical elements. Arms deliveries had been necessary to establish Soviet influence, and the United States estimated that this influence was now being exercised with prudence. In January 1967 General Salah Jadid, head of Syria's Left-Ba'athist regime, had led a large military delegation to Moscow for discussions on increased aid, seeking SAM-2 missiles, other modern weapons, accelerated agreement on the Euphrates dam project and a tougher stand against Israel. The Soviet Union had agreed to supply more tanks and aircraft and had endorsed the Syrian position on the dam, but in the first apparent show of restraint, she refused the missiles – according to Syrian sources, on the grounds that she did not want 'to participate in creating new unrest in the Middle East'. Also she had committed herself only to reiterating a moderate stand on Israel (i.e. to condemn Israel's 'aggressive policies') and to support Syria politically, and had refused to endorse

---

[4] Walter Laqueur, *The Struggle for the Middle East* (London: Macmillan, 1969), p. 89.
[5] Tanjug, 29 March 1967.

46

Syrian demands for support for the liberation of Palestine and the elimination of the state of Israel.[6]

It is not known whether this restraint was due to reservations about the political reliability of the new Syrian regime or to awareness of the potential destabilizing effect of the delivery of advanced new systems. Nonetheless, this was the first indication of deliberate Soviet restraint and circumspection over her involvement in the growing crisis. In the case of Egypt, also, serious shortfalls in spare parts and ammunition were not made up at the onset of hostilities in June, which suggested either the imposition of additional constraints on Egypt or, more likely, an overestimate of the extent to which events could be controlled.

As tensions rose, Syria sent a formal note to the UN Security Council on 18 April, warning of an imminent Israeli attack. Two days later the commander of the Egyptian Air Force arrived in Damascus on a mission to restrain Syria by asserting that deterrence could be restored through closer solidarity with Cairo and firmer control over Fatah. In his May Day speech, Nasser pledged aircraft and pilots to Syria to strengthen joint deterrence.[7] But the pace of terror increased sharply, and in his Independence Day speech Prime Minister Levi Eskhol warned of increased retaliation.

It was thought at the time that the most likely scenario would be an Israeli air and paratroop attack on Damascus, with the aim of overthrowing the radical regime and creating conditions in which the conservative Right-Ba'athists, exiled in Jordan, could return to power – a major reverse for Cairo and Moscow.[8] No major troop build-up along the Syrian border would be required for such an attack.[9] On 13 May the Soviet Union warned that Israel would attack on the 17th with 13 brigades, and Nasser, apparently convinced of the plausibility and imminence of such an attack, ordered two divisions into the Sinai to support the reinforced division already there and, it was hoped, to restore the alliance's deterrence.[10] He later said that after this deployment there was only a twenty per cent chance of war.

On 16 May Egypt ordered the commander of UNEF to withdraw his forces to their two base camps.[11] The UN Secretary General, U Thant, replied that UNEF must be allowed to conduct its mission unimpeded or be withdrawn; Nasser was therefore compelled to request withdrawal. By 19 May UNEF ceased to exist, and Egyptian units occupied their positions along the Israeli border. U Thant's precipitate decision generated genuine alarm in the United States, which launched major moves in the UN to offset the adverse effects of the withdrawal. However, American indignation with U Thant was soon overshadowed by the closure of the Straits of Tiran. When UNEF troops left Sharm el-Sheikh, overlooking the straits, Egyptian paratroops were dropped in and quickly reinforced so as to preclude Israel seizing this vital position.

The speed of the combined service operation to capture Sharm el-Sheikh strongly suggests that it had been planned in advance. However, the use of the position to enforce a blockade was more problematic. In a major speech on 21 May, Eshkol called for moderation and for peace with Israel's neighbours, but he did not mention the Straits or Sharm el-Sheikh. Nasser interpreted this as an indication of their low priority for Israel, and the next day he announced the blockade of Israeli ships and strategic goods, at the same time accelerating the movement of forces into the Sinai. Ignoring American guarantees regarding the Straits, given to Israel in 1957, Nasser justified his action before the UN by asserting that Egypt was attempting to deter Israel from attacking Syria and had merely restored conditions along the Israeli border and in the Straits to their pre-1956 state. He argued that this was consistent with General Assembly resolutions condemning conquest and with the existing state of belligerency with Israel.[12] In his 23 May speech, Nasser stated that even after the blockade of the Straits, there was only a fifty per cent chance of war occurring.

[6] Kimche and Bawly, *op. cit.* in note 1, p. 49.
[7] *Al Ahram*, 2 May 1967.
[8] *Israel Digest*, 19 May 1967.
[9] Charles W. Yost, 'The Arab–Israeli War: How It Began', *Foreign Affairs*, January 1968.
[10] Fred J. Khouri, *The Arab–Israeli Dilemma* (Syracuse N.Y.: Syracuse University Press, 1968), p. 245. In his

23 May speech Nasser stated that the Russians informed visiting Egyptian parliamentarians that the Israeli attack was imminent.
[11] *Al Ahram*, 24 July 1967.
[12] For the UN debate on the issue see UN Doc. S/7896, 19 May, to S/7906, 27 May 1967, and S/PV 1342, 24 May, to S/PV 1346, 3 June 1967.

On 30 May King Hussein of Jordan felt compelled to drop his antagonism towards Nasser, join a five-year mutual defence pact with the UAR and to place his forces under the Unified Arab Command. On 4 June Iraq signed a similar agreement with Cairo. At that point, Nasser estimated that he had raised the price of war so high that the United States would be unwilling to pay and would therefore modify her guarantees to Israel; Israel would thus be isolated and effectively deterred. He was in the strongest political bargaining position of his career. Yet he had no comprehensive political plan for negotiation (except the return to the 1947 borders), and no grand strategy which would prescribe his next step – he had to await Israeli reactions.[13]

Israel watched Nasser's moves with growing alarm. His attempts to achieve Arab unity over the Israeli question required that he compensate for the weakness of his own forces by accepting the radicals' demands for the destruction of Israel as the common denominator for co-ordinated action, without being able to develop adequate control. The tail soon wagged the dog. After her successful shooting down of the Syrian MiG-21s in April and her strong warnings delivered at the same time, Israel expected Damascus to exercise restraint. She was surprised by the continuation of terror and the Arabs' use of Israeli warnings as justifications for mobilization, but she was not unduly alarmed until 19 May. Then the military centre of gravity swiftly shifted to the south, and the threat developed of multiple-front engagement entailing full mobilization, which was far more costly for Israel than for the Arabs. In itself the closure of the Straits of Tiran was economically unimportant, for few Israeli vessels used Eilath. It was, however, politically significant, since it

showed how far the Arabs would go in provoking international opinion in order to force Israel to accept conditions that would enhance the Arab bargaining position. More important, it was a clear test of the credibility of American guarantees. As the situation deteriorated, Israel did two things: she resolved a searing five-day cabinet crisis by appointing a national government, and she conducted extensive probes of American intentions.

Analyses of great-power behaviour during this period have conventionally stressed American perfidy and Soviet complicity. From the outset the Soviet Union saw a distinct advantage in moving the deadlocked issue of Palestine off dead centre, as evidenced by the Kosygin–Gromyko visits and her intransigence at the UN. Her restraint over arms deliveries and her actions during the crisis suggest that her aim was to create conditions for a negotiated settlement in which she would be a partner or guarantor, and to prevent the level of violence from escalating to the point where it would provoke American–Israeli collusion, leading to war. Israel's successful operations against Syria in April must have raised reservations in Moscow about the reliability of Arab analyses, and by May the Soviet Union was sufficiently worried to issue a series of diplomatic notes to Israel, calling for restraint and warning against further aggression against Syria, and to Damascus and Cairo, also calling for restraint and for curbs against Fatah. A statement of 23 May made clear her increasing anxiety. She pledged support for the Arabs, but only if they were attacked – not for a 'holy war' against Israel. (At the same time she gave Israel the strongest warning yet against attacking Syria.[14]) The Soviet Union may have received an up-dated briefing by Egyptian War Minister Shams Badran, who was in Moscow on 25 May to seek sorely needed spare parts and munitions. He reported back to Nasser that the supplies would be delivered, but that the Soviet Union would not intervene militarily unless the United States did so first.[15]

Thus the Soviet Union set distinct limitations to her involvement in the crisis, assisted perhaps

---

[13] Muhammad Haikal, *Al Ahram*, 26 May 1967. 'War is inevitable. For the first time the Arabs can impose their will on Israel. It has no choice but to strike hard, but we are waiting and will strike back equally hard.' Thus Nasser expected to compel Israel to attack his fortified positions – fighting on his terms. This would account for his refusal to pre-empt after being warned by the United States on 2 June of an attack within three days. At any rate, he only expected a drive into the Gaza and the El Arish region, not a frontal attack. For an insight into official Egyptian intelligence estimates see Kimche and Bawly, *op. cit.* in note 1 pp. 97–99, 109–110. On 2 June the High Command expected an Israeli attack within two weeks.

[14] Tass, 23 May 1967.
[15] Nasser said in his Address to the National Assembly 'from Badran's report ... the Soviet Union is standing by our side' (Middle East News Agency, 29 May 1967).

48

by assurances from Washington that the United States foresaw no need to intervene militarily. It is not clear from available evidence if firm commitments were ever made or by whom; most likely they were informal reflections about intelligence estimates at the time that minimized the necessity for great-power military intervention. Nonetheless, this American self-restraint was passed to Egypt and incorporated into Battle Order No. 2: 'because of the firm stand taken by the Soviet Union and her readiness to intervene if any great power enters into war with Egypt, it is now clear that the American government will not on any account enter into any military adventure on the side of Israel'.[16] A basic planning premise of the Soviet Union and the Arab countries, then, was that symmetrical constraints had been imposed on direct intervention by the great powers. From the Arab viewpoint the merit of such symmetrical constraints was that they were expected to be self-enforcing.

The Tiran Straits issue was apparently the key miscalculation in this seemingly tidy scheme. In none of the released diplomatic notes or government statements of the four states, except Israel, were the Straits even mentioned until after the blockade was imposed. The Soviet press tried to minimize the issue, complaining that a crisis could not be created over whether two or three ships passed the Straits or not.[17] This reticence suggests that Moscow was unaware of the impending blockade and indeed, as the Arabs insist, was informed only shortly before the Egyptian announcement.

The blockade was troublesome to the Soviet Union for several reasons. First, she had a strong interest in upholding international law governing international waterways, otherwise her access to the Danish and Turkish Straits might be jeopardized. Second, the blockade challenged the validity of the 1957 American guarantees to Israel, and so might endanger the scheme for self-enforcing mutual constraints. Clearly the United States would have to act, and

the interval between 22 May and the first UN Resolution proposed by the Soviet Union on 26 May was probably used to devise means for defusing the issue and diluting American commitment to her guarantees.

In the wake of the blockade announcement the United States increased her forces in the Mediterranean and alerted additional units. President Johnson gave a major address on 23 May and sent a formal note to Cairo. He rejected Egypt's right to interfere with the shipping of any nation in international waterways and informed Cairo that the United States was firmly committed to the support of the political independence and territorial integrity of all states in the Middle East, including Israel. Moreover, she strongly opposed aggression by anyone in the area in any form, overt or clandestine.[18] The next day reporters were told, off the record, that the government had quietly reassured Israel that the United States would meet her obligations to oppose an Arab invasion of Israel.[19] On 26 May Mr Kosygin proposed to President Johnson that they should act mutually to reduce tension, and they agreed to send virtually identical notes the next day to both Egypt and Israel. The notes urged restraint and stated that aggressive action would have severe consequences for the entire world. Kosygin's second note to Eshkol stated that the Soviet Union was doing her best to restrain the Arabs, and subsequently Soviet diplomats repeatedly reassured Israeli officials that they had nothing to fear, a solution would soon be found. But by then Israel was plunged into a national political crisis over her very existence and was no longer interested in Soviet entreaties.

The Soviet Union had also lost control of Egypt. She had to support Cairo in any action short of aggression, or risk undermining her prestige throughout the Arab world, yet she could propose no political solution that would both reduce tensions and be acceptable to the Arabs. Indeed, she could not even take an active and positive part in settling the blockade issue without endangering her relations with Egypt and the Arab world. The Soviet mistake was not to have anticipated that Nasser would be compelled by Arab pride and the ridicule of

[16] Kimche and Bawly, *op. cit.* in note 1, p. 109.
[17] *Izvestia,* 20 and 30 May; *Pravda,* 21 May and 1 June 1967. Soviet UN Ambassador Fedorenko stated on 24 May that there were insufficient grounds on this issue to hastily convene the Security Council. See Arthur Lall, *The UN and the Middle East Crisis* (New York: Columbia University Press, 1968), p. 29.

[18] *New York Times,* 24 May 1967.
[19] *Ibid.*

the conservatives to close the Straits, and that he had failed to lay any alternative plans to maintain the momentum of the Arab campaign towards a political solution or to prevent a deterioration into war. After 23 May the Soviet Union was confined to frenetic activity, either jointly with the United States or independently, to allay what they called 'exaggerated fears'. The fulcrum of leverage for external powers had shifted to the United States.

Israel had warned repeatedly that blockade of the Straits would be regarded as an act of aggression and that she would react accordingly. The United States' response to the announcement of the blockade was to try and forestall any Israeli retaliation so that she could attempt to reopen the Straits, and during the first forty-eight hours, Israel was told that Washington hoped to solve the problem itself.[20] President Johnson began his 'good offices' by issuing a formal statement of the American position, namely that the United States regarded the Gulf of Aqaba as an international waterway, and that the blockade of Israeli shipping was illegal and potentially dangerous to peace. He called on U Thant, then in Cairo, to place the highest priority on reopening the Straits. Finally, he stated a firm American commitment to support the political independence and territorial integrity of all nations in the area – a commitment made by three previous American presidents.[21] On the same day he sent a friendly personal letter to Nasser urging restraint, as well as a formal, firmly-worded Aide Memoire citing American support for the freedom of innocent passage through the Gulf. Egypt responded to neither, but on the 24 May announced that the Straits had been closed by mines, coastal artillery and armed patrols. This effectively terminated U Thant's mission, which he suspended and returned home.

The United States then took the problem to the Security Council, where debate continued inconclusively for the next two weeks. Meanwhile, Israel's Foreign Minister, Abba Eban, made his historic visit to Washington to present the Israeli case for firm action to uphold American obligations. Washington regarded the Israeli move as a step toward confrontation and

as undue pressure. Eban was kept waiting a day before being curtly told, first by Secretary of State Dean Rusk and then by President Johnson, that if Israel initiated hostilities the United States would not intervene. Johnson pointed out that any American action would require Congressional approval, which would take time and that the United States could not take unilateral action and would need at least two weeks to consult other maritime nations; Eban remained non-committal about deferring retaliation beyond the original forty-eight hour period the United States had requested. While he was in Washington Eban received an urgent message that the issue was no longer the Straits but the number of troops and tanks in the Sinai. He concluded that an Egyptian attack was imminent, which was discounted by American military authorities.[22]

Eban's visit altered American perceptions. Before it, the United States had concluded that Israel was tough and militant and had expected that hostile operations would already have erupted; Eban's presentation, however, gave an impression of an Israeli government that was politically divided and irresolute. His demands that American obligations should be honoured, when Israel was clearly stronger than Egypt, was seen as a move to bring the two countries into collusion, a coupling that the United States wanted to avoid. If Israel did not want to seek an independent military solution, then American efforts to seek a solution through multilateral agreement could ill-afford to be impeded by a demonstration of partiality. Eban's visit was followed by the strongly worded Soviet and American notes to Israel and Egypt, designed in Washington's eyes to provide it more latitude by urging restraint and demonstrating impartiality.

But the American position in the Middle East was seriously weakened when Hussein joined the United Arab Command; it seemed that American influence might effectively be eliminated from the region and Soviet stature enhanced, largely by default. The American plan, proposed to Eban and now implemented, was intended to avoid both appeasement and compromise. It provided for a Congressional resolution upholding the freedom of navigation, endorsement of this by the Security Council,

[20] Interview with Premier Levi Eshkol, *Maariv*, 4 October 1967.
[21] *USIS Bulletin*, 24 May 1967.

[22] Kimche and Bawly, *op. cit.* in note 1, p. 128.

approval by the maritime nations and, finally, the formation of a multinational flotilla to force its way if necessary through the Straits.[23]

Such a cumbersome undertaking had virtually no chance of success and must have been regarded as a smokescreen for more resolute action. It would take days for a resolution to pass Congress which would then be subjected to interminable delays in the Security Council, if not a Soviet veto (indeed the Soviet Union had already rejected American resolution S/7916, calling for a cooling-off period, because it implied opening the Straits). The convocation of the international conference could be stymied over which were the maritime nations and how many were necessary to constitute a quorum for defining international law. On 30 May the British Foreign Minister, George Brown, sought to short-circuit the process by immediately convening an international conference.[24] Twenty nations were contacted and invited to endorse the principles of freedom of navigation and to support them by the use of force, if necessary. Only the Netherlands, Iceland, Australia and New Zealand gave their unqualified support, and France formally boycotted both the procedure and the substance of the conference. De Gaulle proposed a four-power conference, which the Soviet Union rejected, and formally warned Israel that the consequence of aggression would be loss of French friendship. Around that time a State Department spokesman issued a statement that the United States was trying to organize a multinational flotilla to force the Straits, but that she was consulting in the United Nations with a view to issuing a joint declaration on the freedom of navigation. Israel urgently dispatched another emissary to Washington to ask about the prospects for the naval flotilla, on which her restraint and hopes for a peaceful solution were claimed to depend. He was told that the prospects were virtually nil: the demonstration of military power was to be replaced by yet another UN resolution. At the same time, however, in order to keep the momentum of American initiative alive, Johnson sent to Cairo on 30 May a special envoy who arranged an exchange of visits by the American and Egyptian Vice Presidents for the highest level of talks yet considered. The arrivals were

[23] USIS Bulletin, 3 June 1967.
[24] New York Times, 2 and 3 June 1967.

confirmed for 7 June: Nasser still estimated that he had one week's grace.

The collapse of the American initiative with the Israeli attack on 5 June was partly the result of ambiguous perceptions and expectations. One faction in the United States government encouraged Israel to pursue her own solutions as soon as militarily possible, thereby conveniently relieving Washington of hard choices about the over-extension of commitments already made in South-east Asia; furthermore, this option could be implemented with minimum loss and danger to Israeli national interests. A second faction, responding to strong domestic pressure and moral obligations, sought to seize the initiative and steer the crisis away from confrontation toward adjustment. (However, the blockade, which was the most tangible issue for accommodation, quickly became less critical for Israel than the Egyptian mobilization, over which Washington had little demonstrable influence.) But President Johnson himself never made it absolutely plain to Israel that the United States would oppose her if she moved first – as Eisenhower had done in October 1956, and De Gaulle in May 1967. Washington's efforts were confined to the single issue of the blockade, which affected Israeli interests and American guarantees, while omitting a solution to Arab grievances; and yet the United States lost control over even this issue by failing to make clear to Israel the American position on the consequences of aggression.

Thus the progress of the military build-up steadily reduced the issues on which both external powers could press for restraint, while the belligerents gained confidence from their respective mobilizations. The presumption of self-enforcing mutual constraint against direct military intervention had successfully dissuaded both great powers from over-involvement, but it has also demonstrated to the local powers that they could and must rely on their own resources, engendering confidence on both sides. Indeed, self-enforcing restraint may have played some part in dissuading the United States from pressing the scheme for a multinational flotilla: the question of whether or not it should include Soviet vessels – and, if not, how Moscow would react – would have been a strong incentive to abandon the idea. The positive feature of self-enforcing restraint, that of reducing the likelihood of the conflict spreading, was partially neutralized by the unexpected implications it had for local states. It has not yet served as a deterrent to localized conflicts.

There were other limits to the self-enforcing restraint, however, especially for the local states involved: both sides were fully aware of previous interventions by external powers to prevent the complete collapse of the Arab side. It is not clear how far the possibility of ultimate rescue by the great powers figured in Nasser's calculations. During the initial planning, when he was cautious and deliberate, it probably provided the necessary reassurance to minimize risks; during the climactic second half of May when his self-confidence suddenly rose, it probably receded in importance. Before mid-May the prospects for intervention were ignored or regarded with disdain on the Israeli side. During the crescendo, however, many Israeli leaders were confident that the United States would act to prevent destruction of the Israeli state – despite Dayan's public comments that Tel Aviv did not expect American or British boys to die for Israel's cause.

This sense of reassurance, however remote in the plans of Israel and the Arabs, increased their latitude and their confidence that the risks of war were acceptable. From this viewpoint, great-power pledges of non-intervention were germane only to relatively moderate levels of violence, and therefore may have had an aggravating effect rather than the desired deterrent one.

The notion of self-enforcing restraint also had several implications for great-power behaviour. Military non-intervention stemmed from the desire to inhibit the degree of any involvement. Unexpected involvement might be caused by unanticipated calls to meet commitments, uncertainties about the opponent's own obligations or expectations, or a sudden change in the tactical situation affecting clients. Such unforeseen developments could intensify pressure on either or both great powers to increase their involvement, short of direct military intervention. Yet the aggregation of involvement held the danger of mutual nudging towards the brink, as occurred in October 1973.

Thus before the June War, both great powers demonstrated an increasing sensitivity to the dangers of over-involvement and systematically attempted to refine the nature of their commitments. Great-power diplomacy was largely exhortatory; no action was taken by either to provide an initiative for a political settlement. Indeed, the American note to Egypt of 23 May merely listed three areas of outstanding differences between the rivals, without offering even a commentary on possible solutions. Likewise the provision of weapons and equipment was not coupled to specified political conditions or obligations on the recipients to seek a political settlement; the external powers deliberately avoided becoming enmeshed in local political controversy through arms deliveries. Thus when the crisis worsened, neither was able to use leverage afforded by military aid or mutual restraint to promote a comprehensive settlement. (Nor, during the period of general mobilization after 22 May, did any of the local states make any proposal for even a limited political settlement.) The fear of over-involvement reinforced the aversion of both great powers to direct intervention, and the sterility of political imagination in the policies of both great powers became so glaring that unprecedented energy was devoted to seeking a settlement immediately after the war.

Four-Power Interactions
On 3 June the newly-formed Israeli national cabinet, which included all major political parties except the Communist, voted overwhelmingly in favour of 'preventive' war. The government's objectives in a pre-emptive attack, according to Defence Minister Dayan, were not territorial conquest and aggrandizement: 'Our sole aim is to bring to naught the attempt of the Arab armies to conquer our country and to destroy the encircling blockade and aggression.'[25] In the United Nations' debates on the war Israel explained her definition of Arab aggression before the Security Council: Israel had the right of self-defence under Article 51 of the UN Charter, because the Arabs were deploying offensive weapons (tanks and aircraft) towards her borders; the blockade was an act of aggression under international law; the armistice accords with the Arabs had not preserved the peace (a reference to the actions of the Palestinian

[25] *New York Times*, 6 June 1967.

52

guerrillas) and were therefore no longer valid.[26] Egypt replied that, since her air force was virtually destroyed on the ground, Israel was guilty of aggression, and that Article 51 should be applied to the Arab case. But Israel was also seeking political goals: by inflicting as much damage as possible on Arab military forces, she hoped to compel her adversaries to accept her terms for a durable peace. The June War ended in a major military triumph for Israel, but the political objectives were denied her.

Under-involvement by the great powers before the war was promptly redressed as soon as hostilities broke out, with both sides becoming increasingly engaged. At 0800 hours on 5 June, shortly after Israel attacked, Mr Kosygin called President Johnson on the 'hot line' and informed him that the Soviet Union intended to work for a cease-fire through her influence with the Egyptians and expressed the hope that the United States would urge restraint on Israel.[27] The Soviet Union rejected military intervention and apparently sought similar restraint on the American side. She made no threats at that time, but only tried to use persuasion to gain co-operation. Nor did she repeat the Arab charge that American aircraft were aiding Israel – a charge later denied (the radar echoes that triggered the rumour were actually 20 *Mirage* fighters being delivered to Israel by French pilots).

The Soviet Ambassador, Mr Fedorenko introduced in the Security Council a draft resolution calling for an immediate cease-fire and the unconditional withdrawal of Israeli forces. The United States presented a counter draft resolution (S/7935), merely requesting an immediate ceasefire. Finally, on 6 June, the Soviet Union dropped her draft, and the American one was adopted as Resolution 233. This was rejected by the Arabs, because it did not condemn Israeli aggression or demand troop withdrawals, and ignored by Israel. A second version, Resolution 234, was adopted on the 7th and accepted first by Jordan, then by Egypt on the 8th, and by Syria on the 9th; Israel agreed to the Resolution, provided that it was accepted by all Arab belligerents. Since minor activity was still occurring on the Syrian front, Israel shifted her full weight against the Golan Heights.

Israel's disregard for the two ceasefire resolutions, and the collapse of Egyptian and Jordanian resistance was most alarming for the Soviet Union. While Egypt was the main military threat, and there were obvious geographic reasons for seizing Jordan's West Bank, Israel nursed a special sense of revenge against Syria. She therefore deliberately defied the UN resolution in order to seize the heights from which Israeli settlements had been shelled, silence the Fatah bases, and humiliate the Left-Ba'athist regime to the point where it might be overthrown. The Soviet Union felt compelled to act decisively to prevent the attainment of at least the last objective. On 9 June she convened in Moscow a summit conference of Communist party leaders, including President Tito, as a show of solidarity with the Arabs and to determine what immediate support could be provided for their cause. The communiqué issued by the conference threatened the imposition of sanctions and decisive action if Israel did not immediately accept the UN cease-fire.[28]

The conferees, except Romania, pledged immediate military aid to the Arabs and agreed to break diplomatic relations with Israel (which Moscow initiated the following day). The Soviet Union also stepped up her pressure in the Security Council by introducing a draft resolution which condemned Israeli aggression, demanded the halt of military operations, insisted upon a withdrawal to the 1949 armistice lines, and required respect for demilitarized zones.[29] On 9 June the Security Council adopted Resolution 235, and, on the next day, Resolution 236, which called for the immediate cessation of hostilities and a 'prompt return of forces to the original cease-fire positions'. (The failure to

---

[26] For the Security Council debate see UN Doc. S/PV 1347, 5 June, through S/PV 1357, 11 June 1967. Israel also stated that one of her 'war aims' was to co-operate closely with the United States to avoid the reactivation of 'that fatal Soviet–American vice whose closing jaws cracked the position of America's friends in 1956 and enabled her opponents to regroup and to recuperate their strength' (Rafael Gideon, 'UN Resolution 242: A Common Denominator', *New Middle East*, June 1973).
[27] Lyndon Baines Johnson, *The Vantage Point: Perspective from the Presidency* (New York: Holt, Rinehart and Winston, 1971), pp. 287, 298.

[28] *Pravda*, 10 June 1967. Romania's presence diluted the tone and substance of the threat.
[29] UN Doc. S/7951/Rev. 1.

include a timetable for withdrawal was a concession to the United States.)

After the fall of Kuneitra on the Golan Front, Kosygin called Johnson on the morning of 10 June and stated that a critical moment had arrived; he warned that if Israel did not immediately accept a ceasefire, the Soviet Union might have to take independent action to avoid a 'grave catastrophe', which might include military operations.[30] The United States informed Israel of this threat and advised that the Soviet Union would probably react vigorously if Damascus itself were threatened, although there was no evidence of a Soviet military alert.[31] Johnson responded by ordering the Sixth Fleet closer to the Syrian coast, as a demonstration that the United States would not be intimidated and so as to be in a better position for air and sea evacuations of her personnel if Israel ignored her advice and pressed the attack. Israel and Syria accepted the ceasefire at 1830 hours GMT on 11 June.

Israeli forces were victorious on all three fronts, but they had been stopped short of marching on Cairo, Amman or Damascus by the physical barriers of the Suez Canal and the topography of the Mountains of Moab on the east side of the Jordan Valley, as well as by more demanding military priorities and, in the final stages, external political pressures. The reactions of the great powers had altered substantially. At the outset, both had been surprised that they had been unable to prevent hostilities and anxious about the uncertain outcome. When it became increasingly clear that Israel was winning, those in Washington who had earlier advocated leaving the crisis to the Israeli General Staff felt vindicated and tended to restrain those who had seen the outbreak of hostilities as a complication for the American position in the Middle East. In this atmosphere, the United States would probably not have acted on her own to prevent Israel cutting the three main highways to Damascus (the presumed operational plan) and thus humiliating the Syrian regime. Indeed, there was a growing feeling in Washington that an Israeli military

victory would provide reasonable insurance against the risks of great-power confrontation in the Middle East, and it was only when the Soviet Union threatened independent action that the United States decided, if she could, to exercise a moderating influence on Israel. Nonetheless, the Arab countries broke off diplomatic relations with Washington over charges of American bias in favour of Israel.[32]

Thus the United States emerged from the June War acutely embarrassed. Had she honoured her 1957 commitments to Israel, she might possibly have prevented hostilities; she had failed to do so, however, and yet accusations of pro-Israeli partiality had still caused a loss of her prestige in the Arab world. The Israeli victory was nonetheless partially reassuring in that no more serious damage had been done to American regional interests, but the success of Israel's decision to act independently and American perfidy over guarantees created a political debt that Israel called on repeatedly over the next seven years.

The Soviet Union also suffered as a result of her efforts to end hostilities on the best possible terms for the Arabs. Her leverage on Israel was nil. Her most credible political actions had been taken in conjunction with the United States, not as solo ventures. There had been no unusual Soviet naval build-up before the War that might have indicated precautionary or provocative intent, and when the Sixth Fleet steamed toward Syrian waters, Soviet vessels merely maintained their trailing positions and did not attempt to screen or block American movements. Furthermore, the seven Soviet airborne divisions were not put on a high state of alert that might have indicated imminent intervention.

The Soviet Union's only recourse was political pressure. But a successful call for UN sanctions against Israel was not rated as likely because of the American veto, and the sympathy Israel had gained abroad from Arab bombast about annihilation, created for her a new image as an embattled underdog. The only penalty the

[30] Johnson, op. cit. in note 27, p. 302.
[31] General Bar Lev later confirmed that American pressure had been the determining factor in halting Israeli forces before they could attack Damascus (New Middle East, March 1971, p. 37).

[32] In order to restore the image of impartiality, Washington directed the US Air Force to launch a massive air-drop of water to Egyptian soldiers stranded in the Sinai. The operation was cancelled at the last minute because of difficulties in co-ordinating the flights with the Israeli Air Force.

Soviet Union could immediately impose on Israel was to break off diplomatic relations. Yet this decision severely restricted her freedom of action in the future, by denying her both direct communication with Israel and any form of direct influence. Indeed, over the next seven years, this lack of relations was to be a greater handicap for the Soviet Union than for Israel, since she had to depend on the United States to relay her intentions and interpretations of various actions to Tel Aviv. All the same, breaking diplomatic relations was probably the least she could do in the light of sharp Arab charges that Moscow had let them down in their hour of direst need.[33]

An alternative avenue open to the Soviet Union was to use her role in the United Nations to project her political influence in the Middle East. However, Israel's defiance of four UN cease-fire proposals was reminiscent of her indifference to its peace-keeping efforts during the first two Arab–Israeli wars. In addition, the sudden dismantling of UNEF raised serious questions about the future utility of the United Nations.

The Soviet Union's other decision – to underwrite the re-arming of the devastated Arab forces – had far greater ramifications. The successful airlift that began half-way through the war and the pledge of aid from the Moscow summit conference were initially underestimated by the United States. It soon became clear, however, that the Soviet decision ranked among one of the most important made by a great power since World War II, and that it signalled a modification and refinement of the Soviet position in the Arab–Israeli conflict. As the scale of the Arab defeat became apparent, Moscow realized that a political settlement acceptable to the Arabs would be impossible unless either Israel proved magnanimous and benevolent or the Arabs were re-armed, at least to the point of demonstrable military parity. The Soviet Union therefore rushed new weapons and equipment to her client states, though at such a rate that their demoralized and dis-

organized armies were unable to absorb them adequately. Nonetheless, the fact of the deliveries made the Arabs aware that the military option was still open – if Israel did not modify her political terms.

The Soviet reinforcement was so impressive that by the September Khartoum summit conference the Arab states, except for Syria, adopted a hard-line, 'no concession, no negotiations, and no peace' stance that governed Arab policies for the next three years. Now that Soviet military deliveries had effectively denied Israel the political fruits of her military victory (thereby shaping the course of the continuing confrontation), the key tasks were for the Arabs to achieve proficiency with the new, more modern weapons, and for the Soviet Union to work out a revised formula for her involvement in the Middle East.

American intervention during the war proved more decisive than Soviet action. The United States chose to intervene 'on Moscow's behalf' not because of the Soviet threat of force but because of the fear that a complete Israeli military victory would be so destabilizing as to destroy the prospect for political settlement. The Israeli forces were victorious, but American constraints had prevented a complete Arab collapse and the imposition of unconditional surrender.

The different interests of the two great powers converged over the salvation of the Syrian government in a coincidence that was to become the basis of their new involvement. The Soviet Union was anxious to preserve the Left-Ba'athist regime as an important disciple of Soviet Middle Eastern policy, and the United States ultimately agreed that, however undesirable the existing government might be, its demise would create new uncertainties at a time when the nature of her own involvement remained unclear. Thus one of the first principles of the new phase of great-power involvement was that irregular changes in the governments or political systems of the main Middle Eastern states should be avoided. Otherwise such changes would introduce into the delicate political relationships unknown factors that would suspend, if not paralyse, settlement efforts and jeopardize the great powers' respective commitments.

---

[33] On 9 June Algeria's President Boumedienne led the Arab attack and followed it up during his subsequent visit to Moscow in July. Soviet embassies in several Arab capitals were stormed by students protesting about Soviet perfidy.

II. THE CANAL WAR

The Canal War, dating from the end of the 1967 June War to the beginning of the 1973 October War (and sometimes referred to, in a more limited sense, by the Egyptian usage 'War of Attrition'), represented a new phase in great-power involvement in the Arab–Israeli conflict. A new sense of responsibility for promoting a just settlement emerged in the wake of the June War, and was not obscured by mutual recriminations over complicity in its outbreak. During this period both powers re-examined their arms-delivery policies and explored the nature and degree of constraints that could be exercised, individually or jointly, both to prevent hostilities and to promote a final accord.

From the outset, Israel insisted upon direct talks with the Arabs, where the full weight of their defeat could be used to extract conditions leading to a formal peace treaty with provisions satisfying Israeli security requirements. In her view, the conclusion of a successful bargain precluded the disclosure of specific demands beforehand. The Arab states, on the other hand, saw these tactics as a demand for unconditional surrender, and in their turn demanded prompt and total withdrawal of all Israeli troops to the borders obtaining before June 1967, condemnation of Israel as an aggressor, and full compensation for all war damage. They refused to open direct or informal talks with Israel while she enjoyed the bargaining advantage of occupying Arab territory. Finally, they introduced, rather unsuccessfully, an oil embargo intended to coerce the largely pro-Israeli Western nations into endorsing the Arab position.

In the days immediately after the War, the great powers were unable to find any common ground between the demands of their respective clients. The United States agreed to a Soviet request to convene a Special Emergency Session of the UN General Assembly on 19 June 1967, where Kosygin delivered one of the harshest speeches in UN history, demanding the condemnation of Israel for aggression. Nonetheless, the Soviet Union did also propose to an Arab caucus that it should accept the formula of recognizing Israel in exchange for Israeli withdrawal; however, Algeria and Syria rejected the suggestion and demanded unconditional withdrawal without recognition. Prior to the Glassboro Summit Conference between Johnson and Kosygin, held during the UN Emergency Session, the Soviet Union had sought to break the deadlock there by stating that she was prepared to drop the condemnation of Israel and the demands for reparations, but would insist on troop withdrawals. The American position at that time was that the Arab states must provide adequate assurances for Israeli security and a binding peace, and, although the Soviet Union could not provide iron-clad guarantees, the positions of the two powers were close enough for agreement to be reached at Glassboro to sponsor jointly a formula calling for recognition in exchange for withdrawal.[34] To Israel's relief, the draft resolution failed because of Arab opposition. Nevertheless, the Soviet Union persuaded Nasser to present the joint great-power formula at the Arab Foreign Ministers' meeting in August, and later at the Khartoum summit meeting; it was rejected at both sessions.

The United States was the first to advance a comprehensive solution, in what was prematurely labelled the five-point Johnson Plan and then the seven-point Rusk Plan. American thinking at that time was to promote a larger settlement by parcelling out individual bilateral accords that would first include an agreement between Israel and Egypt, then one with Jordan, and finally a treaty with Syria. Neither American initiative received encouragement from any of the belligerents.

By the autumn Egyptian confidence had improved. Nasser had instituted draconian reforms within the armed forces and had withstood an attempted military coup. Soviet arms deliveries were virtually complete, and the Khartoum summit conference had demonstrated in defeat the degree of Arab solidarity he had sought to ensure by victory. By November 1967 the Soviet Union informed the United States that Egypt was now prepared to accept in principle the joint American–Soviet formula rejected in July. On 22 November Security

---

[34] The Glassboro communiqué cited the need for a prompt and durable peace, the right of every state to live in peace and troop withdrawals under the proper conditions (*New York Times*, 25 June 1967).

Council Resolution 242 was adopted, calling for the withdrawal of Israeli forces, termination of belligerency, recognition of the right of all states to peace and security, freedom of navigation, a just settlement for the refugees, guarantees of territorial integrity, and the appointment of a UN Special Representative to assist in negotiations for a settlement. This indicated that enough common ground existed between the great powers to justify their efforts to achieve an agreement; yet only Egypt was prepared to accept Resolution 242 in principle.

Gunnar Jarring was appointed as the UN Special Representative, and he spent the winter and spring of 1968 trying to establish the minimum conditions for negotiation. No movement was registered on either side, but in October Israel agreed in principle that Resolution 242 could be considered the basis for an established peace. After intermittent false starts, Jarring resumed his mission in January 1971 and attempted to resolve the continuing deadlock by acting as a mediator. He sought written replies from both sides to his suggestions for specific accords. Egypt responded generally in line with her endorsement of Resolution 242, but Israel complained that he had exceeded his mandate in acting as a mediator, and virtually terminated his mission by quietly refusing further co-operation.[35]

Israel's stand on Jarring's mediation effort became a hallmark of her position on negotiations: she insisted on direct talks with the Arabs – though she later accepted the idea of informal talks at the opening stages, with formal negotiations reserved for crucial or final deliberations. Any efforts by third parties to introduce their own initiatives interfered with Israel's insistence on dealing from a position of strength and in gaining maximum political leverage from her military victory. Furthermore, she argued that local solutions to local problems were more durable than those introduced or imposed by third parties, and rejection of such external 'interference' was a dominant feature of her policy until the October War.

The failure of Jarring's efforts stemmed also from developments on the military side of the equation. Since there was no indication from Jarring that Israel intended to moderate her

[35] Documentation on his mission is contained in UN Doc S/10070, 4 January 1971.

political stand, Nasser felt compelled to reopen his military option and to force political movement by demonstrating Arab military strength. A central consideration in the military contest between the Arabs and Israelis has always been the requirement of gaining advantage by forcing the opponent to fight on one's own terms: in the Arab case, positional warfare, where artillery and fortifications could be used to inflict heavy casualties while at the same time providing protection; in Israel's case, open warfare, where tanks and aircraft could achieve tactical success through mobility and firepower. After the reorganization and retraining of the Egyptian Army in 1967–8 Nasser concluded that his forces in the Canal Zone were strong enough to resume fighting. On 15 October 1968 Egypt started a systematic artillery bombardment of Israeli positions on the canal and sustained it intermittently for several weeks. The Israeli forces were surprised and lost 15 dead in the first night; they had not fortified their positions and could not engage in effective counter-battery fire. At first the Egyptian High Command estimated that they were achieving their main objective – inflicting unacceptable casualties on the IDF – but Israel staged commando raids deep into the interior along the Nile Valley, demonstrating Egypt's continuing vulnerability. The raids had the desired impact, and Egypt suspended the shellings. Both sides then launched massive efforts to strengthen their positions along each side of the Canal.

The First Rogers Peace Plan

Six months later, in April 1969, Nasser launched his War of Attrition. Israeli raids were infuriating, but militarily insignificant so long as Egypt could confine the heavy fighting to the Canal Zone itself; this was the goal of the new phase. By late spring and early summer the systematic shelling was taking an increasing toll of Israeli lives (29 dead in July). Egypt had succeeded in her objective during this phase, and Israel was forced to escalate the conflict by introducing her air force into the first Battle of the West Bank: the contest for air superiority prior to artillery suppression.

When the War of Attrition was launched, a new dimension in great-power contacts was also opened. The new Nixon Administration in the United States invited the Soviet Union to participate in informal two-power talks about the Arab–Israeli crisis – an important step in granting the Soviet Union the recognition she desired that she was co-responsible for regional stability and security. The purpose of the talks was to determine what common ground existed between the participants, what solutions were most feasible, and whether the two powers should assume the initiative. The American decision had followed indications that the Soviet Union was prepared to play an active and responsible role in seeking a political settlement. On 30 December 1968 she sent a note to Washington outlining a new approach which envisaged full implementation of the provisions of Resolution 242 according to a definite timetable, beginning with a formal affirmation by all belligerents that they intended to implement the resolution. Each would then declare its intention to reach a peaceful settlement, and Israel would commit herself to a withdrawal at a fixed date. Contacts between both sides could then be arranged to consider substantive issues of borders, navigation, and refugees, and a system of guarantees through the Security Council would provide the final matrix.[36]

US Secretary of State William Rogers later discussed the initial conclusions reached during the talks. It was agreed that both had a direct responsibility for promoting a settlement and that continuation of the conflict would benefit nobody. Both powers, rejecting Israel's contention that third parties had no other responsibility than to bring the belligerents together, examined the entire spectrum of the controversy and were able to agree on specific proposals for recommended accords. Finally, enough progress was made for both to agree on appropriate procedural means for conducting talks among the belligerents.[37]

Implicit in the two-power talks was a general understanding that a new relationship was emerging that would govern their behaviour. Both were now firmly committed actively to pursue a political settlement, which indicated the highest degree of involvement yet demonstrated by either power. They had rejected the

constraints that Israel sought to impose on their engagement and had established ground rules for their behaviour; it was agreed that neither had vital interests in the region for which they were prepared to go to war. The holding of the talks implied that both powers were seeking an accord to demonstrate their credibility after their ineffectual performance before the June War. Since agreement required the concurrence of existing regimes, both powers would focus on substantive issues and not on the alteration of present political structures and philosophies. From this it might be inferred that both would act promptly, and possibly jointly, to restore a cease-fire if hostilities broke out, but each probably reserved the right to act independently if the political structure or social fabric of its client were endangered. With this understanding, both powers cautiously increased their stakes in the achievement of a political solution.

Israel's position was now gradually deteriorating. She had lost the political initiative to the external powers, and military pressure along the Canal was steadily increasing. Indeed, Egypt felt sufficiently confident militarily to indicate to the great powers that she would accept some form of indirect talks if Israel agreed to accept Resolution 242 as a point of departure. The great powers were encouraged, and jointly drafted two comprehensive treaties for Israel, Egypt, and Jordan.[38] Accordingly, Israel saw that both political and military developments were on the verge of moving beyond her control, possibly denying her the bargaining leverage of her military superiority. These events prompted the decision to escalate the war.

By the beginning of October, the Israeli air force (IAF) had virtually won the air-superiority battle over the West Bank and was targeting dug-in artillery positions. Both the military and political situations now rapidly collapsed. Because of the IAF's imminent victory on the West Bank, and the loss of the image of Egyptian military parity, the Soviet Union withdrew its co-sponsorship of the draft treaties. The United States pressed the issue and finally on 28 October, sent the three belligerent countries the proposals – in the light of Soviet reticence, referred to by the American

[36] *Al Anwar*, 10 January 1969.
[37] 'Secretary Rogers' Galaxy Conference Speech, 9 December 1969', *Department of State Bulletin*, 5 January 1970; see also *ibid.*, 12 and 19 January 1970.

[38] *New York Times*, 22 December 1969.

appelation of the First Rogers Peace Plan. Nasser reacted by identifying the United States before the National Assembly as the 'number one enemy of the Arabs'.[39] Mrs Meir (who had succeeded Mr Eshkol as Israeli Prime Minister on his death in February 1969) reported her Cabinet's rejection of the proposal to the Knesset and stated categorically, 'We have the right to demand that US policy should not be conducted at the expense of our vital interests'.[40] Such schemes by external powers, she explained, threatened Israel's existence and reduced the chances for a settlement with the Arabs. The Soviet Union refused to be associated with the initiative in any way.

The First Rogers Plan was thus doomed by the imperatives of Israel's bargaining position and Egypt's reverses on the battlefield. By the end of December, the Israel Defence Force (IDF) had virtually eliminated any resistance on the Canal. Egyptian casualties had reached excessive levels, and army morale had again fallen to the June War level; over one million civilians had been evacuated from the Canal cities, giving Egypt the largest refugee population in the Middle East. The initiative had clearly been restored to Israel.

The problem for Israeli leaders was how to convert this new manifestation of military supremacy into political advantage. They could show benevolence and modify their intransigent bargaining line, confident that their humiliation of Nasser further underscored the durability of Israel's military prowess; or they could continue to maintain military pressure, on the assumption that political contingencies within the Arab world, such as factional in-fighting or the overthrow of a key leader, would divert Arab attention towards their own problems, giving Israel more time to gain international acceptability. The Meir Government chose to increase pressure. The IDF could have crossed the Canal against little resistance, but the possession of the entire Canal Zone would bring serious risks of international censure. Accordingly, it was decided to escalate the air war by conducting strategic air raids against Egypt's interior, and military targets throughout the Nile Valley, the

Delta and the Western Desert were attacked.[41]

Nasser was confronted with a militarily untenable position and growing public protest. On 22 January he flew to Moscow to solicit Soviet aid. He first asked for strategic defensive systems, such as the MiG-25 *Foxbat*, to counter Israel's F-4 *Phantoms* or a deterrent system, such as the short-range surface-to-surface *Scud* missiles that could strike Israeli cities. Possession of either would limit Israel's strategic options, and Egypt could then rebuild her air defences with improved Soviet equipment.

The Soviet Union immediately saw the problems. The United States, perhaps inadvertently, had permitted aircraft supplied to Israel for the ground-attack mission to be used in a strategic role that seriously jeopardized Soviet objectives. To make good her pledge to ensure Arab parity, the Soviet Union was now faced with reduced options. She could press the United States to restrain Israel; she could supply highly sophisticated deterrence systems, which would require long training periods and carried the risk of Egyptian forces being defeated before the systems became operational; or she could deploy her own combat units and equipment to participate directly in the air defence of Egypt. There were risks associated with each option. Even if the United States recognized the disparities her policy had created, there was no assurance that she could influence Israel. The complexity of the ultra-modern systems was an order of magnitude greater than existing Egyptian skill levels, thus presenting a high risk of premature engagement and defeat by the IAF, further discrediting Soviet arms and possibly compromising secret technologies. Finally, the deployment of Soviet combat crews for the immediate defence of a non-Socialist country was unprecedented and fraught with risks for the Soviet Union's Warsaw Pact and world-wide commitments; it also represented a new threshold for her political involvement and military intervention in the Middle East that raised uncertainties about American reactions.

[39] Middle East News Agency, 6 November 1969.
[40] 'Mrs Meir's Knesset Statement', New Middle East, February 1970.
[41] By 25 January Defence Minister Dayan publicly stated that four-fifths of Egypt's air defence capability had been destroyed and that all Egypt was Israel's field of battle; the purpose of the strategic raids was to topple Nasser by demonstrating to Egyptians that he could not protect them (New York Times, 25 January, and Washington Post, 28 January 1970).

The Soviet leaders agreed to supply Egypt, within thirty days, with MiG-21J interceptor aircraft, SAM-2 and -3 missile batteries and enough pilots and crews to provide, in Nasser's words, 'area and point defence for only *civilian* and *economic* targets'.[42] Eventually, 150 Soviet aircraft were assigned to six main operating bases controlled by the Soviet Union, and on 13 April Soviet pilots began defensive patrols along the Nile Valley. Since Soviet deployments were highly circumspect, committed only to the defence of urban centres, Moscow was apparently signalling that this was a minimal reaction and was awaiting the response of the other actors.

Israel's reaction was prompt. Dayan claimed that this was the first stage of the 'Sovietization of the Egyptian military disposition', and that the Russians had thrown down the gauntlet;[43] the character of the war had changed. During the first four months of 1970 the IAF had flown 3,300 sorties and dropped 8,000 tons of munitions on Egyptian territory,[44] but the Soviet presence and involvement forced Israel to suspend strategic bombing in mid-April.

Following prudent military practice, the IAF attempted to measure the intentions and proficiencies of its new opponent by flying periodic probes into the presumed Soviet defensive perimeters. In the light of American inability to restrain Israel, each probe was seen by the Soviet Union as an audacious challenge to a great power and its efforts to stabilize the crisis. Accordingly, the Soviet responsibilities were gradually expanded to include all the Nile Valley, the Mediterranean and Red Sea approaches to Egypt and, finally, the support area for the Canal Zone itself.

On the political side, the two-power talks had proved barren after the collapse of the Rogers Plan, but when the decision was reached to deploy combat units to Egypt, Moscow opened a direct channel to the White House to explain the seriousness of the new military situation. On 31 January 1970 Kosygin¯ sent his first personal letter to Nixon, pointing out firmly that Israel was attacking Egypt at will and that

the entire country was vulnerable to strategic bombing. If the United States could not restrain Israel and confine hostilities to the tactical battlefield, the Soviet Union would have no alternative but to supply new arms to Egypt.[45]

Less than a week later, on 4 February, Nixon responded in a routine manner. He denied responsibility for the escalation of hostilities and asked that both powers seek an early cease-fire. He charged that Soviet arms deliveries were the destabilizing factor and offered to discuss an arms ceiling (at roughly the existing level); if no agreed ceilings could be established, the United States would arm Israel appropriately. Finally, he tried to rekindle Soviet interest in the Rogers Peace Plan as the soundest approach to a settlement.[46]

While the United States had observed the massive Soviet air and sealift to Egypt during March, her genuine surprise when the Soviet Union launched the first air patrols, indicated that a serious misperception had occurred. A Soviet diplomat remarked at the time that the Americans forgot that the Soviet Union was as committed to the defence of Egypt as they were to the defence of Israel. In the June War, the threat was seemingly against Israel, but now it was unquestionably against Egypt, and decisive deterrent action must be taken.[47] From press releases on the President's Report to Congress on Foreign Relations, Washington at that time was thinking of 'preserving' or 'maintaining' the existing military balance in the Middle East – a balance which was not a quantifiable sum of arms and equipment, but a subjective evaluation of the qualitative or technological advantage needed by Israel to offset the greater Arab resources in men and material. The United States had such a fixation about the merits of the First Rogers Plan, the failure of which was blamed on the Soviet Union, that a distinct drift beset American policy during the winter of 1969–70 as the position was reassessed.[48] Furthermore, there was a strong feeling in Washington that strategic bombing might be the only way to impress upon the Soviet Union and Egypt the necessity of endorsing the Peace

[42] *New York Times*, 15 February 1970; also Nasser's speech to the Arab Socialist Union Congress, Middle East News Agency, 23 July 1970.
[43] *Christian Science Monitor*, 23 May; *Jerusalem Post*, 5 May 1970.
[44] *Strategic Survey 1971* (London: IISS, 1972), p. 46.

[45] *Pravda*, 13 February 1970.
[46] *New York Times*, 4 February 1970.
[47] An interview with the author.
[48] As late as the spring 1970 Rogers called on other states to rethink the peace proposal, which was sound (*Department of State Bulletin*, 2 March 1970, p. 222).

Plan. Washington was indifferent to, or ignorant of, the basic premise of Moscow's Canal War position: that political discussion could only proceed from the basis of mutually accepted military parity or stalemate.

By May Egyptian forces demonstrated renewed vigour, raiding Elath and conducting minor Canal crossings and ambushes. But such incidents fell far short of establishing parity, which required returning the tactical battle to the Canal Zone. Egyptian forces attempted to reinsert their ground air-defence network but were defeated by the IAF; if they were to demonstrate their control of the West Bank and re-engage the IDF on the East Bank, then Soviet air protection would have to be provided. The Soviet Union constructed an extensive logistic base for rapid resupply along the two roads leading from the Nile to the Canal Zone and then, on the night of 29–30 June, moved up to the Zone twelve SAM-2 and three SAM-3 batteries, plus supporting equipment and anti-aircraft guns. The next morning they shot down their first two F-4s. The Israelis immediately accepted the challenge in the Second Battle for the West Bank, which they had come to regard as vital to their national security.

The Second Rogers Peace Plan
On the political side, several developments during the spring of 1970 forced the United States to reassess her position on the Peace Plan. First, the unexpected Soviet intervention was becoming alarming in its political implications and military potential. Second, Nasser had concluded that combined Egyptian–Soviet deterrence gave him the minimum military capability to risk testing the political waters. In his May Day speech, he asked President Nixon personally to explore the prospects for a political settlement. Third, Mrs Meir accepted in principle Resolution 242, and presumably its implications, and also the formula of indirect talks during the opening phase.[49]

A noteworthy lesson emerged from the formation of the second American initiative. The United States accepted Israel's constraints on the involvement of external powers and agreed not to provide model solutions, package agreements, or even substantive suggestions. The dangers inherent in Soviet military intervention outweighed the American sense of responsibility enunciated in the two-power talks and embodied in the First Plan, and she agreed to confine herself to a role acceptable to Israel. (In the summer Dr Kissinger told reporters confidentially that Washington's main concern was the withdrawal of Soviet forces from the Canal.) This role should merely be to provide an atmosphere conducive to Arab–Israeli talks or negotiations. Thus, preliminary discussions about a second American initiative were devoid of substantive considerations, except to gain endorsement of Resolution 242, and dealt with the procedural problems related to organizing the exchange of views. Most important, the main axis of discussion was between Washington and Tel Aviv, with Moscow being informed through the information circuit of the two-power talks. (Because of the Soviet intervention, the United States was now sensitive about the degree of confidentiality she should maintain at the two-power talks, and was satisfied to keep them correct, informal, informative, but discreet.)

On 19 June the United States transmitted the Second Rogers Peace Plan to the interested parties. It called for a 90-day in-place cease-fire supervised by the United States, and the activation of informal talks between Israel, Egypt and Jordan about their respective problems. The Soviet Union endorsed the Plan, though at the two-power level she continued to promote her version, which she felt was more comprehensive and in the mutual interest of all parties. This was a modification of her December 1968 proposal, emphasizing the time-table for commitments and withdrawals that had become the hallmark of the Soviet positions. Instead of the generally accepted need for a culminating peace treaty, the Soviet Union now proposed accords below the treaty level that would establish a web of normalized relations, without codifying unneccessary principles and responsibilities. She cited as a model her pragmatic relations with Japan, worked out without a formal peace treaty.[50] The United States rejected the suggestion as unacceptable to Israel.

[49] For an American justification for the renewal of her efforts, see Rogers' press conference, USIS Bulletin, No. 122, 26 June 1970.

[50] I. Belzaev, 'How the Soviet Union Visualizes a Middle East Settlement', International Affairs (Moscow), reprinted in New Middle East, June 1970, pp. 30–33.

The Soviet proposal was made at the last two-power meeting before Nasser arrived in Moscow for an unprecedented 19-day stay, and indicated that the Soviet Union expected the toughest bargaining yet to gain Egypt's endorsement of the Second Rogers Plan. (Speeches by Egyptian officials before the Moscow trip reflected Cairo's over-confidence that the military balance had shifted in its favour.) However, she had a high stake in promoting a settlement: she could claim credit for any accord, because of her decisive intervention on the Arabs' behalf; the need for Soviet troops along the Canal would ultimately diminish; and a favourable settlement would provide some assurance that the Soviet Union would remain an important influence in the future regime of the Canal.

Nasser succumbed to Soviet pressure and on 23 July announced to the Arab Socialist Union Party Congress Egypt's acceptance of the Second Rogers Peace Plan.[51] Nasser's decision shocked the Arab world. Egypt's military subsidies from the Arab oil countries were suspended, riots occurred in the radical Arab states, and a civil war erupted in Jordan. Nasser had become the first Arab leader to break the Khartoum pact by accepting the principle of negotiations with Israel. His decision was prompted by two main factors. As he told the Party Congress, it was imperative for Cairo to take action to halt the continuing supply of advanced arms to Israel; the arms race was costing the Arabs far more in resources than it was the Israelis. Secondly, the Soviet–Egyptian air defence crews were winning the Second Battle of the West Bank. For one month the Israelis had heavily bombed the surface-to-air missile complexes, and, even though direct hits were reported, the launchers were soon operational again. The penalty, however, had been the loss of seven expensive modern IAF fighter-bombers, and Israel later admitted that with available equipment she could not have defeated the missile build-up. Before finally succumbing to strong American pressure to accept the cease-fire, however, she sought to redress the military situation by deliberately 'baiting' Soviet fighters and shooting down four MiG-21s on 30 July. The next day she

[51] Middle East News Agency, 23 July 1970.

accepted the cease-fire, which went into effect on 7 August.

The decision to attack the forces of an intervening great power was one of the most momentous choices during the entire Canal War and was reminiscent of Israel's shooting down of five British aircraft in 1948 before accepting London's withdrawal ultimatum. Israel was demonstrating to all parties concerned that she would deal with the Arabs only from a position of strength, so that the terms for her security would not represent a compromise or the lowest common denominator attainable through an international forum. She would not modify this stand, even if it meant demonstrating to the Arabs that she was prepared to challenge the Soviet Union herself; Israeli security could not become the subject of external manipulation, whatever the cost. (Of course, there was also the element of military revenge. But it was bittersweet: 4 MiG-21s are not worth 5 F-4s, 2 A-4s and the loss of the military initiative.)

Egypt did not react initially, apparently awaiting Soviet responses. Within forty-eight hours, the Commander-in-Chief of the Soviet Air Forces, Air Marshal Paval S. Kutakhov, was in Cairo to investigate the incident. As seen from Moscow, it was a flagrant violation of the principles set up in the two-power talks; it was also a direct challenge to a great power, apparently intended to undermine its basic political assurance to the Arabs of parity, and one that weakened the Arab political bargaining position. Thus, the entire purpose of the Soviet military intervention was jeopardized. Further, such cavalier handling of Soviet pilots by the IAF could have serious implications for the Warsaw Pact–NATO confrontation, and might reduce the prestige of Soviet weapons generally throughout the Third World.

On these grounds, the Soviet Union decided that she must honour her commitment to the Arabs and increase the level of her military intervention, even if this hampered relations with the United States. The first SAM launchers were reported moving into the Zone on 2 August (before the cease-fire went into effect). The Soviet Union had decided to strengthen the ground rather than the air component of their air-defence network, and within weeks (and despite the cease-fire) she had built along the canal the most formidable air-defence complex in the history of air power. She was determined to deter Israel from embarrassing her further. In Brezhnev's words, 'those who have been trying in recent years to impose their will from a position of strength on Arab countries now have a new opportunity to reconsider their adventuristic policy'.[52]

The shooting down of the aircraft and the subsequent construction of the 'missile wall' that violated the cease-fire agreement was infuriating and perplexing for the United States, for the political talks were never seriously opened. With the Soviet decision to support the Arab position at what seemed to be considerable political cost to relations with the United States, Soviet–Egyptian relations were at an all-time high. Once more the question of implementation of the peace initiative centred on American–Israeli relations, and the interactions between the four parties had once again become verticalized.[53]

From the Israeli viewpoint there were three separate aspects of the cease-fire that related to great-power involvement. First, the Soviet violations of the cease-fire agreement constituted an obvious effort to constrain Israel in the event of renewed fighting; the provocation of the Soviet forces had proved counter-productive. The Soviet Union had prudently confined intervention to a defensive role, and had not delivered major offensive systems to Egypt, but in Israeli thinking at the time, air superiority was essential to deter Egypt from resuming artillery shelling. The new air defence system on the West Bank was designed to engage the IAF successfully so that ground positions could be systematically shelled. The seeming disparity between Israel's position before the Soviet intervention and the constraints imposed by that intervention was the justification for her re-

quests to the United States for an additional 48 F-4 aircraft.

This disparity was reinforced by the problem of guarantees. As Israel saw it, the central questions about the Second Rogers Plan were whether the Arabs would adhere to an agreement, and whether the external powers would be able to enforce compliance in the event of any violations. She ignored the fact that American reactions to the violations were partially conditioned by the Israeli provocation against the Soviet Union. For the next six months, Israel successfully diverted American attention from the primary motive behind the Second Rogers Plan (launching the political talks) to her own main concern: security matters. She charged the United States with being unable or unwilling to rectify the violations, and therefore unable to provide adequate guarantees for Israel's security. 'If the United States cannot guarantee a simple standstill 90-day cease-fire, how can it provide any assurance for a durable settlement?' Nixon was faced with retribution by Israel and expanding Soviet intervention: he ordered the suspension of the two-power talks, in retaliation for Soviet complicity in the violations, and another reassessment of American Middle Eastern policy – a political signal that the issue has been consigned to indefinite bureaucratic limbo.

During this phase Israel began to show awareness of the fact that procedural manipulations might have serious political overtones. When she saw that she was losing the military preponderance she had enjoyed during the period of strategic raids, without having compelled Egyptian acceptance of her conditions for talks, she quickly sought a surrogate issue – great-power guarantees – that was both critical to her own interests and subject to manipulation. The shooting down of the Soviet aircraft, the rejection of the talks, and palaver about guarantees all indicated a new Israeli sensitivity about negotiating procedures that affected substantive interests of the great powers. When her military options were inhibited, Israel showed an awareness of the need to use procedural limitations to limit Egyptian bargaining latitude to the same extent as she could do by means of military superiority. This syndrome of imposing a bargaining straitjacket gradually became the underpinning for Israeli negotiating strategy.

---

[52] Tass, 28 August 1970.
[53] The United States sought to minimize the violation and stress the importance of getting the talks under way. 'I think the important thing for us,' said Secretary Laird, 'is to move forward toward negotiations, and not debate what went on 12 hours before the cease-fire and 12 hours after.' State Department spokesman Robert McCloskey said, 'The immediate question is whether Egypt, with Soviet support, is indeed attempting to achieve a decisive military advantage under cover of the cease-fire . . . All indications are that Egypt is not undertaking an offensive build-up on the West Bank of the Suez Canal . . . Israel still has overall military superiority'. *USIS Bulletin*, 14 and 17 September 1970.

The Third Rogers Peace Plan
On the Egyptian side, President Sadat (who had succeeded Nasser, at the latter's death on 28 September 1970) held lengthy and confidential talks with both great powers in January 1971 on the issue of guarantees for an interim settlement. The United States convinced him that a great-power physical presence would be counter-productive, and that any accord would have to be self-enforcing. Indeed, it was argued that self-enforcement would be more appealing to Israel and would also probably be more durable, especially if guarantees were attached only to a breakdown of the agreement, and not to minor infractions. This understanding became the basis for a new Egyptian initiative for a political settlement. On 4 February Sadat told the National Assembly that he would extend the cease-fire for another 90 days. During this period he hoped to explore an interim accord for the reopening of the Canal and 'called on the Big Four powers to assume their duties and responsibilities to preserve peace in view of . . . their direct interest in the crisis'.[54] A week later he even agreed to negotiate a final peace agreement if the interim accord proved successful (this was the first time any Egyptian leader had accepted the principle of peace with Israel). He originally envisaged an Israeli withdrawal in Sinai to a line from El Arish on the Mediterranean to Ras Mohammed on the Red Sea, leaving Sharm el-Sheikh temporarily in Israeli hands, followed by a final withdrawal to the 1967 borders.

Mrs Meir responded that Israel would agree to talks on reopening the Canal, but not on Sadat's terms. She also forewarned that any withdrawal would have to be supervised and guaranteed by the United States.[55] President Nixon then replied in a press conference, 'Egypt has been more forthcoming than we expected, and I believe Israel has been somewhat forthcoming'.[56]

On a separate course, Ambassador Gunnar Jarring's final initiative (see p. 57) arrived in Tel Aviv on 8 February, and it appeared to Israel that she faced a Jarring–Rogers–Sadat collusion that might at any time include the Soviet Union. This mistaken perception of encirclement led to one of the worst crises in Israeli–American relations.

In March and April 1971 the United States was in the odd situation of having to reaffirm her good faith to Israel, while gaining sufficient credibility with Egypt to promote Sadat's new initiative. In these circumstances she had no interest in bringing the Soviet Union back into the deliberations, directly, though the Soviet ambassador to Washington, Mr Dobrynin, was periodically briefed on developments.

By May sufficient progress had been made for the United States to risk sending Secretary of State Rogers to the Middle East to meet Arab and Israeli leaders directly and intensify discussions on the interim agreement; the new understanding had been so strongly endorsed by Washington that it became the Third Rogers Peace Plan. Just before Mr Rogers' arrival, a series of political upheavals cast a long shadow over future Soviet involvement in the Canal War. First a pro-Moscow left-wing faction under Ali Sabri, and then a right-wing group of Cabinet Ministers, attempted to topple President Sadat. Both efforts were foiled, and in the process it was discovered that a detachment of East German intelligence experts in Egypt, ostensibly providing technical assistance, had in fact maintained extensive electronic surveillance of Egyptian governmental operations, including those of Sadat's office. Sadat was a marked man. Whether or not the Soviet Union was involved in Sabri's coup attempt, it appeared that she knew of the enterprise and had failed to warn her client. This episode increased the pressure on Sadat to exploit his new American connection in order to secure positive results from his initiative.

The issues to be discussed while Mr Rogers was in the Middle East included the depth of the withdrawal, the number and type of Egyptian forces permitted on the East Bank, how Egyptian sovereignty would be demonstrated, termination of a state of belligerency, freedom of navigation through the Canal, and the connection between the interim and a final agreement. Both sides were close to agreeing on the more technical issues, such as withdrawal distances and types of Egyptian troops, but Rogers was unable to advance the substantive issues of the length of the accord and the state of belligerency. He returned to Washington, after a stormy final session with Mrs Meir, with agreement only on

---

[54] Middle East News Agency, 4 February 1971.
[55] *New York Times*, 10 February 1971.
[56] *USIS Bulletin*, No. 33, 18 February 1971.

the reconsideration of positions and without formulating any positive recommendations.[57]

In the wake of the abortive Rogers mission, the Soviet Union gave Egypt only forty-eight hours notice that President Podgorny would arrive on 25 May to work out a long-dormant Soviet–Egyptian Friendship Treaty. This was signed two days later. The Treaty was not the major historic turning point the Soviet Union claimed;[58] it merely confirmed existing relations between the two states and did not enhance Soviet authority over Egyptian policy, as many had feared. Indeed, it included specific constraints on Soviet interference in Egyptian domestic affairs (as may have occurred two weeks earlier). The importance of the treaty was that it demonstrated the Soviet Union's sensitivity about her preferential position in Egypt and served as a warning that Cairo could not abuse Soviet interests with impunity.

The character of the Canal War now changed, and with it great-power behaviour. The two-power talks had been indefinitely suspended. The United States had been unable to get the Soviet 'garrison' removed from the Canal Zone and had also been unable to capitalize on her new relationship with Egypt. The Soviet Union re-emerged as the most important external influence in Egypt. The failure of all three American peace initiatives indicated that there was insufficient political will among the belligerents to secure even a limited accord, yet the Soviet presence in the Canal Zone ensured that the cease-fire would hold. Once again the interactions became verticalized, with each great power focusing on immediate relations with its client and ignoring further movement on the horizontal level of talks among the belligerents.

For the next six months, the United States again tried to establish a joint understanding with Israel about the role she should play in stimulating agreement. Israel insisted upon non-intervention and the exercise only of US 'good offices'. A compromise was reached after

the United States agreed to transfer to Israel licences and technological know-how for the local manufacture of military spare parts already in Israeli possession, and agreed to deliver additional aircraft and other weapons. The compromise announced in February 1972 (the so-called 'proximity talks') provided for the exercise of American good offices, with the reservation that Washington could introduce its own suggestions – but only after all attempts at resolution had been exhausted by the belligerents. Drift now beset American policy once more.

The proximity talks might have become the Fourth Rogers Peace Plan if they had attracted any Arab attention, but Sadat was bitter that the United States had not been able to deliver Israeli agreement. By September he had concluded that he could make no further political concessions and had no other option than to resume hostilities, which meant mending his fences with Moscow. The Soviet Union had informed him in the spring that she was reviewing her entire Middle Eastern policy, and her attitude toward Egypt in particular; the results would be implemented in the autumn. Sadat visited Moscow in October to examine the new phase in Egyptian–Soviet relations and to request additional weapons, especially 'decisive' weapons that would counter Israel's strategic option. Brezhnev promised to provide MiG-25 aircraft, though only four reconnaissance models eventually arrived after repeated Egyptian entreaties. With the eclipse of the American overture and the restatement of Egyptian dependence on Soviet arms deliveries, the Soviet Union did not noticeably alter the substance or conduct of her relations with Cairo.

Towards Renewed Hostilities

The issue of decisive weapons had again become the crucial problem in relations between the two states, however. In her 1969 build-up in Egypt the Soviet Union had prudently followed a self-imposed policy of restraint or 'adequacy'. This allowed the delivery to Egypt of weapons sufficient in both quantity and quality to ensure the country's defence and the demonstration of parity with Israel, but it precluded delivery of those categories of weapon that permitted all-out offensive attack. The deployment of Soviet forces in Egypt had also been exclusively for

[57] When Assistant Secretary of State, Joseph Sisco, arrived in Tel Aviv on 28 July to explore further progress, Mrs Meir rejected the Egyptian offer of a two- to three-year armistice in return for a thirty-mile pullback. Instead, she insisted upon an additional allotment of 48 F-4s. The Third Rogers Plan was dead.
[58] Tass, 27 May 1971. See also the American assessment in *USIS Bulletin*, No. 102, 2 June, and No. 105, 5 June 1971.

defensive and deterrent missions. Egypt had received medium-range bombers, but not in sufficient quantities to pose a serious threat to Israeli cities; she had also received bridging equipment and amphibious craft, but without air superiority such equipment was mainly of psychological and training value. Such constraints on arms supply had been decisive in shaping Egyptian behaviour, as the Soviet Union had envisaged. Israel, however, had not been similarly affected; indeed, the Soviet Union was more rigorous than the United States in limiting arms deliveries.

In order to resume hostilities, Egypt would have to overcome these limitations or find alternative sources of supply. She must first train and then use Egyptian crews for all missions carried out by Soviet units and then secure strategic weapons. Like all small countries embroiled in a seemingly interminable crisis, she also had to keep the international spotlight on the crisis if public opinion was to be used to promote her cause. When Sadat visited Moscow before the May 1972 Soviet–American Summit Conference, he received the distinct impression, conveyed also in the conference communiqué, that both great powers had agreed to play down the Middle Eastern problem and thereby demonstrate to the belligerents that great-power interests would not be seriously impaired by non-settlement. Great-power indifference also implied a tacit understanding of constraints on arms delivery that might freeze Egypt at its existing qualitative level.[59]

Sadat returned with a new sense of urgency. He had already announced that the preceding year was to be 'decisive in the war with Israel'; now he was threatened with complete immobilization. On 1 June he sent Brezhnev an urgent query about the delivery of advanced weapons, and followed it up two weeks later with an additional plea. On 7 July Brezhnev responded, completely ignoring Sadat's request and blaming Egyptian War Minister Sadek and others for the worsening relations between the two countries. In the presence of the Soviet Ambassador to Cairo, Mr Vinogradov, Sadat decided to expel the 17,000-man Soviet Advisory Mission and issued the appropriate orders, effective from 17 July 1972. In early August both

countries recalled their ambassadors to review the future of their relations.[60]

The expulsion of the Soviet advisers was a major turning point in the Canal War; it gained Sadat badly-needed public support, relieved pressure from other Arab states and restored his prestige among the military. Yet the prospects for resumed fighting on a go-it-alone basis were dim. Munition stockpiles were not adequate for a war of attrition, and spare parts would soon become available only by cannibalizing existing weapons and equipment. The most promising aspect of the expulsion was that it provided the United States with an ideal opportunity to resume exploration of a political settlement. Egypt, not the United States, had achieved Washington's precondition for a stable situation: elimination of the Soviet military presence. The Arabs openly solicited a new American initiative,[61] but the United States had been so badly buffeted by the local belligerents before in her effort to secure a settlement that she was reluctant to become involved again. Besides, the understanding reached with the Soviet Union only two months before to downgrade the Middle East crisis might be jeopardized. Furthermore, a new approach would be an uphill fight with Israel, which saw no need to 'rescue' Sadat. Indeed, Israel interpreted the expulsion as a vindication of her tough view that the strengthening of her security would reduce the prospects of war.

The expulsion was a major setback for the Soviet Union. Her policy of guaranteeing Arab parity had seemingly been treated with disdain; the basis of her influence in Egypt and her authority in a future regime of the Suez Canal had been eroded; her claims to be a regional power with sufficient local influence to assist in regulating regional stability had been compromised. Further, other Middle Eastern countries, such as Syria or Iraq, offered no comparable power-base that could provide a similar degree of influence as Egypt. The Soviet Union had not been able to devise a reliable formula for cultivating and exercising political influence in the Middle East and her behaviour here was

---

[59] For Sadat's reasoning on his relations with Moscow, see his interviews in *Newsweek*, 6 March and 31 July 1972.

[60] Middle East News Agency, 16 and 23 July 1972: *New York Times*, 27 July 1972; and *Al Ahram*, 21 July, 7 August 1972.
[61] See an interview with President Boumedienne, *International Herald Tribune*, 28 July 1972.

governed by the same rules as governed that of the Western states. With the basis of her influence in Egypt amputated, and diplomatic relations with Israel severed, the Soviet Union would be virtually isolated if tensions should again increase, and she might have to yield the diplomatic field to the United States.

The rectangular interactions between the four parties had now lost their symmetrical shape. Both horizontal and vertical axes were deteriorating as a means of routine communication, and negotiations stagnated. This was the ideal situation for Israel. Both great powers had been virtually removed from future interactions – indeed, they appeared nearly paralysed – and, without the military support of the Soviet Union or the political encouragement of the United States, Egypt could hardly act on her own to upset the inertia. Indeed, the interactions between the four powers shrank so noticeably that the great powers' objective of moving the crisis into cold storage appeared to be achieved. This analysis was so comforting for Israel that it was the main reason for her failure to recognize Egypt's dexterity in overcoming this isolation, and for her being taken by surprise in October 1973.

For Egypt the crumbling of the rectangular system could only momentarily fan Arab pride; it could not advance her national interests. Sadat understood the subtle relationship between these two factors. He could not move militarily without Soviet assistance, yet Arab nationalism prevented him from returning to Moscow like a repentant supplicant. The Soviet Union realized that her re-entrance and participation in the Arab–Israeli conflict now hinged upon reaching an accommodation with Sadat that also did not incur loss of face.

The reconciliation was probably worked out during the period between the visit to Moscow of Egyptian Prime Minister Sidqi in October 1972 and that of Sadat's national security adviser Hafiz Ismail in February 1973, when the communiqué mentioned for the first time the need for strengthening Egypt's military potential.[62] Egypt's Minister of War, Ahmed Ali, arrived two weeks later and concluded the final agreement.

In the compromise that was reached the Soviet Union was to provide, as deterrent weapons, two battalions of *Scud* B missiles and crews and to re-institute delivery of munitions and spare parts, as well as increasing the inventory of modern weapons to ensure the success of the anticipated cross-Canal operation. This was a major change in Moscow's dogmatically held rule of 'adequacy'. In return, Egypt agreed to limit her war aims to the recapture of a limited strip of the East Bank that could provide adequate defensive assurance for the reopening of the Canal. Both sides apparently concluded that secrecy was imperative for success and agreed to keep their reconciliation confidential. As a further means of prudent deception, they apparently agreed to minimize the number of states involved in the planning. One vertical axis of the rectangle had been restored to full operation and the groundwork was now laid for the renewal of fighting.

III. GREAT-POWER BEHAVIOUR DURING AND AFTER THE OCTOBER WAR

Preparations for the October war indicated how rapidly the Moscow–Cairo axis could be repaired when national interests dictated conciliatory political will. Shortly after War Minister Ali's visit to Moscow, a Soviet military delegation arrived in Cairo, apparently a liaison mission for the massive new arms deliveries that began in March. The Cairo daily *Al Akhbar* reported on 24 March that in 'importing arms from the Soviet Union these days, Egypt is no longer concerned with the question of the types of weapons' (meaning the quality or 'decisiveness' of weapons). Sadat also expressed his satisfaction: The Soviet Union was 'providing us now with everything that is possible for them to supply. I am now quite satisfied'. War with Israel was now inevitable.[63] The deliveries, however, were not without shortfalls, delays or

---

[62] Tass, 10 February 1973.
[63] Interview in *Newsweek*, 9 April 1973. On 5 April 1973 in response to a question about renewed Soviet arms deliveries Kosygin stated in Stockholm that Egypt had the right to possess a powerful army in order 'to liberate its own lands' – quoted in Foy D. Kohler, Leon Gouré and Mose L. Harvey, *The Soviet Union and the October 1973 Middle East War* (Miami, Fla: Center for Advanced International Studies, University of Miami, 1974).

deliberate denials; for example, 12 Tu-22 *Blinder* supersonic medium bombers were delivered to Iraq and none to Egypt. In July Sadat complained openly about the delay in delivery of weapons.[64] Such statements may have been for deception purposes, but it seems more likely that the Soviet Union was indeed exercising some restraint, because of anxieties that the build-up would again trigger uncontrollable Arab euphoria, or that the deliveries would be detected and precipitate a new arms race or premature hostilities. One apparent indication of Soviet prudence was the delivery of a limited number of *Scud* missiles in April (perhaps as a sign of good faith), while withholding the remainder until September.[65]

The Soviet Union maintained a dual approach to the crisis until at least mid-summer. On the one hand, she had agreed to resupply a wide variety of offensive-type weapons that even 'Israel does not possess'[66] and to use any means necessary to liberate occupied territories (meaning types of arms rather than terrorism and hijackings). On the other hand, according to Sadat, the Soviet Union in March 'persisted in the view that a military battle must be ruled out and that the question [of hostilities] must await a peaceful solution'.[67] Moscow apparently wanted to moderate Egyptian expectations until after the 22 June summit conference with the Americans.

Political Alignments
The internal timing of the adjustment is an important indicator of the motives involved. Sadat claims that Soviet–Egyptian relations remained frozen until February 1973.[68] On 1 February Sadat renewed the 1968 Soviet lease of Egyptian naval facilities, and a week later, his Security Adviser, Hafiz Ismail, was received by Brezhnev. This must have been, however, the final consummation of a preliminary

understanding reached earlier, because Sadat insists that on 21 December he ordered military preparations for the resumption of hostilities within six months – a decision he could not have made without a firm Soviet commitment to supply essential weapons.[69] After the adjustment with Moscow was reached, Sadat sent Hafiz Ismail on a tour of Western capitals to determine if any new interest in a settlement could be generated and to demonstrate that Egypt had left no stone unturned on the subject before resorting to war. The mission was fruitless, and Sadat announced to the National Assembly on 26 March that 'the military situation must be made to move, with all the sacrifices this entails'.[70]

Sadat's reasons for renewing the fighting were apparently: (1) that the deadlock could only be broken if the Arab political position were taken seriously by Israel and the external powers, and at that juncture this could only be achieved by military means; (2) he felt it imperative to regain enough territory to demonstrate Arab military competence and restore public morale and confidence; (3) even a military draw or stalemate would destroy the myth of Israeli invincibility and provide sufficient land for the Canal to be reopened unmolested; (4) he was convinced that both great powers had such a stake in the new detente that they would act quickly in order to impose a cease-fire upon the combatants.[71]

On the other hand, the Egyptian pledge to confine Arab war aims merely to the liberation of specific territories was apparently acceptable to the Soviet Union for several reasons: (1) it appeared to be militarily feasible, because the Arab states, primarily Egypt, would be able to fight on their preferred pattern of positional warfare, where their fire-power advantages could be exploited from under effective air cover; (2) such limited war aims would increase the probability that Israel could be deterred from her strategic option by the deployment of a minimal number of Soviet-manned strategic missiles; (3) a low profile for Soviet military re-intervention would mean a low risk of provoking an American reaction; and (4)

[64] Galia Golan, *The Soviet Union and the Arab–Israel War of October 1973*, Jerusalem Peace Papers, No. 7, June 1974, p. 11; and *New York Times*, 30 October 1973.
[65] This seems the most plausible explanation for the discrepancies in delivery dates. See Gen. Chaim Herzog, 'The Middle East War', *Journal of the Royal United Services Institute*, March 1975; and *Aviation Week and Space Technology*, 22 October and 5 November 1973.
[66] Cited in Kohler *et al.*, *op. cit.* in note 63.
[67] Middle East News Agency, 3 April 1973.
[68] *Ibid.*, 23 July 1973.

[69] *Ibid.*, 3 April 1973.
[70] *Sunday Times*, 14 October 1973.
[71] See Heykal's statement on these limited aims in *Der Spiegel*, 21 January 1974.

reduced war aims would restrict the number of Arab states involved and possibly avoid the disastrous bombast that cost Soviet Union control of events in the period before the 1967 June War.

In developing the appropriate political alignments within the Arab world for the resumption of war, Sadat wisely avoided the basic error of his predecessor – seeking military preponderance through the widest possible demonstration of Arab unity, requiring general acceptance of the lowest common denominator in political ambitions. Sadat expected Arab unity would result from the war itself and foresaw the necessity for conducting the operation on a highly exclusive basis, in order to ensure that the aims would remain restricted. This meant confining the fighting to only two fronts and including only Syria in the initial planning.

Sadat's most formidable obstacle with this scheme was gaining the endorsement of Syria, which strongly advocated launching a general war to gain agreement on a final political settlement. Between 3 April and 12 September, when a summit conference was held between Egypt, Syria and Jordan (and diplomatic relations were restored among the three) the press reported at least eighteen high-level visits by Egyptian and Syrian political and military officials to Cairo and Damascus and other Arab capitals.[72] Yet, it is unclear when within this period President Assad finally committed Syria to participating in a limited war[73] (planning for the operation had been conducted under the aegis of the United Arab Command since January,[74] without formal political endorsement by Damascus). Syrian preparations, however, began to accelerate after February, when Moroccan troops were accepted and deployed to the front (a second contingent arrived in July) and 40 to 50 new Soviet SAM

batteries and additional T-62 tanks were delivered. Iraq, Jordan and Saudi Arabia apparently had a limited foreknowledge that planning was under way, which was evident from the arrival of new Soviet arms, but were not informed about D-day, even though they were expected to provide forces for the United Arab Command. Other Arab leaders were deliberately excluded, especially the Palestinians – indeed Palestinian radio stations were closed down in October to prevent inflammatory broadcasts. Even the Soviet Union was not informed of D-day until 2 October, when she precipitately evacuated Soviet dependants from Damascus.[75]

The available evidence suggests that Moscow had substantially altered her objectives and tactics between the June and October Wars, in part because of the lessons learned during the Canal War. She had abandoned her former policy of arms restraint and accepted the necessity of resumed hostilities. She recognized the dangers of military posturing to secure political bargaining positions, as attempted before the June War. She also acknowledged the futility of attempting to demonstrate Arab parity, even with direct Soviet military intervention. Given the Soviet Union's priority for consolidating political influence among the Arabs, she was prepared to accept the risks of resumed fighting, with sufficient constraints imposed to ensure that there was a low probability that great-power relations would become endangered.

Deception, Warning and Surprise

After the adjustment was reached with Cairo, the Soviet Union adopted an ambiguous policy toward the Arab–Israeli confrontation: supporting the Arabs, threatening Israel and warning the United States. Content analysis of the Soviet media indicates that from about January 1973 Moscow was advancing several themes: (1) the Arabs had rejected the partial settlement plans of the United States and were seeking a general peace accord that would guarantee regional peace; (2) the Soviet Union was providing all the military means necessary to achieve the Arabs' political objectives; and (3)

---

[72] For a partial list, see my *Canal War* (Cambridge, Mass.: MIT Press, 1974), pp. 236–237.
[73] Herzog, *op. cit.* in note 65. Maj.-Gen. Farrar-Hockley places it as late as March and claims that only by midsummer was a joint Egyptian–Syrian operational plan agreed upon in principle; Elizabeth Monroe and A. H. Farrar-Hockley, *The Arab–Israel War, October 1973: Background and Events*, Adelphi Paper No. 111 (London: IISS, Winter 1974/5).
[74] In January Ahmad Ismail was appointed Commander-in-Chief of the Armed Forces of the Arab Federal Republic, meaning both Egyptian and Syrian forces.

[75] See Sadat's interviews in *Al Nawar*, 1 March and 28 March 1974, and *Newsweek*, 25 March 1974.

Israeli intransigence remained the chief threat to regional security and stability.[76]

In a remarkable repetition of history, Israel retaliated against continuing terrorist activities on 13 September 1973, 'baiting' the Syrian air force by flying a provocative penetration course over the Mediterranean toward Latakia. In the ensuing engagement some 13 Syrian aircraft were shot down without Israeli loss. Moscow promptly blamed Israel for aggressive intentions and shifted the focus of the Soviet media attack. On the one hand, Israel was portrayed as being in a relatively weak military position compared to the combined Arab forces. On the other, there was a return to the May 1967 theme of the imminence of an Israeli attack intended to 'intimidate the Arab people' and nullify the joint efforts of the Arabs to recover the occupied lands. The crescendo of charges increased up to 6 October with allegations that Israel was 'concentrating forces on the cease-fire line with Syria', 'stepping up military preparation' and increasing tensions along the Suez Canal that were likely to 'trigger a new military explosion in the Middle East'. Pravda stated on 6 October, 'tensions are increasing on the cease-fire line between Syria and Israel. According to the Egyptian press, Tel Aviv is preparing a massed attack. Israeli tank units and heavy artillery have been brought up to the Syrian cease-fire line. Israeli aircraft are also patrolling the entire length of the Lebanese border'.[77]

While the Soviet media were trying to construct an image of an imminent Israeli attack and thereby warn Tel Aviv against further military reprisals, Moscow also took limited precautions to ensure that detente was not impaired as tensions rose. Under Article 3 of the 'Basic Principles' signed in 1972 as a guide for great-power behaviour, both parties agreed to warn each other in the event of a threatened local conflict and 'to do everything in their power so that conflicts or situations do not arise which would seem to increase international tensions'. But the Soviet Union could obviously not provide the type of explicit warning the

United States expected in such a situation without openly acknowledging her complicity in the Arab military preparations. After the war, however, she claimed to have honoured her responsibilities. Brezhnev stated in his World Peace Congress speech on 26 October 1973, 'During recent years the Soviet Union has repeatedly, I stress repeatedly, warned that the situation in the Near East was explosively dangerous'.[78] Indeed, Brezhnev did raise the issue with Nixon and Kissinger at San Clemente, but apparently in sufficiently vague terms for the Soviet claims to be discounted as alarmist. A sample of the blurred nature of Soviet warnings at the official level was displayed by Gromyko in his UN General Assembly speech on 26 September: 'The Israeli leaders must know that in the final analysis this adventurism (criminal aggressive acts against the Arab states) inevitably brings retribution in its wake'.

According to the American viewpoint, Washington had the right to an explicit warning. Secretary Kissinger asserted at his 12 October press conference that this was consistent with, and indeed required under, the agreement on 'Basic Principles' for each side to inform the other if it 'has certain knowledge of imminent military operations in any explosive part of the world'. He went on to suggest that he did not believe the Soviet Union had any direct forewarning of Arab intentions. This presumption was based in part on intelligence estimates. 'We asked our own intelligence,' Kissinger asserted, 'as well as Israeli intelligence, on three separate occasions during the week prior to the outbreak of hostilities, to give us their assessment of what might happen. There was the unanimous view that hostilities were unlikely to the point of there being no chance of it happening.'[79]

There is no doubt now that the Soviet Union was fully aware of Arab intentions but probably did not know the exact timing until roughly seventy-two hours before hostilities.[80] She has defended her interpretation of the adequacy

---

[76] The most elaborate survey of Soviet media and literature on this period is found in Kohler, et al., op. cit. in note 63.

[77] For more particular charges, see Tass, 13–16 September, Izvestia, 18 September and 3 October, Krasnaya Zvezda, 18 and 23 September and Tass, 6 October.

[78] Pravda, 27 October 1973.

[79] USIS Bulletin, No. 192, 15 October 1973. Golan (op. cit. in note 64, p. 15) claims that the Soviet Union formally informed Washington on 5 October, but there is no evidence to support this from official sources. Indeed, Kissinger repeatedly insisted at his press conference that he was informed only three hours before hostilities, but declined to say from what source.

[80] See interviews cited in note 75.

of the warning given to the United States, however, with the argument that there are different types of crisis and levels of tension, based on their implications for Soviet national interests. Those crises dealing with national liberation movements, which she has an obligation to support, are exempt from great-power discussions provided for in the Basic Principles. By the dual criteria of the liberation of the occupied Arab lands and the promotion of the just rights of the Palestinians, the Arab–Israeli conflict qualifies as a national liberation struggle in which the Soviet Union must have a unique vested interest, and one which the United States must recognize need not damage the detente process in other issues.[81]

The Soviet media campaign was not reflected in the Egyptian press either in coverage or intensity, which was apparently part of the comprehensive Arab plan of deception (indeed there was still substantial criticism of the Soviet Union). One aspect of this 'grand design' was the exclusive nature of the planning, restricting knowledge on a 'need-to-know' basis to Egyptian and Syrian General Staff officers and several Soviet officials. As a result, an unusual degree of secrecy was imposed on the planning and training phases on the preparations. General Herzog has commended the Arabs in these terms: 'Ninety-five per cent of the Egyptian officers taken prisoner by Israel knew for the first time that this exercise [the field manoeuvres] would turn into a war only on the morning of 6 October. One or two knew two days before, one knew three days before, but very senior officers did not know . . . One divisional commander was told the night before and called his brigade commanders the next morning to tell them. . . . This deception plan was eminently successful, extremely well conceived and very well carried out.'[82]

Though the evidence is not conclusive, most analysts agree that Egypt's six-monthly field manoeuvres in May were staged as a massive ruse to draw Israel on to alert, and were not preparations for actual war that were cancelled because of the American–Soviet summit meeting. Israel did assemble her first line reserves and went through the first stages of mobilization at

a cost of 4·5 million Israeli pounds. Even though Defence Minister Dayan told senior members of the General Staff after the Egyptian exercise ended, 'A renewal of the war in the second half of the summer must be taken into account', the cost of the May mobilization was to be a serious deterrent to a second alert in the autumn.[83] When the semi-annual autumn exercises began as usual with the equinox, Israeli intelligence relied heavily on the precedent established in the May manoeuvres and played down the build-up.

Israel had adequate tactical military warning but misinterpreted its full meaning. By the end of September a substantial portion of the Egyptian Army had been moved up to the Canal in full battle formation six times. Communications chatter would die down nightly after the announced end of manoeuvres, yet night observation devices detected continuing unloading of supplies and equipment at the fortifications along the West Bank. Nine days before the War, Egyptian engineers brought rubber rafts and bridging equipment down to the Canal's edge as part of a manoeuvre. At the beginning of October both Egypt's and Syria's air defence systems went on alert. The Egyptian troop build-up on the West Bank now exceeded all previous exercises. Syria redeployed units from the Jordanian border to the Golan Heights, and on 2 October mobilized her reserves; the next day the Soviet Union hastily evacuated her dependants from Syria. On 5 October Egypt began a major exercise toward the Canal which coincided with American signals interceptions indicating the imminence of hostilities.

Israel misinterpreted Arab intentions for both military and political reasons. According to the Agranat Commission, charged by the Knesset to investigate the reasons for Israel's surprise, the majority of the senior IDF officers concluded that the Arabs would not risk a war until they had achieved parity in the air, both in aircraft and proficiency. This estimate, clearly a reflection of Israel's traditional appraisal of the value of air power, rejected the evidence that the Arabs were concentrating on the ground environment of air defence, not aircraft. This grave misjudgment also failed to comprehend the type of war the Arabs preferred to fight

[81] See, for example, Radio Moscow Broadcast to the Middle East on 4 April 1974.
[82] Herzog, *op. cit.* in note 65, p. 5.
[83] Monroe and Farrar-Hockley, *op. cit.* in note 73, p. 17.

and the possibility that they might seek only limited objectives. Finally, Herzog has pointed out that before the Suez and June Wars, warning was based on estimates of enemy capabilities; afterwards it was predicated upon intentions. Intelligence estimating becomes more complicated as the number of perceptions of intention vary. The final product is often a bureaucratic compromise, representing the lowest common denominator of the interested parties.

The second aspect of Israel's miscalculations was political. Her leaders became rather complacent after Egypt expelled the Soviet advisers in July 1972 and the failure of the Rogers peace initiatives had generated drift and indifference in American Middle Eastern policy. Israel was confident that without the active involvement of at least one external power the Arabs would not be able politically or militarily to launch even a limited war.

Great-Power Diplomacy

The United States was completely surprised both tactically and strategically by the Arab attack. Dr Kissinger saw events as indications of a possible Israeli assault on the Arabs and repeatedly warned Tel Aviv not to pre-empt. On 4 October he asked Foreign Minister Eban if Israel would agree to conduct 'corridor conversations' with Egypt at the United Nations under American good offices; Eban readily accepted, as did Egypt's Foreign Minister al-Zayyet.[84] Thus reassured, the United States failed to launch a reconnaissance satellite and, when hostilities broke, she was virtually dependent on Tel Aviv for tactical intelligence, which proved less reliable than during the June War and created suspicions that Israeli aid requests were exaggerated.

In the three hours before hostilities began the United States contacted all parties concerned and attempted to prevent open conflict by acting as a mediator. She sought assurances from each, so that she could provide assurances to the others that no one had any aggressive intentions. After war broke out the United States set herself two main objectives: to end hostilities as soon as possible, and to do so in a manner that would promote a permanent settlement. As Kissinger explained on 12

October, she opened and maintained contacts with all parties (she did not have formal diplomatic relations with either Syria or Egypt at that time) and, rather than risk the hardening of positions by forcing the issue at the UN, attempted to crystallize a consensus. (On 7 October the Soviet Union strongly pressed the United States at the Security Council not to press for a cease-fire.) Assurances were given by both the Arabs and Israel that when a cease-fire was accepted Washington was prepared to assume a major role in promoting negotiations for a durable settlement – an important secondary motive for the Arab attack. Thus, the United States rebounded from complete strategic and tactical surprise at the Arab aggression to a commitment to more intensive political involvement in the crisis.

The American attitude toward Soviet involvement tended to reflect the fortunes of war. On 8 October Kissinger warned that 'detente cannot survive irresponsibility in any area, including the Middle East'. The next day the Syrian thrust was reversed, and the Soviet involvement was intensified with the launching of an airlift and publication of a letter from Brezhnev to President Boumedienne calling for united Arab assistance for Egypt and Syria. On the 10th the Soviet Union performed a *volte-face* and asked for an immediate cease-fire; Israel rejected this. By 12 October Kissinger was arguing to reporters that Soviet actions had not reached an irresponsible level; the airlift was only moderate and the level of Soviet involvement 'acceptable'; the Brezhnev appeal was not 'helpful', but the Soviet Union was exercising relative restraint to prevent an escalation into a confrontation. 'If you compare their conduct in this crisis to their conduct in 1967, one has to say that Soviet behaviour has been less provocative, less incendiary and less geared to military threats than in the previous crisis.[85]

---

[84] Marvin and Bernard Kalb, *Kissinger* (Boston, Mass.: Little and Brown, 1974).

[85] *USIS Bulletin*, 12 and 26 October 1973. The American airlift was slow in starting because of a controversy between Kissinger and Schlesinger over the true nature of Israeli needs, the necessity for maintaining a low profile for any American intervention, and unexpected obstacles, such as the refusal of commercial carriers to participate, the mechanical breakdown of half the C-5A aircraft, and adverse winds over the Azores. The White House created further delays by imposing impractical solutions, resulting from political urgency. Nixon feared that, in the wake of Vice-President Agnew's resignation in

On 13 October, when the Arab forces on the Northern Front had been pushed back to the main fortified line at Saasa, some 20 miles from Damascus, and Israel began redeploying forces southward, the Soviet Union accepted a British cease-fire proposal.[86] On 14 October, in order to ease pressure on Syria and deter Israel from attacking Damascus, and against the advice of his senior officers, Sadat ordered a general offensive by his forces on the West Bank. By 16 October the Egyptian thrust had been repulsed and the junction between the Second and Third Armies penetrated by the Israeli crossing to the West Bank of the Canal. Kosygin arrived in Cairo on the same day and returned three days later with Sadat's terms for accepting a cease-fire.[87]

On 20 October Kissinger left for Moscow to negotiate the provisions of the Security Council cease-fire resolution, which was adopted two days later and accepted by Israel and Egypt. Resolution 338 contained three substantive parts. It called for an immediate in-place cease-fire and the prompt implementation of Resolution 242. Finally, it called for negotiations between the parties concerned, under appropriate auspices, to bring about a just accord. This third provision represented a major concession by the Arabs: it was the first time they had formally authorized negotiations, rather than informal talks, with Israel. To soften the impact, both great powers agreed to offer their good offices, if so desired by the parties concerned. The understanding between the great powers was that they would jointly sponsor some form of international conference that would bring the parties together at an appropriate juncture in the bargaining process.

On 23 October the cease-fire was broken, and Israeli forces completed the encirclement of the Egyptian Third Army by seizing Suez City on the West Bank. The IDF had encountered fierce resistance: nearly half their total tank losses were inflicted in the Sinai. The Egyptian air defence system was completely destroyed in the southern half of the Canal Zone, but the road to Cairo was not cleared, as Israel frequently asserts; to do so would have required protracted fighting and mounting Israeli casualties. Even so, Israel held important bargaining chips in the trapped Third Army – though IDF units were themselves soon encircled by larger Egyptian forces, and tension continued high.

There is considerable evidence that the Soviet Union was at least partially surprised by the Arab attack, and that she genuinely attempted to control hostilities.[88] She sent Ambassador Vinogradov to Sadat a few hours after hostilities began, and again the next day, falsely claiming that the Syrians had accepted a cease-fire and urging the Egyptians to do likewise. She also apparently sent Politburo member Kirilenko on an unannounced visit to Damascus to discuss a cease-fire.[89] Both Sadat and Assad rejected the suggestion. It is unclear whether the Soviet Union was acting in collaboration with the United States, whether she was trying to develop a unilateral initiative that might enhance her posture and ensure her full participation in the post-war settlement, or whether she was simply sounding out Arab terms for an early cease-fire, so that their military advantages might be preserved.

Content analysis of Soviet media during the war reinforces Kissinger's contention that Moscow was more restrained than she had been during previous Middle Eastern crises. Israeli aggression was denounced, but in terms mild enough not to be alarmist, and only after the sinking of a Soviet ship in Latakia on 12 October, which caused loss of Soviet lives and property, did Tass caution Israel against further criminal actions. Likewise, when Israel launched strategic

---

disgrace on the 10th and the dismissal of Cox and Richardson while Kissinger was in Moscow, accompanied by calls for impeachment, an Israeli public complaint of American perfidy over commitments to Tel Aviv might topple his administration. Eventually 569 sorties were flown delivering 22,500 tons of material.

[86] Golan, op. cit. in note 64, p. 18.

[87] Kosygin proposed: (1) an in-place cease-fire; (2) Israeli withdrawal to 1967 boundaries, with adjustments; (3) an international peace conference; and (4) guarantees of the peace agreement by the Soviet Union and the United States. Sadat agreed reluctantly – on condition that the Soviet Union guaranteed the plan's implementation, with or without American co-operation – and accepted the principle of direct talks (Kalb, op. cit. in note 84, pp. 480–481).

[88] Brezhnev assured the World Peace Congress, 'from the moment of the outbreak of military action in the Near East . . . the Soviet Union has done everything in its power, taken all political measures, to help bring about an end to the war and to create conditions in which peace in the Near East would become truly secure'. Pravda, 27 October 1973.

[89] Reported in Al Ahram, 13 December 1973.

bombing raids against Syrian cities, Moscow warned of 'grave consequences' if Arab urban targets were subjected to further attacks – which was bland indeed for the Soviet press.

At the same time, however, the Soviet Union took several military precautions. On 8 October three of her airborne divisions were placed on alert, but their transport aircraft were committed to the airlift supply operation. During the first two weeks of the war, the Soviet Mediterranean Fleet was augmented by ten additional surface combatants, reaching a total of 30 warships (on 5 October three were actually returned to the Black Sea), and was deployed to the principal Mediterranean choke points: the straits of Gibraltar, the straits of Sicily, the straits of Messina and the Aegean Sea. Other warships were moved within striking distances of the Sixth Fleet carrier forces on station in the Ionian Sea and south-east of Crete. All Soviet vessels were removed from the war zone along the Egyptian eastern coast, and after the Israeli attack on Latakia Soviet warships sailed into the war zone off the Syrian coast to protect the Soviet sealift operation. It is estimated that Soviet re-supply operations delivered ten times the total tonnage that the United States airlifted into Israel, the bulk of it arriving by surface, and such an extensive operation required lines of communication to be kept open.

Soviet naval forces actually peaked on 1 November at 40 surface combatants, *after* the brief confrontation with the United States. This delay was due to the constraints of the Montreux Convention which required the Soviet Union to notify Turkey eight days in advance of any ship passing through the Dardanelles; as a result it took her three weeks to double the number of surface combatants. The United States deployed an additional carrier task force into the Mediterranean on 18 October. It should be noted that during the September 1970 Jordanian crisis, the Sixth Fleet and the accompanying Soviet forces had been on station south-east of Cyprus. At the peak of the 1973 crisis all three American carriers were held in non-dispersed formations further west, off Crete, indicating that the probability of American intervention was reduced in the latter case. It should also be stressed that both crises demonstrate that the primary Soviet naval mission in the Mediterranean during any period of tension

is to counter American naval moves at any level of anticipated hostilities, regardless of the nature and source of the tensions.

Confrontation with the United States erupted over the alleged Israeli cease-fire violations. The Soviet Union was incensed by the violations of 23 October,[90] interpreting them as clear indications of the limits of American influence on Israel and as dangerous symptoms of an Israeli stubbornness that jeopardized the predictability and controllability of the crisis. The Soviet Union had delivered the Arabs' endorsement of the cease-fire and the United States could not produce Israeli approval. Most important, the violations were reminiscent of similar Israeli violations in all the earlier crises, demonstrating Israeli defiance of the interests of the external powers and determination to deal with the Arabs only from a position of strength – the antithesis of Soviet policy objectives in the Middle East.[91] If Israel continued to disregard the concerted efforts of the great powers to promote a cease-fire and settlement, the whole Soviet policy of guaranteeing Arab parity would be jeopardized and her position in the Middle East potentially undermined. Finally, the arrival of 38 F-4 replacement aircraft, late-model electronic counter-measures equipment, *Shrike* anti-radiation missiles, and the capture of the air defence system along the southern half of the Canal gave Israel air superiority in that sector and – despite the presence of Soviet *Scud* missiles – raised the possibility of strategic bombing of Egyptian cities, Israel's preferred option for demonstrating her superiority.

Based on these apprehensions, the Soviet Union gained American endorsement of a second Security Council Resolution, SCR 339, calling for strict observance of the provisions of SCR 338 and an immediate withdrawal of forces to lines held on 22 October. Moscow also insisted on American acceptance of Sadat's plea that the great powers intervene by sending military observers to ensure compliance with the cease-fire provisions. The demand for the presence of great-power military personnel

---

[90] See Brezhnev's explanation, *Pravda*, 27 October 1973.
[91] Indeed, Major-General Peled told IAF pilots on 21 October that Tel Aviv's objective was to 'bring the enemy to the point where we can dictate the terms of a cease-fire' (*International Herald Tribune*, 23 October 1973).

indicated that the Soviet Union was now more concerned with redressing the military balance and freeing the 20,000 trapped Egyptians than with the formalities of the cease-fire.

Israel accepted the cease-fire on 24 October, but refused to comply with Resolution 339, arguing that it was impossible to determine where the lines of the two armies had actually been on the 22nd. She indicated, however, that she would be prepared to open negotiations with the Arabs in accordance with Resolution 338. This stance was unacceptable to both great powers, and the Soviet Union concluded that a more tangible manifestation of her insistence on some form of mutually recognized military stalemate as the only premise for a durable settlement was called for.

Accordingly she initiated the following actions on 24 October. She publicly criticized Israel for her continuing provocations and condemned the United States at the UN for her apparent perfidy on the cease-fire issue and for stimulating Israeli intransigence by providing massive military aid (Nixon had pledged $2·2 billion for Israeli support); she diverted military transport aircraft from the airlift operation to assembly points in Hungary and the Soviet Union for possible embarkation of the 45,000 man airborne force. The Soviet naval presence had been augmented to 85 ships, and an airborne command post had been established in the south of the Soviet Union. Twelve An-22 transports had been detected *en route* to Cairo, possibly carrying troops, and communications indicating possible intervention had been intercepted. These activities suggested that Moscow might be prepared to honour her pledge to Cairo and Sadat's subsequent request for the reintroduction of Soviet combat forces. On the evening of the 24th Brezhnev sent a personal letter to Nixon, reminiscent of the Kosygin note of January 1970 but later described as 'brutal' in content. The key passage indicated Soviet intentions; 'I will say it straight, that if you find it impossible to act together with us in this matter, we should be faced with the necessity urgently to consider the question of taking appropriate steps unilaterally. Israel cannot be allowed to get away with the violations.'[92]

Nixon authorized Kissinger to signal the Soviet Union negatively, and a National Security Council meeting decided to place all American military forces on a Defence Condition Three Alert (troops placed on standby and awaiting orders). From the military viewpoint this was the minimum action that could be taken and was itself rather innocuous. It caused more consternation in NATO capitals and among the American public than it probably did in Moscow.[93] In explaining Washington's decision the next day, Kissinger stated, 'It is inconceivable that the forces of the great powers should be introduced in the numbers that would be necessary to overpower both of the participants. The United States is even more opposed to the unilateral introduction by any great power, especially by any nuclear power, of military forces into the Middle East in whatever guise those forces should be introduced.'[94]

While the primary objective was clearly to deter Soviet intervention and stalemate the tactical situation, there was an important secondary aim of signalling to the local contestants, mainly Israel, that the United States had larger interests at stake than their respective bargaining positions. This message was promptly followed up by a direct threat from Kissinger that the United States would undertake to supply the humanitarian needs of the trapped Third Army unless Israel accepted Resolution 339 and commenced military disengagement talks. American transport aircraft were diverted from the airlift into Israel to European bases in preparation for an airlift to the Egyptians, and logistic supplies were prepared for a sustained air drop. It was the direct pressure on Israel, not the military alert, that had the desired effect of inducing Israeli acceptance of SCR 339, thereby deterring Soviet intervention.

The acrimonious exchanges and military posturing of the two great powers were cited by Nixon as the most serious international crisis since the Cuban missile crisis. At his November press conference, Kissinger admitted that a

---

[92] Ray S. Cline, 'Policy Without Intelligence', *Foreign Policy*, Winter 1974–5, p. 127. It is difficult to determine the extent to which the Soviet Union was probing to test American domestic weakness in light of the 'Saturday Night Massacre' and Watergate.
[93] Indeed alerting the Southern Command in Panama and Alaskan Commands, and the deployment of B-52s from Guam to the United States was later admitted to be irrelevant to the crisis.
[94] *USIS Bulletin*, No. 200, 26 October 1973.

confrontation had occurred, but observed that, while the detente process had not been firm enough to prevent the confrontation, it had played an important role in settling the crisis quickly and in restoring good relations between the great powers.[95]

Unilateral American Initiatives
Kissinger I
This seemingly defensive explanation reflected a reappraisal in Washington of the Soviet role in the Arab preparation. It was concluded that this role smacked of duplicity and led to the decision to minimize Soviet participation in the settlement process. Consequently, the United States restated her earlier willingness to afford both sides her good offices and, when they were accepted, launched the first of several unilateral undertakings to secure a settlement through 'step-by-step' procedures. Instead of stalling in order to let tempers cool, as in earlier crises, Kissinger acted promptly, first to consolidate the cease-fire by reducing the causes for infractions, and then to construct it in a manner that would contribute to the settlement process. His formula was a cease-fire linked with direct talks that could lead to withdrawal and a negotiated settlement.

On 25 October, the Security Council called for the establishment of a peace-keeping force to supervise the cease-fire. Consistent with her new policy, the United States withdrew the earlier offer to furnish military personnel and rejected the Soviet demand for the inclusion of observers from both great powers. A compromise was reached whereby two allies of the great powers, Poland and Canada, would provide non-combatant support units for the force. Egypt readily accepted the force and, after protracted soul-searching, Israel reversed her traditional stand that it was unnecessary to maintain a UN military presence on territory she controlled.

On the more difficult issue of the functions to be performed by the UN force, Israel adopted a tougher stand. The great powers envisaged its function as supervising the cease-fire and subsequent troop withdrawals. Because of the threatened American airlift to the besieged Egyptian troops and beleaguered civilians, Israel allowed a convoy of 125 trucks through

to the Third Army, but then refused further relief supplies until Egypt furnished a list of prisoners and lifted the naval blockade of the Red Sea which was isolating Israel's port of Eilath. Egypt insisted on an Israeli troop withdrawal first.

In order to break the deadlock, Kissinger conducted the first of a series of personal diplomatic efforts in the Middle East, dubbed 'shuttle diplomacy'. He succeeded in convincing Sadat of Israel's good faith, and Cairo accepted a six-point plan providing for Israeli troop withdrawal, the activation of the UN operations and the exchange of prisoners.[96] Soon after agreement was reached by both sides, however, it broke down over Israeli insistence that all prisoners should be released before her troops were withdrawn. Egypt, having lifted her blockade, finally made this second concession, based on perceived changes in the Israeli position. Israel had quietly dropped her traditional dogma that the external powers must refrain from acting as mediators or providing any initiatives that might interfere with the settlement process, and she accepted Kissinger and his ideas where she had rejected Rogers and his various plans. On the other side, Egypt overlooking her earlier refusal to deal directly with Israel while Israeli forces occupied Arab land, negotiated with Israeli generals about the exchange of prisoners and about disengagement.

The disengagement talks went beyond withdrawal to the 22 October lines. Kissinger attempted to move the Egyptian–Israeli talks into the settlement process by encouraging acceptance of an interim agreement. On 18 January 1974 Egypt and Israel approved a disengagement accord that paralleled Cairo's bargaining position during the Third Rogers Peace Plan of 1971. According to the fixed timetable, Israel was to withdraw her forces, first from the West Bank of the Canal and then from the East Bank to a new line approximately 13 miles from it. Egypt was to be allowed to reoccupy the East Bank and reopen the Canal without taking a formal position on the passage of Israeli ships or goods. A zone between the two sides was to be patrolled by the UN force, and the military forces of both sides in the

---

[95] *Ibid.*, No. 217, 23 November 1973.

[96] The full text was released in *USIS Bulletin*, No. 210, 12 November 1973.

forward areas were to be sharply reduced and balanced (only 7,000 lightly armed troops and 35 guns were permitted, air defences were reduced and tank units completely withdrawn). Moreover, both sides agreed to allow the monitoring of compliance with the agreement by American aircraft or satellites, thereby overcoming a central obstacle to the Second Rogers Peace Plan and the problem of guarantees.

Thus, Egypt achieved her goals in an interim accord sought since 1971, and Israel lost the bargaining leverage gained by the occupation of further Egyptian territory, without forcing any significant concessions from Cairo. On the other hand, the momentum of shuttle diplomacy produced a similar disengagement agreement between Israel and Syria on the Golan Heights, providing Israel with a vital breathing spell in which to restore her confidence and reorganize her armed forces.

Other results of the October War and the initial round of negotiations had more subtle and far-reaching implications for great-power policies. The one most immediately apparent was the rise in American diplomatic fortunes throughout the Middle East, culminating in June with Nixon's triumphal tour – the first by any American President.

To consolidate the leverage earned from shuttle diplomacy, Kissinger persuaded Sadat to re-establish the full diplomatic relations with Washington which had been broken off after the June War; he also gained unhindered entrée into Syria and other Arab countries, regardless of the status of diplomatic relations. This proved a singularly important move. The United States now had direct communications with all belligerents, while the Soviet Union had ties with only one side. Therefore, in place of vertical relations between the external powers and client states, a new triangular situation now emerged, with the United States at the apex. As the only external power with influence in both the Arab countries and Israel, only she could deliver both sides of the settlement process.

Kissinger insisted on perpetuating the step-by-step procedure and his personal diplomacy as the most appropriate means of bargaining for several reasons: (1) it would widen the influence of the United States among the Arabs and break her isolated tandem position as Israel's sole

supporter; (2) it would strengthen Israel's bargaining position without alienating the Arabs, if satisfactory progress could be achieved; (3) if progress could be made, then a practical oil embargo could be avoided; (4) it would preserve the advantages the United States gained from the triangular situation; and (5) it would reduce the Soviet Union's participation to merely guaranteeing Arab military parity and erode her claims to be the protector of Arab political interests.

The Soviet Union paid a heavy penalty for the duplicity of her detente policy in the Middle East, being confined to the wings of the Middle Eastern diplomatic stage. She was kept informed via the periodic meetings between Gromyko and Kissinger, but neither her views nor the use of her influence on the Arabs were solicited. Initially, she seemed content to let the United States try her hand at promoting a settlement once again, apparently confident that Washington would receive yet another setback, which would rejuvenate her influence among the Arabs. Her preferred mode of settlement was an international peace conference under the aegis of both great powers. This would ensure her full participation in the settlement process and guarantee her involvement in such details as the creation of a Palestinian state. Soviet pressure for convening a conference as an alternative to shuttle diplomacy began to abate in 1975, however, when the question arose of the presence, authority and function of the Palestinians at the conference. When the Arabs themselves could not resolve this problem, and the Palestinians were unable to organize the provisional government called for by both the Soviet Union and Egypt, it was apparent that convening a conference would not help. When Kissinger's efforts to promote a second interim accord between Egypt and Israel failed in April 1975, the Soviet Union seemed more satisfied with her role and took a historic perspective of her Middle Eastern interests; the reopening of the Canal on 5 June 1975 made her the closest naval power to the Red Sea, the Persian Gulf and the Indian Ocean, the areas of new Soviet attention.

On the Israeli side, complacency before the war had taken a heavy toll in lives and material. More important, the country's near-defeat on 7 October created a crisis of confidence on a national scale. Never since June 1948 had public morale sustained such a shock and slumped so sharply. In the ensuing search for causes everything – from the quality of Israeli life, to personalities, to a national psychological block against fighting wars – was blamed. Dayan finally resigned from the Meir government, and Chief of Staff Elazar and several senior army officers were retired. It was in this mood of self-criticism and self-inflicted humiliation that Israel made her principal concessions to the Arabs. However, public confidence was gradually restored as the necessary changes were instituted, and this resilience prompted a toughening in the government's bargaining position and a virtual stalemate that deadlocked both sides for over a year and a half.

From the Arab viewpoint, the War was politically successful. The Arab countries had seized the initiative and forced Israel to fight mainly on their terms, thereby destroying the myth of Israeli invincibility that had haunted Arabs for a quarter of a century. Arab confidence had been restored, and national honour vindicated sufficiently for limited political concessions to be risked. Detente had worked well enough for the great powers to intervene in time to preserve these gains, and massive Soviet arms deliveries – including 50 MiG-23s, more than a thousand T-62 tanks and 30 *Scud* missiles to Syria and Iraq (and to a lesser extent Egypt), plus $800 million in arms to Libya – restored the military balance and the appearance of military parity.

In another vein, the use of the oil weapon had equally far-reaching implications. The embargo effectively demonstrated the vulnerability of the industrial nations and created a major crisis for the Atlantic Alliance. The quadrupling of oil prices set a precedent for raw material producing countries that exacerbated the world economic recession and fundamentally altered the North–South relationship. Achievements on this scale could not have been accomplished without the manifestation of Arab solidarity. With surprising unity, the Arabs implemented political summitry as a means of facilitating decision-making, reinforcing their own self-confidence and per-petrating the cohesion of the Arab world demon-strated in October 1973.

The transformation of the Palestinian problem into a Lebanese civil war, however, has shattered that solidarity for the time being. Regional politics have been polarized as in the mid-1960s, when Arabs were fighting Arabs. Renewed factionalism has reduced Arab influence on the larger international arena, relieving the urgency in the settlement process, and has been a distinct blow to the PLO, as evidenced by the heavy casualties among its fighting forces, the severe clampdown on Palestinians by Bahrain and Kuwait and the weakening of its leaderÊ»ship's authority.

Kissinger II: Aborted

Nearly every month during the summer and autumn of 1974 Kissinger met Arab and Israeli diplomats in Washington to explore the terms for a second withdrawal in the Sinai. Pressure on Israel began to mount with the unexpected success of the Rabat summit conference in October (denying King Hussein the right to speak for the Palestinians), the unprecedented speech by Yasser Arafat before the UN General Assembly on 13 November, UNESCO's denuncia-tion of Israel for her rule of Jerusalem, and Syria's refusal to renew the mandate of the UN observation forces on the Golan Heights until Kissinger personally intervened. Finally, in December, Israel's Deputy Prime Minister Yigal Allon presented President Ford with an Israeli proposal. He offered a withdrawal of roughly 31 miles from the Canal (double the distance of the first withdrawal) to a line from Nahal Yom (an Israeli settlement) to Abu Zeniema on the Gulf of Suez. Israeli forces would not, however, withdraw from the key Abu Rudeis oilfield or from the Giddi and Mitla passes. No Egyptian troops were to occupy the territory from which Israel had pulled back. In return she wanted the Canal reopened to Israeli ships and a commit-ment that the new fortified position would serve as an armistice line for as long as ten years. This amounted to a bilateral termination of the war.

Ford informed Allon that these terms were unacceptable to Egypt, that Israel would have to settle for substantially less stringent conditions, and that this was no time for stalling tactics, in spite of Prime Minister Rabin's public plea that Israel needed to buy time 'to recuperate', since a renewed oil embargo, according to the President, would be disastrous for the industrial nations. The Israeli Cabinet, however, would not alter its stand.

78

Egypt's position had been made clear during the autumn. She wanted the passes and their approaches, plus the oil fields and sufficient territory for their security; in return she would reopen the Canal, privately agree to the passage of Israeli goods (but not ships) and would accept a truce for a year or more, provided there was satisfactory progress toward a final settlement. Finally, she insisted on an agreement with Israel on the overall objectives of the settlement process and an appropriate timetable. Without consensus on goals, the piecemeal tactics of the step-by-step procedure, with their built-in delays, would be unacceptable to any Arab government; they would extend the time schedule rather than contracting it, and positions would harden before the distance to the ultimate aims had been narrowed.[97]

The American stand also began to crystallize. The United States wanted a second-phase accord in the Sinai and the opening of talks with Syria before the mandate for the UN forces on the Golan Heights expired on 24 April 1975. If the focus had not shifted to Syria by that time, Damascus had warned that it would refuse to renew the mandate or to deal further with Israel on a bilateral basis, demanding instead the convening of the peace conference, where Israel would be confronted by an Arab phalanx. To prevent a breakdown and the failure of yet another American peace initiative, compromises would have to be forthcoming on both sides, and strong measures might be necessary.

During the first week in January Kissinger and Ford both issued official warnings that the United States would not tolerate an oil embargo that might inflict 'strangulation' on the industrialized world and, as a final resort, might use military force. Indeed selected American units began training apparently for intervention and protracted occupation of individual Arab countries (most likely Libya).

The United States was attempting to demonstrate her grave concern about the growing prospects of resumed full-scale fighting and the imposition of another oil embargo. Clearly the threat was aimed at deterring precipitous Arab actions. But, since it is widely assumed in the Middle East that Israel cannot afford to be surprised again and will pre-empt the Arabs if

tensions warrant, the main object was probably to reassure Israel. Both sides were being notified that the United States had increasing interests in the settlement process and would resort to more forceful leverage if intransigence dominated the bargaining.

The threat of military intervention was aimed at Israel for other, more obscure reasons. In the past when her options had appeared to narrow, as in the case of the August 1970 cease-fire proposal and the 1971 proposed Interim Agreement, Israel had tried to probe the context in which the United States commitments or Middle Eastern military presence might be reduced. President Nixon reiterated in personal letters to Mrs Meir, on 16 May and 23 July 1970, his affirmation that the Sixth Fleet would remain in the Mediterranean as long as there was a Soviet threat and regional instability. Now, a continuing American presence is the ultimate assurance that the integrity of the Israeli state will remain guaranteed by a great power. Persistent PLO threats to eliminate Israel as a state are rendered incredible by the size of the United States' presence and her political determination, even in a changing international environment. When Ambassador Dinitz was informed by Kissinger that a delay or a deliberate submission of unacceptable terms at that juncture could prove fatal to the cease-fire, Israel reportedly replied with her strongest claims yet that the United States was prepared to stampede and militarily abandon her. In this light Washington's warning may be seen as an indication to both sides that the United States has important strategic interests in the region, which she is determined to preserve, and as the strongest pledge yet that she would use military force or economic reprisals if necessary to ensure regional stability.

In an unexpected turn of events, Egyptian Foreign Minister Fahmy and War Minister Gamassy were urgently summoned to Moscow in December 1974 and met Brezhnev, apparently in connection with his official visit to Cairo, scheduled for 14 January 1975, and the Egyptian request for advanced weapons systems. Brezhnev's visit was cancelled, and the failure to announce a substitute date indicated that the trip was not postponed – a deliberate affront to the Egyptians. Several days later Sadat explained that the reason for the trip to Moscow

[97] Sadat's Statement in *An Nahar*, 16 January 1975.

was to secure replacements for all lost equipment and to request new systems, but the Soviet Union had refused them (other comments by Sadat suggested that the refusal was partly tied to unpaid debts and additional credits). Since the October War, Sadat claimed that the Soviet Union had supplied Egypt with only 'some' weapons and spare parts, which had been paid for by Algeria; no decisive weapons had been furnished, as they had been to Syria. He alleged that the Soviet refusal was on the grounds of Arab irresponsibility (which, he asserted, was disproved by the October War) and Egypt's new American connection, which was seen as undermining the Soviet position in the Middle East.[98]

Sadat responded to this hardening Soviet position by seeking armament production plants in France and Britain and by giving the appearance of intensifying the American connection. He dropped further reference to the peace conference for the time being, praised the achievements of Kissinger, saying that the slowdown in American mediation efforts was due to the change in Administration, and expressed confidence in the outcome of the next round. On 14 January Allon returned to Washington and, before leaving three days later, issued a statement calling for an interim agreement with Egypt; Sadat responded favourably on the 21st. In March Kissinger concluded that the signals from both sides were sufficiently propitious to launch another round of shuttle diplomacy between the Middle Eastern capitals. The issues were soon refined to the central questions of the amount of territory to be exchanged and the duration of the agreement.

Israel's position was based on her estimate of Egyptian bargaining strength. The recovery of the Canal had enhanced Egypt's political prestige to the point that she again enjoyed the pre-eminence among other Arab states that she had had under Nasser (this did not mean that other Arab countries could be ignored, but that a settlement with Sadat would establish important precedents for them). Paradoxically, however, Egypt was economically the least important Arab state, and the reopening of the Canal would provide sorely needed revenues (in 1974

Egypt's GNP had actually declined by 7 per cent). Furthermore, having already won widespread European support, Sadat might now be tempted to curry favour with the American public by implying that American influence might ultimately replace Soviet influence in Egypt. Finally, Israel estimated that Egypt did not want war, but could not ignore the possibility of a coalition developing among her northern allies that might precipitate a pre-emptive Israeli attack.[99]

To temper the territorial issue, Israel raised the question of the type of military surveillance equipment that could be strategically located to prevent mutual surprise. Egypt refused to consider the matter until there was first a decision on where the line would be drawn. Israel could not respond until there was a firm Egyptian commitment to an armistice, an agreement on the renunciation of force, and guarantees for the durability of the line. The final Israeli concession on the time frame was a minimum of four years. Egypt's maximum condition was 18 months with provision for prolongation and with an annual review of the UN mandate. Israel responded that she could not accept such a short time limit without a formal accord terminating the state of war, because of the unpredictability of the Security Council, where either the Soviet Union or China could control the mandate and the UN presence.[100] She then accused Kissinger of introducing his own conditions, namely that Israel must accept Egyptian territorial demands, open negotiations with Syria in three months and within six months be able to discuss 'sweeping peace proposals with the various parties concerned'. In return Sadat would give a private pledge not to resume hostilities while the settlement process remained unobstructed.

These demands were unacceptable to Israel for several reasons. First, the United States had departed from the established ground rules for American–Israeli relations by acting as a media-

[98] Interviews in *Al Anwar*, 8 January and *Le Monde*, 12 January 1975.

[99] Interview of the author with Defence Minister Shimon Peres, 8 April 1975. See also his interview in *Jerusalem Post*, 13 April 1975.
[100] Israel is under no illusions about the UN presence: it is purely symbolic. If either side decides to renew hostilities it will do so, regardless of the nationality of the policemen manning the demilitarized zones. Yet the UN presence has a psychological importance for world opinion that Israel cannot ignore. (Interview with the author and Chief of Staff Maj.-Gen. Gur, 7 April 1975.)

tor and was demonstrating partiality towards Egypt. Second, Kissinger had allegedly created a crisis atmosphere to apply pressure on Israel. Third, telescoping the time schedule in the settlement process was the antithesis of Israeli objectives: to accept comprehensive peace talks within six months would put Israel at the mercy of the Arab countries in the negotiations, since she had not fully recovered from the October War. Finally, Israel could not move so quickly toward a final settlement because, even after a quarter century of conflict, the government did not have a detailed outline of the goals and values it wished to see embodied in the ultimate accord. Accordingly, she rejected the compromise and Kissinger's second peace plan was aborted. One side of the triangle of American policy was temporarily blocked, and the crisis again became vertical, with a deterioration in American–Israeli relations.

There was widespread dismay in Israel in the wake of Kissinger's departure, which he declared was a 'sad day for Israel', and the announcement on 24 March 1975 that the United States was reappraising her entire Middle Eastern policy – meaning that the matter would again be placed in bureaucratic limbo until the attitude of the local contestants changed. In a rare display of near-consensus most Israelis agreed that the round should have been postponed while Washington dealt with the collapse of South Vietnam. There was even greater agreement on rejecting the renewed Soviet call for convening the peace conference. It was generally believed that a solution to the interim agreement with Egypt was feasible, but that little adjustment was foreseeable with Syria. The main problem, ultimately, would be the final disposition of the West Bank.[101]

Regeneration of the settlement process was frequently advocated, but there was an unwillingness to offer Egypt a *quid pro quo* for reopening the talks. There was also a sense of the imminence of hostilities. The gravest danger would be posed by a Syrian-inspired coalition with Iraq and Jordan, and the effective subordination of the PLO; if this occurred,

Israel would have no choice but to pre-empt an Arab attack. Pre-emptive possibilities canvassed reflected Israeli advantages of command and control under mobile conditions, such as a drive through Lebanon or northern Jordan, or both, in order to inflict maximum destruction on allied Arab armed forces, or else a major invasion across the Red Sea and a strike into the Middle Nile that might topple the government.[102] The next war was thus to be conducted on Israeli terms with the object of destroying as much of Arab military capability – and possibly also economic potential – as possible in the shortest possible time (i.e., before the inevitable great-power intervention).[103]

The American assessment of the collapse of the second Kissinger Plan was that Israel had conducted her diplomacy in an unprecedentedly ham-handed manner. Israel opened the negotiations by presenting her maximum demands, not her minimum stance, and in addition had no fall-back position. This was uncharacteristic of the normally sophisticated Israeli diplomacy, and indicated strains within the Israeli Cabinet. Prime Minister Rabin was showing signs of indecisive leadership, and it was Shimon Peres who organized the Cabinet against the American 'ultimatum' by threatening to resign. But if Rabin fell because of American pressure, as he nearly did in April 1975 (and February 1976), a complete change of ministers would be required, which would result in additional delays and uncertainties. Continued discussion with the Rabin government after the American policy reappraisal had been completed was therefore preferable to a change of leadership, unless Rabin adopted an even harder bargaining position.

The virtue of the recurring American policy reappraisals is that they can be terminated or prolonged at will. During this period both the Israeli Embassy in Washington and the Ford

---

[101] Israeli proposals ranged from Allon's Plan for its reunification with Jordan while Israel retained a militarized zone along the Jordan River, to Peres's Plan for an autonomous West Bank within a confederated Israeli–Jordanian state.

[102] See Hussein's confirmation of these plans in *International Herald Tribune*, 24 July 1975. Also Lt-Gen. David Elazar, retired Chief of Staff, stated, 'I believe that a pre-emptive strike is to be considered the most effective means of reaction'. A fellow general claimed that the next war 'would set the Arabs back 15 years', indicating the possibility of economic targeting. Interviews, *International Herald Tribune*, 14–15 February 1976.

[103] These impressions were gained from personal interviews in the Middle East during March and April 1975.

Administration engaged in extensive evaluations of American public and Congressional opinion, especially in the wake of the suspension of arms deliveries to Turkey, the curtailment of the supply of air defence equipment to Jordan and the ceilings on aid to South Vietnam and Cambodia. The collapse in South-east Asia caused grave concern about a balance between American obligations and prospective liabilities, but the Ford Administration seemed determined to reaffirm existing commitments. This reassurance stimulated renewed Israeli confidence in the feasibility of further bilateral bargaining with Egypt. Moreover, Israel correctly concluded that the American policy reappraisal was not a bluff or deliberate stall intended to put pressure on her, but a genuine effort to explore other policy options, so as to advance Washington's interests in the settlement process. In other words, there were no signs of the drift or indifference, present in earlier reappraisals, which had worked in Israel's favour. Israel would therefore have to make adjustments, such as offering Egypt some incentive to reactivate the bilateral exchanges, before the United States completed her reassessment.

In the interval Sadat went ahead with plans for reopening the Canal, despite the lack of a second accord that would remove the military threat to shipping, and accelerated the reconstruction of the Canal cities with contributions from the Shah of Iran and King Feisal of Saudi Arabia. On 5 June the Canal was formally reopened, and Sadat announced that the passage of non-strategic Israeli goods through the Canal would depend upon concrete measures that would demonstrate Israel's peaceful intentions. Then, on 22 June, after meeting Ford in Salzburg three weeks earlier, Sadat pledged recognition of the reality of Israel's existence, a concession already made by Saudi Arabia on 24 May. Neither leader was moving towards diplomatic recognition with these gestures; they were merely endorsing Israel's insistence that the Arab countries should acknowledge her right to exist. Sadat's justification was that Israel had become an accomplished fact, because the two leading world blocs were protecting that reality.[104]

In the light of the stalled bilateral exchanges Sadat hoped that Israel would make some gesture toward 'disengagement by mutual example' that would reciprocate his unilateral gestures of good faith. Rabin announced that Israel viewed the reopening of the Canal as a positive move in the settlement process and would unilaterally withdraw half her forces in the limited military zone along the Canal. This move would substantially reduce the physical threat to shipping. On 20 June Rabin announced a second gesture, more symbolic than practical. The myriad working groups, organized after the collapse of the second Kissinger plan by virtually every ministry and department to chart Israel's aims in the settlement, produced a preliminary report. For the first time the government was able to meet the Arab demands that the two sides discuss the ends before the means. Rabin issued a statement outlining the rough borders Israel expected to retain. She would annex the Gaza Strip, Sharm el-Sheik and a land corridor connecting it with Elath. Some portion of the Golan Heights would also have to be retained permanently, though the border would be negotiable. On the West Bank the outline combined the essential points of the Peres and Allon Plans, calling for autonomy within Jordanian sovereignty, a united Jerusalem (the Old City was annexed in July 1967), open borders with Jordan, Israeli control of security, and Jewish rights to settlement.[105]

Unilateral moves toward disengagement by mutual example thus had the positive effect of

[104] 'The four times I travelled to the Soviet Union, they pointed out to me that Israel was a fact and Israel should not be attacked within her 1967 borders. Even more than

that, they asked us not to undertake any military operation at all, even in our own territory.' On the American side, he stated, 'When I wanted to liquidate the Israeli pocket [west of the Canal] in December 1973, and I was ready to do this, Kissinger came on 11 and 12 December and I told him the situation and asked what would be America's position. Kissinger replied, "We will enter the war with Israel against you, because we will not allow Soviet weapons to win over American weapons again" [indicating, incidentally, that a firm American position had apparently been taken towards both sides during the exchanges over the first Kissinger Plan]'. Interview on *Al Anwar*, 22 June 1975.
[105] Rabin stated that he had discussed the outline with President Ford, and that he acknowledged the importance of providing for the first time an Israeli view of the final borders, but he also expressed reservations about Arab reactions. (In fact, Israel is likely to insist that the line on the Golan Heights include the 25 newly-established Jewish settlements – a certain non-starter for Syria.) *Maariv*, 20 June 1975.

demonstrating enough good faith on both sides for bilateral exchanges to be restarted. It is interesting to note that during the second phase of the second Kissinger Plan the United States symbolically increased her stake by conducting the initial soundings at presidential level, through summit conferences, first with Sadat and then with Rabin. Subsequently criticisms of the Israeli stand were addressed to Rabin by President Ford, indicating continuing American interest at the highest level.

At Salzburg Sadat restated the Egyptian demands: Israeli withdrawal from the passes and oilfields and sufficient territory for their defence. In return Cairo would accept a renunciation-of-force statement, binding for three to four years, with the expectation that the settlement process would continue to advance. This was a major concession that portended possible splits within the Arab world.

Rabin counter-proposed a withdrawal only to the Western slopes of the passes, retaining the five-mile-wide approaches as adequate security for lines of communication and for the base at Rifidim, and adequate early-warning radars in the passes that could be monitored by both sides to detect military movements. Egypt rejected the suggestion out of hand, and Ford warned Rabin that Israel would have to give up the passes and seek compensation elsewhere. He also repeated that the United States would not accept continuing delay and that, if Israel could not reach an agreeable compromise within the near future, the entire question would have to be referred to the peace conference, where Israel could not count on unquestioned American support.

Members of the Knesset and press referred to Ford's assertions as an ultimatum, and ministers warned the United States against developing a new initiative or propelling Israel into intolerable compromises.[106] As Rabin appeared to face his worst political crisis, the Cabinet promptly sought clarification from Washington on several points: (1) whether Egypt would agree to placing a radar early-warning system in the passes; (2) exactly where Egypt wanted to draw the new line; (3) whether the United States would agree not to push Israel into new concessions elsewhere as soon as the agreement under consideration was concluded; and (4) what was the status of the American policy reappraisal and how would it affect future political support for Israel.[107] The last query was unquestionably the most urgent, as it had been in earlier times of national dismay and foreboding. Was the American commitment still credible or would Israel be the next Vietnam?

On 27 June Ford told the Israeli Ambassador that Israel must come up with new ideas within the next several months, or war would be almost inevitable. To avoid such an eventuality the United States would abandon the bilateral approach, shift the problem to the peace conference and recommend a solution to the dispute. The only American commitment at the peace conference would be to impartiality and to seek a just settlement as early as possible.[108] Then Kissinger went on record as saying that the degree of future American support for Israel would be linked to whether she took the chance to make a territorial concession needed for an interim accord.[109] Clearly pressure was being exercised on Israel's most sensitive spot: American support. On the other hand, Israel appeared to be pressing the United States to make the most extensive military and political guarantees of her security yet, as the counterbalance to an iron-clad non-belligerency treaty with Egypt. Washington was tempted to balance heavy commitments to Israel against countervailing obligations to Egypt, thus preserving the triangular relationship.

Kissinger II: Concluded

While the second Kissinger Plan failed in March 1975, the cyclical process of increased American pressure on Israel, leading to greater Israeli demands for demonstrable American involvement in the Middle East, which cut across the mutual desire of the United States and Egypt to

---

[106] Rabin struck a hawkish public stance. 'We say to our friends, "Do not expect us to squander away our vital security interests as we were compelled to do in the past ... As a nation that has always defended itself, by itself, we have the right and we shall exercise that right to decide for ourselves what we can do and what we dare not do as we strike for peace with our neighbours".' *International Herald Tribune*, 4 July 1975.

[107] *Ibid.*, 1 July 1975.
[108] Interview with *Washington Post*, 30 June 1975.
[109] 'The United States will stand behind them [Israelis] in conditions which we can reasonably say to our people that progress is being made.' *New York Times*, 6 July 1975.

amplify their new relationship, led to a new round of shuttle diplomacy in August. The result was a package agreement signed on 1 September 1975, ending this phase of the step-by-step disengagement agreements, and opening the way for a triumphal visit to the United States by Sadat in November. Underpinning the agreements was the most extensive American commitment yet made to regional stability.[110]

The provisions of the accords that are relevant to the earlier positions of the three powers includes:

(1) renunciation of the use of force and the resolution of conflict by peaceful means;
(2) incorporation of this agreement as an integral part of the settlement process envisaged in Security Council Resolution 338;
(3) termination of the accord in connection with the annual review of the UNEF mandate;
(4) creation of a joint commission to resolve any problems arising from implementation of the agreements;
(5) passage through the Canal of non-military cargoes destined for or coming from Israel.

The implementing annexes define the new demilitarized buffer zone, manned by the UNEF, that extends to the eastern approaches of the Mitla and Giddi passes, and the limited forces zones on either side of it. One Israeli and one Egyptian strategic early-warning surveillance station, manned by 250 technicians, are located at either end of the Giddi Pass. Two unmanned electronic sensor fields and one early-warning station are staffed by 200 American civilian technicians. Withdrawal of American personnel will be made upon proper notification: either by the United States or upon joint request by the other two parties.

The military aspects of the accords permit aircraft of both sides to fly freely up to the forward line of that side's zone, reconnaissance aircraft can fly up to the centre line of the buffer zone on an agreed schedule. The United States will continue to fly aerial surveillance of the entire zone at a frequency of one mission every 7 to 10 days, or at the request of either side; the results will be made readily available to both parties. Within the area of limited forces, only

[110] Complete texts of the accords and the accompanying map are reprinted in *Survival* November–December 1975.

8,000 troops will be permitted on both sides, including eight standard infantry battalions, 75 tanks and 60 artillery pieces with ranges no greater than 12 km. Furthermore, no weapons will be deployed within this area that can reach the other side, no anti-aircraft missiles will be placed within 10 km of the edge of the limited forces zone and no new fortifications will be constructed within this zone.

This is the most comprehensive package yet negotiated in the Arab–Israeli conflict. The principle of the renunciation of force, the creation of a joint commission and the extent of the demilitarization were promptly denounced by Syria in a move that split the Arab world, but among the moderate Arabs Sadat had become the 'man of the year 1975'. However, the accords had the paradoxical effect of re-moving the Sinai from the international limelight and allowing Damascus to assume the initiative in promoting the Arab cause. President Assad's stature rose momentarily, when the Security Council debated the Middle East crisis with PLO representation as the price for renewing in November the UNEF mandate on the Golan Heights, but it receded again over the issue of political control of Lebanon.

Sadat's central reason for accepting the agreements and the accompanying risks, as he explained to the American Congress on 5 November 1975, was that the accords were providing for unprecedented American involve-ment in the conflict. In large part, therefore, the accords were successfully concluded because of a coincidence of views, for different reasons, between Israel and Egypt about the necessity and price of enhanced American involvement. In an unpublished Protocol to the agreements the United States Administration undertook to ask Congress for large sums in aid for both parties: $2·5 billion for Israel and $1 billion for Egypt; Kissinger later told the Senate Finance Committee that requests of this magnitude could be expected on an annual basis. Israel saw Congressional approval of the huge grants, and endorsement of American personnel being employed in the Sinai, as reconfirmation of her standing with Congress and of American commitment to Israeli security. Egypt saw the American technicians and the largest American grant ever as the first step in enmeshing American interests in the Middle East conflict and as an opportunity to expand her political and economic relations with the West on an increasingly reliable, long-term basis. Kissinger concluded, after the agreements were reached, that the present close relations between the United States and the Arab countries was now 'irreversible'. From Sadat's viewpoint the 27 secret American commitments made to Israel, including the supply of oil and the 'institutionalization' of continuing consultations on Israel's economic and military needs, binds the United States closer than ever to Israeli security, and thereby to the guarantee of Egyptian borders which only she can provide; but it binds her through involvement and not through intervention.

IV. CONCLUSIONS

These general observations about what the great powers seem to have learned, or failed to learn, from their experiences should be followed by some concluding comments about the impact this limited learning process has had on present policies and future trends.[111]

The Soviet Union does not seem excessively resentful or embittered because of her declining influence in the Arab world. She has apparently concluded that a policy like her anti-Nasser campaign of the early 1960s would again prove counter-productive, and that Israeli intransigence and American disenchantment or indifference will once again compound Arab frustrations and bring about the resurrection of the Soviet option. Meanwhile, the Soviet Union can afford to wait while the period of post-election restructuring of the American Administration forces the United States to adopt a passive policy toward the Middle East. Nonetheless, the Soviet Union appears convinced that the basic tenets of her Middle East policy remain sound – i.e., the guarantee of clients' military parity and negotiating equality or superiority, and the organization of clients into a 'progressive regional bloc' under Soviet leadership.[112]

During the interval of reduced activity in the Middle East, she seems content to adopt the same model for establishing influence abroad and apply it to Black Africa, where there are now opportunities for foreign involvement. The development of a viable Soviet policy of African involvement would both outflank Arab interests strategically (hazy as they may be) and demonstrate that co-operation with the Soviet-led 'progressive bloc' is essential for the promotion of Arab interests in Africa – implying as a corollary greater Arab respect for Soviet Middle Eastern interests.

The Soviet Union also appears confident that, if she can remain aloof from the deepening Palestinian morass, she may retain sufficient leverage against the United States to ensure for herself full participation in the final peace negotiations. She has demonstrated to all concerned that she is prepared to play the role of a great power in prescribing the terms for regional stability – a great power whose interests cannot be ignored if durable stability is expected.

However, it would appear that the Soviet Union does acknowledge several constraints on any future attempt to renew her involvement. The United States retains some influence with Israel, however circumscribed, and is cautiously optimistic that the Arab countries' growing contacts with, and leverage on, the West are becoming a viable basis for mutual influence. The Soviet Union, on the other hand, has virtually no direct influence on Israel and could only re-establish her authority among the Arabs on the previous basis of arms transfers which proved to be insufficient to create influence. Regardless of what demands military contingencies might make, the influence the Soviet Union gained through arms shipments is unlikely to reach the 1970–72 level. These constraints on her Arab policy are likely to increase her interest in strengthening an African connection, despite the risks of strategic interdiction and further estrangement from the Arab world.

For her part, the United States has learned from the fate of the Rogers Plans that her role as a great power is highly circumscribed by

---

[111] Charles A. McClelland made the initial study of the learning process in 'Decisional Opportunity and Political Controversy: The Quemoy Case', *Journal of Conflict Resolution*, September 1962.

[112] William E. Griffith, 'The Decline of Soviet Influence in the Middle East', in Lawrence L. Whetten (ed.), *Political Implications for Soviet Military Power* (New York: Crane, Russak, 1976).

Israel. Indeed, she has been confined to performing largely procedural, rather than substantive, functions. Even when the October War created an unprecedented crisis (see pp. 33ff above), she only attempted to reactivate interest in the abortive Third Rogers Plan of step-by-step negotiations, abandoning earlier efforts to achieve a comprehensive settlement at the outset of the reconciliation process.

The United States had long sought to establish reliable ties with Arab states, but failed because Israeli intransigence prevented her from reciprocating Arab concessions. She now recognizes that further moves in the settlement process require greater confidence on both sides, and that she is genuinely involved in the conflict and in the promotion of the respective interests. This would seem to indicate a firm American commitment to the settlement process and provide a justification for the unprecedented American aid commitments still being made to both sides. Finally, in recognizing the importance to the settlement process of her influence among the Arabs and of the need for greater impartiality (the Arabs can receive some aid as long as Israel gets more) the United States seems increasingly prepared to accept the risks she encountered earlier in the interest of promoting a comprehensive settlement. When the Arabs can resolve their differences and Washington returns to active leadership, she may call for the reconvening of the Geneva Peace Conference.

At the conference the United States, confident of the strength of her influence in both camps, could co-opt Moscow as co-responsible for maintaining regional stability. While in the past some observers have argued that co-sponsorship implies recognition of political equality, previous experience suggests that it is a more reliable method of ensuring Soviet restraint (which is the basic American concern) than a policy of discrimination and ostracism. The Soviet Union's self-interest could be engaged in such a restrictive embrace – for example, by means of joint guarantees for both Arab countries and Israel – that her stake in stability could be enhanced and the incentives to seek unilateral advantage reduced. If the guarantees were reasonably self-enforcing, the great powers' obligations would acquire the same status as their obligations under other jointly-sponsored treaties, such as

the ban on weapons of mass destruction in Antarctica, the seabed and outer space. Such a schema could serve the multiple purpose of providing adequate local security, assuring limited Soviet involvement and preserving a privileged American position.

Of the local actors, Egypt in particular has clearly been the quickest to apply the lessons of previous experience. The military option was employed in a variety of modes, as was the oil weapon, but political probes were also periodically made. Sadat offered to negotiate a final peace agreement and an interim accord, breaking a three-year-old common Arab stance against concessions. He also sponsored a new role for the United States in the settlement process; the Soviet Union could deliver arms, but only the Americans could deliver Israel. Sadat's perceptiveness about the changing nature of great-power influence resulted in a kaleidoscopic scenario: (1) the expulsion of the Soviet forces; (2) Moscow's subsequent agreement to supply decisive weapons; (3) a further worsening of Soviet–Egyptian relations; (4) negotiation of a disengagement accord with Israel; (5) restoration of diplomatic ties with Washington; and finally, (6), a triumphal state visit by Sadat to the United States – all this in three years. Egypt has not yet achieved her ultimate objectives in the conflict, but adroit shifting of them has permitted her to make important secondary gains – for example, greater security, foreign investment and economic relief. While Cairo remained the focal point of Arab policy through the conclusion of the Sinai accord, other Arabs drew different conclusions about the settlement process and the initiative shifted to Damascus and Riyadh.

Israel, on the other hand, has probably learned the least. After nearly thirty years of intermittent war, she remains unable to convert her military strength into diplomatic initiative. She has been politically incapable of visualizing a comprehensive formula for peace and has become increasingly dependent on a single external protector for her ultimate security.[113] (The complex proportional representational of her political system gives small marginal parties a stranglehold over the inevitable coalition and makes leadership by consensus virtually im-

[113] Richard H. Ullman, 'Alliance with Israel?' *Foreign Policy*, Summer 1975.

86

possible – yet the issues are vital to all.) During each war Israel has sought enhanced security by extending her borders, and each war has resulted in external intervention. Military success, based on self-reliance and the unreliability of previous external guarantees, created a consensus that national survival was dependent upon Israeli military prowess. But Israel drew the wrong inferences from these lessons. The siege mentality that inevitably accompanies a constant state of vigilance can be counter-productive: confidence in self-defence often nurtures isolation, first from the outside world, then from reality. The failure of the previous guarantees to defuse tensions or deter aggression was due to the nature of the guarantees, not to the principle itself.

Israel's reluctance to give up territory for external assurances or some form of military stalemate is reinforced by innate confidence in the indestructibility of Jewish character. Israelis believe they will survive as they did before, living Jewish life on the margin of other societies, and indeed enjoying not being integrated into regional structure or entities.[114] But living on the margin of Middle Eastern life is too risky until Israel defines more precisely her terms for accommodation with her Arab citizens and neighbours.

The main lessons of the last war are that renewed fighting can buy Israel only a limited respite, not security;[115] that time is not on her side; and that the credibility of guarantees must be reassessed.

The classical dilemma in military confrontations is whether priority should be given to reaching a political adjustment that would permit military disengagement, or to a reduction of forces designed to create a climate conducive to political negotiation. Defusing the confrontation failed in the past, because Israel inflicted military penalties and demanded political concessions before offering even an outline of the expected settlement. But a settlement that anticipates enforcement by self-compliance and external guarantees neutralizes the dilemma of political adjustment or military disengagement if confidence in compliance is reasonably high. Thus, a settlement may be facilitated if emphasis

is shifted to problems of compliance, rather than the preliminary issues of representation and jurisdiction.

A final lesson was learned by all actors, though probably not by all equally: the effectiveness of the oil weapon and the impact of the oil boycott. The Arabs, learning from their earlier experience, achieved an unprecedented degree of cohesion and applied the oil boycott with discretion and firmness. Pressure was placed on Western Europe that was transmitted to Washington. (The Soviet Union, on its part, did not support the boycott, however; indeed, she exploited the embargo to advance her own oil sales.) The West reacted initially in a confused manner, generally pursuing independent national interests, rather than a coherent policy. The friction generated within NATO, resulting from European unwillingness to assist the American resupply operation to Israel during the war, was relieved mainly by a shift in Washington's position and by Western Europe's support for an Oil Consumers' Group authorized to share supplies. Finally, Israel apparently fully grasped how critical the oil embargo was only during Rabin's 1974 Washington visit. Arab cohesion assumed a new dimension for Tel Aviv.

The role of guarantees should be to give Israel the assurance she needs to withdraw from the occupied territories and to demonstrate to the PLO that Arafat's 'dream' of a multiracial, bilingual, secular state encompassing the whole of the former British mandate is quite unrealistic in the foreseeable future. The survival and security of Israel is simply not open to question. The great powers could then guarantee the territorial integrity of all states in the former Palestine, either by means of UN supervision and a mandate from the Security Council alone (and not the local states), or by the presence of foreign (though not great-power) combat forces.

The presence of foreign troops would serve the important initial function of a surrogate for normalized relations. Ultimately, however, the guarantees must be self-enforcing among the potential belligerents. The necessary first step would be withdrawal and (provided terrorism is suspended) demilitarization of zones behind adjusted 1967 borders. Political and military confidence-building measures directly related to the guarantees would be a second step. These might include joint stock companies for ex-

---

114 Amos Elon and Sana Hassan, 'Dialogue between Arab and Jew', *Encounter*, December 1974.
115 Interview by the author with Maj.-Gen. Gur, Army Chief-of-Staff, 8 April 1975.

ploitation of resources and prior notification of military manoeuvres. The aim of confidence-building is to increase the stakes of all powers in compliance, so that assurance in self-enforcement is mutually perceived.

The final feature of the proposed guarantees must be the inclusion of equal participation, however remote, by both great powers. Their involvement in the Arab–Israeli conflict for a quarter-century is sufficient evidence that neither will be content if excluded from this role.

If demands for credible guarantees from the great powers should wane, their behaviour could either take the form of benign neglect (as was attempted in 1972) or else of competition for unilateral advantage. Acceleration of rivalry in the Middle East could be conducted under these circumstances if either power were prepared to amplify other regional issues to crisis pro-portions, or to compromise its guarantees and involvement in the settlement of the Arab–Israeli conflict.

It is too early to predict whether great-power behaviour in the Middle East will become co-operative or mutually complementary. Either way, relations are not likely to conform to their concepts of detente and coexistence – a situation that is not likely to become dangerous unless the present belligerents remain unable to reach a settlement.

3 THE SOVIET RECORD IN THE MIDDLE EAST

PETER MANGOLD

It is now more than twenty very eventful years since the Soviet Union first emerged as an important actor in the Middle East. During a period which has, to cite only some of the more dramatic developments, witnessed four Arab–Israeli wars, an Arab cold war between radicalism and conservatism, and serious internal disturbances in Lebanon, Jordan and Iraq, Soviet fortunes have fluctuated, sometimes dramatically. The initial establishment of close relations with Cairo, Damascus and Baghdad, which took place between 1955 and 1958, was both swift and dramatic. It was followed in the late 1950s and early 1960s by a reaction affecting links with all three countries. But the tensions which then emerged did not last. By the early 1970s the Soviet Union had established naval facilities in Egypt and Syria, and signed Treaties of Friendship and Cooperation with Egypt and Iraq. To the original list of Soviet clients could now be added the former South Arabian Federation (now the People's Democratic Republic of Yemen [PDRY]), the Palestine Liberation Organization (PLO) and Libya. Since then, however, there has been a second reaction, this time of a rather more serious nature. Relations with Egypt have deteriorated to the point of hostility, so that by the beginning of 1978 the Soviet Union not only finds herself virtually excluded from influence with the most important country in the Arab world, but her own former privileged political position in Cairo has been supplanted by the United States. Soviet links are now effectively confined to a group of radical countries which are in many ways the mavericks of a region experiencing a resurgence of political conservatism, and which, with the exception of Syria, exercise little direct influence on the central Arab–Israeli conflict.

Whether these reverses should be regarded as essentially temporary, or whether they do in fact represent a fundamental weakening of the Soviet position in the Middle East, is a matter for

Peter Mangold is a former member of the Foreign and Commonwealth Office Research Department.

debate. Still, after more than twenty years it is possible to assess the strengths and weaknesses of Soviet policy in the region, and to come to at least some provisional conclusions about the Soviet achievements there.

Early Gains

Perhaps one should begin by recalling the substantial advantages which Moscow has enjoyed in its dealings with Middle Eastern countries. The 1950s was a period in which Western influence and Arab conservatism were both on the defensive. The radical regimes emerging in the region tended, as they still do, to look East rather than West, and in so far as it has affected the general orientation of the foreign policies of Middle Eastern countries, ideology has been a significant factor in determining the extent of Soviet involvement. More important, however, was the fact that countries as diverse in political outlook as Syria and the Imamate of the Yemen were seeking a political counter-weight to Western influence as well as economic and military aid which, for various reasons, Western countries were unwilling to provide.

Once established, Soviet–Arab relations continued to develop, if somewhat fitfully, partly because they remained advantageous to the countries concerned, but partly also because the latter found themselves with little alternative. The more radical regimes, which feared Western-inspired intervention, saw the Soviet connection as important to their security, a view that Moscow tended to encourage, while nevertheless carefully eschewing any formal commitments. But even those Soviet clients who wanted to keep open their lines to the West experienced difficulty in doing so. The problem was not simply that they had accepted Soviet aid at a particularly critical moment of the cold war. More serious were the repeated attempts made during the late 1950s and much of the 1960s by radical states, notably Nasser's Egypt, to subvert the remaining Western colonies and allies in the region. If that were not enough, there was the impact of the

89

Arab–Israeli conflict, and in particular the legacy of the Six Day War.

The advantage that this conflict afforded the Soviet Union lay not just in her own willingness to provide military and political support to the Arab countries, but in the inability of the United States, at least until 1973, to exert sufficient pressure on Israel to make territorial concessions. For the period between the Six Day and the October 1973 Wars witnessed an action-reaction cycle in which Israel emerged as Washington's most-valued proxy in the eastern Mediterranean and Moscow as the attorney, armourer and protector of last resort to Egypt and Syria. These Soviet roles were based on a close military relationship involving the transfer of substantial quantities of Soviet arms and military skills which were used by Arab forces during the War of Attrition and the 1973 October War to try to weaken the Israeli hold over the territories captured in 1967. In addition, the Soviet Union provided, or rather was manoeuvred into providing a *de facto* guarantee that Israel would not be allowed to score further major victories in the process. Hence, to mention only two of a number of incidents, the deployment of Soviet airforce squadrons and missile crews to Egypt during the latter stages of the War of Attrition, and the alerting of airborne divisions and other military signals intended to enforce the Soviet–American cease-fire agreement at the end of the 1973 October War. What the Soviet Union gained from these involvements were military bases and a crucial diplomatic role in the periods of maximum polarization of the Arab–Israeli conflict. Indeed, it is notable that the major Soviet role in wartime diplomacy was achieved despite, and in some degree because of the poor performance of her clients on the battlefields, since the worse this performance, the greater was the threat of more active Soviet involvement and hence of super-power confrontation.

What is uncertain is whether the military dependence thereby established could provide the basis for long-term political influence. It certainly is the case that confrontation states militarily dependent on the Soviet Union cannot readily pursue a political strategy widely at variance with the interests of Moscow. This fact has been clearly recognized by President Assad, whose forces are still almost exclusively equipped with Soviet arms. It is more dramatically under-lined by the experience of Egypt since 1973. The Egyptian bargaining position has almost certainly been weakened by the military sanctions imposed by the Soviet Union in the wake of the Egyptian–American rapprochement, while the country's security has to some extent been undermined by the large-scale acquisition of Soviet arms by Libya, with whom there was a brief military flare-up, following months of tension, in July 1977. These considerations help to explain why, at least until the time of the Fahmi-Gromyko talks which had preceded this incident, Egypt was ready to explore the possibility of some rapprochement with Moscow, a move still favoured by some Egyptian officials. It is indeed arguable that the option of a complete break with Moscow was open only to a country like North Yemen – a country which was small, poor, uninvolved in the Arab–Israeli conflict, and assured that all her military and economic needs would be taken care of by a new patron, in this case Saudi Arabia.

Unenthusiastic Clients
Yet if few could afford to go to this extreme, nearly all Moscow's clients have experienced some measure of disillusion with the policies of their patron. The Soviet position has proved to be nowhere near as strong as it had seemed to those Western policy-makers and observers who, from the mid-1950s onwards, had been promulgating a Middle Eastern domino theory culminating in Soviet domination of the region. What this theory failed to take into account was that the same nationalism, rivalries and instabilities which had first facilitated Soviet penetrations would also serve to constrain and complicate the Soviet role. The Soviet Union has never found a really stable ally in the region. She has, on the contrary, found herself heavily dependent on the loyalty of individuals and movements which were extreme, insecure or impulsive. The pot may have been calling the kettle black when Khruschchev publicly brought the latter charge against Nasser in 1959. Still, Nasser was relatively easy to live with. His position *vis-à-vis* Israel was not as extreme as that of Syria, who for a long time rejected United Nations Resolution 242; his power base was far more secure and united than that of the PLO or the Syrian neo-Ba'ath in the late 1960s; and he did not, like Qasim and Sadat, turn against his patron.

90

These then were problems largely beyond Soviet control. However, the strains in Moscow's relations with its clients also owe a great deal to Soviet behaviour. It was not just the insensitivity with which the Soviet policy was frequently conducted, the insensitivity of the Soviet advisory corps which Heikal describes in *The Road to Ramadan* being but one example.[1] Much more important was the basic incompatability between a number of Soviet objectives and those of her clients. It soon became evident that Soviet policy had many of the characteristics of traditional Western imperialism. The Soviet quest for bases in the Arab world had begun within six years of the final British withdrawal from the Suez Canal Zone base, and a decade later, in 1971, Egypt was described in *Strategic Survey* as being in many respects a Soviet forward base area.[2] By 1969 General Assad, then Minister of Defence, was publicly accusing the Soviet Union of interfering in Syria's internal affairs, and similar and far more detailed accusations covering the same period have been made by President Sadat. In 1971 the Soviet Union tried to consolidate her position in Egypt by insisting on the signature of a treaty covering relations over a broad spectrum of political, military, economic, scientific and cultural matters. Egypt was thereby required to make a formal move away from non-alignment in foreign affairs and towards socialism in domestic policy.

The Soviet Union held the Treaty as a model for relations with other Third World countries pursuing the non-capitalist path to socialism. Egypt saw it very differently. It did not, as she had hoped, serve to limit the extent of Soviet interference in Egyptian affairs. It smacked of the hated Anglo–Egyptian treaty of 1936, and coming as it did shortly after the Ali Sabri affair,[3] it must have made Egypt acutely aware that her patron bore the double stigma of imperialism and Communism. Within a matter of months, Egypt had made her attitude clear by helping in the suppression of a Communist coup in the Sudan, a precursor of more recent attempts by

the Sadat government to combat Soviet influence in Africa.

The Soviet Union did, of course, usually recognize the need to avoid too close an identification with the mostly weak local Communist parties, and provided persecution was not too blatant, it was frequently ignored. What was much more difficult was to avoid taking sides when local rivalries came to boiling-point. Moscow's clients inevitably looked to their patron for whole-hearted support. But this the Soviet Union, like her Western rivals, was frequently unable to give, even though she recognized that her influence was often at stake. The dilemma first made itself felt as early as 1956, when the risk of a super-power confrontation and the absence of effective interventionary forces confined Soviet activities during the Suez crisis to the level of propaganda. The Iraqi coup of 1958 created further difficulties in that Nasser was originally disappointed by the absence of any forcible Soviet reaction to Western intervention in Lebanon and Jordan, and then angered by subsequent Soviet support for Qasim. Since then the Soviet Union has had to steer a careful line between the rivalries of the Syrian and Iraqi Ba'ath parties, the tensions between Iraq and Iran, Egypt and Libya and the two Yemens, and of course, most important of all, in the fighting between Arab states and Israel.

What is important here, however, is less the quarrels between the Soviet Union and confrontation states over arms supplies than Moscow's relatively poor record as an attorney for its clients. It was not until the 1973 October War that Soviet attempts to manipulate the local balance of power in favour of her allies began to have any significant impact on the Israeli bargaining position. The Soviet Union was unable to exert any direct influence over Israel, and the total break in communications between Moscow and Jerusalem, which can be seen as an inevitable corollary of Soviet support for the Arab cause, combined with the various other strains in Soviet–Egyptian relations, meant that the Soviet Union could not exploit her military contribution once this had fulfilled its immediate purpose of breaking the deadlock brought about by the Six Day War. In other words, Moscow has less to offer its clients as a peace mediator than as an armourer, and consequently Mr Gromyko does not have the freedom to shuttle

---

[1] Mohamed Heikal, *The Road to Ramadan* (London: Collins, 1975).
[2] *Strategic Survey 1971* (London: IISS, 1972), p. 31.
[3] In May 1971 Ali Sabri, among others, was involved in a plot to take over the government. Sabri, a close associate of President Nasser, was a leader of the 'left-wing' pro-Soviet group in the leadership.

between the confrontation parties enjoyed by Dr Kissinger or Mr Vance.

Countermeasures and Setbacks

This situation may not prove permanent, given the difficulties the Carter Administration is in its turn experiencing in forging dependence on the United States into an effective instrument of pressure *vis-à-vis* Israel. But it does underline one other difficulty which has faced Soviet policy in the Middle East: the success of Western countermeasures. It was the United States which largely was responsible for politically neutralizing the impact of Soviet military resources transfers to Egypt and Syria between 1967 and 1973, just as it was the United States, together with Britain, which helped to shore up the conservative order in the Middle East during much of the two previous decades. The success of this latter policy is particularly evident in the Gulf area, and over the last few years two beneficiaries of Western support, Saudi Arabia and Iran, have emerged as formidable opponents of the Soviet Union in their own right, both in the Middle East and in Africa.

The impact of all of these problems is to be seen in certain limitations on Soviet influence in the Middle East. In the first place, that influence has been confined to a limited number of countries. Although Moscow of course has diplomatic relations with some of the conservative capitals of the region, several of which bought small quantities of Soviet arms, the area of Soviet influence is largely bounded by the limits of radical influence. In so far as Egypt has been moving from the radical to the conservative camp since Nasser's death, the area for potential access has been contracting. Moreover, even in the radical states it proved extremely difficult to move from a position of involvement to one of influence, particularly when this included attempts at political penetration. The reaction was most violent in Egypt, where Soviet imperialism had taken its most blatant form, and Soviet restrictions on arms transfers had been especially resented. In contrast, the relatively smoother pattern of Soviet–Syrian relations owes something to Syria's ability to forestall some of those incursions which had most offended Egypt's sense of pride and independence. Still, the basic problem was the same in both cases: the Soviet Union offered too little (arms and an acceptable Arab–Israeli settlement) and demanded too much (bases and political dependence). Where the Soviet Union shared a common interest with these clients, the latter frequently proved invaluable as local proxies. But where interests have diverged, as they have done over a host of matters, many of which proved of vital importance to the Arab states concerned, Moscow has been able to exert only limited or temporary leverage over its clients. The intensity of nationalist feeling, the threat to look elsewhere, whether to China or the West, and the extent to which the commitment of its prestige determined subsequent Soviet policy in the face of defeat, proved ultimately to be more important in the complex Soviet–Arab relationship than the fact that for several of its clients, Soviet military aid was almost literally a matter of life or death.

Some twenty years on, therefore, the observer is more conscious of the weaknesses of the Soviet position than of its strengths. The Soviet Union has suffered a number of very public and humiliating setbacks, and her search for alternative *points d'appui* in Iraq, Libya and with the PLO are unlikely to provide any real political or military substitute for the Soviet–Egyptian relationship in its heyday of the late 1960s. All of this reflects not only the essential instability of the Soviet position but also the fact that the most substantial Soviet achievements turned out to be the least permanent and in a sense the most negative. Soviet policy, particularly in the 1950s, helped reduce Western influence in the Middle East, and in particular to hasten the process of British withdrawal. Soviet support for Nasser – arms and finance for the Aswan dam – gave an added impetus to an anti-colonialist movement which spread well beyond the Middle East. Within the Arab world the result was to be seen in the weakening and frequent destruction of those regimes on which Western influence had been based. These were clear Soviet gains and, together with the failure of the Baghdad Pact, which owed much to well-timed Soviet diplomacy, and the improvement in the 1960s in relations with Turkey and Iran, meant an enhancement of Soviet security as far as the threat from the south-west was concerned. In addition, the Soviet Union gained some useful military information as a result of the War of Attrition and the 1973 October War, as well as welcome hard currency from more recent arms transfers.

A Middle East Power

But if undermining Western influence proved relatively easy at a time when indigenous nationalist sentiment was already strong, replacing it with Soviet influence was quite a different proposition. There are instances where the Soviet Union gained access to ports or airfields vacated by Britain or France, but for the most part Soviet military planners must be disappointed with their inability to gain anything other than the limited facilities allowed them in Syria, Iraq, Libya and the PDRY. The Egyptian bases, like the 1971 Treaty, the Egyptian experiment with socialism, and the Soviet penetration of the single Egyptian political party, the Arab Socialist Union, did not last. The special relationships which at one time appeared possible with Iraq and Syria do not appear to have materialized, although relatively little is known about details of Soviet–Syrian relations during the key period of the late 1960s.

These developments must have been disappointing for the Soviet Union. However, they have not affected vital Soviet interests and they are, to some extent at least, offset by the fact that while involvement has not automatically been translated into influence as far as bilateral relationships are concerned, it has allowed the Soviet Union to become a Middle East power. She is, in other words, an actor who, by virtue of her network of political connections, nearby fleets and relatively open armoury, has to be consulted and taken into consideration both by regional states and by the rival super-power. Even if Moscow could not by itself control events or impose an Arab–Israeli settlement, it has made itself into one of the important factors in the Arab–Israeli equation. Washington has thus had to deal direct with its rival to control crises and, to some extent at least, to negotiate a settlement: hence the two-power peace talks of 1969 and Dr Kissinger's visit to Moscow during the last days of the 1973 October War to arrange a cease-fire. In what can be seen as a formal recognition of parity with the United States in the Middle East, the Soviet Union subsequently became co-chairman of a regional peace conference. Here perhaps lies the most significant achievement of Soviet policy over the last two decades. In an expansion of influence unparalleled in any other part of the world – before, that is, the recent Soviet incursions into Africa –

the Soviet Union has become a Middle East power. Even if she does not exercise the influence enjoyed by the earlier Middle Eastern powers of this century, the Soviet Union has enhanced the deference due to her as a super-power and taken a further step towards achieving overall political parity with her rival. She has also gone some way in imposing her concept of detente on the United States, at least in so far as joint crisis management is concerned.

Does this verdict still stand, however, in the wake of the events which have succeeded the 1973 October War? Is there not a case for saying that the months between October 1973 and the convening of the Geneva Peace Conference marked the apogee of the Soviet role as a Middle East power? Perhaps, but there is also good reason for treating such judgments with reservation. It is true that Moscow's credentials as an equal negotiating partner with the United States have declined over recent years. The deterioration in relations with Cairo have left the Soviet Union heavily dependent on Syria and the PLO. The latter connection has obvious value at a time when it is generally recognized that the Palestine issue must be an integral element of any viable settlement, and when Washington is still deprived of direct contact with the PLO. But the Soviet Union is wary of giving the organization unqualified support, and she cannot be sure that the PLO, as opposed to some other Palestinian group, will play the key role in a settlement. Moreover, anxious as Syria is to maintain close links with Moscow, the Soviet Union cannot have overlooked the fact that it was Dr Kissinger who negotiated the Syrian–Israeli disengagement agreement of 1974 (incidentally after a mini Syrian–Israeli War of Attrition for which the Soviet Union had as usual provided the arms). Nor can she have overlooked Syria's willingness to cast an at least sympathetic eye towards President Carter's peace proposals. The risk of exclusion from the peace-making process has thus worried Moscow, all the more so as this course would be favoured by both Egypt and Israel.

It is in this context that the Joint Soviet–American Declaration on the Middle East of 1 October 1977 assumed importance, for it reflected renewed willingness on the part of the United States, after the unilateral nature of Dr Kissinger's step-by-step diplomacy, to co-operate with the Soviet Union. Indeed, it is difficult to see how, having decided on the need for a comprehensive settlement to be negotiated at Geneva, the United States could for much longer have refused to work with Moscow. The Soviet Union also wanted a settlement; her position, as characterized by President Carter, was a 'balanced' one, and there were repeated hints during 1977 that Moscow might be able to use its contacts with the PLO to help negotiate a compromise formula for Palestinian participation at Geneva. Conversely, there was always the danger that, if excluded for too long, the Soviet Union might again begin to play a spoiler's role. This ability was in fact demonstrated a couple of months later, when the Soviet Union helped to co-ordinate the anti-Sadat summit held in Tripoli in December 1977, in an attempt to bring under a wider Arab control President Sadat's unilateral peace initiative launched in Jerusalem.

The Prospects

The real issue remains that of *how much* influence Moscow can hope to exercise in the future. The difficulty from the Soviet point of view is that she is now operating under far less favourable conditions than she has done in the past. The legacy of disappointment and suspicion can only complicate future diplomacy, particularly if the Soviet Union continues to play an active role in the Horn of Africa. Moreover, she now has less to offer. Economic aid is available from the conservative treasury on the Arabian Peninsula, and there is a clear preference for Western technology, both in conservative and radical states. Western arms are again being supplied to Egypt, and the Soviet Union is less well-equipped than the United States to cope with the current, primarily diplomatic phase of the Arab–Israeli conflict. At the same time, the Soviet Union does still enjoy many of her former advantages. The radical states continue to look first to Moscow, not perhaps because they trust the Soviet Union, but because they distrust the United States more. This trend has if anything been strengthened by Cairo's rapprochement with Washington and President Sadat's unilateral peace diplomacy. They also recognize that in military terms they remain dependent on the Soviet Union for arms, significant deals having been concluded with Moscow in recent years by Iraq, Libya and Syria. But there is a further consideration, one

that could again apply to Egypt. Few Middle Eastern countries, and particularly not those directly involved in the Arab–Israeli conflict, are in the long run easy with a foreign policy relying exclusively on only one of the super-powers.

Much therefore will continue to depend on local circumstances largely beyond Soviet control, primarily the future of the Arab–Israeli conflict and, closely related, the future of the conservative order in the Middle East. Since the 1973 October War the main emphasis has been on the achievement of a settlement. This aim has been supported by the Soviet Union, provided of course that it is negotiated within the framework of the Geneva Conference. Assuming for a moment that such a settlement is now feasible, the question is what kind of settlement it will be and how much it will give to Moscow. If the settlement is a 'good' one, i.e. one broadly acceptable to all the confrontation states, plus Saudi Arabia and the Palestinian mainstream, and if it allows them to help guarantee at least some of the constituent agreements, the Soviet Union could probably look forward to modest, although relatively durable gains, in the reasonable certainty that the most dangerous flashpoint for super-power confrontation had now been removed. The role of guarantor would confer prestige and ensure some degree of long-term involvement which would lend itself to exploitation in a variety of dealings with Middle Eastern capitals, as well as with Washington. Much would depend on the details of the settlement, but there should at least be the basis for a rapprochement with Egypt and Israel, possibly even for the establishment of diplomatic relations with Saudi Arabia.

Against this would have to be set the likely distancing of relations with Syria, for whom a settlement may provide a welcome opportunity to diversify ties further to the West, and a possible loosening of the Palestinian connection. This would almost certainly be the case if the Palestinian entity turns out to be part of a Jordanian confederation (assuming of course that the Hashemite monarchy remains in in power). Even if an independent Palestinian state is formed, its ties to Moscow would be constricted by a number of factors, one of the most important of which would be the influence of Gulf money. A settlement may also reduce the long-term opportunities for Soviet penetration by helping to consolidate the conservative order in the Middle East. But it would be as well not to confuse an Arab–Israeli settlement with a solution of all the problems of the region, and Moscow would probably be able to complement its role as a respectable settlement guarantor with the exploitation of other tensions. The concept of a 'good' settlement does not preclude the survival of some rejectionist sentiment, whether among Palestinians or in Tripoli and Baghdad. This could cause difficulties for Moscow in so far as it could only lend support at the expense of the settlement it was itself underwriting, and would in any case be compromised in rejectionist eyes. But the Arab–Israeli conflict has never been the dominant factor in Soviet relations with Libya, Iraq or the PDRY. Much more important have been internal or inter-Arab tensions which could intensify once the cement of anti-Israeli sentiment is removed from the uncertain structure of Arab unity.

Consideration of this possibility leads to another alternative – a 'flawed' settlement, i.e. a settlement rejected by one or more of the parties concerned. This situation could be of advantage to Moscow. It would be relatively safer than the *status quo* in the sense that Israel would no longer be facing a united front of Arab neighbours and that the risk of renewed conflict would thereby be lower. It would leave the conservative order more vulnerable and would provide Moscow if not with more, then possibly with relatively more dependent clients. But at what cost? Military dependence, as past experience has shown, is both dangerous in that it helps establish a degree of *de facto* Soviet commitment, and unreliable as a basis for political influence. A Soviet refusal to participate could cause problems with Washington, potentially very serious ones if the settlement were to break down and the United States were in some way involved as a guarantor. Furthermore, failure to participate would affect Soviet relations with the local signatories and could prove the cause of a total rupture in Soviet–Egyptian relations.

Some of these dilemmas would become even more acute if the peace initiative were finally to run into the sands. The road would then be open for a major improvement in bilateral Soviet relations with the confrontation states, including Egypt, and for a much greater Soviet involvement in Middle Eastern affairs than there has been seen since the end of 1973. Such a situation could be very attractive provided that Moscow were able to prove itself a more effective attorney for its clients than it has in the past. That is possible, but it depends on the United States being more sensitive to the risk of a new war than she was before 1973. The case for this assumption rests on the fact that Israel is now a less valuable anti-Soviet proxy than at the beginning of the decade; that American opinion could become less sympathetic towards Israel if a breakdown in peace negotiations could be attributed to Israeli obduracy; and that the United States has become increasingly vulnerable to the pressures exerted by a group of states which supply a significant proportion of American oil needs and maintain substantial reserves in dollars. These arguments are hardly new. But their impact on American policy could become much more immediate and pressing once the prospects of peace had begun to recede and arms were again flowing in significant quantities from the Soviet Union to all the confrontation states.

But if the United States cannot afford the risk of another war, neither can the Soviet Union, and recognition of this fact may well be reflected in the willingness of Moscow to put forward constructive proposals of its own, and, on the whole, to avoid obstructing American peace diplomacy. Perhaps the most likely response to a breakdown in negotiations would be a return to the traditional two-track Soviet policy – a broadening of the arms conduit, accompanied by a continued and possibly more active search for a diplomatic solution. But here again the Soviet Union would depend on the support of others – a Middle East power with severe limitations.

4 REVOLUTION IN IRAN

The beginning of the year had seen the Shah of Iran at what seemed the height of his power, undisputed ruler of his own country and host to the President of the United States. A year later the Shah had been forced to leave his throne and his country and to seek refuge abroad as the guest of Morocco's King Hassan II, while Iran, bruised and weakened, was under the tenuous control of a religious leader, Ayatollah Khomeini, and faced an uncertain future.

With hindsight, it became clear that the appearance of complete control by the Shah had been deceptive. After nearly fifteen years of political stability and a decade of remarkable real economic growth (averaging over 10% a year), Iran seemed set on a course of modernization and on the way to joining the ranks of the developed world. Active opposition to the Shah during this period had been limited to radical urban guerrilla groups on the Left and obscurantist religious figures on the Right. Despite sporadic and isolated minor disturbances since 1970, the government's strength appeared to assure its continued control, and its striking economic success – though creating social strains – seemed sufficient to alleviate what promised to be temporary difficulties of inflation, speculation, power failures, pollution and congestion. Yet in just twelve months many of these assumptions were shown to be unfounded.

Causes of Unrest

How did the Shah's authority deteriorate so quickly after Iran's rapid economic growth? The sudden infusion of oil wealth into the country after 1973 both aggravated many of the problems inherent in modernization and obscured them. It reinforced tendencies towards social engineering and technological tinkering unrelated to the social context. Always arrogant in leadership, the Shah became intolerant of competing ideas and impervious to alternative programmes. Political repression became doubly oppressive when corruption was rampant at all levels. The crassest forms of materialism flourished in a cultural and spiritual wasteland. This materialism, being essentially alien and imported with other Western goods and values, came to symbolize to many the 'godlessness' of a regime whose ruling style had become increasingly anachronous, even by Middle Eastern standards.

Practical difficulties exacerbated the Shah's problems, as economic growth accelerated social dislocations. The agricultural sector's deterioration, a partial consequence of the emphasis on rapid industrialization, was particularly serious, since half the population lived in the rural areas. An attempt at land reform fifteen years earlier had failed to achieve its promise, and, while the richer peasantry continued to prosper, some 1¾ million families were left landless. Urban incomes, up to five times higher than rural ones, attracted labour to the cities, weakening traditional family structures and further depleting the agricultural sector (by 1978 it had become necessary to import $2 bn worth of food a year). Once in the cities, many peasants were better off in absolute terms, but this was offset by high rents and inflation running at over 35%. Furthermore, the widening gap between rich and poor (10% of the population accounting for 40% of consumption) became strikingly conspicuous and a source of additional discontent. Real growth slackened after 1976 to 3.2%, leaving the migrants from the countryside unemployed on the streets. Uprooted and adrift in a strange environment, they gravitated towards the only social institution that was familiar: the Mosque. The urban proletariat, sharing the difficulties of congested cities and without the right to organize or strike, also sought solace in religion. The urban traditionalists of the bazaar, too, though profiting from economic growth, felt victimized by the government's selective 'anti-profiteering' campaigns and joined in providing support for the mullahs and, in particular, their most forceful representative, the exiled Ayatollah Khomeini. In addition, the middle classes – 800,000 civil servants and perhaps 750,000 workers in industrial plants – found the prospect of material reward progressively less satisfying and the impulse for political participation more intensely moving. Finally, the Shah's traditional opponents, the intelligentsia, students and clergy (180,000 mullahs), who had been ignored or slighted in recent years, formed the core of this disenchanted populace.

The apparent revival of Islam (manifested in attacks on banks, casinos and women's equality) represented a traditionalist backlash against the regime. It was in part a rallying cry against excessive and indiscriminate Westernization, in part a protest against the erosion of traditional values and a reaffirmation of them as the basis of a search for enduring values to guide a society in transition. The pervasive discontent coalesced around the belief that the system itself was the root cause of Iran's social, cultural, economic and political problems and must therefore be radically reformed. The Shah's opponents came to equate the regime with 'foreigners', and specifically with the West, which had assumed a major and conspicuous role in Iran's economic and military modernization programmes (with over 100,000 Westerners in the country, and about 50,000 from the US alone).

The very broad cross-section of Iranian society opposed to the Shah was reflected in a diversity of political groups of varying popularity and degrees of organization. Traditional leftist groups, such as the banned *Tudeh* (Communist) party, co-existed with guerrilla groups, such as the *Fedayin-e-Khalq* (Strugglers for the People) and *Mujahedin-e-Khalq* (Holy Warriors for the People). In the centre stood the National Front, a loose coalition which inherited the constitutional tradition and much of the aura of the Mossadeg period but lacked a strong organizational structure. The Front, led by Karim Sanjabi and Shahpour Bakhtiar (expelled in late December for agreeing to form a civilian

government at the Shah's request), although divided into factions, agreed on a programme calling for restoration of political freedoms, curbs on the Shah's powers, and punishment for those guilty of corruption. The socialist, democratic and secular content of the Front's platform differentiated it from the smaller and more Islamic-oriented Iran Liberation Movement under Mehdi Bazargan (whom the Ayatollah Khomeini appointed as his first Prime Minister in February 1979).

Despite the inchoateness of much of the opposition's political programmes and the dangers of regression if Islamic law were strictly enforced (it would, for instance, prohibit charging interest on loans), the Shah was unable to neutralize this appeal by mobilizing his natural constituency, the urban middle class (up to 25% of the population). In part this was due to his earlier failure to establish any basis for loyalty to his regime other than fear and material reward. The conspicuous apathy of the middle-class response demonstrated collective disaffection with the regime, even though the crisis threatened middle-class interests. Moreover, the Shah continued to dispute the legitimacy of the moderate opposition, and as late as August he was still denying its existence and equating criticism with treason. This largely self-created political polarization came to haunt the Shah when, in the second half of the year, he vainly sought to win over those elements which did not make his deposition a precondition for dialogue and support of the government.

Yet, even these strong currents of discontent and opposition to the Shah's regime would not have brought it down, but for two factors: the central role played by the religious leaders (above all the Ayatollah Khomeini) and the power wielded by Iran's 67,000 oil workers who, by stopping oil production, paralysed the government's authority.

Khomeini was not the only religious critic of the Shah and his regime, but he became the most forceful. He emphasized traditional Shi'ite and Persian values, in contrast to the regime's ready acceptance of Western culture; he was incorruptible, in contrast to the corruption of the Iranian system; he refused to compromise as the Shah sought to appease the current of unrest. Combined with the impact of modern communications, these attributes provide Khomeini with unchallengeable authority – particularly in relation to the one objective which united all opponents: the overthrow of the Shah and the political regime he stood for. The diversity of views among the various forces of the 'opposition' was to come to the fore the moment this objective had been achieved. Until then, however, from his exile (since 1963 in Iraq – then, from October 1978, in Paris) the Ayatollah determined the strategy of revolt: the replacement of the monarchy by an Islamic republic.

As the Ayatollah's appeal grew, so other options for resolving the crisis were progressively swept aside as politically unrealistic. His hold on large sections of the Iranian people and his refusal to compromise with the Shah's 'illegal and usurping regime' undercut the more moderate domestic-based religious opposition, led by Ayatollah Shariatmadari in Qom, and forced the more secular groups, such as the National Front, to avoid negotiating with the Shah for fear of isolating themselves. As a result, the most vocal element in a diverse tactical coalition of opposition groups belonged to the religious group which initially called for a return to the 1906 constitution, emphasizing the neglected provision which required the creation of a committee of five religious leaders to ensure the conformity of legislation with Islamic law (*Sharia*) by right of veto. But by the year-end Khomeini's immense influence had brought about the adoption of his personal preference for the establishment of an Islamic republic.

But it was the effectiveness of the strike weapon – particularly in the oil fields – which more than anything else rendered the country ungovernable. It was proof against persuasion by moderates and remedy by force alike. The striking oil workers reduced an oil production of over 6 million barrels per day to less than half a million barrels in November-December – well below even domestic requirements – and the consequent loss of some $3 billion in revenues flattened a government already besieged by widespread strikes in its vital administrative centres. The ease with which this tactic was employed raised fears lest it should set a precedent for workers in other oil-producing states in the area, and it stressed the weakness of states dependent on one major extractive industry.

From Unrest to Revolution

Growing and almost continuous political upheaval shook Iran throughout 1978, and at least 2,000 people were killed. Starting in Qom (the religious city in central Iran) during January, rioting spread in February to Tabriz in the north-west and then to other provincial towns. In June the government attempted to meet opposition demands by replacing the head of the secret police (SAVAK), Gen. Nehmatollah Nasiri, with a known moderate, Gen. Nasser Moghadam, but this had little effect, and major violence in Isfahan led to the imposition of martial law in August. A subsequent incendiary attack on a cinema in Abadan, where 430 people died, resulted in Jamshid Amuzegar's replacement as Prime Minister by Jafaar Sharif-Emami, a more traditional figure and a man with strong religious connections, and the promise of free elections by June 1979. These attempts by the Shah to appease his critics failed, and in September massive demonstrations against the Emami government led to martial law being declared in Tehran and ten other major cities. This was answered by a series of strikes in the public sector, including the oil fields, and further violence in Tehran in early November. A military government was installed under Gen. Gholam Reza Azhari, but it was as helpless as its predecessor to cope with the situation. The Shah's mixture of concessions, promises and stern measures were increasingly ineffective. Releasing political prisoners, granting amnesty to political opponents, reinstating the Islamic calendar, banning the Royal Family's business activities, granting large wage claims, the Shah directly admitting past mistakes in a broadcast to the nation in November, weakening SAVAK and promising rectification and compensation for its past excesses – all were insufficient to stem the tide. On the contrary, they seemed to encourage the Shah's increasingly confident opponents rather than encourage compromise.

In a final attempt to save his power, the Shah dismissed the military government at the year-end and appointed Shahpour Bakhtiar, a firm opponent for the past 25 years and one of the leaders of the National Front, to form a new civilian government. But Bakhtiar was unable to win support from either the mosques or the oilfields, and the Shah, by delaying his departure for a 'temporary holiday', deprived the new premier of the major initial success that might just have shored up his authority. The Shah did not leave Iran until 16 January 1979, after Bakhtiar's government was given a vote of confidence in the Shah-controlled parliament. The Regency Council set up to maintain the monarchy disintegrated quickly, and the morale of the military hierarchy, uncertain of its role without its royal commander-in-chief, was gravely undermined.

Bakhtiar's attempts to assure a position from which to induce the Ayatollah Khomeini and his supporters to move to a more secular and less religiously rigid system of government were vain. The leaderless military proved indecisive, first wanting to block Khomeini's return from exile, then acquiescing in it; first repressing demonstrations against Bakhtiar and in favour of Khomeini's prime ministerial nominee Mehdi Bazargan, then (as important units, particularly in the air force, began to side with Khomeini) on 9 February announcing its neutrality in the domestic power struggle. The armed forces were no longer a cohesive instrument of power in the state, and their abdication from loyalty to the monarchy sealed the fate of the government. Bakhtiar immediately resigned. Within forty-eight hours of Khomeini's return to Iran Dr Bazargan's skeletal cabinet was installed and soon afterwards was recognized by most foreign governments.

The transfer of power was bloody (over 1,000 killed in Tehran plus thousands of casualties) and yet incomplete. Some elements that had joined the opposition to the Shah under the Khomeini banner were not satisfied with the revolution's pace or direction. Foremost among these were the highly armed urban guerrillas, the leftist-secular *Fedayin-e-Khalq* group and the Islamic-Marxist radicals of *Mujahedin-e-Khalq*. In addition there was the Iranian Communist party (*Tudeh*), which appeared to be well organized in the oil fields. Singly or in combination, these groups posed a serious obstacle to the less doctrinaire approach to Iran's problems that Bazargan wanted to adopt. The disintegration of the armed forces left the provisional government without reliable means to enforce its authority, and the resultant near anarchy boded ill for a speedy reassertion of central authority.

The Soviet Union and the Crisis

Soviet interest in events in adjacent Iran reflected the two countries' mixed relationship. Hostility in the post-war years had been replaced by pragmatic economic relations in the 1960s, including the construction of a steel mill in Iran, the exchange of Iranian gas for Soviet goods, agreement on transit rights and the sale of limited quantities of Soviet arms. In the 1970s their trade increased rapidly, with Iran becoming the largest market for Soviet non-military goods in the Middle East. Soviet exports to Iran rose by 50% in 1977 to $515 million, and Soviet technicians to about 3,000, the largest such contingent among less developed countries. An important exchange agreement in 1975 on the transfer of gas from Iran to the Southern USSR, and from western Siberia to Europe, was due to be implemented in 1981. In other respects, however, relations were competitive. The Soviet Union regularly criticized Iran's arms acquisitions and activist foreign policy, particularly in the Persian Gulf, and viewed the growing Western presence in the country with concern. Moreover, Iran under the Shah demonstrated a self-confidence which the USSR found difficult to accept in a neighbour, and the Shah left no doubt of his firmly pro-Western and anti-Communist attitude.

The initial Soviet reaction to the events of 1978 reflected the complexity of the relationship. Any developments that weakened the Shah and undermined his policies – in particular his pro-Western orientation, assertive foreign policy and military expansion programme – were welcomed, since they could make Iran more sensitive to Soviet interests. But the USSR showed no inclination to foster Iran's disintegration or encourage anarchy there. Recurrent large-scale disorder might weaken the Shah's regime, but it could also threaten the security of Soviet frontiers by inviting outside interference. Also, and most important, endemic instability might provide the breeding ground for a new autocrat in Iran, whether in military or religious guise, who could be unpredictable, particularly if driven by a new-found nationalist zeal. Only in November, when the opposition appeared irresistible, did Soviet commentaries explicitly support it. Soviet propaganda then played up the social discontent, arguing that it reflected great opposition to the Shah's arms purchases and to continued Iranian participation in the Central Treaty Organization, thus constituting a major setback for the West. By posing as a sympathetic and impartial neighbour, the USSR sought to ingratiate herself with the opposition.

Though some of the more militant Iranian opposition groups had received Soviet arms through third parties, they did not represent a decisive threat to a regime that had already provoked the coalescence of such an extraordinarily diverse opposition. There was therefore little reason to doubt the Soviet Union's claims of non-involvement – indeed there was no necessity for her to be involved. Consequently she could deny any intention of becoming involved and, by demanding a reciprocal assurance from the United States, could use the Iranian issue to embarrass her publicly. In addition, President Brezhnev's November statement warning that 'military interference in the affairs of Iran would be regarded as a matter affecting Soviet security interests', suggested that Moscow also wanted to discourage any US attempt to diminish the set-back for the West.

The United States and the Crisis
The impact and consequences of the Iranian revolution were much graver for the United States, Iran's *de facto* protector for over two decades. Yet the developments of

1978 were such as to deprive the United States of any leverage, and while President Carter's administration might have made a more consistent and positive response it seems unlikely that this would have significantly altered the course of events.

In the United States the Iranian crisis provoked first disbelief and then a search for evidence of foreign involvement. As late as August US intelligence authorities had not understood the magnitude of the opposition to the Shah – over-reliance on Iranian security sources for intelligence having deprived them of precisely the kind of objective analysis that was crucial in a time of change. Unwilling to risk the Shah's personal displeasure or short-term bilateral goals, the US (especially under Presidents Nixon and Ford and Secretary Kissinger) had signally failed to exercise an influence commensurate with her large and growing interest in Iran. Oblivious to the mounting evidence of mismanagement and corruption, successive US governments had failed to impress upon the Shah the need for reform and the decentralization of authority. Ironically her entanglement had made the US dependent: unwilling to use her influence, she became a captive of indigenous and local circumstance.

By the year's end, as the Shah's weakness became crystal clear, a special committee chaired by former Under Secretary of State George Ball examined the premises of relations with Iran and the Persian Gulf in light of the crisis. Perhaps too late, the United States delicately sought to put some distance between herself and the Shah and to search for possible alternatives without precipitating his fall by a sudden withdrawal of support. She therefore encouraged an orderly process of transition to allow the Shah to disengage himself from political responsibility by handing over power to a civilian government headed by Dr Bakhtiar. But the process of political change had become too powerful for the United States to shape it at this stage, and, despite her considerable interests, the US found few instruments of influence readily available. Even those at hand were mismanaged. A decision on 29 December to send a Seventh Fleet task force into the Indian Ocean region was reversed five days later, and President Carter implied that it might 'inflame' the situation. No more effective in symbolizing US decisiveness or power to reassure her allies in the region was the decision on 10 January 1979 temporarily to deploy an F-15 squadron to Saudi Arabia, ostensibly to demonstrate an 'interest in the security of the Kingdom'. Though the aircraft (which were refused landing rights in Spain and consequently had to be aerially refuelled) were unarmed, their deployment two months after the Brezhnev warning was neither timely nor impressive.

Prospects

The diverse forces within Iran which coalesced in 1978 were perhaps united on only one issue other than opposition to the Shah – nationalism. Whether they will be able to translate this emotional consensus into a government with a working programme is unclear. But whatever the form of government – republic, military government or even constitutional monarchy – it is most unlikely that a strong leadership will emerge soon in Iran. The most likely prognosis is one of drift, of uneasy coalitions and sporadic unrest.

Preoccupation with internal politics and economic consolidation will take priority, with less attention paid to foreign policy and a correspondingly narrower definition of Iran's security interests. The effect will be fewer initiatives and less assertiveness in foreign policy, combined with a greater tendency to avoid major disagreements with the USSR. One can expect stronger support for the Arab cause against Israel, greater distance from the Western states, a stronger line over North/South issues and non-alignment, and militant support for maximum oil-price increases, combined with conservation or cuts in production.

There are, however, several structural constraints on Iran that will prevent too sharp a swing away from the West, whatever the government. Primary among these is the desire for oil revenue which can buy technology and knowledge. This will drive any future Iranian government (albeit more gradually than hitherto) into commercial links with the West, and the many Iranian students educated abroad over the past generation will continue to see the West as the most desirable source for technical expertise. Similarly in foreign policy, after an initial reaction against what some in Iran see as over-reliance on the West, an equilibrium may be established that maintains security links to offset the Soviet Union's proximate power. Dependence on the West (and particularly on the US and Britain for spare parts and replacements for practically her entire armed forces) should for several years militate against any precipitate action which could jeopardize Iran's security and entail long and costly dislocations while searching for alternative sources. But this depends on the nature of the leadership that emerges and how it defines security.

For the West two consequences stand out in particular. First, the Iran that emerged from the revolution of 1978 will no longer be the close ally of previous years, identifying with Western concepts of regional security or stability of energy supply. Iran will no longer be the second largest oil exporter and a dependable supplier, she will no longer be the West's bastion in a turbulent region, promoting stability in the Middle East, controlling the Hormuz Straits, and providing the backbone of regional stability. Internally the revolution implied a return to more traditional values of society; externally it implied a return to the fold of the non-aligned world.

Second, the Iranian revolution demonstrated the weaknesses in the political structures of countries on whose stability the industrial Western states depend – weaknesses which existing means of outside influence can do little to affect. It thus emphasized the need to reassess Western strategies to develop a more resiliant framework for co-operation and mutual advantage between the industrial and the raw-material-producing countries than that implied by bilateral military and economic alliances.

The Regional Impact

Whatever the outcome of the revolution in Iran considerable damage had already been done to the region's security, a fact quickly recognized in the immediate area. Saudi Arabia, in particular, had often expressed her support for the Shah and claimed that his removal would harm the region's security and well-being; the small Gulf states followed suit, and Iraq, too, acted in a conciliatory manner. These reactions were in large part predictable, reflecting as they did the considerable progress that had been made in the creation of a regional detente in the Gulf. Although the detente was unlikely to be translated into formal co-operation among the littoral states, there had been substantial agreement on two points: first, non-intervention in each other's affairs and, second, the creation of a basis for limited co-operation on security issues. This general pragmatism had two consequences: the defusing of immediate, local threats to Gulf security and the reintegration of Iraq into Persian Gulf politics.

Saudi and Iraqi interests in Iran's stability were of course more concrete than this. For Saudi Arabia, despite occasional prestige rivalry, Iran under the Shah constituted the best guarantee of moderation in foreign policy and a parallel pro-Western orientation. This relieved her concerns about her security in the East, reduced the likelihood that she would be isolated in OPEC, and gave extra protection to the smaller Gulf states. The Shah's secular pragmatism was predictable and hence preferable to any likely alternatives, whether left-wing or religious rightist, which would be more volatile and probably aggressively nationalist in foreign policy. For the Ba'ath regime in Iraq the prospect of a religious revival in Iran, followed by the installation of a Shi'ite religious government, was viewed with great alarm. Any religious appeal by a new regime in Tehran might mobilize the Iraqi Shi'ite majority and create difficulties for the Sunni minority which controls the government machinery.

If any common thread ran through the instability not only in Iran but in Pakistan and Afghanistan as well, it was the persistence and reassertion of traditional Islamic values sorely buffeted in the scramble for modernization. In this sense, states changing in different degrees and speeds have encountered a formidable fundamentalist back-lash, with Islam providing a rallying point for criticism of excessive, uneven or indiscriminate growth and appealing to popular nostalgia for predictability and identity in the face of social dislocations and alienation.

The surfacing of this nostalgic appeal in 1978 represented the slow maturing of a long-standing resentment, and its success was largely due to the political ineptitude of the regimes it helped supplant. This is an important reminder to the West that it cannot take for granted that states in which it has important interests will make a peaceful transition to modernity, particularly if the leaders of those states do not live as simply as the Islamic fundamentalists demand and do not improve the common man's economic lot. Since Westernization is the most intrusive force in the area, much of the focus of the religious appeal is bound to be anti-Western, even where politicians have not deliberately cultivated it.

The present Islamic revival is basically different from those of the past because it is national, and not pan-Islamic, in character. The role that Islam plays in each state will vary according to the society and formulas evolved to balance the old and the new. In Shi'ite Iran the reassertion of Islam has been frankly political – a protest movement against excesses fuelled by a large oil income and against a government increasingly detached from its people. In Egypt, where there is no comparable wealth, Islam in the guise of the Muslim Brotherhood constitutes an important focus for traditionalist or right-wing sentiment and a warning against 'godless' modernization. In Afghanistan, by contrast, Islamic fervour is likely to act as a brake on the new Marxist government. In Pakistan, where the army overthrew Mr Bhutto when the Islamic-led opposition parties created the sort of turmoil later repeated in Iran, the present government obviously hopes that institutionalizing Islamic law and practices and thus harnessing the appeal of Islam (Pakistan's original *raison d'être*) will enable it to counterbalance fissiparous tendencies in the provinces and sharpen a sense of national identity.

However, it is still unclear whether the official cultivation of Islam, with all its attendant inconveniences for governmental operations, will provide sufficient unity to bind together nations beset by separatist sentiments. In none of the countries mentioned does Islam provide an alternative direction or a competing programme for government.

The religious upheaval will sharply curtail Iran's role in the area's security arrangements for some time to come. The removal of one pillar of the security edifice has therefore increased the load that the other, Saudi Arabia, has to bear in maintaining regional order. Yet, even if Saudi Arabia were able to assume large responsibilities in this area (and she is not), she does not appear willing to do so. For her, Washington's lack of positive action over the crisis in Iran – coming on the heels of the coup in Afghanistan and the war in the Horn of Africa – cast doubt on the value of the US connection for her security and made the alternative of seeking refuge in an Arab consensus and playing down ties with the US more attractive. Although it is still too early to assess how this may affect Saudi Arabia's attitude to the proposed Camp David arrangements, more cautious Saudi diplomacy appears to be the most likely outcome.

The crisis in Iran has also undermined Western thinking about security in the Persian Gulf, where the West is now faced with a choice between responding directly to or ignoring local conflicts. A mobile interventionary force for military contingencies in such regions would meet only half the problem, since the efficacy of its deployment would rest on two assumptions – that the projection of the force to distant areas would be politically acceptable within the US; and that the deployment would not exacerbate local feeling nor increase regional polarization. Neither of these conditions prevailed in Iran. In addition, what happened there has reminded the West that the cutting off of oil need not be caused by interdiction at the choke points or government embargoes. The political foundation of the oil-producing governments may be their weakest point, and the one least susceptible to remedy by the use of outside force.

5 REPERCUSSIONS OF THE CRISIS IN IRAN

SHAHRAM CHUBIN

The 'lessons' of Iran will be debated even as that country's uncertain future unfolds. There can be little doubt that the collapse of the Shah was a blow to the West. But to what extent did Western – especially American – actions contribute to the 'loss' of Iran, when the Shah had instruments of power but none relevant to his political future? And how should the West respond to future disorder, primarily internal, in third-world states that are its allies or key resource producers? Shahram Chubin provides answers to these and other questions about the implications of events in Iran – for Iran herself, for the region and for American and Soviet policies. While agreeing that actions by outside powers could not have affected the course of the Iranian revolution decisively, he is strongly critical of American policy. He regards it as ill-formed during Iran's vital period of development (1972–6), and the actions of the Carter Administration during the Iranian crisis as at best half-hearted and contradictory.

The revolution in Iran removing the Shah after a thirty-seven-year rule will have a profound effect both on the political balance in the Middle East and the East–West strategic balance. Whatever the new regime, its policies will be less favourable to Western interests than before: it will be politically non-aligned, militarily and diplomatically passive, militant on oil prices and conservationist in production policy. The upheaval in Iran is also important as a model of an authentically and markedly anti-Western populist national revolt. Furthermore, throughout the months of turmoil, Western, especially American, policy has been ineffective either in anticipating events or in limiting their damaging consequences for other interests in the region. Certainly this was due in part to the policy inherited by the Carter Administration and to the intractability of Iran's domestic problems to external influence, but it was equally due to Washington's inconsistency, incoherence and equivocation.

Outlook for Iran

With the Shah's departure and the disintegration of the army there remain few independent bases of power in Iran. The revolutionary clergy in the Mosques, the militant, secular and Marxist–Leninist guerrillas in the cities and the moderate intellectuals in the National Front will contend for power, though with unequal resources. Without a strong central authority, there will

Shahram Chubin is Assistant to the Director of the IISS.

be a reassertion of local power in the provinces. Although it is still too early to define with any precision the nature of politics in republican Iran, the forces affecting transition are discernible.

First, the revolution has eroded the traditional channels of authority and overturned two major national institutions, the monarchy and the army. The wide-ranging coalition in opposition to the previous regime is cemented by no concensus on the future shape of Iran and authority is divided, with Ayatollah Khomeini a symbol of legitimacy, the revolutionary militants holding the guns and the *Tudeh* (Communist) Party in control of a strategic asset – the oil fields. How these groups reconcile their divergent goals will determine the policies of the new government, although it will be operating within certain parameters whatever its composition.

If the government of moderate technocrats appointed by Prime Minister Bazargan manages to gain actual rather than titular authority, it will act pragmatically. In the aftermath of the revolution, people's expectations will be greatly aroused even as the social and bureaucratic disruptions will have made their realization more difficult. The government will need to demonstrate quickly that the revolution has benefitted the people, which will necessitate some caution in economic planning. At present the writ of the provisional government does not extend very far, and the reassertion of authority throughout the country will be a high priority

104

for any government in Tehran, giving it little time for an assertive foreign policy in the near-term.

Still, the broad outline of Iran's foreign policy are clear: she will be neutralist or non-aligned, having left the Central Treaty Organization.[1] Her definition of security will be narrowed to coincide with national territory; consequently she will neither play an active role in the Persian Gulf nor extend assistance to nearby states threatened by subversion. Furthermore, Iran's military build-up will be arrested and fewer resources spent on defence.

Spare parts and training, especially for the air force, are practical necessities, so the new government will probably continue Iran's military relationship with the United States, though on a reduced scale. However, existing American missile-monitoring and early-warning stations in Iran will have to be dismantled and, despite the important American role in training Iran's officer-corps,[2] sources may gradually be further diversified, especially through purchases from France.[3]

Iran has now taken direct interest in the Arab–Israeli conflict, which some elements of the new regime define as one of religion. The visit of Yasser Arafat as a 'head of state' and a delegation of the Palestine Liberation Organization (PLO) to Tehran in mid-February underscored this interest. Apart from the element of *quid pro quo* in which Iranian revolutionaries acknowledge the military assistance and training received in southern Lebanon over the past decade, this theme – political involvement arising from religious concern – bids fair to become a focal point of Iran's foreign policy in the Middle East. Whether it is pursued vigorously with military manpower and financial support for the Palestinians, or is restricted to merely verbal encouragement, the effect on the political balance in the Middle East will be significant.

In sum, Iran's foreign policy will be more concentrated, with less emphasis on military security and more on declarations of militant nationalism. At best, this sensitivity to the condition of the Third World could produce an Iranian foreign policy comprised of equal parts of nationalism and pragmatism, similar to Algeria's. At worst, it could degenerate into indiscriminate interference and the export of revolution, on the Libyan model. Neither

approach is obviously more beneficial to Iran, but there is also no doubt that both are less consistent with Western interests than was the Shah's foreign policy.

Regional Reverberations

Very few governments in the Middle East are insulated from the wider ramifications of the turmoil in Iran: from Turkey, where economic problems and political violence have led to the imposition of martial law, to Egypt and Morocco, where President Sadat and King Hassan are vulnerable to a similar Left–Right coalition able to exploit the gulf between rich and poor. However, the immediate effects of the crisis will be felt by Iran's smaller neighbours, since her weakness, internal preoccupations and changed foreign policy will alter the balance of power in the Persian Gulf: Iraq's importance will increase, but the smaller sheikhdoms will be weakened.

If the central government is unable to reimpose its authority on outlying areas, the revival of tribalism and demands for provincial autonomy, or even secession, could have international repercussions. For example, current unrest in Tabriz in north-western Iran could lead to a repeat of the events in 1945, when a provisional government seeking to secede was set up in Azerbaijan with active Soviet support. Less dramatically, the current signs of a revival of Kurdish nationalism in Iran could have profound effects in Iraq and Turkey, whose Kurdish population number two and three million respectively. Similarly, the parallel weakening of the governments in Tehran and Islamabad may encourage the Baluchi populations straddling the Iran–Pakistan border to co-ordinate their efforts. A revival of ethnic or tribal, to the exclusion of national, loyalties could scarcely pass by the Arab population in Khuzestan in southern Iran, reviving friction with Iraq and Syria, which had supported their claims to the autonomy of 'Arabistan' in the 1960s.

Assuming that Iran remains intact and the government does regain control, the revolution would challenge her neighbours in two distinct ways: first as a model; second as a result of policy changes. The revolt brought together the Left and Right, the secular and sometimes doctrinaire Marxists with the religious traditionalists. It was in part a protest against an over-rapid, indiscriminate Westernization, the erosion of traditional values and life-styles and the pervasiveness of corruption, and in part a demand for political participation. The sheer mass of the opposition, combined with well-organized strikes in a key extractive industry, finally brought down the old order.

Iran's oil-rich neighbours are not equally susceptible to such a coalition. Saudi Arabia has more revenue, is more conscious of the religious element in planning modernization, and lacks a comparable middle class. Nevertheless, she can be criticized on human rights issues, corruption, an unequal income distribution, over-rapid growth and, especially, subservience to Western influence. In varying degrees all the oil-producing states are vulnerable to popular discontent, given the disjunction between economic growth and political institutions. In addition, the effect of the strikes in Iran on the attitudes of workers in key industries may have an enduring legacy in the Gulf.

Changes in Iran's policy have already had an effect. Perhaps of most strategic significance is the case of Oman, Iran's closest Arab ally before the revolution and the one most exposed to local subversion. Iran's decision not to continue support for that government has underscored the effect of the regime change in Tehran on Gulf security. Overlooking the main shipping channel from the Musandam Peninsula, Oman has few resources and fewer friends to secure her against either internal disorder or subversion instigated from across the border in the People's Democratic Republic of Yemen (PDRY), where a Soviet–Cuban presence has increased in recent years. The withdrawal of the Iranian guarantee leaves few acceptable alternatives. Britain is unwilling to increase her commitment, and Saudi Arabia, traditionally cool to Oman, cannot provide military assistance.

The change has affected the overall balance of forces in the Middle East, where the 'moderates' have been weakened, and will have a profound impact on Saudi Arabia. First, lacking the bond of kingship, the prospect for rivalry has increased. Second, since Iran has broken away from their common security partner – the West – bilateral dialogue will have to be more direct, increasing the possibility of friction. Third, and most important, Iran's revision to neutralism exposes Saudi Arabia's uncomfortable isolation

in Persian Gulf and OPEC politics. This exposure and pressure is further increased by the Iraqi–Syrian *rapprochement* since November, and by the failure of the Camp David formula to date. There will be considerable incentive for Saudi Arabia not to isolate herself further by supporting Camp David, or by increasing her production so as to freeze oil prices. The strain of the revolt in Iran will thus be felt in Saudi–US relations, since it will accentuate Saudi Arabia's vulnerability to local criticism as a supporter of the West, and increase Riyadh's pressure on Washington to demonstrate that this connection is mutually beneficial.

The crisis in Iran prompted the immediate revival of the moribund discussions on Gulf security. Saudi Arabia reached an agreement with Kuwait on the long-disputed neutral zone on their joint border, and Iraq reassured Kuwait about her territorial claims. Bahrain and Oman also showed a keen interest in concrete measures of co-operation, arguing that the upheaval in Iran affected their interests. Having had reasonable working relations with the Shah's regime since 1975, Iraq felt acutely threatened. In February her Foreign Minister expressed the hope that events in Iran would lead to co-operation between Iraq and Saudi Arabia in ensuring security in the Persian Gulf.

However, though the need for regional co-operation was underlined, the events in Iran contributed little to a clarification of how to deal with what are largely internal threats. The decline of Iran's power and contraction of her responsibilities raised serious questions about the kinds of response regional states could offer should guerrilla warfare revive in southern Oman. Saudi money may buy off irritants, but it cannot deal with specifically military threats. In the upper Gulf, Saudi co-operation with the sheikhdoms in ensuring their internal security should be sufficient for the present. To fill the void in Oman, Egypt has offered, at considerable political risk, to act as an all-purpose policeman, in exchange for modern weapons, worth billions of dollars, from the United States. This offer, contingent on the achievement of a peace settlement with Israel, reflects Egypt's changed security perceptions, and as an earnest Cairo has dispatched 200 troops to Oman to replace the contingent withdrawn by Iran.

Paradoxically, although both Israel and Egypt were alarmed at developments in Iran and its implications for the region, both hardened their terms for a Middle East settlement. Disturbed by the United States' inaction during the crisis, and reinforced in the belief that it has increased her value to the West as a strategic asset and as a dependable ally, Israel became more obdurate. Egypt, keenly aware of the changed balance between moderates and radicals in the region, was even less disposed than before to complete a settlement which would further isolate her among the Arab states. If the pressure on Saudi Arabia not to support the Camp David formula does increase, the prospect for a general agreement will have been wrecked as a direct result of events in Iran, which have also made the achievement of a settlement more urgent and costly.

In the longer run the effect of a change in policy may be felt most keenly in Iraq. If, for example, the new regime in Tehran saw itself as the protector of Shi'ites, the most natural focus for its attention would be Iraq, the location of the sect's most revered shrines. The political discrimination against Shi'ites in Iraq (there are none in the Cabinet), and their occasional clashes with the authorities (as in January 1977), have tended to encourage their radicalization – they are, for example, disproportionately involved in the Iraqi Communist Party. This would provide fertile ground for religious agitation from Iran. A policy of protection would also promote ties with Syria, since President Assad is himself an 'Alawi – an offshoot of Shi'ism. In sum, the revolution in Iran has implications for both monarchies and republics in the Middle East.

American Policy

The revolution in Iran is the greatest setback for American interests in the Middle East in the post-war era. The relationship with the Shah had deepened and intensified over thirty-seven years and the tenure of seven Presidents. In the early 1970s Iran became important not only as a dependable source of oil and as a stabilizing power in the Persian Gulf, but as a force for moderation in a wider Asian setting. In this she had been encouraged by the United States, whose longstanding involvement in Iran had grown in proportion to her stake in the region. For convenience, the United States equated the Shah with the nation, and dealt directly and exclusively with the monarch. The King was charming and brilliant but also extremely sensitive to slights, and Washington preferred not to upset him by raising unwelcome questions. Consequently, in the vital period of rapid economic growth (1972–6) the United States failed to encourage the Shah to build political institutions or decentralize authority.

It was an Iran on the brink of civil unrest that the Carter Administration inherited and embraced as an ally, despite doubts about her human rights record. Yet as events unfolded in 1978, the Administration's policies appeared half-hearted and even contradictory. There were errors of omission and commission; foremost among them was the failure to appreciate the gravity of the situation in time and devote systematic presidential attention to it. Washington's assessments were behind those of virtually every other government and independent observer, and this failure in simple analysis (*not* intelligence) narrowed its already thin margin of influence. This influence was further squandered by the style in which the Administration conducted its foreign policy.[4] Inconsistent statements, contradictory assessments, bureaucratic jockeying and inspired leaks were greatly amplified in the volatile political setting of Iran. The myths of pervasive Western influence and cunning Occidentals congenitally conspiring die hard in the Middle East, and Washington's curiously equivocal statements and desultory responses to the crisis lent credence to the Iranian view that Carter was 'dumping' the Shah. In the cacophony of voices one theme stood out: that the United States could not and would not intervene in Iran's internal affairs. After more than thirty years of pervasive interference, this statement during a crisis was an advertisement of retreat; to Iranians it signalled the withdrawal of the American veto against opposition to the Shah.

In other respects, too, Carter's policy was uninspiring. The response to President Brezhnev's 19 November warning regarding interference lacked the firmness required to protect an embattled ally.[5] Indeed, many interpreted the American response as tacit acquiescence in Iran's 'instant neutralization'. The poorly timed and executed dispatch of twelve unarmed F-15s

107

to Saudi Arabia and Sudan, and the indecision about deploying a naval contingent did little to limit the loss of confidence in the US.

Implications for the United States

The immediate practical problems created for the United States by a neutralist regime in Iran were clear: to minimize the disruption in the relationship so as to conserve access to oil, protect her technological secrets (e.g., in the avionics packages on the F-14s,) protect her citizens, and salvage as much as possible in the way of bases, facilities and monitoring stations on Iranian territory. These problems are in some respects the easiest to settle, for the new Iranian government still needs markets for her oil and technical assistance and spare parts to maintain her armed forces. Nevertheless, the withdrawal of guaranteed access to Iranian air and naval facilities – on which much of American contingency planning for the Persian Gulf was based – means Washington has to revise her assumptions and probably search for substitutes.

However, the more profound challenge to the West is less practical than conceptual. First, the reverse in Iran concerns Western assumptions about regional security and the 'twin-pillars' that were supposed to support it. More fundamentally, it raises questions about the precise meaning of security in areas undergoing rapid growth and disrupted by often lop-sided modernization. This growth largely results from the revenues generated by oil exports which the West is eager to encourage. Yet the social strains arising from rapid growth are likely to undermine the reliability of these countries as long-term suppliers, or indeed as allies.

If the United States embraces the dynastic leaders on the southern littoral of the Gulf, the opposition, if it comes to power, could reject the West as the defender of the old order. How closely should American ties be identified with a particular leadership if the country and region is subject to change and revolution? On the other hand, given the immense stakes involved, how can the West avoid this identification and still hope to secure oil on beneficial terms?

President Carter has reiterated that the United States cannot 'control events' in other countries and does not 'oppose change'.[6] However, the issue is not one of controlling change but of seeking to affect its pace and direction. The timely use of influence (intervention, if you will) may go a long way towards conserving important interests. The role of virtuous spectator does little to reassure allies of the depth of the American commitment, or to protect Western interests – far better that the United States should use more influence, encourage reform, promote human rights and political institutionalization.

The Iranian crisis has set the issue of American influence and commitment into sharp relief. Clearly the current political mood in the United States discourages activism, and Congressional constraints on covert and limited commitments of troops in the War Powers Act further restrict the President's options. In this setting it is difficult to see how Secretary of Defense Brown's visit to the Persian Gulf in February could 'reassure' the United States' remaining allies. Assertions that Saudi Arabia's security was 'pivotal' for American interests and that the United States would take concrete measures to arm and defend the Gulf states simply lack credibility. The asymmetry in US–Soviet instruments for covert activity, in the use of proxies, and in the reliance on force as a political instrument, strengthen these doubts. The relevance of the American commitment to defending the oil-producing states is also in question if it is limited to defence against external agression. The design of 'interventionary forces' for as yet undefined contingencies in the Persian Gulf would be more reassuring if the Gulf rulers were not in doubt about American policy short of the apocalypse.

Harold Brown's tour of the area suggested that a larger, more visible Western presence might be in the offing. This might include, in addition to arms sales to friendly regional states (the Yemen Arab Republic and Egypt), new military bases, more frequent naval deployments to show the flag, and occasional military exercises on land. Diego Garcia might be expanded to facilitate access and airlift into the area, or Oman's Masirah island developed. It is important that any increased involvement is not given a purely military flavour. Interventionary forces will need to be assessed with reference to the political setting and constraints operating on local regimes as well as by comparison with Soviet capabilities. But it appears most unlikely that the West will be able to continue its present relationship with these states unless it is prepared to become more intensively engaged in the region.

Soviet Involvement

After 1964 the Soviet government established correct, if not cordial, relations with the Shah. Commerce between the two countries had developed to a point where Iran was the largest market for Soviet goods in the Middle East, and the host for over 3,500 Soviet technicians. In addition, the Shah's pragmatism and long rule gave the relationship a degree of stability and predictability welcome to the Soviet Union. However, after 1973 Iran's relatively equidistant stance between the two blocs was supplanted by a move towards the West, involving a tighter military integration, an arms build-up, increased trade, and a wider and more assertive diplomacy in Asia. The last increased the points at which Iran and the Soviet Union clashed, whether in Oman, Somalia or support for President Sadat. The strain in the relationship was evident after 1976 as the Shah sought greater independence, which Moscow defined as provocative.

Despite a clear preference for a more accommodating government, the Soviet Union was careful not to alienate the existing regime totally. Only after mid-December, when the overthrow of the monarchy seemed certain, did the Soviet Union increase her criticism, but even then she was careful not to support a particular person or faction. A common theme in Soviet broadcasts was the necessity for the diminution of Western influence. Prominence was also given to the view of the *Tudeh* (Communist) Party that the naming of a provisional government 'is only the completion of the first stage on the people's road to final victory'.[7]

The degree of Soviet involvement in the revolt is difficult to assess. Direct involvement appears to have been limited within Iran to covert assistance to the opposition in the publication of political leaflets. Outside Iran, support for the *Tudeh* Party has been appreciable, and it may have extended to the political organization of the oil-workers in southern Iran. Indirectly, Soviet support for the opposi-

tion has been notable in the supply of arms directly to the PLO, the Popular Front for the Liberation of Palestine and Afghanistan, which found their way to Iran. None of these activities determined the revolt's outcome, but cumulatively they affected its course.

Repercussions and Implications

The Soviet Union stands to gain from the revolt in Iran. Since the Shah was identified with the West, his removal was widely considered a direct set-back for his Western allies. It exposed the limits of their influence and undermined the credibility of their commitments. In addition, the upheaval in Iran was anti-Western in a deeper cultural-spiritual sense; as a protest movement against indiscriminate modernization it served as a warning to other Muslim nations.

The current political situation in Iran is of course unpredictable. For both the Soviet Union and the West the outcome is uncertain, and they share a desire for some predictability or stability. Continued turmoil, economic dislocations and national disintegration pose problems for both blocs, interrupting the supply of oil for the West and gas for the East. But this shared interest, whether for access to resources or in the avoidance of super-power confrontation, does not go much further. The West's desire for a strong centre to ensure Iran's national unity and the maintenance of her territorial integrity contrasts with the Soviet preference for a weak central government with looser control.

Soviet support for the revolutionary opposition is therefore understandable. Despite the religious overtones which gave it a cloak of legitimacy, the opposition never seriously threatened to become a stong Islamic government, for its predictable splintering into groups of varying degrees of radicalism and secularism guaranteed unstable coalitions and weak governments unable to challenge the Soviet Union.[8] Tehran will now be much weakened in its relations with Moscow, more susceptible to pressure and more tempted to accommodate her interests. The one important exception is the price of gas supplied to the southern provinces of the Soviet Union, which will be increased to the prevailing world price.[9] In this, as in all decisions relating to Iran's natural resources, the new government will be more militantly nationalist, pressing for maximum returns. It may therefore be reluctant to engage in the barter of Iran's oil for East European goods which the Shah encouraged. Whether or not the new regime in Iran will be sufficiently strong to resist Soviet blandishments, Soviet interest in Iran will continue to grow, as a neighbour, a potential supplier of Eastern Europe, and as an entry point into Persian Gulf politics. Moscow's overtures to Saudi Arabia have already increased in the wake of Iran's collapse, encouraging any tendencies Riyadh may have to secure her position further. Iran's removal as a strong buffer, combined with the unravelling of the CENTO states, has improved the prospects for Soviet access to and influence in the Arabian peninsula.

Oil

Iran has accounted for 10 per cent of all oil production and has been the world's second largest exporter. Of a total daily production of 5·9 million barrels, approximately 800,000 barrels were retained for domestic consumption, the balance exported. Equally important, as the largest non-Arab exporter Iran was a dependable source of supply, immune to pressures to embargo. This was critical to Israel and South Africa, which were disproportionately dependent on Iranian supplies (60 per cent and 90 per cent respectively).

Oil exports, disrupted in October, ground to a halt by the end of December. The effect was not immediately felt by most states because of the transit time for delivery and the existence of large stocks. Nevertheless, it was clear that the prolonged withdrawal of 5 million barrels a day (b/d) from the international market would have severe consequences. The United States depended on Iranian oil for 5 per cent of her total consumption (10 per cent of imports), some 900,000 b/d. Europe was more heavily dependent, varying from 7 per cent for France, 18 per cent for Britain and 20 per cent for West Germany. (Iran also accounted for 18 per cent of Japan's oil needs.)

South Africa and Israel were naturally affected most quickly and severely by the termination of supplies. The former resorted to expensive spot-purchases on the international market and sought to increase (expensive) domestic

substitutes. The latter, already engaged in negotiations with Egypt, appraised the withdrawal from the Sinai in a new light. Although the Alma oil-fields in the Gulf of Suez produce only 15 per cent of Israel's oil needs, their importance as a proximate and dependable source of supply suddenly increased and Israel's attitude to them hardened: first, because the new Iranian government's policy of forbidding all exports to Israel is likely to be permanent; second, the assurance of American supplies extended to Israel by Henry Kissinger in 1975 raised a different kind of problem in terms of dependence and susceptibility to American leverage, unwelcome to Israel. Nor could alternative suppliers, such as Mexico, be expected to supply the bulk of Israel's oil needs without becoming subject to pressure.

The immediate effects of the drop in supplies was cushioned by increased production in other states, particularly Saudi Arabia, leaving a net short-fall globally in early 1979 of 2 million b/d. Thus, in practice, the United States lost half a million b/d, corresponding to 2½ per cent of total consumption. But on top of this it was clear that an extended disruption of Iran's exports would be much more costly. The turning point came in early March, when the last shipments from Iran reached their destinations and when importers traditionally increased their purchases to build up stocks for the autumn. Furthermore, increased exports by other oil-producing states cannot go on indefinitely, and certainly not at current prices. Saudi Arabia, which increased her production in December from 8·5 to 10·5 million b/d, cut back to 9·5 million b/d by February 1979. This is still 1 million b/d more than she wants to produce, and to underline the point she has charged a premium on it. Continued imbalance between supply and demand will inexorably drive oil prices above the staggered 14·5 per cent increase agreed by OPEC for 1979. In early 1979 several oil-producing states (Qatar, Abu Dhabi, Kuwait and Venezuela) announced increases, with the prospect of a much larger concerted increase by the year's end.

More important than the economic will be the political pressures on the oil-producing states, in particular Saudi Arabia, as a result of developments in Iran. Even assuming the technical capability and the acquiescence of the more radical oil-field workers, there is considerable confusion as to the Iranian government's attitude on oil exports. At the very least it is likely to be militant on oil prices within OPEC and conservationist in the levels of production permitted. Preliminary indications suggest that, since oil exports will be geared to the need for revenues, which will be used to sustain a lower level of growth, they will not exceed 3 million b/d. Even though there may be strong short-term pressures within Iran to restore the economy through larger exports, it appears unlikely that this figure will be exceeded.[10] To a revolutionary regime requiring revenues, a more attractive solution will be to raise prices or conduct spot-sales on the open market.

As a result of Iran's example, Saudi Arabia will become vulnerable to the charge of over-producing oil to keep prices low – a charge less easy to deflect now that she is isolated within OPEC, and a policy more difficult to defend in the absence of American pressure on Israel to conclude a Middle East settlement. Other pressures against production beyond her economic needs may build up within Saudi-Arabia, given the salient lesson of Iran regarding over-rapid development. Saudi Arabia may consequently be reluctant to continue to fill the shortfall created by Iran's crisis and be passive in OPEC councils in order to escape charges of acting as a 'Western agent'.

Conclusions

The ripples of the crisis in Iran have been far-reaching. Few countries have been left unaffected, the industrial states by their dependence on oil and interest in stable prices, the West by the undermining of its assumptions about security, China by her rivalry with the Soviet Union, and Iran's neighbours in the Middle East and the Muslim world in general.

A recognition of the limits to the United States' power and the ability to involve herself world-wide was the original rationale underlying the Nixon Doctrine. This policy of retrenchment, or selective engagement, involved building up friendly states in important regions. In the Persian Gulf this policy resulted in arms transfers, technical assistance, and training which, paradoxically, necessitated greater involvement. Inevitably it meant identification with the ruling regimes. It also entailed the devolution of greater responsibilities onto regional states to assure their own security. It is now evident that both consequences may be costly – the states' political foundations may be too narrow for the assumption of those responsibilities which exacerbate their weaknesses and are no substitute for American involvement. The problems for the West remain how to protect its own interests without too close an identification with regimes which may be swept away in the process of modernization.

There are no simple formulas. The political constraints on activism as well as a recognition of the limits to American power pervasively condition the diplomacy of the current US government. Yet the inability to 'order events' should not become an excuse for the abdication of responsibility for influencing them. Western interests are not easy to defend – for example, a simple interest in the flow of oil would be much easier to ensure than the need for its flow at a certain rate and price level. This complex requirement is unlikely to be achieved by passivity. Regional allies have a right to demand a coherent and forthright policy which minimizes their confusion and anxiety. Pending the development of alternative sources, or radical conservation measures, the dependence of the West and Japan on Persian Gulf oil will increase, and there are strong indications that Soviet bloc interest is also increasing. Given the immense stakes, a code of conduct in this region will have to be worked out to guarantee the flow of oil and reduce the risk of superpower confrontation.

Threats to the region which originate locally must also be met, although the needs are various and often contradictory. For example, the attempt to settle one local conflict (the Arab–Israeli) which affects Persian Gulf security, if pursued according to a particular formula such as Camp David, may complicate rather than ameliorate Saudi security. To defuse sources of local conflict on the Arabian peninsula is somewhat easier and requires less external assistance. Existing structures, such as the Arab League, should be revitalized to sanction peaceful settlements. The encouragement of regional co-operation through aid and trade (a policy pursued by the Shah) will now have to be borne principally by Saudi Arabia, which has followed the course with mixed success in Oman, the Yemen Arab Republic and the PDRY. The role of outside powers will be limited to the provision of arms and diplomatic support, and should include receptivity to states which appear prepared to pursue less disruptive policies, such as Iraq since 1975 (and the PDRY briefly until July 1978). If small local conflicts become endemic, selective guarantees, such as on oil installations, or freedom of access to supplies, may be needed. The least disruptive guarantors would be Europeans – Britain has already played a limited role in Oman.

Finally, there are threats to the region's security which originate in domestic politics and are the most resistant to outside influence. They may stem from economic failures, cultural confusion, or the inadequacies of the central government, taking the form of coups, revolutions or demands for autonomy. Separatist forces exist in Iran, Iraq, Pakistan, Oman and potentially in Turkey; as a newly formed nation-state, Saudi Arabia is not immune to similar pressures.

Few of these domestic sources of instability are without international ramifications. Strengthening the pattern of non-intervention among the states concerned will help to contain these threats – witness the evolution of Iranian–Iraqi relations after 1975. But the influence of external powers will also be important if it is used to encourage local allies to nurture political institutions and governments responsive to their citizens. Constructive involvement and timely advice will be needed if political change, which is inevitable, is to be accommodated with minimum disruption. A definition of security which encompasses the possibility of change but which seeks to moderate it will necessitate a diplomacy that avoids the twin extremes of outright dictation and excessive deference to the alleged uniqueness of indigenous cultures. It will also require economic assistance, and the European nations should participate in multinational consortia which extend aid to the most needy states – Egypt, Sudan, Turkey, the YAR and the PDRY.

The revolt in Iran has lent fresh urgency to the need for a flexible but comprehensive policy towards this vital area. It will require not fresh declarations of reassurance but systematic involvement equal to the stakes concerned. The lesson of Iran may well be that, without such involvement, much greater risks will be run.

NOTES

[1] The US was only an associate member of CENTO. To acknowledge the importance of Iran, which was not covered by any defence arrangement with the US, a bilateral Executive Agreement was concluded in 1959. Its wording was loose, requiring in the event of aggression such appropriate action as may subsequently be agreed. This is the only formal defence agreement between the two states; its fate is still unclear.

[2] Since 1945 some 12,000 Iranian students and officers have been trained by the United States.

[3] The Shah sought various suppliers for the naval and ground forces but the air force was exclusively American-supplied, partly for logistical convenience.

[4] The influence, such as it was, was not enhanced by President Carter's repeated advertisement of the United States' limited power in January and February 1979.

[5] Mr Brezhnev said that 'any interference, especially military interference, in the affairs of Iran' would be considered by the Soviet Union 'as a matter affecting its security interests'.

[6] President Carter's speech, 'America's role in the Changing World', at the Georgia Institute of Technology, 20 February 1979.

[7] Radio Moscow, 'World Service', 15 February 1979. Text in BBC Summary of World Broadcasts, SU/6045/A4/1, 17 February 1979.

[8] Although the Muslim population in the Soviet Central Asian Republics are becoming increasingly important in the demographic balance, and Soviet sensitivity about their loyalties are expected to grow correspondingly, there is no evidence of a religious revival in the Soviet Union. In addition, although Iran's 1,250-mile border with the Soviet Union is highly permeable, it has tended to be so in one direction, North to South.

[9] Iran's export of gas to the Soviet Union started in 1970 and is due to expand with the completion of a second pipeline in 1981. By this practical, if complicated, arrangement both Iran and the Soviet Union gain hard currency. The price Iran has charged for gas delivered for Soviet consumption has nonetheless been below market prices. This owed something to the Shah's acknowledgement that the arrangement was part of a political relationship, rather than a purely commercial transaction.

[10] Iran is estimated to have lost some $6 billion from the interruption of oil exports between November 1978 and March 1979.

6   SHIFTS IN THE ARAB WORLD

In 1978 Egypt's moves towards establishing a peace agreement with Israel profoundly affected all alignments within the Arab world. Superficially, Egypt's action united against her the Palestine Liberation Organization (PLO) and all the Arab states with the exceptions of Oman and Sudan and the qualified exceptions of Morocco and North Yemen. But the apparent Arab unity against President Sadat – endorsed in early November at a summit meeting of twenty states and the PLO in Baghdad – concealed deep differences of approach within the opposition camp. For the sake of unanimity the moderate pro-Western Arab states, such as Saudi Arabia, the Gulf states and Jordan, agreed on a series of sanctions to be taken against Egypt if she signed a separate agreement with Israel, and in return Libya, Iraq and other hard-line states for the first time accepted the principle of a political solution to the Arab–Israeli dispute. But the extent to which either group had modified its real attitude was doubtful. Saudi Arabia and Jordan hesitated to declare total opposition to US policy, while the hard-line states did not abandon their hope for the destruction of Israel.

The most significant development in Baghdad was that the rival Ba'athist regimes of Iraq and Syria, which had patched up their differences just before the meeting, were now working together. These differences had hitherto prevented Iraq from joining Syria, Libya, Algeria, South Yemem and the PLO in the self-styled 'Front of Steadfastness' established after President Sadat's visit to Jerusalem in November 1977. This new entente, which seemed more serious than any of the two countries' previous attempts at reconciliation, was the most important change in the Arab spectrum in 1978. However, it remains uncertain how far they will fulfil their declared intention to move towards full political union or to reinforce the Syrian front with Israel with Iraqi troops.

Saudi Arabia and the Arabian Peninsula

During 1978 Saudi Arabia continued to act (and to be perceived) as the foremost stabilizing power in the area. From her massive capital surplus, she extended foreign aid to several Middle Eastern and Islamic countries in order to achieve her fundamental goals: to help Arab states, especially those confronting Israel; to back up conservative powers in repelling Soviet and Communist influence; and to assist Muslim states in re-establishing or reinforcing Islamic social values. Thus, some 90% of Saudi aid in 1978 went to Islamic countries, with the Arab Middle Eastern and Gulf states receiving the lion's share.

Saudi Arabia's predominance among the Gulf sheikhdoms was extended when the intelligence instruments of the United Arab Emirates, Kuwait, Bahrain, Qatar and Oman were linked to her own security agency. Hoping to prevent a resurgence of the Dhofari revolt in Oman, she increased aid to that country in 1978 by some $800 million, of which about $250 million was earmarked for the development of Dhofar province and $350 million for defence. North Yemen (Yemen Arab Republic, or YAR) received similar extensive aid, with Saudi Arabia taking almost total responsibility for balancing the country's budget as well as making large subventions to the YAR armed forces. Saudi Arabia's influence in North Yemen was such that her military attaché maintained direct and privileged automatic access to the YAR officer corps. And without Saudi blessings, Col. Ali Abdullah Sabih would certainly not have been able to succeed to power in Sana in June when a South Yemeni envoy assassinated President Ghashmi (whose predecessor had been murdered in October 1977 on the eve of a conciliatory visit to South Yemen).

Two days after Ghashmi's death President Ali of the South Yemen (People's Democratic Republic of Yemen, or PDRY), who favoured improving his country's relations with Saudi Arabia, was executed after a coup by a pro-Soviet faction in Aden. This extraordinary conjunction of events exacerbated the long-standing antagonism between the PDRY and Saudi Arabia, and the latter sponsored an Arab League meeting in July which imposed sanctions on the PDRY, including the suspension of financial and technical assistance.

Throughout the remainder of the year instability in both Yemens was punctuated by occasional border clashes, continuing a relationship which, reflecting the bitter legacy of the civil war which ended a decade ago, has alternated between discussions about unity and outright hostilities. The divisions between the more conservative YAR and the Marxist PDRY have been further complicated by their foreign-policy alignments, with Saudi Arabia's dominant influence in Sana being matched by Soviet, Iraqi and Libyan influence in Aden. Saudi Arabia has always viewed the secretive and rigidly ideological regime in Aden (the closest approximation to a Communist state there is in the Arab world) as the primary destabilizing agent in the region. Rich, vulnerable and underpopulated in relation to both her resources and her neighbours, she has been cautious about any moves towards unity between Sana and Aden, since a united Yemen, whatever its political orientation, would exercise great power in the Arabian peninsula. Moreover, Saudi Arabia depends on Sana for at least a million labourers who, if organized or politicized, could pose a serious problem of internal security.

The PDRY's closer alignment with the USSR in 1978, combined with Soviet influence in Ethiopia, gave the USSR a considerable foothold for exerting pressure on the Arabian peninsula, and intensified Saudi fears of disruption in the region. In February King Khalid publicly called on members of the Arab League to support Somalia in her conflict with Ethiopia, saying that Saudi Arabia had already provided her with moral and financial aid, and would give more if Somalia requested it. Indeed, in 1978 Saudi aid, primarily intended to bolster Somalia's war effort against Ethiopia, was estimated at about $300 million. In April the Foreign Minister, Prince Faisal, reiterated Saudi fears by declaring that 'foreign presence in the Horn of Africa was a major factor leading to instability and insecurity in the region'.

One of Saudi Arabia's most crucial concerns during 1978 was the perpetuation and development of her friendly relations with the United States. She supplied over 25% of US oil needs in 1978, and some 85% of her accumulated financial surpluses was held in dollars. Moreover, nearly $35 billion of her 1978 foreign assests were estimated to be in US government securities, with a further $24 billion in other US interests, and the Joint Saudi-US Committee for Economic Co-operation handled contracts worth over $650 million. However, Saudi Arabia was almost totally dependent on American military and technological aid, with various US companies and government agencies providing support for her regular army, National Guard, coast guard, air defence and national airline. It was primarily for this reason that Saudi Arabia embarked on the long, sometimes bitter and eventually successful struggle, involving fierce lobbying of the US Congress, to obtain the F-15 fighter. To the Riadh government, getting Washington to sell it this aircraft was a political rather than a strategic matter, representing a continuing American commitment to its security.

A major and persistent point of tension in Saudi-American relations during 1978 related to US support for Israel. Saudi Arabia consistently urged Washington to exert far greater pressure on Israel to relinquish the occupied territories. As the foremost Islamic country, she could not condone continuing Israeli jurisdiction over Jerusalem (the third most venerated city in Islam) and thus felt unable to support the Camp David agreement, in which there was no mention of Jerusalem. More important, she doubted that the agreement would provide a long-term solution. Yet, Saudi Arabia was not prepared publicly to condemn President Sadat's policies. Consequently, in the November Baghdad summit meeting of Arab states opposed to the Egyptian initiative, she was the primary sponsor of the moderate resolutions that stopped short of completely isolating Egypt and President Sadat. In this as in her other diplomatic initiatives in 1978, Saudi Arabia used her influence to moderate political activities in the area, and particularly to act as an arbiter in inter-Arab relations.

Whether this policy could be sustained indefinitely in the light of the Syrian-Iraqi reconciliation and Saudi anxiety over events in Iran was not clear at the end of the year, but the decision taken at the December OPEC meeting in Abu Dhabi to raise the oil price by 14.5% over the next year suggested Saudi unwillingness to take decisions unpopular in the Arab world. Sheikh Yamani's comment that 'Unless the situation in Iran is rectified [the West] will have to pay much higher prices than the current OPEC increase' referred as much to the political as to the economic implications of developments in Iran.

Iraq

Potentially one of the most significant events in the Arab world in 1978 was the reintegration of Iraq into the mainstream of Arab politics. In the first nine months of the year, Iraq's isolation was greater than ever. The Ba'athist leadership in Baghdad continued its militant 'rejectionist' stand on Israel, advocating, along with the Libyan government, the maximalist position of not recognizing Israel and accepting only a 'secular democratic Palestine'. In the first six months Iraq also pursued an abusive propaganda campaign against the 'capitulationist' and 'client' Egyptian and Saudi governments, although in practice her policies towards them were far less intransigent. Routine cultural and economic relations with Egypt, which had been revived in the wake of the October 1973 war, if unspectacular, were unaffected by the ideological invective, and Iraqi-Saudi relations tended towards regional co-operation rather than conflict.

In contrast, Iraq's relations with Syria and the PLO during the same period were antagonistic in both word and deed. Iraq continued to accuse the 'Syrian ruling clique' of 'selling out' to Israel, calling President Assad's position 'traitorous' and a 'stab in the back of the Arab nation'. Because of her quarrel with Syria, whom she accused of being no better than Egypt in accepting the principle of a political settlement with Israel, Iraq remained outside the 'Front of Steadfastness'. Relations between the two became so bad that they denied air space to each other's airlines, closed borders and reduced their embassies to an almost skeletal representation. Also a running feud between the PLO and the Iraqi-backed guerrilla group, the Arab Liberation Movement (ALM), resulted in the assassination of several moderate PLO leaders in London and Paris, the reprisal bombing of ALM offices in Beirut, and the attempted assassination of Iraqi ambassadors in London and Karachi.

The Egyptian-Israeli Camp David agreement enabled Iraq to free herself from this self-imposed isolation and return to mainstream Arab politics, and she immediately issued an invitation for an Arab summit to be held in Baghdad to discuss the effect of Egypt's apparent withdrawal from the Arab-Israeli conflict, declared her willingness to station troops on the Golan Heights in Syria and suspended all propaganda campaigns against the Syrian government. High-level envoys were then sent to Damascus, Riadh and Amman to emphasize the new-found Iraqi spirit of co-operation. The intensive diplomatic activity led to the Baghdad summit during the first week of November, which brought to a culmination dramatic reconciliations between Iraq, Syria and the PLO (Iraq giving her first tacit support for the formula embodied in General Assembly Resolution 242 as a basis for peace negotiations) and between the PLO and Jordan.

On 24–26 October, just before the Baghdad summit, President Assad of Syria had travelled to Iraq for a historic meeting with President Bakr which resulted in a 'Charter of Joint Action', ending ten years of overt hostility and pledging future co-operation. The Charter called for the establishment of a joint steering committee to oversee military, political, economic and cultural co-operation and established, in principle, a joint military command. At the end of January 1979 a further meeting was held between Assad and Saddam Hussein (Vice-Chairman of the Revolutionary Council, but in practice Iraq's real ruler) in Damascus, a mutual defence pact was concluded, and guidelines for a future unified state were established. There was clearly still a long way to go before such a state (with, it was claimed, one name, one flag, one national anthem and one President, alternately Iraqi and Syrian) came into being, but the two countries continued to move towards greater co-operation, if not unity. At the end of February the 650-km oil line that links the Iraqi oilfields with the Syrian port of Banias was reopened after a two-year closure, and a further meeting of the two heads of government was planned for sometime in April 1979.

In other respects, too, Iraq shed her earlier image, establishing greater independence from the USSR. Although the Soviet Union remained Iraq's principal arms supplier, the war in the Horn of Africa divided them, with Iraq maintaining her long-standing support for the Eritrean secessionists and Arab Somalia, and Moscow switching its support to Ethiopia – and, ironically, finding itself side by side with Israeli experts. In May 1978 the Iraqi government executed 21 Communists for attempting to organize cells within the armed forces 'to subvert the state', and in an important interview in July the Iraqi leader, Saddam Hussein, acknowledged that this had been intended as a warning against outside interference. Deeply concerned about the Soviet-assisted April coup in Afghanistan, the Iraqi regime was clearly anxious to maintain its autonomy and put some distance between itself and the USSR. Baghdad continued to support the Eritreans (mainly with small arms) and refused to allow either Soviet overflights or the use of Iraqi soil for staging facilities for equipment destined for Ethiopia.

By the end of 1978 the Iraqi leaders had successfully discarded their reputation as the 'wild men of Arab politics'. Strong mutual interests suggested that the Syrian-Iraqi entente might last longer than other similar associations in the Arab world and might gradually overcome the deep-rooted antipathy between the two Ba'ath regimes. Iraq's immense oil reserves (probably second only to Saudi Arabia's), in conjunction with Iran's current difficulties, gave Iraq special significance in the Middle East. In Saddam Hussein she has an energetic leader with increasing influence in the Arab world. To return to active participation in Arab politics Iraq had to modify her extremism by, *inter alia*, reaching agreement with Arafat's faction of the PLO, which had strongly suggested a willingness to accept a political arrangement based on a

Palestinian West Bank–Gaza state (see p. 62). This pragmatism in Iraqi policy is a precondition for her increased influence in the Arab world.

Syria and Lebanon

President Sadat's peace initiative placed Syria in a clear dilemma which lasted throughout 1978, as she tried to maintain a balance between support for the PLO and outright opposition to Egyptian policies, on the one hand, and avoidance of a war with Israel which could only be disastrous, on the other. In January there was an increase in Soviet military supplies, including surface-to-air missiles, tanks and aircraft, and later in the year Syria also received some French and West German arms, partly financed by Libya. The defence allocation in Syria's 1978 budget was $1,100 million, about one quarter of the total and a 10% increase on 1977. But the quarrel with Iraq represented a fatal weakness in the northern front with Israel, and even relations with Jordan were cool in the earlier part of 1978, because of King Hussein's refusal to condemn President Sadat's peace initiative outright. Following Camp David there came an improvement in relations with Jordan and at the end of October, when President Assad made his first visit to Baghdad, a reconciliation with Iraq.

Syria's immediate preoccupation remained the Lebanon, where 30,000 of her troops continued to form the bulk of the Arab Deterrent Force and cost her an estimated $70 million a month. In January there seemed to be better prospects of an entente between the various political factions which could lead to a strengthening of President Sarkis' authority and assist the building up of new Lebanese security forces, more representative of the whole Lebanese population and less dominated by right-wing Christians. But in February there occurred the first serious clash between Syrian troops and Christian militia backed by some Lebanese right-wing officers. Relations between Syria and most of the Maronites (her former allies of 1976) deteriorated throughout the summer.

The Syrian dilemma was clearly demonstrated when Israel invaded southern Lebanon on 14 March to try to clear the area of Palestinian guerrillas and their bases. Syrian forces remained north of the Litani River in order to avoid war with Israel, and it was left to Iraq to send arms and volunteers to help the Palestinians and their Lebanese leftist allies. Although Israeli forces withdrew in stages from the Lebanese territory they had occupied, handing most of it over to the newly-arrived UN Interim Force in Lebanon (UNIFIL), they gave clear support to the Lebanese Christian militia and handed the last strip of territory along the border over to them. In this strip the militia continued to defy both UNIFIL and newly-constituted units of the Lebanese army sent to take up positions south of the Litani. In May, Syria warned the Palestinians against their continuing clashes with UNIFIL and also agreed to a renewal of the mandate of the UN peace-keeping force in the Golan Heights. On the other hand, she roundly condemned the 27 April declaration signed by 74 of 99 members of the Lebanese parliament calling for an end to all Palestinian (and non-Palestinian) armed action on Lebanese territory. The contradiction in the Syrian position was evident.

The increasingly open alliance between Lebanese Christians and Israel, vaunted by the Maronite leadership, further exacerbated Syria's relations with the Christians. So did the murderous struggle which developed during the summer between the Lebanese Falangists, the largest body of organized Christians, and the supporters of ex-President Franjieh in the north, Syria's only remaining allies in Lebanon. There were severe clashes in July and again in September and October. Tension rose in the area as everyone expected Syrian and Palestinian action to try to nullify the effects of Camp David. Syrian forces surrounded and bombarded Christian east Beirut, and Israeli planes regularly overflew the city to demonstrate their support for the Christians. Syria allowed the PLO to take up advanced positions against the Christians, and the situation became so threatening that a hastily-convened meeting of Arab foreign ministers in Lebanon arranged for Syrian forces to be withdrawn from the perimeter of east Beirut and replaced by non-Syrian troops.

117

An uneasy calm was restored, but the Lebanon's effort to recover from civil war had received a terrible setback. The port of Beirut was closed, security was so bad that most employees in the city were afraid to go to work, and many factories in east Beirut were destroyed. Perhaps the most serious effect was that the revival of bitter sectarian antagonisms seemed to have destroyed President Sarkis' last opportunity of restoring a unitary state with Syrian support. The only sign of anything favouring Lebanese unity was that the Maronites had learned how little effective support they could expect from the West, which tended to blame them for the latest fighting.

Within Syria President Assad retained a strong hold on the country. There were, however, continued sporadic incidents of sabotage and murder, directed mainly against the Alawite minority of which the President is a member, and in April his government announced an increase in counter-terrorist security measures. A plebiscite on 8 February elected Assad to a second five-year presidential term by a high majority. Syria's financial problems seemed likely to be eased by the results of the Baghdad summit in November, when the Arab oil states, including Iraq, decided to increase aid to Syria so as to strengthen the northern front with Israel. The morale of Syrian troops in Lebanon, who suffered severe casualties in the fighting with the Christian militia in the late summer, remained a major concern. Syria continued to find herself entangled in a situation in which she had little to gain and much to lose and from which she could see no way to disentangle herself. Additional Syrian troops were sent to Mount Lebanon in November and December, and there was no prospect of Syria being able to remove the bulk of her army from Lebanon.

The PLO and Jordan

The apparent unity of the PLO in total opposition first to President Sadat's peace initiative and then to the Camp David agreements concealed considerable differences of opinion and attitude. During the year, the moderate faction of the PLO, led by Arafat, attempting to assure its own position, willingly talked with a wide variety of states with differing views on the accords in ways that could not have been supported by important elements in the PLO or by some of its allies in the Front of Steadfastness.

Arafat mended his fences with Iraq, held meetings with Sadat and the USSR, sent a message to Washington via a US Congressman that the PLO would renounce the use of force against Israel if a Palestinian state were created in the West Bank and the Gaza Strip, treated Syria with great care so as to avoid conflict in Lebanon, and renewed a dialogue with Jordan. In his talk with King Hussein in November, the first meeting between Hussein and a PLO leader since 1972, Arafat suggested that the two should 'co-ordinate' their activities in regard to the West Bank and also requested that the PLO be allowed once more to operate along the Jordan Valley. Hussein agreed to the first, loosely expressed proposal and flatly rejected the second, recognizing the dangers that it involved for his own position. Arafat's motive in attempting to reconcile the long-standing enmity between Jordan and the PLO seems to have been to ensure that Jordan would not join in the negotiations.

The question of who should negotiate for the Palestinians under occupation was a crucial one in the jockeying within the Arab world. Because the United States was unable to give Hussein satisfactory answers to the series of questions he had posed on sovereignty for the Palestinians, the King had already reluctantly decided that he would be forced to align himself with the rejectionists. Thus Arafat's action, which was regarded by the hard-liners as diluting the 1974 Rabat resolution (proclaiming the PLO as the sole legitimate negotiator for the Palestinians), merely strengthened Hussein's position as a potential accredited negotiator for the West Bank.

While the PLO enjoyed considerable popularity on the West Bank, even moderate leaders regarding it as the sole legitimate representative, King Hussein had been using his considerable assets to improve his position. For example, it was he who channelled Saudi subsidies to the Palestinians under occupation, because Saudi Arabia was unwilling to allow the PLO to handle this. It is true that the leaders of the Palestinians under the occupation, caught between Israel, Jordan and the PLO, were unable to take any clear-cut line on the Camp David agreements; because the PLO was excluded, it was impossible for them to come out publicly for the accords.

Yet, when and if the negotiations ever get to the point of seriously discussing Arab sovereignty for the West Bank and the Gaza strip, many of these leaders may refuse to accept PLO directions, and may instead insist on playing a central role either alone or in conjunction with Jordan.

7 EGYPT AND ISRAEL:
The search for peace

It was clear from the beginning of the year that in seeking a settlement it would be impractical to work for simultaneous resolution of all the outstanding issues which had resulted in Arab-Israeli hostilities for over thirty years. It also was clear that to sustain the momentum established by President Sadat's historic visit to Israel in late 1977 would take more than US help – it would require full US participation. But even with this participation, the two sides found it impossible to make the remaining compromises necessary to assure the signing of a treaty by the end of the year. Egypt found the pressure exerted by other Arab states, culminating in the November meeting in Baghdad, more vigorous and serious than expected. Israeli leaders were buffeted by internal factional problems, and Prime Minister Begin would have found it difficult to accommodate all the demands being made by Presidents Sadat and Carter even if he wanted to. At the year's end, while much progress had been made there was still a large gap between the two sides, and the award of the Nobel Peace Prize to President Sadat and Prime Minister Begin had begun to look more than premature.

The Negotiations
The prolonged negotiations during the year – in Jerusalem in January, in Alexandria in February, in England in July, and finally at Camp David in September and in Washington from October to December – fully exposed the deep suspicions and differing attitudes of Egypt and Israel. From the outset it was evident that the major stumbling block was the problem of the Palestinians and the role they would play in the West Bank and the Gaza strip.

The positions of the two sides were set forth in the starkest way in the beginning of the year. Israel's plan, which she billed as providing 'autonomy' for the Palestinians, envisaged a move towards limited self-rule under a continuous Israeli military presence with a review after five years. In fact, Israel was attempting to perpetuate the *status quo* in a way which would preclude any form of Arab sovereignty over the territories in question. The Egyptian position, set forth in President Sadat's six-point proposal in early January, called for immediate abolition of Israeli military government in the West Bank and the Gaza strip and a five-year transitional period, after which the Palestinians would determine their own future. Supervision of the two areas during the transitional period would be the responsibility of Jordan and Egypt respectively, who would guarantee that security arrangements to be worked out would be respected in their areas.

The gulf between these two positions was exacerbated by the public posturing of the two sides. By carrying out their negotiations in the glare of the television cameras, both Sadat and Begin increased the pressures not to yield that were being exerted by their constituencies. Begin was attacked by those who feared that this search for peace with Egypt would adversely affect Israeli security by creating a hostile Palestinian state on Israel's borders. Sadat's freedom of action was constrained by those in the Arab world who accused him of seeking a separate peace with Israel while ignoring the just demands of the Palestinians.

Throughout 1978 President Sadat never seriously wavered from his declared intention to make peace with Israel; his periodic adoption of a hard line – even to the extent of threatening another war if there were no progress towards peace – was no more than tactical. The basis of Sadat's strategy was simple. He believed that only the US could force Israel into the concessions necessary for a Middle East settlement. His primary objective was therefore to involve her directly in the peace negotiations and exclude the Soviet Union as far as possible. In publicly placing his trust in the United States and thus incurring the anger of many Arab states, and the USSR, Sadat aimed to place Washington under a heavy obligation, which he believed would take the form of increasing pressure on Israel.

Prime Minister Begin's strategy was equally consistent throughout the year, equally simple, but short-sighted. He believed that Egypt was so eager for a peace which would give her back control of the whole of the Sinai that she would adjust her position on the Palestinian question so as to meet Israeli needs. He pinned his hopes on the Arab rejectionist camp, which declared its adamant refusal to participate in the process, believing that, once it was clear that neither Jordan nor the local Palestinians were prepared to join the peace talks, Sadat would drop his insistence on their participation. To help this process, Begin was willing to accommodate what was regarded as 'Sadat's needs in the Arab world' by paying lip service to the Palestinian question, though not intending to relinquish any control over the political fate of the West Bank and Gaza, to which he believed Israel had an inalienable right. Eventually, however, Begin came to realize that, if he wanted an agreement with Egypt, he would have to make some verbal concessions on the question of the West Bank and Gaza, and clearly link these to his agreement to dismantling the thinly-populated settlements in the Sinai and his agreement to a withdrawal by stages to the 1967 border with Egypt.

Before Begin reached this conclusion, and ratified it in the ambiguous 'Frameworks' worked out at Camp David, there was a series of difficult confrontations. In early January, before any real negotiations could get under way, Sadat abruptly withdrew the Egyptian delegation to the meeting of the Egyptian–Israeli Political Committee in Jerusalem, denouncing Israeli intransigence, but making it clear that this was not the end of peace

negotiations. He then toured the United States and European countries to promote the peace initiative he had begun with his late 1977 visit to Jerusalem. While Sadat was in the US, President Carter agreed to supply 50 F-5E fighters to Egypt, and this was approved by the US Senate on 15 May. Though this move left the Arab-Israeli military balance unchanged (it also included the supply of F-15s to Israel and Saudi Arabia), Sadat could claim that it marked an important shift in US policy towards the Arabs – especially since the deal was bitterly opposed by Israel.

The Camp David Talks

In August, after the deadlock in direct talks had become clear, President Sadat secured the breakthrough he had been hoping for: President Carter invited Sadat and Begin to meet him at Camp David in the United States on 5 September to discuss a Middle East peace settlement. The United States, and Carter's own prestige, were now fully involved, and the US had changed her role from 'honest broker' to direct participant. During the meeting, which lasted two weeks, Carter proved to be the indispensable practical mediator and the architect of a document which bore all the signs of a hard-fought compromise.

Like Sadat, Carter was convinced that if the Palestinian question and the Syrian aspect of the problem were not attended to, the new Egyptian-Israeli relationship would founder. The US argued that a separate peace could not last and that any real progress in implementing the agreement between Egypt and Israel would be impossible without the participation of the Palestinians, Jordan and Syria. Rather than attempting a wholly new proposal, both the US and Egypt preferred to modify Israel's 1977 autonomy scheme, hoping thereby to lessen Prime Minister Begin's opposition. The results of two weeks of hard bargaining at Camp David were two implicitly linked 'Framework' documents (reprinted in *Survival*, November/December 1978 pp. 271–4), one covering Egyptian-Israeli relations, the other setting out the direction that future negotiations concerning the West Bank and Gaza strip would take. Their major significance lay in the fact that

Begin found it necessary to acknowledge publicly that the Palestinian question was an essential issue that must be addressed in any Middle East peace process.

It was agreed that a new locally-elected Palestinian self-governing authority would replace the Israeli civilian and military administration; that the authority for this body would derive from an international agreement involving Jordan, Egypt and Israel; that a strong local police force would be set up under it; and that Israel would re-locate her remaining reduced military forces in specified locations in the West Bank to provide for Israel's security needs. Although the agreement was at times loosely worded and ambivalent, because the negotiators deliberately did not attempt to answer all the many difficult questions, a sound basis for Palestinian participation was stipulated by the accord. Israel had to recognize 'the legitimate rights of the Palestinian people and their just requirements' and the participation of the Palestinians 'in the determination of their own future'. Provisions were made for the return to proper homes in the West Bank of the Palestinian refugees displaced in 1967 (who mostly live in Jordan), and a decision was reached to establish a mechanism for dealing with the larger, more complicated question of the refugees displaced in 1948–9 in a way which took account of all the relevant UN resolutions. The complicated, sensitive question of Jerusalem was purposely left unresolved, with each side merely reiterating its position.

The Washington Talks

On 12 October Egyptian and Israeli negotiators again met in Washington to try to translate the framework agreements into a peace treaty within the three-month deadline established at Camp David. It was soon realized, however, that the many details still to be worked out made quick settlement of even the bilateral problems a far from easy task. As time passed, more and more complications and obstacles emerged, calling time and again for American intervention – even in technical matters, which seemed to preoccupy both sides. The more protracted the discussions, the clearer it became that Egypt was not after a separate peace treaty, particularly not the one envisaged by Israel. Israel, meanwhile, continually expressed displeasure at the pressures being exerted by the US and feared that the same methods would be applied in the future if she were to negotiate the substance of the autonomy scheme.

Now that the two countries faced the necessity for forging a final, rather than tentative and incomplete, agreement, each manoeuvred to secure a better package than it had agreed at Camp David. Both returned to presenting positions through the media, and declarations and intentions thus announced again proved obstructive to the peace-making process. Egypt now insisted on a clear connection between the bilateral settlement and the loosely agreed autonomy for the Palestinians under occupation. The debate within Israel, on the other hand, made it clear that, even if a vague connection were agreed to, Israel would not accept that progress in the relationship with Egypt must be made contingent on the implementation of the autonomy scheme – about which more and more Israelis were anyway now expressing reservations. Israel refused to allow a connection between the two problems to be embodied in the treaty, fearing that this would enable Egypt to postpone establishing diplomatic relations with Israel if Palestinian actions made it impossible to meet the deadline so established. However, she did agree to start negotiations on the autonomy scheme once the peace treaty was signed. This was not enough for either Egypt or the US, who, mistrusting Begin's vague assurances, demanded a final date for West Bank autonomy.

Other issues arose which highlighted the rift that had developed between the United States and Israel during the course of 1978. Even the combined Egyptian-Saudi-Israeli arms deal, which Congress had approved on 15 May, had failed to bring home to Israeli leaders that there had been a significant shift of opinion in the United States. But developments in November forced Israel to a different view. Right-wing members of the Israeli government, concerned at the direction that the negotiations were taking, leaked Israeli plans to 'thicken' the existing settlements on the

West Bank and establish new ones. This, together with Begin's statements that Security Council Resolution 242 did not include the West Bank (which he viewed as part of traditional Israel) further eroded US support for Israel. The Administration, sharply critical of Israel's settlement policy as well as of her way of conducting the negotiations, began to exert economic pressure, indicating that the United States would not pay all the expenses of a new defence line in the Negev or removing Israeli settlements in the Sinai. This revived dormant anxieties in Israel about the future of American-Israeli relations, strained confidence over the value of American security guarantees should a treaty be signed, and stiffened Israeli opposition.

Events in Iran reinforced this concern and made Israel more intractable over another question: the oil fields in the Sinai. Egypt had been demanding compensation for the oil Israel had used since 1967, while Israel argued that, as the developer of old fields and the discoverer of new ones, she had a legal right to the oil. Israel now went further and demanded that Egypt should undertake to guarantee her regular oil supplies.

Encouraged by the rift between Israel and the United States, Sadat made further demands for explicit linkage and a tight autonomy schedule. He also raised new problems, insisting on alterations in an American compromise plan which Israel had accepted in principle on 21 November. In a letter to Begin on 1 December, he reiterated his rejection of item 6 of the proposed peace treaty, which gave the Egyptian-Israeli agreement priority over all the two countries' previous obligations and which clearly affected Egypt's defence pacts with other Arab states still in a state of war with Israel. In a new tactical move he did agree on an extension of the schedule for the Israeli interim withdrawal in Sinai from nine to twelve months, to coincide with the American proposed deadline of December 1979 for the holding of elections in the West Bank.

Not only did Israel reject Sadat's proposals, she now made public her plans to create 84 new settlements in the West Bank and reminded the world of her interpre-

tation of the Camp David Agreements on this question: she would only refrain from establishing new settlements until 17 December, the date on which the peace treaty was supposed to be signed. President Carter attacked the Israeli decision, repeating his understanding that there were to be no new settlements established during the five-year transitional autonomy period. In a last effort to move the talks forward, Secretary Vance travelled to the Middle East and met Sadat on 10 December (while Begin was in Oslo accepting the Nobel Peace Prize) in an attempt to work out the wording of a number of letters intended to accompany the disputed treaty text in hopes of satisfying both sides. But Vance's trip failed to bridge the gaps between the Egyptian and Israeli positions before the 17 December deadline was reached. This did not mean an end to the search for a peace treaty, for, with encouragement from the United States, Egypt and Israel agreed to another round of talks at foreign minister level to begin at the end of February 1979. Sadat's shrewd tactics and events in Iran had combined to increase the pressure on Israel. The United States was now a direct participant in the negotiations, and the reminder which Iranian developments provided of the West's need for Saudi Arabia's support reduced such patience with Israeli tactics as still remained. However, whether Israel would bow to these pressures or show her traditional response to adversity by hardening her position remained uncertain.

Egypt

The motivating factor in Egyptian behaviour throughout the year was the belief of President Sadat and his closest advisers that if a peace agreement could be reached with Israel an impetus would be created that Jordan and Saudi Arabia, and ultimately Syria, would find difficult to resist. Yet Jordan, Saudi Arabia and the Gulf States attended the summit meeting in Baghdad in early November, along with Syria and other more uncompromising Arab states. There they approved a series of sanctions for use against Egypt if she signed a separate peace with Israel and threatened to transfer the Arab League headquarters from Cairo to Tunis or

123

Kuwait. While Egypt's social and economic problems made peace seem not only desirable but absolutely essential to the Egyptian people, the possibility of an effective boycott by the other Arab states was alarming. Since 1973 Egypt has received more than $17½ billion in aid from them, and the remittances of over 1½ million Egyptians employed in those states amount to about a third of Egyptian national income. No amount of aid that a grateful US could or would provide for signing a separate agreement with Israel would compensate Egypt for loss of these advantages.

In addition, there were political forces within Egypt which reflected concern and disagreement with Sadat's policy. While they posed no direct threat to his political authority, they nevertheless indicated the strains which prolonged negotiations with Israel imposed on the political fabric of the country. Of these, the left-wing opposition – expressed through the small Progressive Unionist Party in parliament, its weekly newspaper *al-Alhali* (when its issues were not seized by the authorities), some leading intellectuals and students – stood out because it was the one on which President Sadat concentrated his attacks. Ever since the widespread rioting of January 1977, Sadat had seemed convinced that there was a danger of left-wing subversion promoted from outside. Although measures he took in May 1978 to silence and restrict the political activities of the opposition were ostensibly directed as much against the *ancien régime* forces represented in the revived *Wafd* Party, there is no doubt that the Left was the main target.

Opposition from within the regime came from individuals such as the former Foreign Minister Ismail Fahmi and the Minister of State Muhammed Riyadh, both of whom resigned during President Sadat's visit to Jerusalem, and Fahmi's successor Muhammed Kamel, who resigned at Camp David. The Secretary-General of the Arab League, Mahmoud Riyadh, also criticized the Sadat policies at the Camp David summit, as did Mohammed Heikal, the former editor of *al-Ahram*.

Opposition to Sadat's peace plans from the Right, still largely below the surface by the end of 1978, was potentially the most serious. Islamic revivalism in the form of the Muslim Brotherhood and other similar groups had been tolerated (even at times encouraged) by Sadat, provided its support came from Saudi Arabia rather than Libya, and the fact that Muslim Brotherhood played a role in the rioting of January 1977 had largely been ignored. Only terrorist groups like *Takfir Wa al-Hijrah* (Repentance and Flight from Sin), responsible for the assassination of a former Minister of Islamic Affairs, had been severely dealt with. But the spread of Islamic revivalism among the younger generation (the Muslim Brotherhood was now the most important active group in the universities) was a threat to President Sadat's entire programme of *Infitah*, the open door, because the Muslim Brotherhood and its kind were in revolt against all forms of Westernization. Events in Iran were thus a serious warning to the Sadat regime. By the end of 1978 the most consistent open criticism of the Sadat peace policy came from the Brotherhood's newspaper *al-Da'wa* (The Call): the whole of Palestine should be under Islamic rule, it argued, and there should be no peace with Zionism.

In October, after Camp David, President Sadat replaced Mamduh Salem with a new Prime Minister, Mustafa Khalil, formerly Secretary-General of the Arab Socialist Union. His cabinet was billed as geared to an 'era of peace' for the first time in thirty years, and had the special task of tackling Egypt's massive internal problems and rooting out corruption and inefficiency. The new premier acknowledged the scale of the task in view of the appalling state of Egypt's public services – water, electricity, telephones and housing – after years of neglect in which the bulk of Egypt's financial resources were devoted to the military sector. This emphasized the need for a period of political stability, peace with Israel and large-scale investments from abroad. But it also underlined that if the peace negotiations did not soon produce a result acceptable to Egypt and conducive to stability in the region, President Sadat's domestic authority, on which his ability to seek an arrangement with Israel depends, might become more tenuous and volatile. This pointed again to the need to reach an

124

agreement between Israel and Egypt during 1979, before the US Presidential election campaign further circumscribed already reduced American diplomatic influence.

Israel

The alternation between progress and deadlock in the Israeli-Egyptian peace negotiations produced even more extreme swings in mood in Israel, ranging from euphoria to disappointment and even despair. Along with these variations in mood went sharp disagreements over the pace of the negotiations and the tactics that should be used in trying to move the Egyptian government to a peace settlement. Many Israelis, and most of the government, felt that the longer the negotiations took the more concessions Israel would be able to extract from Egypt.

This view was challenged, particularly by the Defence Minister Ezer Weizman, who calculated that without a quick settlement Israel would lose her bargaining flexibility and become increasingly subject to American pressure. Prime Minister Begin and the majority of the government, however, insisted that Israel should be firm in her negotiations with Sadat and advocated a hard line on the question of the West Bank and the Israeli settlements there. While the January talks were under way Agriculture Minister Ariel Sharon, with the Prime Minister's approval announced the establishment of eight new settlements in the Rafah salient, and throughout the year the settlements issue continued to create doubts over Israel's sincerity in the search for a durable peace.

In early March, Israel faced a difficult decision, when PLO commandos attacked a bus near Tel Aviv and many of the passengers were killed. Despite the dangers that a large-scale reprisal might harden Egyptian attitudes in the negotiations, she decided that such action was necessary, and on 14 March Israeli troops invaded south Lebanon in an attempt to destroy the PLO bases there. Although the Israeli advance was swift, PLO units, anticipating a reprisal, had left the area and suffered few casualties. Indeed, if anything the attack helped the Palestinian cause, since the PLO, having

provoked Israel into a large-scale and expensive operation which brought her small profit, not only gained popularity among the Palestinians but was also a direct participant in the talks which resulted in UN troops replacing the Israelis who were forced to withdraw from southern Lebanon. Nonetheless, Israel was right in judging that her action would not cause Sadat to suspend the peace talks.

Prime Minister Begin's tactics in these drawn-out negotiations, however, promoted rifts within Israel and the government itself. The 'Peace Now' movement of reserve officers and liberals began to attack the government's intransigence on the West Bank and its settlement policies; it was confronted by a small group called 'Secure Peace', composed mostly of Begin's followers. Both these groups restricted themselves to marches, rallies and publications to make their points, but the ultra-nationalist militant religious *Gush Emunim* (Bloc of the Faithful) was more forceful. Ideologically committed to retention of the West Bank, which they believed was a part of historic Israel which should never be relinquished, its members moved in and attempted to start new settlements, but without government approval. When Begin ordered the settlements to be forcibly removed, because the timing of their establishment was felt to be wrong, the government split, with some hard-liners wanting to continue the expansion of the settlements. The 'Peace Now' movement profited from this. Having gained strength during the year and now being able to mount very large-scale demonstrations, it brought 100,000 people to demonstrate in Tel Aviv on the eve of Begin's departure for the Camp David talks, appealing to him to change his policies regarding settlements on the West Bank.

The news from Washington throughout the conference raised fears and anxieties as to the outcome. The resignation of Communications Minister Meir Amit, former head of Army Intelligence, in protest over the government's rigid stand was seen as proof that the talks were moving towards deadlock. The effect of the announcement of the Camp David agreements was therefore electric, and Begin was received on his return with unprecedented spontaneous enthusiasm, even his opponents congratulating him for modifying his adamant position. But the enthusiasm soon evaporated. Once again it was *Gush Emunim* which reacted most strongly against the Agreements, fearing that the dismantling of settlements in Sinai would create a precedent for the West Bank. Some sixty of its members defied the government, bringing a few tents and a flagpole to establish a settlement on the hill overlooking Nablus. But the authorities' quick evacuation of these and the other settlers who tried to establish themselves on other sites exposed *Gush Emunim*'s numerical and political weakness, for there had not been widespread support for these efforts.

There was wider support, however, for the view that Begin's position of sacrificing the territory and settlements in the Sinai would not necessarily assure a foothold in the West Bank and the Gaza Strip. Begin found that, although his popularity among the people was still high as a result of Camp David, support within his coalition government was being eroded, and in an attempt to consolidate his position, he insisted on the imposition of coalition discipline in the Knesset vote on the Agreements. He also linked both Framework Agreements together in one vote, although he had originally claimed that he would allow a free vote on the issues separately. He realized that this would make it difficult for the right wing of the coalition, as well as the opposition, to oppose the whole package rather than just the settlements question by itself.

Although Begin was able to assure Knesset approval for the agreements in this way (by 84 votes to 19 with 17 abstentions), the debate which took place highlighted the deep disaffection of the right-wing of his coalition. Faced with this, he decided to demand modifications to the agreements from Egypt and the United States. To appease the hard-liners further, and to silence *Gush Emunim* which was exerting strong pressure on the National Religious Party, he ordered the execution of certain development schemes, such as the appropriation of land from some Arab villages, which had been temporarily frozen.

The issue of the settlements raised a series of questions relating to the political nature of the plan for Palestinian autonomy under the occupation. Many Israelis believed that it was time for the government to make use of available 'government' land and to acquire private land in the name of security. However, the government found itself faced by a number of Arab land-owners who appealed to the Israeli High Court of Justice and in some cases managed to prevent the acquisition or expropriation of their land by the Israeli authorities. As a result, the number of land transactions dwindled sharply. If the government wanted to establish new settlements it would have to use 'government' land, but little of this was in arable areas.

Although Begin took every opportunity to make it clear that the proposed five-year transitional period did not mean that Israel would relinquish her claims to sovereignty over the West Bank and the Gaza Strip, nor that she would totally withdraw her forces from the occupied territories after that period, both his followers and his opponents charged that his autonomy scheme, especially in its modified version, was a possible nucleus for an independent state. At the beginning of November, Begin gave tacit approval for the formation of a new regional Israeli Council in the West Bank called the 'Judea and Benjamin Council' (after the Israelite tribes that lived there in biblical times) to represent 13 existing settlements. He also authorized a large budget for an East-West road linking new settlements with Israel, along with plans for the development of Jerusalem and its surroundings. But even these moves did not reduce the growing mistrust within Cabinet ranks, and in the National Religious Party, which insisted on having a more influential role in the negotiations.

Economic Problems
Coalition members' disapproval of the government's policy and the process of decision making was not confined to political issues, but was also reflected in their abstention, or even support for the opposition, on issues which had little to do with the peace negotiations. Indeed, in mid-November, the government narrowly sur-

vived a Labour Party no-confidence motion on its economic policy.

Israel had been plagued by high inflation long before the Begin government came to power, but that government has exacerbated the situation. Its policies, which aimed at liberalizing the economy and reducing public sector expenditure, the newly-introduced relaxation of foreign-currency restrictions, increased incentives for exports and the 2% per month devaluations of the Israeli pound against a basket of currencies had little immediate effect; they could not create the new base necessary for economic growth. Instead Israel's balance-of-payments gap widened again during 1978, foreign currency reserves were depleted, and the State's external debt rose. The flight of capital, the reduced level of exports and increased imports of luxury goods only contributed to the constantly rising inflation, which had reached 70% by the year's end.

Yet, while the cost of living rose, so did the standard of living of many Israelis. More of them travelled abroad and more people invested in an attempt to better their living conditions, though in short-term (mainly stock market) transactions and property, rather than in long-term savings as the government wanted. The government attempted to soak up excess liquidity by selling long-term government bonds, while simultaneously trying to control inflation by limiting wage increases; it also tried, but failed, to improve tax collection. Although it succeeded in attracting buyers for the bonds, it was confronted by a chain reaction of strikes and forced to give up some of the economic measures by which it hoped to contain inflation.

The Arabs in Israel

The Arab sector of Israel's population numbered some 600,000 out of a total population of 3½ million living within the pre-1967 borders. There were two opportunities to sense its mood during 1978: the Camp David Agreements and the municipal elections in November. In general, the Israeli Arabs gave the Agreements a warm welcome, despite their blunt rejection by the PLO. And in the municipal elections the Arabs of Jerusalem voted in four times greater numbers than they had in the previous election, despite the fact that the PLO had asked them to abstain as a way of expressing Palestinian separatism. But of the Arabs living within Israel's old borders, more voted for 'Raqah' (the Soviet-guided 'New Communist List' composed mostly of Arabs but jointly led by Jews), not because it was Communist but because it reflected their views on political and national questions.

The shift towards extremism, signalled in the elections, developed hand in hand with the rapid growth of higher education among the young Arabs. Some 75% of Israeli Arabs are under 30, and many increasingly identify themselves with the PLO, even if they do not fully endorse its official policies. The constant increase in the numbers of well educated Arabs was an important factor in the continuing gradual change in the economic, social and political structure of the Arab population in Israel. Contrary to the government's expectations, it did not bring moderation or growing acquiescence; instead there rose from among the educated Arab population hostility to Israel's right to exist as a state and calls for the establishment of a Palestinian Arab state in its place.

The voting strength shown by the 'front' formed by *Raqah* and the newly established and more radical organization *Abna' al-Balad* (Sons of the Village) in the municipal elections was a sharp reminder that thirty years as Israeli citizens had not reconciled the Arabs of Israel to willing membership of that state. Along with the other components of the complicated Palestinian problem the status of the Arabs within Israel is likely to trouble Israel increasingly in the years to come.

8 A HOMELAND FOR THE PALESTINIANS?

AVI PLASCOV

Any discussion which separates the Palestinian question and therefore the political fate of the West Bank and Gaza from the bitter and prolonged Middle East dispute is artificial and pointless. Agreement about these territories needs at least the consent of Jordan, Israel and the Palestinians, each motivated and influenced by a different set of pressures and considerations. A basic distinction must be drawn between the different parties' tactics and convictions. This article aims to define some of the problems and attitudes of the main actors regarding the new American initiative which calls for a homeland for the Palestinians and to consider a number of questions this raises.

The use of terror brought the Palestinians back into the world's political focus. They are no longer just a pawn in the Middle East chess-board, but an independent factor that must be taken into account and satisfied. Ironically it was *not* the Palestinian resistance in the occupied territories nor the activities of the Palestine Liberation Organization (PLO) against Israel that earned the Palestinians this position but rather their success inside the Arab camp. They can no longer be ignored, and while many Arabs consider them a nuisance, 'something' has to be done for them beyond mere declarations. In that respect the Palestinians have achieved what they longed for.

They have become a factor which may be strong enough, despite its military weakening in Lebanon, to upset the delicate balances in the area. Today they have some 'power of veto' over any comprehensive Middle East settlement. It is this fact which lies behind the recent shift of policy undertaken by the new American administration. The United States is convinced more than ever before of the centrality of the Palestinian Question and is not prepared to continue to ignore it. By raising this proposal she seeks to encourage the moderate element within

Avi Plascov is an Israeli scholar on Palestinian affairs and is now a doctoral student at the School of Oriental and African Studies, University of London. This article was written before President Sadat's visit to Jerusalem.

the PLO and provide Mr 'Arafāt with a much needed boost *vis-à-vis* his other partners. This implies three new equations: no peace can be achieved without the Palestinians; the Palestinian representatives are the PLO; a new State should be set up in the West Bank and Gaza to provide a homeland for the stateless Palestinians. A *de facto* recognition between the Palestinians and the Israelis, made by seating them together at the Geneva Conference, would, it is hoped, enable each party to avoid the painful and apparently inconceivable process of going back on their respective positions.

Thus, twenty years after it was rejected by the Arabs, a modified Partition Scheme for Palestine has been re-introduced to satisfy in part the aspirations of the 'have nots' – the Palestinians. The alternatives for the future of the West Bank and Gaza have been reduced to two: total separation or autonomy within a federation with Jordan.

Those who advocate a 'homeland' do this for a variety of political reasons. They hope the plan will fulfil the wishes of most Palestinians who would have, for the first time, a say in their own political fate. They believe that this can be achieved without harming Israel's security or undermining the pro-Western Jordanian monarchy. They seem to minimize both the influence of those Palestinians who oppose the idea and the possible strategic danger that such a homeland might pose. They do not accept Israel's contention that this future State would necessarily become uncontrollable, hostile, turn into a Soviet base and harm the interests of Israel, Jordan and the United States.

Rather, they believe that once a Palestinian leader, regardless of all his previous declarations, became the ruler of such a 'State', he would seek to pacify any radical opposition, especially those who brought him to power, aiming to preserve his own position in order to prevent an invasion by Jordan or Israel. This means in essence that any ruler would need the assistance of the old notables who are basically pro-Hashemite. Furthermore, the fact that this state

128

would be deprived of the right to have its own army would make it militarily weak and vulnerable. A unit like this, it is argued, would be incapable of upsetting the Middle East balance while at the same time placating a major element of controversy and potential conflict. This would turn the conflict between Israel and the other Arab states primarily into a question of border determination, which would perhaps be easier to settle or at least to defuse.

The Soviet Union for her part supports the proposal in principle as a means of enhancing her own interests in the area. She does not accept the PLO postulate that Israel should be destroyed but believes that such an arrangement would maintain that level of tension in the Middle East conducive to Soviet interests.

What is the reaction of the parties concerned to such a proposal? The different ways of viewing the American proposal range between two extremes of rejection. One extreme sees the new state being sandwiched from both sides and essentially as an element of stability; the other sees it as a time bomb which some event is bound to trigger sooner or later and hence as an element of instability. Jordan and Israel take the second view and the few rejectionists groups among the PLO leadership take the first. All the other actors support the new state for various and often contradictory reasons: some only tacitly; some with reservations, regarding it as the least of many evils.

The Arab Countries' Attitude

Whatever its basis, the Arab commitment to the Palestinians since the 1974 Rabat Conference, Syria's attempts to prevent Egypt reaching another agreement with Israel and the PLO's unintended achievements in the Lebanon all made the Palestinians a useful partner in the step-by-step Arab strategy of warfare against Israel. The creation of the proposed new state has become a major component of the new Arab strategy of regaining occupied Arab territory by stages, 'slicing the salami' as it is commonly put. The idea is to cut Israel back to a more vulnerable size. Moreover, in supporting this proposal they see it as a way of isolating Israel from the United States.

With the exception of Jordan, all the Arab countries basically want the state although they differ over the tactics for achieving it

and over the role they assign to it in their overall strategy. In this respect, there are two main axes in the Arab World: Syria on the one hand and Egypt and Saudi Arabia on the other. The latter are more inclined to be flexible in their position, fearing Syria's intransigence. They are uneasy about the possibility of the PLO coming unwillingly under Syrian control and Egypt is therefore trying to consolidate her position amongst the Palestinians by gaining support for them. Syria is more ideologically committed and finds it difficult to work like them. Either way, the Arab commitment to the Palestinians has been stiffened by an awareness that all bargaining with Israel was held up by the Lebanon affair, a dispute which is still not resolved.

By appeasing the Palestinians the Arab countries hope to postpone hostilities, rid themselves of some of the political burden involved, isolate the rejectionists and regain control over the Palestinians under the guise of a 'co-ordinated all-Arab' strategy. A Palestinian state would enable them to ease out the Palestinian contingent amidst them, which is regarded as a potentially subversive element.

This does not exclude the fact that some Arab regimes are apprehensive about the new state's future. Thus Saudi Arabia, fearing her interests would be seriously threatened by a new war, regards a Palestinian State as one way of acquiring greater control over the Middle East situation: she would hope to hold some of the economic reins of the new state and keep it stable and quiet. She would even go so far as to pressurize the only other monarchy in the Middle East, Jordan, to accept such a solution.

The other major Arab countries are worried about who might control the new state and how it would align itself internationally and within the Arab world. Egypt and Iraq fear a possible takeover by Syria as part of her plan to create, eventually, a Greater Syria to include Lebanon, the West Bank and even Jordan. Hence Egypt would like to see a link between Jordan and the new state. Syria, on the other hand, suspects that, because of its geographical and economic vulnerability, the state might rally to the conservative Arab countries. All are uneasy that it might become a Soviet client which could either isolate them or reduce their bargaining power with the Soviet Union.

The Palestinian Positions

To the Palestinians, the creation of a West Bank–Gaza state is both a sensitive and controversial subject. While united in their aspirations they are divided and uncertain as to how to achieve them. Some support the scheme as a solution to their present predicament – remembering where extreme stands led them in the past. Others see it as the first step on the road to achieve the final goal – a secular democratic State covering all Palestine.[1] Both groups find it difficult, however, to come out in its support since this would entail overt recognition of Israel and imply that they are willing to compromise over their aims. They also fear the reaction of that group which preaches rejection of such a 'mini-State'. All three groups are found in all quarters of the dispersed Palestinian community. However, the large majority of the Palestinians, particularly those living under Israeli occupation or in Jordan, favour this solution, although they do not necessarily regard it as final.

The PLO

Operating from Lebanon and surrounded by one of the smallest Palestinian communities in the Middle East, this organization, which clearly represents the Palestinian community as a whole, is divided over its position.

The rejectionists amongst its leadership justify their position on ideological as well as pragmatic grounds. To them, regaining only part of Palestine would be an unacceptable compromise since this 'Palestinistan' would not only exclude the continuation of the struggle for a larger Palestine but would also mean fraternizing with their enemies from east and west, on whom they would be dependent. Furthermore, they claim it could not survive for very long before Jordan or Israel tried to further their 'expansionist policy'.

They know that this land-locked state would have to rely economically on the goodwill of

both Jordan and Israel, who could always cut it off from their markets and consequently the rest of the world. They contend that such an area could not contain all Palestinians nor could it be an adequate substitute for the refugees' full return to their places of origin in other parts of Palestine, outside the proposed State. They accuse the 'reactionary' Arab governments of being willing to compromise on the Palestinians' behalf by accepting this area as a final solution – although no Arab government has yet made a statement expressing such acceptance.

They fear that even a temporary acceptance of the new State would soon become a permanent solution to the Palestinian Question; the Palestinians would be bogged down within the new State and would neglect to strive for the ultimate goal. They claim it is a trap for the Palestinians, advocating instead a continued struggle and preferring to drag the Arab armies into a large scale war to destroy Israel. Then and only then would they set up the Palestinian Republic as part of the United Arab world.

Whether 'Arafāt would be content with such a framework as a final solution is hard to tell and perhaps not all that important. Like many other Palestinians, he badly wants something to grasp, knowing that if this idea materializes the Palestinians will at least have something of their own. A state in the West Bank would manoeuvre Jordan out of the picture, enable the Palestinian leadership to control the Palestinians directly by giving them a territorial base of power and making them an independent factor in Arab politics. 'Arafāt knows that he will not be able to get far beyond the proposed borders without confronting Israeli, Jordanian and American opposition, even if he is backed by other powers. He realizes that, at least for the time being, this is the maximum that can be achieved and it is a case of 'better a bird in the hand than two in the bush', though in the present state of PLO politics he cannot come out in its favour. He hopes to allay his comrades' fears and get their support by arguing that this would be a bridgehead for regaining the lost lands.

However, 'Arafāt must also know that most Palestinians support the pragmatic solution which would give them something with which

---

[1] The terms *dāʾim* and *marhali* respectively standing for 'permanent' or 'temporary' are used by Palestinian writers when reflecting on both long-term final goals and tactics for immediate political gains, in their strategy of progress by stages. Accordingly the secular democratic state, being the final solution to the Palestinian Question, would emerge after (at least) two stages (*marāhil*): a West Bank–Gaza State, followed by territorial changes in accordance with the 1947 Partition Plan.

to identify even if they live elsewhere and even if they continue to long for their lost lands. Like the Jews, perhaps only a minority of all Palestinians, who are now partly integrated into the various societies in which they live, would opt for 'going back home' but many would need this State as a focus for identification. This is true of the numerous Palestinians living in the United States and in Latin America as well as for those living in the countries of the Middle East, including Israel of pre-1967 borders, and for all who realize that while the PLO can force the issue into the open it cannot dismantle Israel nor coerce her government to negotiate. Knowing that Israel is there to stay at least for the forseeable future, the Palestinian 'diaspora' are impatient and willing to compromise.

The Attitude of the West Bankers

Although no one has asked or can ask them, given the chance, most ordinary Jordanian Palestinians would opt for a West Bank state. The few rejectionists among them carry little influence. They are generally more realistic about Israel's existence and see the State as a chance to regain some of their lost honour and pride and rid themselves of Israeli tutelage.

The PLO has gained more of their support by the change in its attitude towards some of the West Bank politicians, seeking to involve them in the political struggle and develop their sense of participation. Yet many see 'Arafāt and the others as their spokesmen, not necessarily as their leaders. After all, they are the only Palestinians who can function openly in world politics. The West Bankers are themselves trapped. The ones who side openly with the PLO risk expulsion by Israeli forces. Those who supported openly the monarch or tried to establish an independent position now see little point in airing their views. They were by turns ignored and encouraged by the Israeli government, sharply criticized by fellow Palestinians, and threatened by the PLO, which fears isolation from the Palestinian community if a local leadership re-emerges.

However, now that Israel wants to revive the idea of granting to the mayors a greater political role, the West Bankers now have no choice but to assert that the PLO is the only representative Palestinian group and that any deal has to be done through it or be approved by it. In that respect Israel underestimated the extent of the PLO's support when she held the last municipal elections early in 1977. The local inhabitants widely supported candidates with an eye to their wider affiliations and connections. The PLO emerged even stronger from these *democratic* elections in which even those previously banned by Jordanian law from voting were allowed to do so. Its grip over the West Bank tightened and that of Jordan loosened.

Israel, it seems, is now paying for her post-1967 policy of preventing the local West Bank leaders organizing themselves and expressing their views on issues beyond municipal problems. The 'Dayan Policy' of disallowing their involvement in political matters only strengthened the PLO's claim to represent all Palestinians. It is not suggested that if those leaders had had their say, they would have acted counter to this organization, but that Israel's claim that the PLO cannot represent all Palestinians would perhaps be more valid. Israel, however, only wanted to hear voices in support of her presence there or reassertions of Jordanian loyalty. Therefore, Israel enabled the Jordanian Government to send money in an attempt to maintain her position in the West Bank. But Israel's policy only further weakened Jordan's position and power, contrary to what both governments had intended. Now any independent political action is itself regarded as anti-PLO and thereby counter-productive to the Palestinian cause.

Israel's denial that the PLO was representative played into the hands of the PLO since her policy itself blurred any possible differentiation. In fact, Israeli occupation has probably sharpened political awareness amongst the Palestinians, helping to crystallize their sense of uniqueness and separateness. Shattered by the total failure of the idea of Arab Unity – being regarded as different or even aliens among their brothers – their feelings of exclusiveness and Palestinian consciousness were reinforced once all Palestine came under Israel's control. The relatively more educated, white-coloured, militant and proud generation is very critical of its father's generally pro-Hashemite orientations.

The occupation not only stopped the emigration of these youngsters but caused many of them to return to the West Bank, attracted by the relatively high salaries and economic well-being.

Better economic conditions have therefore not eased the problem but rather laid the foundations for the support of the radical young, morally at least, for the PLO. Yet the economic improvement did have an important long-term effect. For the Palestinians on the West Bank, a Palestinian State must be one to which neither the Jordanian market (and through it all other Arab markets) nor the Israeli markets should be closed. The economy of the West Bank and Gaza is interwoven with both Israel and Jordan. The new situation created after 1967 has made the economy of the envisaged new Palestinian State and that of Israel dependent on one another for employment, finance, labour, marketing, etc. No political arrangement can undo this symbiosis. The West Bank's economic expansion through its integration into the Israeli economy, on the one hand, and the importance of the East Bank, on the other, make it all the more natural for the borders to remain open once arrangements are finalized. The economic composition of those three units is the foundation for any political structure yet to come.

None the less, the economy of the area should not be treated as a serious consideration for or against the State's creation. As it is argued, the interested parties, be they the United States or the oil Arab countries, all of whom have a common interest in promoting stability in the area, would ensure that the new framework would not be economically handicapped.

The political alternative, of coming under Jordanian domination, is completely ruled out. This is not to say an anti-Hashemite spirit prevails but that the West Bankers are likely to accept nothing less than arrangements which put them on an equal footing with the Jordanians.

Yet many West Bankers still fear that they might wake up one morning to find Jordanian units had replaced the Israeli after a secret agreement between the two countries. However, King Hussein's commitment to the all-Arab position certainly precludes any such organized takeover, much as he may desire it. To date all meetings on this between the King and Israel have been fruitless.

The greatest fear of the West Bankers, however, is that a rigid PLO position will lose

them what they regard as their golden opportunity. If the PLO rejects recognition and acceptance of Israel in principle, the idea of a homeland might lose its political momentum. However, they could not openly criticize their 'sole representatives' since such a step could be regarded as disassociative.

The East Bank Palestinians

This group naturally welcomes any scheme which could ease their predicament of belonging to two peoples simultaneously. The proposed new State could solve many of their persisting problems of identity and identification. They would no longer be trapped between two limited choices and torn between two loyalties. Possibilities of movement between the two states would make living with this much easier. On the other hand, conflict between Jordan and the new state could further divide their loyalties. Thus their fear of being pushed out of the East Bank is constant. They could lose much that they have built up and saved through years of hard work. The trauma of becoming refugees in their own country is salient in their thinking, but their position could not be isolated from that of the Jordanian regime.

Jordanian Views

Jordan gained economically from the Lebanon crisis, when many Western firms moved their Middle East headquarters to 'Amman and rich Christians as well as wealthy Muslim Palestinians arrived in Jordan, transferring their assets with them. Furthermore the East Bank's accelerated economic and educational development in the last decade or so, effected through huge direct and indirect Western and United Nations (UN) contributions, closed the economic and social differences between the original Trans-Jordanians and the Palestinians.

Politically, however, the gap is wider than before. The bitter memory and lessons of September 1970 and the period leading up to it remains. Regardless of all future Arab manoeuvres to renew the dialogue between the monarch and the PLO, co-existence in its true sense between the PLO and the present Jordanian regime is simply not possible.[2] The

[2] The meetings held between PLO representatives and Jordan at the end of February 1977, following Syrian

King also has the memory of the PLO's response to his 1972 proposal for an Hashemite Federation[3] which aimed to incorporate the West Bank, recognizing the Palestinian uniqueness, though not the full implications of their being a political entity. Moreover, the continued clash since 1948 between Jordan and the distrusted Palestinians in Jordan crystallized Jordan's position and accelerated the process of the Jordanization of the inhabitants rather than the Palestinianization of the Kingdom.

The distinctiveness of each of the reluctant partners only suggests that they do not intend giving up their final goals. The idea advocated by some Palestinians of trying to take over Jordan and create a direct front with both the West Bank and Israel is still the threat the monarch fears most. It seems the King would prefer a West Bank under his rule, in spite of all the problems it poses, rather than an independent State there, which he feels would threaten his position. Therefore the extent of Jordan's direct involvement in the proposed State's affairs could prove crucial to all parties concerned.

However, the opinion is increasingly being held in Jordan that the West Bank might be more of a burden than an asset because, even if the Jordanian regime re-accepted control of it, it would be practically impossible to govern without employing harsh measures. Such control would serve little purpose and could create unease amongst the numerous Palestinians in both parts. The Jordanians know the Palestinians have not endured Israeli occupation only to come once again under the monarchy; although many of them respect it, this respect is tinged with fear and suspicion. The King is aware of the new situation in the West Bank emanating from the occupation, which taught the Palestinians to appreciate certain features of the freewheeling style of Israeli democracy.

Many in Jordan would still like to see the return of the Hashemite government to the West Bank, but their fear is that Israel would hand over only its administrative, not its

military control, since Israel would not allow Jordanian troops there. To accept Israel's terms would inevitably be seen as treason and would completely upset their relations with the Palestinians and the Arab countries.

Unable to have its own way, the regime – which has more confidence in the policy of the present right-wing Israeli government on the West Bank and is now content with the Rabat resolutions which could expose the PLO's weakness as a potential negotiator – has chosen for the present to leave the West Bank as an occupied territory. The Crown Prince and others in the Royal family are the main proponents of this policy.

Even the other alternative – a Federation – does not enjoy wide support amongst the Jordanians proper. They do not wish to embark on such a venture, fearing that the next stage would be representation according to numbers, making them a minority in their own country (including within the armed forces), or having to rule a frustrated majority. They take comfort from the knowledge that they need not control the West Bank directly in order to make it dependent on the East Bank. The policy – while paying lip-service to the Palestinian struggle – remains one of striving to minimize the role of the PLO and to neutralize its efforts to become the accredited negotiator for the West Bank.

Israel's Dilemma

While the Arab positions are vague, Israel makes no bones about her position. Israel made it clear that she is only willing to discuss Palestinian affairs with Palestinians under her control. For Israel, talks with the PLO mean recognition of the right to self-determination. That in turn means negotiating the formation of a Palestinian independent political framework, i.e. giving up most of the West Bank territory she holds. At present this is simply not acceptable. The new Government is more ideologically committed and strongly emotional about the issue of Palestinian entity, especially now it is forced to view it in terms of territorial concession rather than merely confronting terrorism. The aim of its policy of building settlements in the West Bank, apart from its patriotic significance, is to create obstacles to a proposed state and to give the Government bargaining counters in the future. The a-political

and Egyptian initiatives, and talks between Hussein and 'Arafāt in Cairo a few days later produced practically nothing. These meetings were opposed by the 'rejectionists' among the PLO.
[3] For the PLO's negative stance on Hussein's renewed call for the set-up of the federation – see Fārūq Qaddūmī's article in al-Ahrām, Cairo, 26 February 1977.

'Bantustan' Israel is proposing in the West Bank could not solve the predicament. Israel wants Jordan as a partner but without allowing her to control the disputed territories. In short, Israel is holding the stick at both ends. Her problem now is how to avoid damaging her special relations with the United States and continue to hold the West Bank without causing stagnation in the diplomatic arena. Knowing that the Arab countries cannot go to war without Egypt, Israel tried anxiously to continue the momentum of interim agreements with Egypt by attempting to satisfy her demands with large territorial concessions. Israel hoped to use the vast Sinai territories to fragment the Arab camp. Whether Egypt will continue to stick reluctantly to the all-Arab stance is, therefore, a crucial question. Hence the question on the agenda between Israel and the United States is Israel's eastern borders.

Common Fears, Unanswered Questions

Jordan and Israel have a common interest in preventing the establishment of a state between them; both fear the Palestinians' intentions to expand east or west once 'given' a State.

These fears are not theirs alone. The PLO members are troubled by the same questions but seen from their side of the fence. If the State is allowed no army, they argue, but has an Israeli force stationed along its Eastern border range of hills, what does its sovereignty amount to? Such an Israeli presence is inconceivable to the Palestinians but it is the absolute minimum Israel is likely to demand. If the Palestinians want peace, she argues, why should they want an army?

On the whole it seems the new state would be a precarious creation whose very existence would depend on the course of events. For example, a bomb fired from the new state against Israeli towns could become a *casus belli* or reason enough for Israel's forces to enter and occupy the area; a similar incident involving Jordan could be a pretext for Jordanian entry. Of course, Israel and Jordan would face outside pressures not to upset the whole arrangement because of an 'odd attack', costly as it may be. This would, however, leave the two countries, and even the Palestinians, dangerously frustrated in their freedom of action: held to ransom by small violent extremist groups, within or outside, or shackled by the major powers. The UN peace-keeping forces could not, as Israel learned in 1967, provide stability; nor could a local government restricted to handling only local affairs, under an Israeli military presence which would lack popular support.

Who would run West Bank affairs? Would it be 'Arafāt or one of his comrades, who have never hesitated to spell out their views and hostility towards those two countries? Can Israel or Jordan trust such a leader to change his views and co-operate with them, accepting and respecting the constraints on his sovereignty? If they do have a direct say, what kind of puppet state would it be, and who amongst the locals would back it and see its leadership as truly representative? What would happen if a new Palestinian leader emerged there declaring he was no longer bound by the treaty that created the State? He might seek support from the Soviet Union or China including military aid and experts and small units to 'safeguard' Palestinian interests. Would that justify Israeli military intervention? With Israel then facing the Soviet Union would the United States not hasten to restrain Israeli action, fearing the risk of potential super-power confrontation?

The most important question for Israel is, of course, whether the Arabs and especially the Paletinians will regard the creation of a West Bank–Gaza State as their *final* goal? In other words, would the creation of this State mean losing the right to demand Jaffa? Would such demands be considered mere rhetoric, or show that the Palestinians do not see it as a final solution? Would calls for implementing the UN resolutions on partition and the return of the refugees follow?

After all, an independent West Bank–Gaza State could not satisfy the refugees. As one refugee living in Qalqilyah, just opposite his home village Kafar Saba, said 'My Palestine starts only two miles westwards from here and nothing in the world can change that'. Needless to say this kind of view would be more vehemently held by a refugee from Haifa living in Syria and who cannot regard Nablus as a replacement for his home town even if the scheme had his support. The refugees claim they did not wait and suffer all these long years to give up their right freely to choose whether to return or to be compensated in accordance with the 194 UN resolution of December 1948 and its reaffirmation ever since. Therefore they regard the new state only as a first step towards the liberation of all Palestine and the destruction of Israel. This is not altered by the fact that most would probably not opt to go back if given the choice.

Moreover, the so-called Israeli-Arabs – the Palestinians living in Israel – could pose yet another sensitive problem by demanding to be incorporated into the new State. The Arabs who populate heavily the Upper Galilee could declare their adherence to it, punishing Israel for not populating this area with Jews. Compared with these uncertainties, questions relating to the fate of the Israeli settlements in the occupied territories, and even that of Jerusalem, seem relatively more manageable.

For Israel such an arrangement seems too risky to accept even if she could be assured that the solution was a final one – which no one can. So why, Israel argues, enter now into a situation which would lead to a repeated threat and danger to her reduced territory? No guarantees can dispel these concerns. Israel will be reluctant if not unable to bring herself to accept such a plan, especially when she has less faith in the American promises – witnessing what she inconveniently regards as a gradual erosion of the United States commitment towards Israel. She refuses to accept the fact that the United States' list of priorities cannot coincide with those of Israel. No wonder the 'Third State' plan, at least in the vague way it is presented, is a nightmare to nearly all Israelis. More Israelis therefore argue that if a war is inevitable, why not fight it soon, under better conditions, rather than face the danger of extermination in a few years time, defending a country which is not even as wide as London?

Some Israelis sadly note that they could perhaps have saved themselves this problem had they agreed a few years ago to the Jordanian demand to sign an agreement with her for the separation of forces. This included granting the Jordanians a limited administrative control over a certain strip west of the river, with the Israelis still controlling the mountains overlooking the Jordan Valley. Such an arrangement would have transferred part of the West Bank to Jordanian hands, creating an important pre-cedent. Now more voices there urge the abandoning of the pro-Hashemite orientation to enable the Palestinians to take over Jordan by revolution, regretting Israel's intervention in September 1970 which, they claim, prevented such an occurrence. If this came about, they argue, it would give the Palestinians a place of their own, with the western part of 'their country' being a demilitarized zone.

The West Bankers could, according to this strategem, vote and participate in all political institutions in the eastern part of the Palestinian–Jordanian 'Arab Republic' with far less frustration. This situation would damage beyond repair their larger claims for self-determination and return. The demilitarization of the West Bank would then become more acceptable. However, this description is rather unrealistic. Although not all Jordanians are staunch supporters of the Hashemites, such a coup is quite difficult to effect. For example, the Transjordanian elements which are the corner stone of the regime, fearing a change in their status, would themselves hasten to try to control the direction of events once an assassination or a sudden take-over occurred. As far as they are concerned, the Palestinians are in no position to inherit the regime. The armed forces, without which any revolution cannot be accomplished smoothly, are mainly manned by the patriotic Transjordanians with little decisive Palestinian representation.

It is also difficult to conceive that, in the event of another clash between the PLO and the Jordanian army, the latter would be defeated fighting for survival on their own ground. Jordan is Lebanon neither topographically nor militarily. None the less, such a change could come about if Syria, Iraq and Israel believed the time was ripe and if the government in 'Amman were totally devoid of internal and external support. Although the United States has shown lately, with regard to some countries in the world, that her list of priorities is far more flexible than ever before, it is difficult to envisage her sacrificing, in the near future, her oldest ally in the Arab world. Thus this scenario is more like Israeli 'wishful thinking'.

In any event the United States has learnt that the Middle East has its own rules of fluctuating patterns to which the competing powers occasionally need to readjust. Trying to appease the Palestinians and partly satisfy their demands, showing them that a moderate line would be to their advantage and that a new state could only be created with American mediation and pressure, she hopes to make the Palestinians dependent on her and to maintain the momentum.

Possible Trends

The problem is to convince each party that its interests would not be harmed by their supporting this scheme, as each of the actors is troubled more by the precise details of a given agreement than by its objectives. The American administration has no illusions about the intentions of the opponents. Yet it believes that such a homeland would have a positive impact on the Arab–Israel relationship, and it certainly prefers it to the present highly explosive situation. Now that it has acquired recognition, it is difficult to see the Palestinian Question being pushed aside for Israel's convenience. It is also impossible to see any overall settlement of the Middle East conflict – if it will ever come about – which does not resolve this issue.

However, the system of interim agreements might be introduced if the Arab camp failed to stick to its united, threatening position. Most members of the PLO may want the scheme but may remain a prisoner of its own uncompromising rhetoric, thus prevented from openly acquiescing to Israel's right to exist. This is the vicious circle: they want the State but an open recognition of Israel is synonymous with treason. They want to be made to extend an unbinding and indirect recognition, and they hope that the United States will engineer something for them. Again the only thing the PLO as a whole can agree upon openly is a 'negative' stance to the process of peace making.[4]

The moment of truth and real decision-making rather than resolutions and declarations could prove extremely painful. After all it is difficult to see the rejectionists remaining aloof

in the face of these developments and refraining from attempts to cripple or at least damage 'Arafāt's position by resorting to action against Israel, international terrorism or other means.

The PLO will find it difficult to decline the American initiative if it wants to retain the backing of most Palestinians and Arab countries, with the exception of Lybia and Iraq. In the event that the 'rejectionist' view should prevail in the PLO, Egypt and perhaps even Syria would be inclined to negotiate with Israel, hoping to recover territories in exchange for their 'willingness' to abandon the Palestinians temporarily. The Arab governments refuse to be committed by a small group of Palestinians to a position which would prevent them from regaining lost territories and risk their involvement in another unpromising military conflict.

As Israel is the one holding the territories and as she can create border tensions and throw into disarray threatening diplomatic initiatives, her fears and considerations need to be taken into account. What her reactions would be if faced with a painful choice between another full scale war which could prove extremely costly, or transferring a certain area to Palestinian control, is difficult to assess. The present Government under Begin could be more inclined to reject the latter, regardless of all American pressures and assurances. Other governments may react differently.

If Israel would eventually opt for such an experiment – and a mutual recognition between the PLO and Israel is a prerequisite of any arrangement – 'stage by stage' movements would be introduced as neither Israel nor Jordan would be expected to agree to an instant change. Owing to the prevailing deep suspicion of all parties, the gradual implementation of the agreement would have to be checked at every stage. Misbehaviour on the part of one of the parties could be counter-productive to its own interests and would baulk completion of the process. Once finalized, it is argued, it would be practically impossible to launch a full scale war without the consent of one of the conflicting super-powers, which know that such hostilities would have to be stopped to avoid adverse international consequences.

One possibility is that Israel may choose to leave the problem in Jordanian hands, agreeing

---

[4] Comparison between the carefully worded 15-point Palestinian National Council Political Declaration adopted on 20 March 1977 and the 24-point Rejection Front programme presented a few days earlier, cannot reveal the differences between the PLO factions. This is simply due to the fact that the PLO wanted to avoid any open friction between its members which would be counter-productive to the PLO and prevent it from seeming to emerge strong and united.

in principal to such a gradual creation only if it would come under Jordanian supervision. Jordan would then face pressures from within and without the country to sign an agreement to that effect. However, it is difficult to see Jordan being pressurized into the act of negotiating with Israel only to regain the area in order to transfer it to the PLO. The King would probably try to consolidate his position there and therefore it is also difficult to see Jordan allowing what she would regard as potentially hostile developments taking place in that territory. As mutual suspicion would shape the movements of each of the Arab actors, a new set of conflicts is bound to arise, enabling Israel to escape the continuation of the process.

An alternative possibility for such a phase could be an arrangement which would transfer a certain strip of land west of the River to Palestinian free domination. This can include a Jericho–Nablus 'finger' which could provide for Palestinian autonomy, creating a basis for future agreements – if such a stage would confirm, after an agreed time, what those who envisaged the state had in mind. This territory would be the base of all Palestinians wherever they are and function as a sovereign state regardless of its territorial size. In the event it would violate the agreement, but Israeli troops, stationed as before on the mountains overlooking the River, would easily prevent any Arab army from crossing while refusing to continue to allow the creation of an independent state. Such a small and vulnerable framework could hardly harm Israel's security as such.

Another possibility, perhaps even a 'safer' one, is to start the scheme in the area where the Palestinians set up their first government in 1948 – the Gaza strip. Isolated and remote from any Arab country, the risks involved there for Israeli and certainly Jordanian interests are even less acute.

Although a West Bank–Gaza State cannot possibly serve as a solution to the Palestinian Question, such possibilities may well lay the foundation for a new kind of coexistence between Israel and the Palestinians, on a somewhat peculiar, though principally equal, basis. This could have positive long-term effects with the new state working towards its consolidation rather than its expansion; the Palestinians would then fear to lose what they have achieved. In that respect the Palestinian homeland may be a stabilizing factor which perhaps could improve Arab–Israeli relations. An agreement which will provide simultaneously for substantial and open Arab concessions in exchange for small territorial parcels on all fronts, and would indicate good will on behalf of all parties, with Israel coming into a defence pact with the United States, would reduce the conflict and allow for a gradual implementation without drastically changing the existing balances.

On the other hand, the proposed arrangement could burden the Middle-East conflict with new and bitter disputes. The process itself and arguments over its continuation could well turn into yet another dangerous deadlock, bringing the whole endeavour more forcefully back to square one.

9 THE SOVIET UNION AND THE PLO

GALIA GOLAN

I. HISTORICAL BACKGROUND

There was no great Soviet reaction to the founding of the Palestine Liberation Organization (PLO) in 1964. The Soviet Union continued then, as previously, to treat the Palestinian problem as one of refugees: their return, and/or their compensation was considered, without recognition of their nationhood or national rights. Indeed, the earliest Soviet approach to the Palestinian problem failed even to recognize it as a legitimate refugee issue, claiming in the UN in 1948 that in fact it was Britain who had created the refugee problem.[1] This more extreme attitude was gradually revised, and by the time of Nasser's visit to the Soviet Union, in 1958, Moscow was willing to include a phrase in the final communiqué on the 'legitimate rights of the Palestinian Arabs', and during Khrushchev's 1964 visit to Egypt the Soviet leader acknowledged the 'inalienable and lawful rights of the Palestinian Arabs'.[2] Nonetheless the approach was still based on the plight of refugees rather than on the demands of a national liberation movement. And so, when the PLO was formed Moscow remained more or less indifferent – so much so that Ahmad Shukeiry, leader of the new organization, claimed that his approaches to Moscow had been rebuffed, presumably leaving him no option but to turn to China (who did respond in a positive and concrete fashion).[3]

The shift in the Soviet position began to appear only after the Six-day War of June 1967, in mid- to late 1968. It is conceivable that the attention and aid given the PLO by China influenced the Soviet Union towards this change. Certainly, consistent Soviet criticism of the pernicious influence of China on the Palestinians would suggest that the Soviet Union did take up the challenge to compete with China for this group. Yet the timing – some four years after the Chinese moves began – suggests that while competition with China may have been a contributing factor to the Soviet decision, the precipitating causes were of another – and possibly related – nature: (1) the PLO, in the form of Al Fatah, was becoming a factor on the Middle East scene, operating more effectively and commanding increasing attention; while (2) Egypt, then the cornerstone of Moscow's Middle-East policy, undertook a *rapprochement* and co-operative position with Al Fatah.[4] Thus in July 1968 President Nasser took Yasser Arafat with him on a visit to the Soviet Union, after which the Soviet media began referring most positively and frequently to the Palestinian 'partisans', the Palestinian resistance movement and, specifically, Al Fatah, lauding their operations and indeed exaggerating their successes.[5] More concretely, the Soviet Union also began supplying arms and equipment for these operations, indirectly, through the medium of the East European countries and the Arab states. Nonetheless, even at this time of decided shift in the Soviet attitude (and apparently policy) towards the PLO, the Soviet Union only rarely called for anything more than solution of the 'refugee' problem, occasionally even stating that there were *two* parties to the Middle East conflict – Israel and the Arab states – and excluding any mention of the Palestinians.[6] Thus, while the Soviet Union was willing to speak more frequently of the legitimate rights and interests of the Palestinians, and actually to assist as well as praise Al Fatah, she did not introduce into the two-power and four-power negotiations of 1968–9 anything more than the refugee issue, insofar as the Palestinians were concerned.

In February 1970 Arafat himself led a delegation to the Soviet Union, upon the invitation of

138

the Soviet Afro-Asian Solidarity Committee, which was to be his host for subsequent visits until 1974, rather than any government or party body. This trip occasioned another elevation of the PLO's status and shift in Soviet attitude for, immediately following the trip, *Pravda* introduced a new phrase which was soon to become the standard characterization, referring to the 'Arab people of Palestine'.[7] However tenuous this change in phraseology might appear to the outside observer, it was interpreted (and apparently intended) as the beginning of Soviet recognition that the Palestinian problem was one of national aspirations. At the same time, however, the Soviet Union also sought to gain more direct access to, and presumably control over, the PLO by creating Al Ansar, a sabotage-guerrilla organization sponsored by the Jordanian Communist Party.[8] In fact little came of this group, and it was apparently superseded in 1973 by the Palestine National Front (PNF), also sponsored by the Jordanian Communist Party, which became a member of the PLO executive in June 1974.[9]

Once again, despite the augmentation of Soviet support, relations were not of the best. The Soviet Union remained somewhat aloof from the fate of the Palestinians during the Jordanian events of 1970–71, considerations of Soviet–Syrian (but particularly Soviet–American) relations weighing more heavily upon Moscow than the plight of the Palestinians. Moreover, in 1971, upon the occasion of a visit to Moscow by a delegation of the Syrian Communist Party (which was suffering serious internal dissension at the time) the Soviet Union explicitly admonished this party for placing too great emphasis upon the Palestinian issue.[10] The contents of these talks, with all that they revealed regarding Moscow's position on the specific issues of the Palestinian case will be discussed below. In terms of the historical development of PLO-Soviet relations, however, this was a clear indication that the Soviet Union continued in a decided ambivalence, only tentatively and gradually improving the relationship.

Another such improvement came with Arafat's visit to Moscow in July 1972, when the PLO leader met Soviet defence ministry officials and succeeded in obtaining direct Soviet arms supplies (which began arriving via Syria in September 1972).[11] This development may well have been influenced by the deterioration of Soviet–Egyptian relations at the time (with the expulsion of Soviet advisers in July), which did in fact occasion a Soviet effort to improve her position and to forge a formal 'progressive front' primarily composed of Syria and Iraq,[12] as well as the Palestinians. Certainly Arafat accommodated the Soviet Union in terms of propaganda by most generous acknowledgement of her support for the Arab cause, at a time when Sadat was exhibiting opposite sentiments.[13] In addition to the direct arms aid, this new augmentation of Soviet support was capped by the inclusion of the demand 'for realization of the legitimate rights of the Arab people of Palestine' in the slogans for the anniversary of the October Revolution. Although the Soviet Union had included such a clause in the resolutions of the 1971 CPSU Congress and repeatedly expounded it in speeches and official statements, this was the first time the formula was to appear among Moscow's slogans, and – as it turned out – the last, for it has not appeared in either October or May Day slogans since. A further and probably most significant elevation of Soviet interest in, and support for, the PLO began in 1973, possibly just before the October War, but most apparently after it. Yet throughout the years since 1968, with their gradual but decided increments of Soviet support, there have remained a number of serious, even quite basic, differences and problems between the Soviet Union and the PLO, and, though the list of issues is not a short one, the most important were as follows: (*1*) Palestinian statehood, including the related problems of borders, Israel's existence and Jordan; (*2*) a negotiated Middle East settlement, including the problem of Security Council Resolution (SCR) 242 and the Geneva Peace Conference; (*3*) the use of terror; (*4*) the character of the PLO and the lack of unity within it; and (*5*) recognition of the PLO as the sole legitimate representative of the Palestinian people.

In the meeting between Soviet and Syrian Communist leaders in 1971 (a purported protocol of which was subsequently published by, among others, the Palestinians themselves), the Soviet Union was outspokenly contemptuous of the idea of a Palestinian state. Their direct comment was 'How big? Where? When? It raises many problems.'[1] Supporting the right to return, and even self-determination after return – defined as the right to determine their own administration and the form and character of the state – the Soviet Union explained that 'the demand for a unified state also comes within the category of the right to self-determination; the right to self-determination does not necessarily imply a separate state'. She urged the Syrian Communists to accept the fact of the existence of Israel rather than to pit one national movement against another's rights to self-determination. Moreover, she argued that the slogan calling for the destruction of Israel was 'unsound not only tactically but also as a matter of principle.... It is permissible to struggle against the racialism of the State of Israel, its reactionary qualities, its colonialist character, but it is not permissible to talk about eliminating the State of Israel.' Indeed on this last point – the existence of the State of Israel – the Soviet position was to remain consistent; the standard Soviet formula for a settlement usually contained the need for guaranteeing or securing the independence, occasionally the sovereignty and territorial integrity, of all the states in the area. This formula often specified Israel as one of the necessary beneficiaries and, upon occasion, linked this phrase with Soviet willingness to provide such guarantees. Apart from Soviet Foreign Minister Gromyko's pronouncements to the Geneva Peace Conference and the reiteration at the United Nations of Moscow's continued recognition of Israel's right to exist,[2] there were other notable examples of official Soviet willingness to recognize, and even to participate in, guarantees of this situation: Gromyko's speech honouring visiting Syrian Foreign Minister Khaddam in April 1975 (in which Moscow expressed her willingness to offer Israel 'the strictest guarantees'),[3] Brezhnev's speech to the 1976 CPSU Congress,[4] and the Soviet government's statement of 28 April 1976.[5] Indeed, the Soviet Union reportedly even

attempted to persuade Arafat, during his April–May and November 1975 visits, to agree to some sort of recognition of Israel's existence, hoping to pave the way for a Soviet resolution in the Security Council in 1976 which would call for mutual recognition by Israel and the PLO.[6]

The Soviet position on a Palestinian state did in fact undergo a transformation immediately following, if not before or during, the October war. While little evidence is available of such a change before the war,[7] and the Soviet Union barely mentioned the Palestinians during the war (presumably so as to prevent complications in the cease-fire negotiations),[8] immediately after it the Soviet Union sent a memorandum to each of the PLO leaders, Arafat, Chabash and Hawatmeh.[9] In this memorandum she reportedly asked the PLO for a precise definition of the term 'legitimate rights', and on 15 November 1973, in a joint communiqué with President Tito of Yugoslavia, she added for the first time the phrase 'national' to the 'legitimate rights' demanded for the Palestinians.[10] While this was not in fact a public mention of the idea of statehood, the use of the term suggested Soviet support for the idea. What occasioned this shift is difficult to determine. It is possible that the Soviet Union estimated that serious negotiations for a Middle East settlement were imminent, necessitating a clarification of the Palestinian issue and the PLO's position; she may well have wanted an additional option for these negotiations, primarily because of the already apparent increase in the importance of the United States in the Middle East conflict and the emerging American–Egyptian relationship, as well as a means of claiming a role in whatever talks concerned the hitherto exclusively American clients, Jordan and Israel.

Still, the Soviet commitment to Palestinian statehood was ambiguous and slow in emerging. Gromyko's speech at the Geneva Peace Conference in December 1973 almost totally ignored the issue; Gromyko did *not* use the new term 'national' legitimate rights and he relegated the Palestinian problem to the secondary position of 'many other aspects of settlement' which would find their solution if the 'root cause' were solved – the 'root cause' was explained only as the Israeli occupation of Arab lands 'that continues for over six years'.[11] Only gradually, in 1974, did the Soviet Union begin regularly to employ the new term, the *national* legitimate rights of the Palestinians' and, finally, in autumn 1974, she made her first official public reference to a Palestinian state.[12] This came first in the form of a speech by President Podgorny in Bulgaria on 8 September 1974, in which the Soviet leader specified the Palestinians' 'right to establish their own statehood in one form or another'.[13] Podgorny himself repeated this in the name of the Politburo in a cable to Algerian President Houari Boumedienne, who made it public on 4 October 1974.[14] The cable may not have been intended for publication, and it was conceivable that Podgorny was expressing a dissenting view, rather than that officially accepted at the time (he had in the past exhibited a tendency to a more radical view on the Middle East).[15] But the fact that these pronouncements did constitute a new official Soviet position was confirmed just a week later; in a speech in Kishinev on 11 October Mr Brezhnev referred for the first time to the rights of the Palestinians to a 'national home' (and this was further confirmed by his speech on 26 November, which changed the phrase to a Palestinian 'state').

This breakthrough, which was not, however, accompanied by any official Soviet comment on a Palestinian government-in-exile, was most likely connected with the Rabat Conference of Arab leaders opening at the end of October.[16] The situation facing Moscow on the eve of this meeting was the serious deterioration which had taken place in Soviet–Egyptian relations since the previous spring,[17] the general belief that Sadat would urge the conference to accept Kissinger's step-by-step approach (as distinct from the Soviet efforts to reconvene the Geneva Conference), and the fact that the United States was trying to promote talks for an Israeli–Jordanian agreement or another Israeli–Egyptian accord. Thus it was no wonder that the Soviet Union sought to strengthen her position – at least with the more radical Arabs – before the meeting in the hope both of countering whatever arguments Sadat might present and forestalling any agreement to procedures or negotiations which would exclude the Soviet Union. Additional support for the Palestinians at this time – at least on this issue – might well provide a vehicle for such objectives.

Yet the issue of Palestinian statehood was a complicated one for a number of reasons, not least of which was a certain hesitancy on the part of the PLO itself to declare for such an objective. Thus the Soviet–PLO communiqué of 24 November 1974, remarkable for its urging of a Palestinian state, linked this position to 'the Soviet side' only.[18] The problem here, particularly between Moscow and the PLO as well as within the PLO, was the locale of such a state. Almost totally ignoring the PLO's demand for a 'secular democratic state' in all of Palestine, the Soviet concept of a Palestinian state was that of a state alongside Israel. In the 1973 memorandum to PLO leaders and in the Soviet exposition of the position of their own PLO affiliate, the Palestinian National Front, as well as in numerous articles and discussions with the Palestinians, the Soviet Union has made clear that her idea of a state corresponds to what the Palestinians term a 'mini-state': i.e., a state to be set up in the territories liberated from Israeli occupation or, as explained by Moscow, on the West Bank and the Gaza Strip.[19] The Soviet Union has on occasion singled out and praised Hawatmeh for accepting this position, although he appears, in fact, to have agreed to the 'mini-state' only as a first step.[20] Similarly, the Soviet Union claimed that Arafat agreed to this idea, and they even hailed what they claimed was the decision of the Palestine National Council, at its meeting in June 1974, to support the idea; in fact, while the Council programme spoke of a 'fighting government', perhaps better translated as 'authority', to be set up in all freed land, the goal of the PLO was to remain 'the liberation of all the Palestinian land'.[21] This programme was, however, a compromise necessitated by the opposition of the more radical PLO leaders, specifically Chabash and Jibril, to any mention of a state at this point.[22] Chabash claimed, however, that Arafat had in fact agreed with the Soviet Union on the mini-state idea, and, in polemics against her on this issue, Chabash explained that he refused to join the July–August 1974 PLO visit to Moscow because of Moscow's position on this issue, as well as on one or two others. He said, for example, that 'the Soviet Union's mistake is her belief that the peaceful solution is the way to settling the Middle East conflict', and added his rejection of what he called 'the proposal of a Palestinian "mini-state",' explaining that 'for the present circumstances the direct result of the establishment of such a state is the recognition of Israel as a state and the acceptance of its peace'.[23] In the statement at the close of Arafat's visit to Moscow in November 1975 the PLO leader did finally agree to join the Soviet call for a Palestinian state but the vague term 'on Palestinian territory' was used rather than the usual 'in the areas to be liberated' or the Palestinians' preferred 'all of Palestine'.[24] The Soviet position remained unchanged, however, as indicated by numerous articles and such things as the comment that Israel and the United States were trying to use the Lebanese events as proof of the '"impossibility" of peaceful coexistence of Muslims and Christians within the framework of one state, [so that] by the same token it could also be possible to prove the impossibility of existence of a Palestinian state alongside Israel', without any reference at all to the PLO's concept of a secular, democratic state in all of Palestine.[25] More important, the Soviet Union continued to demand that Israel withdraw from the territories 'occupied in 1967', and in the Soviet government's statements of January and April 1976 this demand was said to be 'linked organically' with the creation of a Palestinian state; the April statement explained *inter alia* that such a withdrawal would not only restore Arab sovereignty of the lands belonging to them, but would also provide the possibility for the Palestinians to express their self-determination in their own state.[26] As the third element of the usual Soviet formula was also present – guaranteed existence, independence, sovereignty for Israel – even 'inviolability of frontiers' – 'linked organically' with the specific area for withdrawal and the Palestinian state – the idea of a state *next* to Israel, rather than instead of her, was confirmed.

This is not to say that the Soviet Union acknowledged the legitimacy of Zionism. Her position continued to be that Zionism was not a national liberation movement of the Jewish people, but rather the bourgeois racist ideology of a small clique which had taken over Israel, operating to the detriment of the interests of the Jewish people.[27] With this arbitrary (and artificial) separation between the State of Israel and the ideology upon which it was founded, the Soviet Union apparently did not find it incumbent upon herself to explain her continued

and publicly reaffirmed acknowledgement of Israel's right to exist, despite the opposition this evoked within the Palestinian movement (as well as in Iraq and probably other Arab States).[28] For example, in response to the PLO talks in Moscow, in November 1973, Chabash said:

The Soviets are friends who have a specific point of view on Resolution 242. Will the balance of forces, taken together with the Soviet point of view, allow us – according to the analysis of the situation by certain comrades – to reach the goal of Palestine national, democratic jurisdiction, followed by total withdrawal from Arab territories *without recognition, without peace, without secure frontiers, without demilitarized zones*, without international forces, without all those safeguards? My answer is *certainly not*.... Because, as I have said, *Israel would survive even if the maximum achieved at the Geneva Conference was the acceptance of the Soviet point of view, since this is the Soviet understanding of a just settlement*. I think you actually heard the Soviet point of view when our delegation went to Moscow. Thus the situation is that our point of view on the question of Israel and secure borders differs from that of another effective party.[29]

Even the ostensibly more moderate Al Fatah, in its draft programme for the 1974 Palestine National Council meeting, proposed a clause calling upon 'friendly states' not only to maintain a break in diplomatic relations with 'the Zionist entity' but to withdraw recognition of the State of Israel as well.[30] Without embarking upon a discussion of the complex problem of Soviet–Israeli relations, one might speculate that when the Soviet Union informed the Syrian Communists in 1971 that her opposition to the destruction-of-Israel slogan was a matter of principle, she was not expressing a commitment to Israel's existence but her realization that Israel is a fact and that any real threat to her existence would most likely invite American intervention, with all that it might entail, including the threat of super-power confrontation.[31]

Yet the issue was not only that raised by the Palestinians (the continued existence of a Jewish state, even next to a Palestinian one) but the 'mini-state' idea itself: i.e., the definition of the borders of each state or – from the Soviet–Israeli point of view – the 1967 versus 1947 partition plan borders. On this point the Soviet position was ambiguous. The standard Soviet position over the years recognized only the 1947 partition plan lines as the borders of Israel. Indeed official Soviet maps always indicated these borders, sometimes adding the 1949–67 lines as 'armistice lines', and the post-1967 lines as 'cease-fire lines'. Official statistical references also made these distinctions, while any discussion of Israel's borders over the years usually referred to the 1947 lines, expanded when Israel conquered an additional '6,700' – or sometimes '7,000' – square kilometres in the 1948–49 war, and an additional 68,700 square kilometres in 1967. Indeed some of the more esoteric journals or anti-semitic publications even referred to such places as Akko, Beersheva, Ramle and Yaffo as areas taken by Israel in 1948, and which would have to be returned (a clear reference to the 1947 lines as the only legitimate borders).[32] As the issue of Palestinian statehood emerged following the October War, and particularly in conjunction with the UN debate on Zionism, even the central Soviet press made references to the 1947 partition plan as the basis for the Palestinians' claim to a state.[33] One important commentator, Izvestia editor Lev Tolkunov, even referred to the often forgotten reservation expressed by Gromyko in his famous 1947 UN speech favouring partition.[34] Undoubtedly hoping to preserve some future option vis-à-vis the Arabs, Gromyko said at that time that Moscow preferred a binational solution in Palestine (i.e., the alternative opposed by Israel and those favouring Israeli statehood as made possible by partition) but that, if this proved impossible for the peoples involved, Moscow would support partition.[35] This qualification was then forgotten, mentioned seldom, if ever, and virtually held in cold storage until 1975, when it could be conveniently brought out for whatever dividends it might earn the Soviet Union in the eyes of the Palestinians. Yet Tolkunov was the only one to make such a reference, and indeed most (though not all) the articles harking back to the 1947 plan as the legitimization of the Palestinian claim to statehood refrained from adding territorial comments which would link such a state to a specific locale defined by the 1947 plan – for example, the claims regarding Israeli annexation of 6,700 square kilometres in 1949. Moreover, even articles which did make such comments, such as those of Tolkunov and Izvestia's commentator Kudryavtsev (chairman of the Afro-Asian Solidarity Committee), not only limited the 1947 references to the principle of legitimacy for the Palestinians but then went on to specify withdrawal from the 1967 territories (as distinct from vaguer wording like 'Israeli withdrawal' or 'liberation of the Arab lands') as a basis for a solution to the Arab–Israeli conflict and the answer to the Palestinians' problem.[36] Tolkunov even praised what was termed the 'realistic' position of Hawatmeh, for example in accepting the limitations of the West Bank and Gaza.[37]

This apparent ambiguity was probably connected with the fact that as early as 1970 the Soviet Union had begun to enunciate a new public attitude towards Israel's legal borders. In that year, as part of the Soviet position presented to the United States in the two-power talks and in response to the Rogers Plan, the two senior Soviet commentators on Middle East affairs, Yevgeny Primakov and Igor Belyaev, expressed the new attitude. Recalling the 1947 lines as the only legally recognized border of Israel, Belyaev concluded his detailed programme for a settlement with the statement that:

The parties involved in the conflict should proceed from the assumption that the secure and acknowledged boundaries between the Arab countries and Israel are those that existed on 5 June 1967.[38]

In the description of a plan which he said the Soviet government had conveyed 'to all the parties involved'[39] Primakov said:

Were the present Israeli leaders really concerned about anything other than expansionist projects for territorial 'acquisitions', Tel Aviv would pay closer heed to proposals guaranteeing the frontiers of the states in the area, including the frontiers of Israel, which could accord with the demarcation lines that existed on 4 June 1967.[40]

The same year a less important commentator reiterated this theme even more explicitly:

The withdrawal problem is directly linked with that of the Israeli–Arab frontiers. The Soviet Union recognizes the legitimate rights and aspirations of every state in the area. This naturally presupposes as an essential condition the establishment of secure and recognized frontiers between Israel and the Arab States. The Security Council Resolution (22 November 1967), in that part which refers to the establishment of such frontiers, condemns the seizure of territory by force of arms. In conformity with this, the Soviet Union proposes formalizing the lines that existed on 5 June 1967, as the permanent and recognized frontiers between Israel and the neighbouring Arab states party to the June conflict. The Arab states agree to this, though it means a certain concession on their part. For it is known that the 5 June 1967 frontiers are more favourable for Israel than those defined by the UN decision on the creation of the State of Israel in 1947.[41]

While these were indeed explicit and quite new formulations clearly acknowledging the 1967 borders as Israel's legal borders, they remained in the realm of unofficial statements, though the pronouncement in *Pravda*, purporting to be the official Soviet position conveyed in the negotiations – which apparently was indeed the case – did give the idea certain authority. Official expression of this new idea came at the Geneva Peace Conference in December 1973 with the plan for a settlement outlined in Gromyko's address. After directly affirming Israel's right to exist, and adding a word on the inadmissibility of 'protecting one's frontiers' by seizure of others' territories, Gromyko said: 'It is only the legitimate frontier recognized by those who are on both its sides that is really safe. In the specific Middle East situation such are the demarcation lines that existed on 4 June 1967.'[42]

That Gromyko was in fact saying that Israel's legitimate borders were the 4 June 1967 lines was confirmed by a *Pravda* reference to this speech which singled out this phrase saying: 'In connection with the border question, it is possible to see only the lines which existed 4 June 1967 as the legal borders.'[43]

As we have seen, this was the mini-state position presented to the PLO leaders in October 1973 and by the Palestine National Front, in the former case as part of Soviet urgings that the PLO adopt a 'realistic and constructive' position. This kind of limitation on the Palestinians' demands was the position for which the Soviet Union

praised Hawatmeh and the Palestine National Council, and over which Chabash challenged her. For example, Gromyko's speech in April 1975, honouring Khaddam and offering 'strictest guarantees' to Israel, was called by Chabash's newspaper *Al-Hadaf* a declaration of the Arab states 'ally to guarantee the borders of Israel, as defined by the 1967 frontiers'.[44] That Chabash's interpretation, echoed by other Palestinian sources, was indeed correct, was confirmed during a Soviet radio round-table discussion by the comments of *Izvestia* commentator Matveyev on the importance of Gromyko's statement on guarantees.[45] It was reportedly also presented to Israel in some of the rumoured talks held through various emissaries between the two countries.[46] While no other high-level Soviet official was to reiterate this position, it was nonetheless repeated even as the Rabat Conference and the Vladivostok summit were approaching, and at the time of Kissinger's unsuccessful efforts to negotiate a second Israeli–Egyptian agreement in the spring of 1975. Because of the obvious significance of the expression of this new Soviet position, as distinct from the more generally known – and oft-repeated – references to the 1947 partition plan, it is worth noting the post-Geneva statements. According to *Mezhdunarodnaya zhizn* of October 1974:

Recognition of the lines of demarcation existing prior to the June 1967 conflict as the final borders between Israel and the Arab countries constitutes the only reasonable basis on which a settlement in the Middle East can be reached. If one considers that, from the point of view of international law, there are no recognized borders between Israel and Arab countries at all so far, then their establishment along the lines defined would signify great progress in Arab–Israeli relations, and would considerably improve the entire political situation in the Middle East.[47]

Thus, for the first time since 1970, the full significance of Gromyko's Geneva formula was spelled out. Two later articles in *Mezhdunarodnaya zhizn* reiterated this position; in February 1975:

It would be greatly in the interests of the people of Israel to use the present opportunity for a stable settlement of the territorial dispute by way of withdrawing Israeli troops back to the borders that existed prior to 5 June 1967, in compliance with Resolutions 242 and 338 of the Security Council, borders that would become secure and recognized.[48]

and in March 1975:

The Israeli expansionists should not forget that their refusal to withdraw their troops from all the Arab territories occupied in 1967 deprives the State of Israel of any real chance of having the Arab states recognize its existence within the boundaries which existed prior to 4 June 1967, that is, of confirming the territorial demarcation between the Arab countries and Israel which resulted from the Palestine war of 1948–9 and which has not yet been formally endorsed by anyone anywhere.[49]

There was also a Moscow radio in Arabic broadcast on 8 October 1975 which said that the solution to the Palestinian problem should be found in the Israeli withdrawal from the territory occupied in 1967, with the Palestinian state to be founded 'in the end', in the territories liberated from Israeli occupation. And in early 1976, following Moscow's unsuccessful bid to introduce a Security Council resolution whereby Israel and the PLO would recognize each other, a Soviet commentator said:

Israeli propaganda constantly repeats that the recognition of the fight of the Arab people of Palestine to establish their own state would be tantamount to demanding the abolition of the Israeli State. . . . However, the draft resolution backed by the overwhelming majority of the Security Council members, including the Soviet Union [resolution presented by the non-aligned nations] proved these claims groundless. This did not pass unnoticed in the American press. Analysing the rejected draft resolution, the *Washington Post* significantly stressed that its formulation meant to leave room for pre-1967 Israel.[50]

While these were but commentaries designed perhaps to spell out the almost totally consistent *official* Soviet references to the 1967 territories as those which Israel had to vacate in order for there to be a settlement, official status does appear to have been bestowed upon the 1967 border idea with the government statements of January 1976 and, especially, 28 April 1976. Here Moscow 'organically' linked Israeli withdrawal from the 1967 territories with the idea of a Palestinian state and 'international guarantees for the security and inviolability of the frontiers of all Middle Eastern states, and their right to independent existence and development', claiming that 'this basis for a settlement' would provide three things. First, for the Arab states, the return of their territories and their sovereignty over these territories, as well as the removal of the danger of war and the consequent possibility of concentrating on their own economic and social problems and playing a greater role in international affairs. Second, for the Palestinians, the possibility of the refugees leaving the camps, gaining freedom from the oppression of the invaders and building their own independent state. Third, for Israel, ensuring 'peace and security within the recognized frontiers', the opportunity for her young people to be free from the danger of war and for all the people of Israel 'to live in conditions of confidence in the morrow', and for the State of Israel to normalize her position among the states of the world.[51] These comments were all accompanied by secondary reporting of such things as 'demonstrations on the West Bank' (as distinct from 'Israel proper'), 'Arabs on the West Bank and Gaza' (as distinct from 'Israeli Arabs'), and other such fine points implying acceptance of Israel as an entity within her 1967 borders.[52]

Thus the Soviet Union apparently has not retreated from her position regarding the 1967 borders even while she continues to refer to the 1947 lines. She would appear to emphasize the 1967 idea particularly when trying to present herself, as a reasonable, moderate and, therefore, acceptable participant in talks from which both Israel and the United States have tried to exclude her. Indeed one can see an almost exact correlation between Soviet efforts to resume the Geneva Conference and Soviet expressions of moderation regarding Israel and her borders. Yet the fact that the Soviet Union has risked complicating her relations with the PLO by advocating the 1967 lines suggests that this position is not merely tactical, though the continuation of references to 1947 may be designed as the stick to whet Israel's appetite for the 1967 carrot, while also serving as a sop to the Palestinians.[53]

It cannot be ruled out that the two positions and resultant ambiguity are due to some differences of opinion within the Soviet leadership over the Palestinian issue. Certainly some papers have anti-semitic overtones and a harder line on Israel than other papers, undoubtedly due to internal considerations (e.g., the Ukrainian press), and greater support for the Palestinians was apparent in the Trade Union paper *Trud* during the period in which Shelepin was head of the Trade Unions.[54] Also, as already pointed out, on at least one occasion Podgorny took a more radical line on the Palestinians than did Brezhnev.

Such differences could be responsible for the apparent contradiction and hesitancies within the Soviet attitude on this issue, although the differences could possibly reflect a natural – possibly even intended – division of labour, designed to get several points of view across to suit various circumstances. So long as no decision is demanded by the Middle East negotiations it is not surprising that the Soviet Union should wish to keep a number of options open. Indeed there is no reason to believe that she views this issue of Palestinian–Israeli borders as a crucial one or one of principle; in fact it is more likely that she is basically indifferent to the position of the border. Her tendency to favour the 1967 lines, evidenced by the fact of her even considering an alternative to the 1947 lines and by her arguments with the Palestinians, would appear merely to be a function of what she herself calls a realistic approach, given Israeli strength, the American commitment and the generally recognized status of Israel from 1949 onwards.

The other border of the Palestinian state, the one with Jordan, is rarely discussed by Moscow though such a border – as distinct from a Palestinian state occupying all of Palestine (which would then include Jordan) or on the West Bank linked with Jordan – is implied by Soviet comments calling upon the Palestinians to accept a state within the territories occupied in 1967. In one conversation with Arafat, when defining the territories to be affected by a settlement, Gromyko specified 'Egyptian territory [Sinai], Syrian [Golan Heights] and those yet to be defined, i.e., the West Bank including Jerusalem, and Gaza'.[55] Thus the ownership or ultimate ownership of the Jordanian territories was ignored, at least in Arafat's version of his 6 May 1974 conversation with Gromyko.

Similarly Jerusalem was rarely mentioned at all when discussing the occupied territories or a Palestinian state. In fact Soviet reporting of the November 1973 Algiers Conference and the February 1974 Lahore Conference *deleted* the resolutions referring to Jerusalem.[56] Indeed the only context in which the Soviet Union did mention Jerusalem was apparently when seeking to please Jordan – specifically, for example, when demanding Israeli compensation for Arab losses, including losses to Jordan from tourism to Jerusalem, or when criticizing the second Egyptian–Israeli agreement.[57] A Jordanian Communist Party official explained, in the April 1974 issue of the *World Marxist Review*, that first a Palestinian state should be set up in the liberated territories and then its future relations with Jordan should be considered.[58] In a talk on 5 March 1974, the Soviet Ambassador to Jordan also implied that some arrangement would have to be worked out with Jordan in the effort to obtain Palestinian self-determination in the 1967 territories.[59]

These early statements made no reference to the Jordanian idea of a federal Jordanian–Palestinian state, but it was not ruled out either. Later, however, an article by Tolkunov in the authoritative Party journal *Kommunist* did explicitly rule out Hussein's two-year-old proposal for a federal solution, calling it an 'American inspired' plan, as did other articles and Moscow broadcasts in Arabic.[60] It is possible that this declared opposition was meant to foil Dr Kissinger's attempts to negotiate a Jordanian–Israeli agreement which, it was now clear, threatened to settle such problems *without* inclusion of either the Soviet Union or the Palestinians. It came in the same period as the first Soviet pronouncements regarding Palestinian statehood, just prior to the Rabat Conference.

Yet the Soviet Union expressed this anti-Jordanian position only briefly, and mildly; indeed, she was even to demonstrate startling objectivity in reporting the PLO–Jordanian dilemma prior to Rabat.[61] Moreover, both before and (particularly) after Rabat she sought generally to emphasize the meeting points or co-operation between the Jordanians and the PLO, rather than the dividing points. Soviet reporting of the Rabat Conference stressed in most positive terms the working-out of a *modus vivendi* between the two as a sign of voluntary and generous co-operation on the part of both.[62] The Palestinian appraisal of this development was not so sanguine,[63] but the Soviet Union was apparently intent upon keeping her own options open with Jordan. Certainly she strove to improve her relations with Jordan even while increasing support for the Palestinians. Thus Mr Vinogradov, the chief Soviet delegate to the Geneva peace talks, was sent to Amman several times for high-level talks (primarily connected with Soviet efforts to reconvene Geneva, as we shall see below); perhaps more significantly in terms of improved official relations, a Supreme Soviet delegation visited Jordan in March 1975, and a high-level Jordanian governmental delegation went to Moscow in December 1975, just a few weeks after Arafat had visited the Soviet capital.

This process reached a climax with King Hussein's visit to the Soviet Union in June 1976 amid a great deal of attention and fanfare. While this visit – and *rapprochement* – could hardly be welcomed by the PLO, it was perhaps less risky for Soviet Middle East interests in 1976 than earlier, because of the intervening Syrian–Jordanian *rapprochement* and the Jordanian move closer to the radical wing of the Arab states, especially since Egypt was becoming identified with American-inspired moderation in the wake of the 1976 Egyptian–Israeli agreement. As part of this Soviet effort *vis-à-vis* Jordan, the Soviet air force commander, Air Marshal Kutakhov was sent to Amman, and King Hussein was offered a surface-to-air missile defence system as a substitute for the complication-ridden American–Jordanian *HAWK* missile deal.[64] Thus the Soviet Union was even willing to jeopardize relations with the PLO in the interests of gaining some foothold in Jordan, mainly to undermine American influence there, but also as a means of gaining a new option in the Middle East (particularly important in view of the steady decline the Soviet Union had been suffering in the area since 1972). While she probably estimated that her link with the PLO would not be seriously endangered by this move (she may have considered that the increased diplomatic and propaganda support she offered the PLO at the same time was sufficient compensation),[65] the move did reflect the general Soviet preference for dealing with established and stable states, with all that they might offer in the way of strategic and other interests. Certainly the Palestinians, even with a state of their own, would be less desirable – though ideologically somewhat (but not entirely) more attractive – given the PLO's clearly unstable and politically uncertain character and unauthoritative status in the world; and in any case the Palestinians were still far from achieving statehood.

III. GENEVA PEACE CONFERENCE

The idea of the Geneva Peace Conference embodies some essential issues in the PLO–Soviet relationship, such as the concept of negotiations, SCR 242 (on which the conference is based) and the two-pronged problem of Soviet commitment and PLO willingness to participate in the conference. Chabash's arguments against the Soviet Union opposed the very idea of a negotiated settlement (as well as SCR 242),[1] because of its implied recognition of Israel as a state. This was also the line taken by Jibril and the Iraqi-sponsored Arab Liberation Front, but the criticism levelled against Arafat by these groups and by Chabash – as well as the image of Arafat the Soviet Union sought to create – suggest that the Fatah leader was more amenable on this issue, though he never made any public declaration to this effect.[2]

As the October War drew to a close, the peace conference became an acute issue in PLO–Soviet relations, for the Soviet–American cease-fire proposal (SCR 338) not only called for negotiations but limited itself specifically to the implementation of SCR 242, which dealt with the Palestinian problem not as a national or political issue but rather as a mere refugee problem. As a result, the PLO added its criticism of the cease-fire to that of Syria (which up to then had also failed to accept SCR 242), Iraq, Libya and Algeria. The Soviet Union, finding herself on the defensive, explained her interpretation of SCR 242 in such a way as to include a specific demand for the

Palestinians' legitimate rights, hoping thereby to pacify Palestinian objections to the cease-fire.[3]

The problem persisted in the period after the October War, even becoming acute with Soviet pressure for a negotiated settlement via the Geneva Peace Conference. The Soviet Union continued to hedge, offering definitions and interpretations of SCR 242 which at least accounted for the Palestinians' legitimate rights.[4] Even the draft programme submitted to the June 1974 Palestine National Council by those elements of the PLO which did not form part of the 'Refusal Front' – Al Fatah, Sai'qa, and Hawatmeh's Popular Democratic Front for the Liberation of Palestine (PDFLP) – argued that 'the Arab political decision accepting the cease-fire resolution 338 met the requirement for ending the battle at the limits of limited war. No one loses sight of the connection this resolution has with resolution 242 and the meaning of this – namely, bypassing the core of the issue and total injustice to our people's national and historic rights.'[5] Given this position on the part of even the ostensibly more moderate Palestinians, the Soviet Union cannot have been surprised when the Council meeting explicitly rejected SCR 242 and 'any action on that basis at any level of Arab and international operation, including the Geneva Conference'.[6] However, both extremes – Chabash on one side and the Soviet Union on the other – claimed that this resolution was merely tactical, concealing what were in fact a different set of intentions. Chabash claimed that Arafat – indeed the PLO executive – did intend to participate in Geneva. The Soviet Union cited this Council meeting as a turning point in the Palestinian attitude toward Geneva,[7] and maintained that the PLO agreed to attend, though she allowed on occasion that the precondition was that the Palestinian problem should be examined there 'as a political question, as a question of securing the lawful national rights of the Arab people of Palestine and is not confined to the "refugee problem".'[8] In fact what the PLO was to demand was an amendment to SCR 242 along these lines.[9] Rumours in Arab circles at the time claimed that the Soviet Union had agreed to support such an amendment,[10] although, given her undoubted awareness of the difficulties and risks involved in tampering with this resolution (the hard-won minimum point of agreement between the Arab states and Israel), she ap-

parently preferred to ignore the idea of *amendment* as such. Her efforts to persuade Arafat to declare in favour of participation continued to be unsuccessful, therefore, and the statement on Arafat's visit to Moscow in July–August 1974 spoke only of the support of *the Soviet side* for PLO participation at Geneva.[11] Indeed, Arafat, defending himself from internal attacks, continued explicitly to reject the idea, because of SCR 242, while the Soviet Union openly criticized Chabash for 'co-operating with the imperialists' in efforts to dissuade the PLO from participating.[12] But none of this ruled out the possibility that Moscow had secured Arafat's agreement in principle, provided she supported the placing of the Palestinian issue before the UN, with the attendant possibility of some new resolution on the issue being passed.

This was indeed what happened, and the Palestinians did in fact gain a new resolution of the General Assembly. While the Soviet Union actively supported this effort and hailed the General Assembly resolution (GAR 3236) when it was passed, she did not follow up Arafat's clear intention of having this new resolution used as a basis for subsequent negotiations. With an eye on the United States and Israel, she apparently did not feel it opportune in 1974 and during most of 1975 even to test the reception of such a linkage; she was presumably too interested in bringing about the reconvening of the Geneva talks to risk making this new demand. Indeed, during Arafat's November 1974 visit to Moscow, after the passage of GAR 3236, the Soviet Union not only refrained from any such linkage of this resolution with Geneva but, reportedly, pressed the PLO leader harder than ever on the Geneva issue, arguing that the only alternative to Geneva was war.[13] As a result, the final communiqué of the visit once again limited support for PLO participation in Geneva to the Soviet side alone.[14] In the communiqué issued at the close of Arafat's next visit to Moscow, after Dr Kissinger's failure to obtain an Israeli–Egyptian agreement in the spring of 1975, the Soviet Union was willing at least to mention the 'decisions of the 29th session of the UN General Assembly', but did not link this with the statement's subsequent comments regarding the Geneva Conference. For the first time, though, Arafat did agree to the formulation of recognition by 'both sides' of the importance of the PLO's participation in all negotiations including Geneva.[15] However, Arafat later denied that this was a firm commitment, reverting to the vague formula that the PLO would decide this issue when actually invited, and the PLO information chief Abu Mayzar claimed that Arafat had told Brezhnev that the PLO rejected any initiative based on SCR 242.[16]

In any case the Soviet Union had apparently already realized, even before her round of consultations with the Arabs, that the various positions were too far apart to permit the Geneva talks to be reconvened. As early as 30 March 1975, just a few days after the suspension of Kissinger's Middle East talks, the Soviet media began to speak of the necessity for preparations, even lengthy preparations, for the reconvening of Geneva. Continuation of this line after the round of consultations indicated that Moscow had apparently not achieved agreement with her Arab friends regarding Palestinian participation there, nor on other issues.

The Soviet Union did eventually show some willingness to accommodate the PLO demands regarding Geneva, though this change did not, as might have been expected, occur in response to the success of Kissinger's effort to obtain an Egyptian–Israeli agreement in August 1975. The Soviet Union did use the neglect of the Palestinian issue in this agreement as part of her propaganda against it, and presumably also as a lever to try to prevent similar negotiations for a Syrian–Israeli agreement. However, her decision finally to link Geneva with GAR 3236 (coinciding with a new emphasis in Soviet insistence upon PLO participation) came only in November 1975, *after* Syria had rejected American overtures for a Syrian agreement and had launched her campaign in the UN to place the Palestinian issue in the centre of discussions, specifically in the Security Council.[17] The Soviet move apparently was designed primarily to support the Syrian initiative, both as a means of isolating Egypt and the United States and as a means of preserving Soviet ties with Syria. While such increased support for the Palestinians carried the risk of preventing the reconvening of Geneva and harming Moscow's broader interests regarding a settlement, the tactical calculation at the time probably placed Soviet–Syrian relations – and the related disarming of Kissinger on this front – temporarily above these broader considerations.

Thus, while the Soviet note to the United States of 9 November 1975, calling for the reconvening of Geneva, specifically added GAR 3236 to SCR 338 as the basis for a settlement there, the Soviet media either omitted to mention this or substituted the much more vague phrase 'appropriate UN decisions'.[18] Subsequent official Soviet initiatives, such as the January and April 1976 statements, also failed to link GAR 3236 with Geneva, and, aside from occasional references to the resolution, particularly in UN speeches by the Soviet representative Mr Malik, it has not yet been made part of the Soviet Union's demands for Geneva or of her conditions for Palestinian participation.[19] Moreover the Soviet Union ignored the Palestinians' demand for an amendment to SCR 242 in the Security Council debate of January 1976. While this need not prevent her from returning to such a linkage in the future, the general retreat suggests that American opposition was sufficiently strong to arouse Soviet concern for reconvening Geneva.

The use of GAR 3236 has not been the only gauge of the Soviet Union's commitment to PLO participation; it merely exemplified her effort to persuade the PLO to participate. The other side of the coin has been her effort to *enable* the Palestinians to participate by convincing the other parties involved. Here, too, her position underwent numerous transformations, exhibiting many inconsistencies and much tactical manoeuvring. She totally ignored the Palestinians in the reference to negotiations in the cease-fire resolution of October 1973, and was most willing to convene the Geneva Conference without them, agreeing to the highly non-committal formula that further Middle East participants would be decided at the conference itself.[20]

In 1973 and 1974 the Soviet Union appeared to support a solution to the problem of participation by means of a combined Jordanian–Palestinian delegation.[21] Following the opening of the Geneva Conference, she began to make more consistent references to the Palestinians' national rights and began officially to call for 'Palestinian participation' in Geneva. This call appeared to be connected with American successes in the Middle East, since the more frequent mention of the Palestinians – and specifically of the need for them to participate in Geneva – occurred just before Kissinger's arrival in the Middle East for the Syrian–Israeli disengagement talks. On this occasion the Soviet Union pointed to American opposition to Palestinian approval as 'proof' that the Americans could not be trusted.[22] She returned to this point after the successful completion of the disengagement talks in May 1974, though her increased support for the Palestinians was by then connected not only with combating American successes but also with the convening of the Palestine National Council in June 1974.[23] Yet during the June 1974 talks between President Nixon and Mr Brezhnev these efforts to persuade the United States to agree to immediate reconvening of the Geneva Conference led to a Soviet retreat on the Palestinian issue; the communiqué on the talks used the pre-Geneva compromise formula that additional participants from the region would be decided at the conference itself.[24] Presumably to compensate for this apparent abandonment of the Palestinians, and perhaps reflecting the actual Soviet proposal to the Americans, a Tass commentary of 4 July claimed that Brezhnev had in fact pressed Nixon to agree to Palestinian participation 'from the outset', but this point was not repeated or emphasized at that time.[25]

One sign that the Soviet Union may not have given up her hopes of solving the problem by means of a PLO-Jordanian delegation was her prematurely enthusiastic response to the Sadat-Hussein communiqué of 18 July 1974. Apparently grossly miscalculating the overwhelmingly negative response it would provoke in the Arab world – because of its division of responsibility for the Palestinians between the PLO (said to represent the Palestinians outside Jordan) and Hussein (by implication considered the legitimate representative of those within Jordan) – she welcomed it as a sign of a Jordanian shift in the direction of the PLO, Egypt and other Arab countries,[26] and emphasized the role such an arrangement provided for the PLO at Geneva. Well aware of Israel's refusal to agree to the Geneva talks if a PLO delegation were present, Moscow may have seen this new development as the basis for a joint Arab or Jordanian delegation which could include the PLO.[27]

In order to compensate for this mistaken interpretation (and probably also in order to disclaim approval of a compromise with Jordan) the Soviet statement issued at the close of Arafat's visit to Moscow on 3 August 1974 included the stipulation that the PLO should participate 'with equal rights with the other participants' at Geneva.[28] However, since this coincided with a shift towards Soviet recognition of the PLO as the sole legitimate representative of the Palestinians also in the communiqué (see section VI below), these steps were not merely recompense for the earlier mistake. Rather they were probably forerunners of the significant increase in Soviet support for the PLO and criticism of Jordan which was to come as the Americans pressed their step-by-step plans (including direct talks between Jordan and Israel, bypassing Geneva) and as the Rabat Conference approached.[29] Thus Brezhnev's Kishinev speech of 11 October 1974, made as Kissinger once again journeyed to the Middle East, called for Palestinian participation in Geneva. But once again commentaries pointing out America's desire for partial agreements excluding certain parties from the negotiations demonstrated that at least one of the reasons for supporting the Palestinians was to impede American gains in the Middle East.[30] Nonetheless the door was left open for compromise should the reconvening of Geneva become feasible, for no mention was made of when the Palestinians were to participate, and, although a statement at the end of a visit to Moscow by the Egyptian Foreign Minister on 18 October did stipulate 'on an equal footing',[31] the Soviet position on these important details fluctuated greatly in this period. In response to the Rabat Conference, the Soviet Union publicly raised the idea of a joint Palestinian–Jordanian delegation, while the Podgorny–Kosygin message to the conference called for a resumption of the Geneva talks without mentioning the Palestinians at all.[32] This relative moderation during, as distinct from before, the Rabat Conference may have been designed to prevent the conference accepting too-strict limitations regarding agreement to reconvene Geneva. (Such limitations were certainly possible, given the position of the more radical Arabs before and during the conference.[33]) Having significantly raised her support for the PLO and the Palestinians' more essential demands, the Soviet Union therefore probably felt free to pursue her goal of the resumption of the Geneva talks as she saw fit.

The Vladivostok talks between President Ford and Mr Brezhnev, unlike the previous summit, did not mention the issue of additional participants in Geneva at all. Given the Arab opposition he would certainly incur if he publicly put off the participation question again, and given the improbability of American agreement to any other, more positive formulation, Brezhnev may simply have preferred to avoid the issue altogether. Yet during the few weeks before and immediately after the summit official Soviet pronouncements failed to mention Palestinian participation at all,[34] although it was mentioned, and the 'equal footing' stipulation repeated, in the communiqué of 30 November at the close of Arafat's visit to Moscow.[35]

The same inconsistencies, retreats and increased demands persisted over the next months and the following year, although a definitely more insistent Soviet line over Palestinian participation became apparent just before the December 1974 meeting of the Central Committee of the Soviet Communist Party.

This coincided with a deterioration of Soviet–Egyptian relations, a crucial factor of which was Sadat's preference for the Kissinger approach over a return to Geneva, and the Soviet Union may have used this new emphasis upon Palestinian participation in Geneva as added pressure on Egypt, as well as a propaganda weapon against the United States.

The new line persisted throughout the period of Kissinger's January–March 1975 efforts to gain a second Israeli–Egyptian agreement, now with relatively frequent references to Palestinian participation on an equal footing, including one by Brezhnev.[36] But, despite her apparent commitment to Palestinian participation, the Soviet Union undertook efforts to seek Israeli and Jordanian agreement to reconvening the Geneva conference – agreement which, at that time, would almost certainly have had to be at the Palestinians' expense, at least in the first stages of a reconvened conference.[37] In what may have been a continuation of earlier efforts to find a suitable framework for Palestinian participation through another delegation, Moscow received Assad's offer of a unified Palestinian–Syrian military and political command as providing a possible means of Palestinian participation in Geneva.[38] (One of the reasons for Chabash's opposition to this proposal was that he, too, saw it as a measure which was designed to bring the PLO to Geneva.[39])

A further clue that the Soviet Union was thinking in terms of linking the Palestinians to some other delegation was *Pravda*'s correction of Gromyko's comments at his meeting with Arafat in Damascus in February 1975; according to Moscow domestic radio, Gromyko called for PLO participation in Geneva 'with full rights as a delegation', but the *Pravda* version omitted 'as a delegation'.[40] The Soviet Union apparently discussed this approach with Jordan when Mr Vinogradov went there on his way to Beirut for talks with Arafat in March.[41] No public mention was made of this trip, but the Soviet ambassador to Beirut reportedly found it necessary to reassure at least some Palestinians that the Soviet Union supported independent PLO representation at Geneva, specifically denying reports that she favoured Jordan representing the Palestinians.[42] The Soviet Union expressed 'understanding' of the Palestinians' opposition to mediation by Hussein, although the Soviet media continued to highlight any sign of PLO–Jordanian co-operation.[43] Moreover, despite the inclusion of the idea of Palestinian participation 'on an equal footing' in all the communiqués on Soviet consultations with Fahmy, Khaddam, Arafat and Iraq's Saddam Hussein in 1975, after the failure of Kissinger's talks, there was no mention of the timing of such participation. Furthermore, not only did the Soviet Union have a hand in approaches involving the inclusion of the PLO in broader delegations, she reportedly indicated to certain parties, such as the United States and Israel, that she would be willing to compromise on the matter of direct PLO representation from the beginning.[44]

In the late summer of 1975, during a period of Jordanian–Soviet contacts on bilateral issues (including an invitation to Hussein to visit the Soviet Union), Soviet references to Palestinian participation at Geneva again decreased. Since this came just as Kissinger was concluding the Israeli–Egyptian interim agreement, it is possible that the Soviet Union believed that Kissinger's efforts, whether successful or not, would be followed by American agreement to reconvene Geneva, and she therefore sought to prepare the compromise position necessary for such a move. But it is also possible that she despaired more than ever of reaching a formula for Palestinian participation acceptable to both the PLO and the United States.

The switch back to demanding Palestinian (indeed PLO) participation – now not only 'on an equal basis' but also 'from the outset' – came in a reference to GAR 3236 supporting the Syrian moves in the UN in November 1975.[45] Even when the Soviet Union dropped the reference to 3236 she continued for some months to demand Palestinian participation, including the stipulations 'from the very beginning' and 'on an equal footing' in the January 1976 statement which coincided with the Syrian campaign in the UN. Yet the April 1976 statement returned to the milder demand which did not specify when the Palestinians should participate, stipulating only that the PLO should participate as 'a' representative, according to the Tass translation. Brezhnev, in his speech to the 25th Congress of the Soviet Communist Party in February 1976, did not even call for Palestinian participation in negotiations; nor has any official Soviet document or any Soviet leader ever specified the PLO as the *sole* representative of the Palestinians (indeed the 9 November 1975 call for Geneva listed Jordan as one of the necessary participants, as did the January 1976 statement).[46]

The picture of Soviet inconsistency on the issue, and especially on the timing of Palestinian representation, has continued, the fuller Soviet support coming when tactically desirable (for example, during the split between Syria and the PLO in the Lebanon in the late spring and summer of 1976, when the Soviet Union sought to provide added support for the PLO). Such tactical manoeuvring strongly suggests that the Soviet position on Palestinian or PLO participation is not as firm as it might at first appear, and when the possibility of reconvening the Geneva Conference has appeared imminent or feasible, the Soviet Union has retreated on the issue, sometimes completely but always on its timing.

Given the Soviet Union's overriding interest in being a party to the Middle East negotiations, primarily by moving the talks back to Geneva, it does not seem likely that she would risk the cancellation of such an event by insisting on Palestinian representation, in the face of American–Israeli refusal to accommodate it. The most she seems willing to do, apart from striving for some sort of joint-delegation solution, is to bring sufficient pressure on the United States via the Arabs to prompt a compromise. But such pressures are of a delicate nature. Although Chabash has indeed accused the Soviet Union of encouraging American contacts with the PLO in order to reach a *modus vivendi* regarding Geneva (and thus to thwart an American-sponsored Israeli–Jordanian agreement),[47] on a more long-term basis she could not be expected to view with favour the risk of yet another of her clients beginning to look to Washington for solutions.

IV. INTERNAL DIFFERENCES IN THE PLO

The lack of unity within the PLO has remained a constant point of criticism by the Soviet Union and may well have contributed to her original reservations about the group. Not only does the lack of unity complicate Soviet efforts to gain control over the main forces of the movement, but it also adds an element of instability, particularly regarding understandings reached by the Soviet Union with the organization or its leadership. Further, the substantive side of the internal PLO differences is of serious concern, focusing as it does on the central issues of ends (statehood, destruction of Israel) and means (terror, negotiations). Besides undermining the stability of the organization, these differences more often than not involve direct opposition to Soviet preferred policies. This situation is further complicated for Moscow by the fact that some of the dissenting groups within the PLO are highly ideologically oriented, the more extremist having received varying degrees of Chinese support over the years, while some of them are linked with, and sponsored by, certain Arab states: i.e., Iraq (the Arab National Front) and Syria (Sai'qa).

The Soviet Union's general concern over the PLO's internal differences has been more or less constant over the years, and few commentaries in the Soviet media fail to mention this problem in one form or another. As the Soviet Union increased her support for the PLO, she did occasionally claim that it was succeeding in overcoming its differences.[1] The June 1974 session of the Palestine National Council was severely criticized, however, for lack of unity and, specifically, for the opposition of the more radical elements to participation in the Geneva talks and in a peaceful settlement. 'Extremism of some of the contingents' of the PLO was cited as one of two sources of the 'real dangers threatening the resistance movement'[2] (the other was imperialist and reactionary quarters).

The Soviet Union has also criticized lack of PLO unity as a barrier to the adoption of a common programme which could be put forward in international efforts to solve the Middle East conflict[3] – though after Arafat's July–August 1974 visit to Moscow, a Soviet commentary did refer to the ascent of the 'realists' in the PLO regarding both the issue of negotiations and the idea of a mini-state.[4] Nonetheless, a comment by Arafat during his November 1974 visit suggests that he had not yet satisfied Moscow on this issue of internal unity. Admitting the existence of differing points of view within the Palestinian movement, despite the 'strengthening and improving' of relations between elements of the movement, he argued that the expression of differing views was 'a sign of the good health of the revolution'. Admitting that there were even 'negative currents', he seemed to challenge the Soviet Union: 'But can there be a revolution without a negative current? Even the established states have negative currents. We cannot expect a revolution without negative currents, and especially the Palestinian revolution and the Palestinian issue.'[5] There are no signs, however, that the Soviet Union accepted this argument, and the issue of unity remained,[6] albeit somewhat altered because of Lebanese events, as we shall see.

As to specific groups and their opinions, the Soviet Union has been relatively cautious, at least in publicly providing details of their preferences and complaints. Because of their extremist views on such things as terror, neither of the two more Marxist-oriented groups of the PLO – Chabash's PFLP and Hawatmeh's PDFLP – was considered a suitable partner for the Soviet Union in the early years of her support.[7] Thus, from the outset the Soviet Union concentrated on the non-Marxist nationalist Arafat, while creating her own grouping: first Al Ansar and later the Palestine National Front. Realizing the

influence wielded by Iraq and Syria via their groups in the PLO, she also sought to increase the role the relevant Communist Parties played in connection with the PLO – though in the case of the faction-torn Syrian Communist party this created unwelcome problems for her, as we have seen.[8] Aside from the constant support for Arafat, there has been a definite tendency, since at least 1973, to improve contacts with, and increase Soviet support for, Hawatmeh and, since 1975 especially, to strengthen the Palestine National Front. With Chabash, however, she had reached the stage of open polemics by 1974, while Lebanese events occasioned some modifications in Soviet attitudes.

The Soviet interest in Hawatmeh – natural because of his Marxist convictions, but difficult because of his extremism – may have been encouraged by his participation in Arafat's delegation to Moscow immediately after the October War. According to the Soviet Union, he then agreed to the idea of a mini-state, though Hawatmeh himself said after the visit that this in no way meant renouncing the Palestinians' 'historic rights' to their 'entire homeland'.[9] A year later, on the day a PLO delegation arrived in Moscow, *Izvestia*'s editor, Tolkunov, criticized those in the PLO who advocated a Palestinian state *instead* of Israel, claiming that 'most' PLO organizations now agreed to a more 'realistic' position, 'many' supporting the idea of a Palestinian state on the West Bank and Gaza; in this context he again used the term 'realistic' of Hawatmeh's 1973 plan for a Palestinian authority on the West Bank and Gaza.[10] Another sample of Soviet efforts to portray Hawatmeh as a moderate was the positive reporting of the interview Hawatmeh had agreed to have published in Israel. Having used this event as 'proof' that Zionism had failed in its attempts to push the Palestinian organizations to extremism, the Soviet Union must have been particularly embarrassed when, six weeks later, the PDFLP staged one of the most barbarous terrorist attacks yet – seizing ninety Israeli schoolchildren at Ma'alot in May 1974 and murdering over twenty of them – in answer to attacks upon Hawatmeh's loyalty from within the PLO.[11] Nonetheless, the Soviet Union increased her support for Hawatmeh by inviting him to Moscow independently of Arafat, first in November 1974 (just after Rabat and before a visit by Arafat in which Hawatmeh nonetheless participated) and again in December 1975, following a visit by Arafat on which Hawatmeh did not accompany him. Although the first trip was given no publicity in the Soviet media, Hawatmeh met Gromyko with the intention, according to comments to *Le Monde* earlier, of discussing the political profile of a Palestinian government-in-exile.[12] The Soviet position and Hawatmeh's were identical (favouring a group which would be a reflection of the PLO executive, rather than including additional, bourgeois, elements), so it was more or less natural for Moscow to seek to strengthen this viewpoint, via Hawatmeh, in the debate that was taking place in the PLO.[13] Hawatmeh was again singled out for praise just before the PLO visit in May 1975 as a 'politically experienced and erudite figure', as distinct from reactionary elements which threatened the progressive nature of the Palestinian state-to-be.[14] His December 1975 visit to Moscow was perhaps of greater significance, for not only did it come instead of participation in Arafat's delegation, but this time he was given some publicity, and a statement (though not a joint communiqué) was even issued at the close of the visit.[15] This suggested a Soviet effort to cultivate Hawatmeh independently of Arafat, even though his delegation had been invited at a lower level (by the Afro-Asian Solidarity Committee), and Hawatmeh was more forthcoming than Arafat in the final statement, praising Moscow's initiative for reconvening the Geneva Conference.[16] This singling out of Hawatmeh was the more significant because his visit came at a time of splits within the PLO as a result of the fighting in Lebanon and of Syrian efforts to take over the PLO through their contingent, the Sai'qa. Its exact significance is harder to assess, however; some rumours claimed that the Lebanese events had brought Hawatmeh closer to Chabash (who was still anathema to the Soviet Union), while others claimed that Arafat himself had drawn closer to Chabash – which could perhaps explain both Arafat's rather less co-operative attitude on the Geneva issue during his November 1975 visit and the Soviet Union's desire to strengthen her position with Hawatmeh, possibly even as an alternative to Arafat. The subsequent months, however, produced no similar juxtaposition of the two leaders on the Soviet horizon (except for

publication of both their telegrams to the CPSU Congress in February 1976, the other PLO groups' cables merely being mentioned), and the Lebanese events have gone through several more convolutions affecting PLO internal alignments.[17]

Although far weaker politically than Hawatmeh, the Palestine National Front (PNF), created by the Jordanian Communist Party, was far more promising to the Soviet Union than any other PLO contingent, provided it could be elevated to a significant position within that organization. A front of Communists and non-Communists, trained to operate on a guerrilla as well as a political basis on the West Bank, it could provide the desired vehicle for Soviet policy preferences amongst the Palestinians and within the PLO organization. The PNF also supported a Palestinian state on the West Bank and Gaza shortly after the October War, acknowledged SCR 242 and echoed Moscow's appeals for the Geneva Conference.[18] The Soviet Union praised the PNF's acceptance into the PLO executive (at the Palestine National Council meeting of June 1974) and began to give the Front greater publicity in the autumn of 1975.[19] Soviet broadcasts in Arabic traced the brief history of the organization (including the Jordanian Communist Party's role in its creation) and cited in particular its positive position on the idea of a state in the occupied territories. That this was part of a Soviet effort to bolster the group was evidenced by the fact that a leader of the Front, Abd al-Jawad Salah was invited to head a delegation to Moscow between 5 and 12 April 1976, and sympathetic publicity was given to this first publicly acknowledged visit to the Soviet Union by the PNF on its own.[20]

While this increased public support by the Soviet Union came as Lebanese events were entering a critical stage, and the PLO was splitting badly in several directions, the move may have been still more directly connected with events in (and Soviet plans for) the West Bank. The Soviet Union seemed to have been grooming the PNF as the leader or representative of the West Bank Arabs, not only as a cover for bringing Communists or Communist sympathizers into the local administrations but also as an alternative to the more extreme PLO line. Thus, although trained for sabotage and guerrilla action in the occupied territories, the

PNF reflected the Soviet preference for political action, such as the riots and demonstrations which took place on the West Bank in late 1975 and early 1976 during the UN discussions on Zionism and the preparations for West Bank elections.[21] This type of action, apparently co-ordinated with the Moscow-oriented New Communist Party of Israel (Rakah), suited the Soviet Union far better – particularly for international purposes – than the PLO style of terror. Thus the Soviet press reported the results of the West Bank elections, at least in the cities, as a victory for 'PNF sympathizers' (without mentioning the PLO) and referred to the group's local support.[22] The PNF's elevation at the expense of the PLO's policy line was relatively short-lived, however, and the Soviet press soon returned to reporting PLO support on the West Bank, without mentioning the PNF. Indeed the Soviet Union has so far shown no inclination to alienate the PLO by this manoeuvring; rather, she appears to be striving to bolster the PNF *within* the PLO without creating an open challenge.

Moscow's attitude towards Chabash and the Refusal Front within the PLO[23] has also undergone a number of changes, mostly in the direction of deterioration. Soviet relations with Chabash were never very good, given his extreme radical position on just about every issue of the Middle East conflict, and even while he advocated co-operation with the Soviet Union for ideological reasons he openly criticized her policies.[24] Chabash openly expressed such criticism as early as the November 1973 PLO visit to Moscow (see Chapter II, p. 5). In the summer of 1974 he pressed this to the point of polemics, refusing to join the July–August delegation to Moscow because of the Soviet position on Geneva and the mini-state, and explaining the refusal in a joint statement with the PFLP General Command and the Arab Liberation Front, published on 19 July, attacking PLO participation in Geneva.[25] Shortly afterwards he said that 'the Soviet Union's mistake is its belief that the peaceful solution is the way to settling the Middle East conflict', adding that 'for the present circumstances the direct result of the establishment of [a Palestinian mini-state] is the recognition of Israel as a state and the acceptance of its peace'.[26]

The Soviet Union responded to Chabash at first indirectly, but a few weeks later by name.

On 14 August 1974 *Literaturnaya gazeta* implied that Chabash was co-operating with the imperialists in efforts to dissuade the PLO from participating in Geneva. (Although this journal is basically oriented towards domestic audiences, the naming of Chabash nonetheless marked an unusually open intervention in internal PLO struggles.) While the Soviet Union may have simply decided that she could not let Chabash's attacks go unanswered, this move may indicate that she believed Arafat to be sufficiently secure to withstand an open break with the Refusal Front. Indeed the exclusion of these radical elements from the PLO was probably desirable in her eyes, and she had in any case decided to provide Arafat with enough support to outweigh the possible attraction or justification of Chabash's anti-negotiation position. Thus the Soviet reaction to Chabash's withdrawal from the PLO executive in September 1974 was only to report a Lebanese paper's brief rebuke of the PFLP for thereby causing delays in the PLO's struggle.[27] The Soviet press did not report any details of the arguments which had led to this move, some of which had been critical of the Soviet position. The Soviet Union may also have welcomed Chabash's last minute refusal to participate in the Rabat Conference; just before the Conference she issued a warning, quite possibly directed against the Refusal Front, about 'attempts of enemies . . . to dictate an agenda completely contrary to the peaceful aspirations of the Arab people.'[28] Just as the Conference was opening, Moscow issued a joint communiqué with a visiting Iraqi Communist Party delegation favouring a Palestinian state in the territories to be liberated and the reconvening of the Geneva Conference.[29]

With the intensification of the Lebanese civil war, the Soviet Union's position *vis-à-vis* the Refusal Front and the various other components of the PLO became much more complicated. She was faced with a Syrian-supported Sai'qa under Zuhair Mohsen trying to take over the PLO at the expense of Arafat, and with a consequent *rapprochement* between Arafat and Chabash, as well as what eventually turned out to be a *rapprochement* between Hawatmeh and the Refusal Front. While Moscow would not have welcomed a weakening of Arafat's position, given the alternative of the anti-Soviet radical elements of the Refusal Front, it may not

155

have been entirely opposed to a Syrian take-over of the PLO with the aim of submerging it in a possibly more amenable Syrian–Jordanian axis.

In 1976, however, as the Syrian intervention in Lebanon began to assume worrying dimensions in Soviet eyes (particularly, no doubt, because of Syria's clearly independent line, supporting the Christian Right against the Muslim–PLO Left and, at least implicitly, serving American interests there), Soviet support of Arafat increased, and Chabash was even occasionally mentioned favourably in the Soviet media.[30] In the late spring and summer of 1976, the Soviet Union indirectly acknowledged the disintegration of the PLO as an umbrella organization in the Lebanese context by reverting to her usage of earlier years and referring to the 'Palestinian Resistance Movement', rather than the PLO. At the same time, however, her general support for the PLO in the Arab–Israeli conflict (on such things as the Geneva Conference or statehood) was stepped up.

But the polarization of the PLO (i.e., Arafat) and Syria, with its effect of putting the Soviet Union behind the Palestinians and against Syria, cannot have been welcome from Moscow's point of view. (This support for Arafat did at one stage give her the opportunity to gain favour with Iraq and Libya, but complications arose in July 1976, when Arafat appeared willing to accept a Syrian-sponsored cease-fire plan while the more radical Chabash and Hawatmeh rejected it.) In theory Syria was a more important client than the PLO, provided she could be brought back to at least a degree of co-operation with the Soviet Union. However, given the ever-changing events and alignments in Lebanon, little more than tactical positions could be expected from the Soviet Union at any given moment, the firmness of her support for the Palestinians, via Arafat, being subject ultimately to her calculations about Soviet–Syrian–American relations in a broader context than that of Lebanon.

V. TERRORISM

A continuous and major problem in Soviet–PLO relations was presented by the extremist, often pro-Chinese elements in the PLO, with their penchant for international terrorism and their belief that only the military destruction of Israel could bring a solution to the Palestinian problem. Terrorism as such has little or no support from official Soviet ideology, the early Bolsheviks, including Lenin, having opposed the idea. While there are plenty of instances in which Soviet ideological tenets have been stretched, distorted or ignored to accommodate the dictates of political tactics, terrorism was and is generally (though not always) seen by the Soviet Union as counter-productive – and in this specific case as harmful to the Arab cause.

This relatively conservative attitude towards terrorism should be considered within the framework of the Soviet attitude towards armed action, revolution and wars of national liberation. With the introduction of the policy of peaceful coexistence, after Stalin's death, the demand for the reduction of world tensions brought a return to Lenin's tactics for Communist parties and to the question of revolution in what was

becoming known as the Third World. The return to the Leninist line meant Communist support for, and alliance with, the national bourgeoisie of the Third World: i.e., pre-capitalist or nascent capitalist societies, in which the non-existence or smallness of the local proletariat precluded socialist revolution or worker leadership of revolutionary action. Generally speaking, this meant postponing genuine revolutionary action during a period of co-operation with a bourgeois regime ostensibly engaged in a national struggle for independence from Western imperialism. Theoretically, it also meant support for non-ruling national liberation movements in their anti-imperialist struggle. However, just as co-operation with bourgeois regimes was largely motivated by the Soviet interest in reducing tension, so as to further the pursuit of certain strategic and economic goals, so support for national liberation movements was tempered by considerations of war and peace, tension and quiet.

One of the points of difference between the Soviet Union and China, therefore, concerned wars of national liberation and the radicality of national liberation movements. Soviet support for armed action, or even wars of liberation, is apparently likely to be forthcoming only when Moscow believes that, (1) they have a genuine chance of success, and (2) there is little or no likelihood of Western (American) intervention. In an area as volatile as the Middle East, with its global as well as regional connections, the Soviet Union prefers stability or, at worst controlled conflict, ruling out almost all armed conflict against Israel except what she may see as limited, controlled, static battles of attrition.

With regard to guerrilla action, the Soviet Union seems to make a distinction between acts of terror on the one hand, and sabotage or resistance on the other. She has therefore encouraged, equipped and trained Palestinians whose task is ostensibly armed action *within* the occupied territories ('resistance') or against strategic and military objectives in Israel; indeed this was the *raison d'être* she put forward for the Palestine National Front: a group geared to resistance, of an armed as well as political nature, against the Israeli occupier on the West Bank.[1] The Soviet Union has therefore sought to depict acts of terror within Israel as the work of *local* Arabs or, at the most, as actions against strategic-military objectives. However, this was not done only for ideological and propaganda reasons; it also stemmed from genuine concern over the escalation that might result from Israeli reprisals against outside incursions. The Soviet Union thus rejected many of these acts, as well as more obviously objectionable international terror, condemning the 'extremism' of some elements of the PLO, just as she condemned the 'leftist adventurism' of other Arab militants anxious for renewed war against Israel.

A sample of Soviet responses to PLO actions will demonstrate this position and some of the complications involved. The September 1972 murder of Israeli athletes at the Munich Olympics and the murder of Western diplomats in Khartoum in March 1973 were both openly condemned by the Soviet Union (however 'understandable' such 'acts of desperation' might be). In these cases she sought to dissociate the PLO from the Black September group – even, on occasion, claiming that the latter belonged to Israel (how else could one explain a group so detrimental to the Palestinian cause and therefore of benefit to Israel?).[2] Nonetheless the Soviet media chastised the PLO

for failing to achieve internal unity leading to control over its armed groups,[3] and such criticism was often expressed in *Sovetskaya Rosiya* – generally known for its nationalistic stand and possibly representing the views of some in the Kremlin who may have opposed Soviet support for the Palestinians and favoured instead reliance upon relations with Arab governments.[4]

The hijacking at Rome and Athens airports on 17–18 December 1973 was apparently particularly irritating to the Soviet Union, coming as it did just before the opening of the Geneva Peace Conference. Although the operation was disowned by the PLO, the Soviet Union found the incident embarrassing, for at the very least it demonstrated a lack of control over her would-be clients at a time of increased Soviet support for the Palestinians, and it forced her to condemn acts of air piracy while weakly hinting that the terrorists might not have been Palestinians but might even have been working for Israel.[5] Moreover, the incident did not help her pre-Conference efforts to portray Israel as the only unreasonable party in the Middle East dispute. By raising tensions above the level desired in order to pressure Israel, it threatened the very convening of the Conference for which the Soviet Union had been striving.

Indeed the Soviet argument against the Palestinians' use of terror focused on this counter-productive effect of such acts. Such criticism continued in the spring of 1974 and may even have been raised in Gromyko's talks with Arafat in March 1974. On 15 March 1974 *New Times*, which since the beginning of the year had also been published in Arabic, saw fit to criticize the leadership of the Palestine Resistance Movement on the issue of terrorism and to condemn the use of terror – specifically the activities of the Black September group – on the grounds that it was harmful to the cause of national liberation.[6] A few days later Moscow radio in Arabic reported Arafat's condemnation of 'armed operations outside Israel' claiming that 'the patriotic forces' of the Palestinian resistance had deplored terrorism.[7] Similarly, a leading Jordanian Communist official, writing in *World Marxist Review* in April 1974, claimed that the influence of 'Marxist and Trotskyite ideas and slogans' such as 'everything comes from the barrel of a gun' was waning and that there was a 'disaffection with adventurous actions which so strongly harmed [the PLO's] reputation, confused world opinion, and diverted attention from the crimes of the Israeli occupying authorities'.[8] Yet the attack by Jibril's PFLP General Command, clearly a PLO member, on a block of flats in the Israeli town of Kiryat Shmona on 11 April 1974 contradicted this. The Soviet Union tried to depict the incident as legitimate resistance by local Arabs, rather than an outside terrorist raid.[9] Nevertheless Arafat was apparently obliged to reassure his Soviet-bloc allies that he did not condone terrorism – which suggested that Moscow had expressed its dissatisfaction to him – and one Soviet Arabic-language broadcast after the attack spoke of 'barbaric actions committed by irresponsible persons'.[10]

It was hard for the Soviet Union to speak of 'irresponsible persons' when Hawatmeh, the man she had acclaimed a moderate, perpetrated the attack on an Israeli school in the town of Ma'alot the following month. But she did condemn this attack, if only indirectly when Pravda, as well as the New Times, reported 'international condemnation' and printed-more press accounts than usual of the incident.[11] Soviet sensitivity was shown by her meticulous effort to shift the blame for the killings to Israel, even calling Dayan a 'Palestinian Eichmann'; for example, on 20 May 1974 Tass carried a story of 'Palestine-born Dayan who perpetrated the Ma'alot tragedy so as to have an excuse to attack the Palestinians, just as the Germans had killed Germans to have a pretext for invading Poland in 1939'. In response to Ma'alot, the Soviet Union clearly stated that she condemned terrorism, claiming, however, that the PLO too had denounced the Ma'alot action.[12] At least one Soviet-bloc paper found it necessary to qualify its support for the Palestinian demands in late May, at the time of the signing of the Syrian-Israeli disengagement agreement, with the statement that it was not always possible to agree with the methods resorted to by 'some members' of the Palestinian resistance movement.[13] Indeed, when the Syrian–Israeli talks had run into a serious delay over the very issue of Palestinian incursions, the Soviet Union reported the delay without specifying the issue involved – a further sign of her sensitivity, especially on the geographic origin of such activities.

For all these efforts to dissociate the PLO from the label of terrorism, and to ignore its actual role in such actions (for example, the continued singling out of Hawatmeh as a moderate just two months after Ma'alot), criticism of such extremist tactics and admonitions to the PLO to put its house in order continued to appear in the Soviet media.[14] On the day of Arafat's arrival in Moscow on 28 July 1974, Izvestia's editor Tolkunov condemned in no uncertain terms such things as hijacking, sending explosive parcels by mail, or 'such action as the seizing and murdering of Israeli sportsmen at the Olympic Games';[15] rejecting terror, he recommended 'proper forms' of struggle, such as sabotage against military targets. A possible difference of opinion may have been reflected by a New Times article (just a week after Tolkunov's criticism), which, while condemning the use of terror by the Chabash and Jibril organizations, presented their case for terror in most sympathetic terms.[16]

The overall line remained firmly against terror. On the occasion of Arafat's next visit to Moscow, in November 1974, a Soviet broadcast in Arabic called for a sense of responsibility on the part of the Palestinians and urged greater 'political activity' in the occupied territories – a line expressed by the Palestine National Front and probably linked with Moscow's preference for the type of civil disorder then encouraged on the West Bank in conjunction with the Palestinian debates in the UN and the Rabat Conference.[17] A Palestinian journalist who apparently accompanied Arafat on this visit was to refer to differences with the Soviet Union, claiming that the latter wanted to avoid armed confrontation by all means, wanted the 'logic of peace in times of crises', while 'we Palestinians' saw the necessity of intensifying the armed struggle.[18] A series of articles the following spring by Izvestia's supporter of the Palestinians, Viktor Kudryatsev, denied the charge that the PLO even used terror and emphasized 'the struggle within the occupied territories' carried out by the Palestine National Front. This presaged increased Soviet publicity for the PNF, but it also clearly reflected Soviet preferences.

Nonetheless, the Soviet Union and the PLO continued not to agree on this question of tactics; a lengthy Soviet Arab-language broadcast of 24 September 1975 on the Palestinians, going into some detail on the lessons of Lenin's book *Left-wing Communism, an Infantile Disorder*, was in fact an admonition against extreme or precipitate actions. This line was also maintained with regard to the hijacking of the Air France plane to Uganda in July 1976. The Soviet Union condemned this action as an act of 'piracy', reporting the fact that Jewish hostages were not released, though non-Jews were, and, even after the Israeli rescue operation (also condemned, as violation of Ugandan sovereignty), the Soviet media continued to characterize the hijacking as inadmissible and abhorrent.[19]

Though the condemnation of hijacking and international terrorism has so far coincided with the Soviet Union's interests, there is no reason to suppose that she will cease to prefer that guerrilla activities should be limited to the occupied territories or, even within these territories, to prefer civil disorder and political activity to more extreme tactics. In the light of the overall Soviet position on wars of liberation, the PLO would have to gain far greater mass support, and the volatility of the Arab–Israeli crisis (with its American factor) would have to be drastically reduced, before the Soviet Union might be expected to alter her position.

VI. RECOGNITION OF THE PLO

While the shift to Soviet support for the PLO which began in 1968, coincided with Soviet acknowledgement of the Palestinian resistance movement as part of the Arab national liberation movement, official recognition was long in coming. To this day, such recognition fails to acknowledge the PLO as the *sole* legitimate representative of the Palestinian people.

The communiqué at the close of Arafat's July 1972 visit to Moscow did state that the Palestine resistance movement 'expresses the interests of the Palestinian Arab people', and prior to the October War the Palestinian resistance was elevated to the role of 'vanguard' or 'leading force' of the Arab struggle.[1] The organization itself was given a significant boost in mid-1973 by the announcement that East Germany had agreed to the opening of a PLO office in East Berlin, generally taken as a sign that Soviet recognition would not be long in coming.[2] This view was further strengthened by the resolution of a meeting of Arab Communist parties in September 1973 which spoke of the 'Palestinian resistance movement' as 'representing the people of Palestine',[3] yet, like most Soviet comments, did not refer to the PLO by name. The Soviet versions of the decisions of the September 1973 Non-aligned Conference in Algiers actually *omitted* the decision to recognize the PLO as the 'legitimate representative of the Palestinian people and its struggle'.[4] As already pointed out, these early inconsistencies at a time

of clear intensification of Soviet support for, and contacts with, the PLO may have been the result of continued indecision – or even differences of opinion – within the Kremlin, or simply of a desire to keep all available options open.

Arafat claimed that the memo the Soviet Union sent him immediately after the October War contained recognition of the 'Palestinian resistance movement' as the only legitimate representative of the Palestinian people. But the delivery of this memo individually to Arafat, Chabash and Hawatmeh – in addition to the continued absence of the term PLO – strongly suggests that the Soviet Union was not yet ready to recognize the organization fully.[5] Arafat's visit to Moscow at the head of a PLO delegation in November 1973 was, as before, at the invitation of the Soviet Afro-Asian Committee, rather than a Party or government body, nor was he received by any high party or government official except Boris Ponomarev, who was responsible for relations with non-ruling Communist Parties and often handled contacts with national liberation movements. Much more indicative of Soviet reticence at this time, however, was the reporting of the resolutions of the Algiers Conference of Arab heads of state just two days after Arafat's visit: the resolution granting the PLO the status of 'sole legitimate representative of the Palestinians' was actually deleted.[6] Only an article by Vladimir Shelepin in the Soviet Trade Union paper *Trud* referred

159

to this resolution; he was careful to attribute it to 'international press reports', while reporting the other resolutions directly. This indicated a realization of the sensitivity of the point but did not stop him from saying what he wanted to say. Indeed, writing in the *New Times* the following week he reported the PLO recognition directly.[7] Similar, though not so exclusive, unofficial recognition was given in a 12 December article by Igor Belyaev in *Literaturnaya gazeta*.[8] However, *Pravda*'s coverage of a resolution of the Syrian Communist Party Central Committee again ignored reference to the PLO as the sole legitimate representative of the Palestinian people, indicating that the official line, at least, remained unchanged.[9] (On this last occasion *Trud* avoided any difference from *Pravda*'s reporting by simply ignoring the Syrian meeting altogether.) Similarly, the entire Soviet media ignored the November 1973 meeting of representatives of the Arab Communist parties and its similar resolution.[10] The official Soviet version of the resolutions of the February 1974 Lahore Muslim Conference deleted the decision recognizing the PLO.[11] As with the Algiers Conference, this official reticence did not prevent less official references to Arab recognition of the PLO, in this case in Arabic broadcasts.[12]

The PLO received a strong boost in the direction of official recognition when the Soviet Foreign Minister met Arafat twice, during the former's March 1974 visit to Egypt and Syria. Although the Soviet Union stopped short of full recognition – neither referring directly to the PLO as the sole legitimate representative of the Palestinians nor issuing a separate official communiqué with Arafat – Gromyko did receive Arafat in the Soviet Embassy in Cairo for official talks which were subsequently summarized in the Soviet–Egyptian communiqué. Moreover, Gromyko reportedly extended to Arafat the latter's first *official* Soviet government invitation to visit the Soviet Union, although the Soviet Union herself did not make the invitation public.[13] These steps towards the PLO were primarily symbolic, taken perhaps for their tactical effect on both the United States and Egypt, but also possibly intended to strengthen Arafat in the debate then going on within PLO about a mini-state and Geneva participation. Moscow herself played up the meeting with Gromyko in her Arabic broadcasts, saying for

example, that the 'Palestine resistance movement' had gained important moral and political support from the visit.[14]

Arafat claimed after these talks that Gromyko had now accorded the PLO the same recognition granted by the Algiers and Lahore Conferences, but Moscow was willing to admit only that the international recognition received by the PLO had been discussed.[15] The admission, although it came only in an Arabic-language Soviet broadcast quoting Arafat, nonetheless implied Soviet approval. This impression was substantiated by a number of semi-official Soviet references to the PLO's authoritative status: for example, mentions of Arafat's claim that 103 countries recognized the PLO as the sole legitimate representative of the Palestinians, the publication in *Pravda* of similar recognition granted by the co-ordination committee of the non-aligned states, and an *Izvestia* report of an interview with Palestinian members of the PNF who said that the inhabitants of the West Bank saw the PLO as their sole representative.[16] It is indeed possible that the Soviet Union did agree – in March 1974, or late October 1973, or even earlier – to recognize the PLO exclusively, but such agreement coupled with this 'unofficial' recognition made her continued reluctance to make an official statement all the more striking. It would seem that she was keeping her options open, possibly as a lever in her relations with the PLO as well as in the broader negotiations over an Arab–Israeli settlement.

In the course of 1974 the Soviet Union referred with increasing frequency to the recognition granted to the PLO by others, culminating in a Ponomarev–Arafat communiqué at the close of Arafat's July–August 1974 visit. This visit was of a more official nature than his others had been; Arafat was housed in an official VIP guest house and was received by Party and government officials, albeit none was higher than Deputy Foreign Minister Kuznetsov. On this occasion the Soviet Union allowed that 'the sides noted with satisfaction the importance of the decisions taken at the conference of the heads of Arab states in Algiers and the Conference of Muslim states in Lahore on the recognition of the PLO as the sole legitimate representative of the Arab people of Palestine'.[17] Another important result of this visit was the announcement of Soviet agreement to the opening of a PLO office in Moscow. This was clearly a turning point in

Soviet relations with the organization, though full official Soviet recognition was not yet granted.[18]

Arafat was shortly to declare that the Soviet Union, Yugoslavia, Romania, East Germany, Czechoslovakia, Bulgaria, Poland and Hungary had all recognized the PLO – meaning presumably that they had agreed to the opening of PLO offices (though quite some time passed before they were opened).[19] Other efforts were being made at this time to increase Soviet support for the Palestinians, following the Soviet Union's mistaken appraisal of the Sadat–Hussein statement,[20] at a time when she was apparently seeking to thwart American efforts to achieve a Jordanian – Israeli agreement on the eve of the Rabat Conference and the Palestinian debate in the UN. As we have seen, this shift was followed by Soviet support for a Palestinian state and a slightly more direct recognition of the PLO, which came on 11 October 1974 in the form of Brezhnev's reference to the PLO by name for the first time in a published speech and his mention of it as one of the partners for negotiations in the Middle East, along with – and by implication on a par with – the Arab states.[21]

The Soviet Union could now enthusiastically report the Rabat resolution recognizing the PLO as sole legitimate representative of the Palestinians. Yet, still anxious to keep her options open with Jordan, particularly over the question of the Geneva Conference, she characterized this resolution as a sign of Jordanian–PLO rapprochement,[22] which was by no means the interpretation applied by the PLO (or, for that matter, by Jordan, who began systematically to dissociate herself from the Palestinian issue). Thus Arafat's November 1974 trip (in which he was received by a still higher level of Soviet officials – Gromyko and, finally, Kosygin) was concluded by a communiqué welcoming recognition by others – in this case the recognition given at Rabat[23] – though still not admitting this to be direct Soviet recognition. This was, of course, a purely formal reservation, given all the other forms of recognition that the Soviet Union was according the PLO, but it was sufficient to leave some small opening for future manoeuvre.

Meanwhile, if pressed, she could point to the implicit recognition contained in these communiqués, speeches and commentaries, as well as to Soviet support for the UN General Assembly resolution according the PLO the status it sought.

This basic approach, of limiting recognition to praise for such by other states or bodies, was maintained throughout the ensuing year. In late 1975 and early 1976, however, there occurred still further refinements of the Soviet position. In her 9 November 1975 initiative for a reconvening of the Geneva Conference, the Soviet Union for the first time *officially* called for participation of 'the Arab people of Palestine *as represented by the PLO*' and *on an equal footing* with, it stipulated, Egypt, Syria and Israel and with Jordan (with whom Moscow was in frequent high-level contact by this time).[24] Subsequently, frequent references to the PLO as 'the representative' or 'the legitimate representative' appeared in the press (although Russian has no definite article, so that the formula was weaker in the Russian original than in Tass translations to English). In particular, Ambassador Malik used these formulations in the UN, where Soviet pronouncements tended to be somewhat more militant than elsewhere. In time, the Soviet press was even to add the word 'sole', while such official Soviet statements as the January 1976 government statement called the PLO 'legitimate representative' of the Arab people of Palestine; the 28 April 1976 government statement, however, reverted to the indirect formula, 'is widely recognized as the lawful representative', and even limited its characterization of the PLO at Geneva as 'a' representative of the Palestinian people.[25]

Thus, even in 1976 references in official Soviet statements, the Soviet Union has refrained from committing herself to the exclusivity of representation that the PLO claims. While this may yet be granted, if she should want to increase her support for the PLO in the rapidly changing context of Middle Eastern events and the superpower competition in the region, the tendency is clearly to retain at least some small option for future manoeuvring.

Soviet–PLO relations have come a long way since 1968, and particularly since the October War of 1973. Moscow shifted from a limited approach to the Palestinian issue as merely a refugee problem, gradually introducing and increasing her support for the Palestinians' right to statehood, first (after the October War) by advocating the Palestinians' national rights, and then, in the autumn of 1974, by advocating a Palestinian state. Similarly, she elevated her recognition of the PLO, promoting it from one of the Palestinian organizations to the status of a national liberation organization. By 1974 its leader was received officially by Party and state functionaries and accorded an office in Moscow and Soviet support in international organizations. Yet the Soviet Union has still held back from full official recognition of the PLO as the *sole* legitimate representative of the Palestinian people; the speeches of Soviet leaders and official communiqués have limited themselves to citing others' recognition of the PLO, or mentioning the PLO without referring to its *exclusive* representation of the Palestinians. Contacts have been maintained – indeed augmented – with Jordan, whom, despite the decisions of the Rabat Conference, Moscow continues to envisage as a party to the Middle-East negotiations.

Moreover, the Soviet Union has yet to resolve a number of serious issues with the PLO, such as the Soviet desire to limit a Palestinian state to the occupied territories (i.e., the West Bank and Gaza), when the Palestinians would prefer to destroy Israel and create a state in all of Palestine. Her insistence on the 1967 borders of Israel tends to suggest that she would not support even the middle road of a return to the 1947 partition plan (although occasional lapses may indicate either internal Soviet differences of opinion or simply a desire to maintain an open position regarding the 1947 borders), but there is no reason for her to be wedded to one border or another except insofar as she deems one position more likely to prove tenable or possible of peaceable implementation. Soviet failure to persuade the PLO to adopt a 'realistic' policy recognizing Israel's existence is compounded by the lack of agreement within the PLO regarding negotiations (including the Geneva Conference) and the value of terror. These basic issues, which

contribute to Moscow's general consternation over the lack of unity within the PLO and the continued activity of extremists, have remained constant throughout all the twists and turns of Moscow's augmented support.

While the Soviet Union may genuinely believe that the Middle East crisis cannot be resolved without some solution of the Palestinian problem, her insistence on her own view as to the desired solution, and her reluctance to commit herself entirely to the PLO as the *only* relevant party concerning the Palestinians' future, strongly suggest that she views the PLO within the framework of tactics rather than as a basic principle. It would seem that she has used the PLO and the Palestinian issue when she wanted to increase Soviet support among the more militant or radical Arab groups, in order to bring pressure to bear on Westward-leaning Egypt, and to discredit the United States when American inroads into the Arab world appeared to be expanding. While such tactical manipulation could conceivably draw the Soviet Union into an irreversible position – for example, on such things as Palestinian participation in Geneva – all the signs indicate that she is striving to keep her options relatively open regarding the PLO itself and the varieties of solutions deemed to be peacefully obtainable.

For its part the PLO and its various components have demonstrated their own awareness of the broad differences between themselves and the Soviet Union on basic issues, maintaining their independence and striving to keep their own organization together despite their obvious need for Soviet aid and support. Yet they probably know that, just as they are ultimately dependent upon the Arab states, so too the Soviet Union has built her Middle East policy on states, not movements. While the PLO's role in Soviet policy has increased markedly – particularly with the deterioration of Soviet–Egyptian relations, and more recently with the Soviet–Syrian problems linked with the Lebanese crisis – there is little likelihood that the Soviet Union sees this as a long-term alternative which is clearly preferable to working through the Arab states. It is still less likely that she would permit the PLO to jeopardize any form of agreement to which she might be party, leading to a settlement of the Middle East conflict.

As the Lebanese crisis polarizes Syrian–PLO and the Soviet–Syrian relations, and as the latter deteriorate over the issue of Syrian independence of action (and even, perhaps, Westward tendencies), there is the very real possibility that the Soviet Union may be left with nothing more than the PLO. There is at present no reason to believe that the Soviet Union considers this desirable, however; the PLO is far too divided and unstable, too little Marxist and too extremist

to be her preferred major partner in the area. As a result of the Lebanese crisis, it is more split than ever, and the chances of Soviet control, or at least influence, are more remote than ever. It is therefore reasonable to assume that, in the future as in the past, Soviet–PLO relations will be governed more by *ad hoc* Soviet tactical decisions than by some overall Soviet strategic plan for the area, and that this will result in a continuation of many of the inconsistencies, shifts and disputes that have characterized these relations in the past.

NOTES

Radio sources are based on the monitoring services of the BBC and FBIS. Arabic sources are taken from the translations of the BBC, FBIS and IMB unless otherwise indicated.

I. HISTORICAL BACKGROUND

[1] See speech by Yacov Malik to Security Council, 18 August 1948 quoted in Yaacov Ro'i, *From Encroachment to Involvement* (New York: John Wiley, 1974), pp. 58–60.
[2] *Ibid.*, pp. 252, 388. See also joint communiqués with Egypt in 1965, with Syria in 1966.
[3] See Moshe Maoz (ed.), *Palestinian Arab Politics* (Jerusalem Academic Press, 1975), pp. 91–2.
[4] Mohammed Heikal, *The Road to Ramadan* (London: Fontana/Collins, 1976), pp. 60–63. See also Oded Eran, 'The Soviet Union and the Palestine Guerilla Organizations', (Tel Aviv University, 1971), pp. 15 ff.
[5] The Soviet Union praised alleged Al Fatah actions against such things as power stations and railway bridges in Israel (sometimes non-existent ones), though she usually claimed that over 90 per cent of even these actions were in the occupied territories. See, for example, V. Kudryavtsev, 'Middle East: Military Situation', *New Times*, no. 14, 1968, pp. 14–15.
[6] L. Zavyalov, 'Tel Aviv Manoeuvres', *New Times*, no. 32, 1969, p. 4.
[7] *Pravda*, 22 February 1970, followed by the communiqué at the close of Nasser's July 1970 visit (Moscow domestic radio, 17 July 1970), and a Brezhnev speech in August 1970 (Moscow domestic radio, 29 August 1970). The 1971 CPSU Congress also included a clause on the 'legitimate rights of the Arab people of Palestine' (Moscow

domestic radio, 13 April 1971).
[8] In 1972 a number of Middle Eastern Communist Parties sponsored the Arab Popular Conference in Beirut, from which grew Kamal Jumblatt's Arab Front for the Support of the Palestine Revolution.
[9] Moscow radio in Arabic, 3 September 1975, gave the history of the PNF.
[10] 'Special Documents: The Soviet Attitude to the Palestine Problem', *Journal of Palestine Studies*, vol. VI, no. 1, 1972, pp. 187–212, Syrian Communist Party protocol of Khaled Bagdesh talks with Suslov and Ponomarev, May 1971.
[11] *New York Times* service, 19 September 1972; *L'Orient le Jour* (Beirut), 27 September 1972 (said the first shipment to the Palestinians had 'recently' arrived in Syria).
[12] The Soviet build-up in Syria and Iraq at the time may well have been a long-planned step, but the break with Egypt made it necessary both to gain bases and facilities in Syria and to emphasize, in propaganda, the fine state of relations with at least these Arab states, as well as the PLO.
[13] See, for example, Voice of Palestine, 20 July 1972, and Soviet references to such expressions of gratitude: Tass, 19, 22 July 1972; Moscow radio in Arabic, 26, 28 July 1972.

II. PALESTINIAN STATEHOOD

[1] For this and the following quotation, see *Journal of Palestine Studies*, vol. II, no. I, 1972, pp. 187–212.
[2] See, for example, Gromyko's speech to the UN General Assembly, *Pravda*, 25 September 1974.
[3] *Pravda*, 24 April 1975.
[4] Moscow domestic radio, 24 February 1976.
[5] Tass, 28 April 1976.
[6] *Le Monde*, 30 April 1975, 3 May 1975. That the demand was made in 1975 was borne out by subsequent internal PLO debates and criticism by Chabash; see *Al-Nahar* (Beirut), 15 May 1975, and *Al-Hadaf* (Beirut, belonging to Chabash's PFLP), 17 May 1975. For the November effort

see *As-Siyasah* (Kuwait), 12 January 1976. In both instances Arafat's failure to agree is supposed to have contributed to the fact that only a 'report', rather than a joint communiqué, was issued at the close of the visit.
[7] Prior to the war, there was a Soviet Arabic-language commentary of 5 March 1973 which explained that the 'right of the Palestinian Arab people to determine their own destiny as they wish and without external interference is the most important of their legitimate rights . . . [they] themselves can deal with the question of the forms of exercising their right to determine their own destiny', and then referred to the 1947 partition decision 'regarding

the creation of an Arab state on the basis of this right . . . to determine their own destiny'. This suggested a change in the Soviet Union's 1971 attitude towards a Palestinian state. So did the fact that *Pravda*, 17 October 1973, carried (albeit without comment) Sadat's remark that if the Palestinians created a government-in-exile Egypt was prepared to recognize it, and also the resolution of the September 1973 meeting of Arab Communist parties referring to the Palestinians' right to self-determination (reported, along with the other resolutions, in *Pravda* almost a month later, on 19 October 1973).

[8] After a brief line in the Soviet government statement on the outbreak of the war (Tass, 7 October 1973) the Palestinians were not mentioned in subsequent official statements (the 12 and 23 October warnings), in speeches of Soviet leaders, in most of the resolutions and statements of protest meetings, or even in the Soviet reports of the official statements of Poland, Hungary, Bulgaria and Czechoslovakia on the war. The only exception to this was the Trade Union paper *Trud* and Trade Union leader, Shelepin's speech to WFTU. This discrepancy had been notable prior to the war as well, suggesting Shelepin's opposition on ideological grounds to Soviet support for bourgeois – even progressive – regimes, rather than (or at the expense of) national liberation movements and local Communist parties. (See Ilana Dimant, 'Pravda and Trud: Divergent Attitudes Towards the Middle East', Soviet and East European Research Centre, Hebrew University of Jerusalem, 1972.) Only after Jordan announced her plan to provide troops did the Soviet press express any particular attention to the Palestinian contribution to the war efforts. Moreover, the Soviet–American cease-fire proposal, based as it was on SCR 242, was in direct contradiction to PLO (as well as Syrian and Iraqi) positions. See Soviet response to Palestinian criticism on this, Moscow radio in Arabic, 22 October 1973.

[9] *Le Monde*, 31 October 1973, 6 November 1973; *New York Times*, 2 November 1973; *Guardian*, 6 November 1973.

[10] Tass, 15 November 1973.

[11] Tass, 21 December 1973.

[12] Soviet Middle East commentator Igor Belyaev had already raised the idea on the Soviet radio on 2 June 1974, and he later told an Arab paper (*Al-Nahar*, 4 November 1974) that, when in Moscow in summer 1974, Arafat was told by the Soviet government that it would support the creation of an independent state.

[13] *Pravda*, 9 September 1974.

[14] Algiers radio, 4 October 1974.

[15] Discernible in a more sceptical attitude towards the Geneva Conference expressed at the end of December 1973, this was particularly apparent during Assad's visit to Moscow in April 1974. On this occasion Podgorny, unlike Brezhnev, referred to the Palestinians' 'national' rights and expressed a harsher warning regarding the Syrian–Israeli disengagement talks.

[16] Despite PLO claims to the contrary, the Soviet Union had made no statements regarding the creation of a government-in-exile, limiting herself only to occasional reports of Egyptian support for the idea. Eric Rouleau claimed in *Le Monde*, 22 May 1975, that the Palestine National Front had approved the idea – as a means of facilitating PLO participation in Geneva – since December

1973, but the Soviet Union made no mention of this in her description of the 1973 PNF position (see Moscow radio in Arabic, 3 September 1975). The first, and almost only Soviet public approval of the idea was voiced by Belyaev in an interview to an Arab paper in November 1974, after the Rabat Conference. He said the Soviet Union would recognize such a government, the creation of which would be considered a positive step. During the post-Rabat debate within the PLO over the character of such a body (a copy of the PLO executive, or an independent politically broader – in the eyes of the world – group), Moscow made known her preference for a PLO-type group. Yet even after Belyaev's comments, the Soviet Union still refrained from public statements urging a government-in-exile. *Pravda*, 17 October 1972; Moscow radio in Arabic, 7 January 1974; *Akhbar al-Yom*, 2 February 1974; *Le Monde*, 6 November 1974; 25–6 May 1975; *Al-Safir*, 14 December 1974; *Al-Nahar*, 4 November 1974; *Journal of Palestine Studies*, vol. IV, no. 3, 1975, pp. 142–4.

[17] A slight improvement had occurred with Fahmy's visit to Moscow in October 1974, but the December cancellation of Brezhnev's planned visit, as well as subsequent comments by Sadat, indicated that Soviet–Egyptian relations had not been totally repaired.

[18] Tass, 30 November 1974.

[19] Moscow radio in Arabic, 26 February 1975, 3 September 1975 (on PNF stand); *Le Monde*, 6 November 1973; Voice of Palestine (on Soviet memo), 30 October 1973; INA (Iraq), 24 November 1973 (on Soviet plan); *Al-Nahar*, 10 May 1974 (Arafat on talks with Gromyko).

[20] *Izvestia*, 30 July 1974; INA, 24 November 1974; Moscow radio in Arabic, 26 February 1975; Naim Ashhab, 'The Palestinian Aspect of the Middle East Crisis', *World Marxist Review*, vol. XVII, no. 4, 1974, p. 29.

[21] Victor Bukharov, 'Palestine National Council Session', *New Times*, no. 25, 1974, p. 13; 'Yasser Arafat on the Problems of the Palestine Movement', *New Times*, no. 32, 1974, p. 11. Palestine National Council programme: Voice of Palestine, 8 June 1974.

[22] See *Journal of Palestine Studies*, vol. IV, no. 2, 1975, p. 167. The use of the term 'authority' or 'entity' was less committal for the Palestinians, since 'state' implied something fixed, permanent, with borders, rather than a temporary unit perceived as a stage on the way to something larger. The Soviet media and officials accommodated these sensitivities for a while, but by the close of 1974 they shifted to using 'state' almost exclusively, despite the PLO position.

[23] *Al-Nahar*, 18 August 1974. See also *Al-Hadaf*, 3 August 1974 and 28 September 1974.

[24] Moscow radio in Arabic, 28 November 1975.

[25] *Krasnaya zvezda*, 16 June 1976 (Tass, 15 June 1976).

[26] Tass, 9 January 1976, 28 April 1976. This idea had also often been spelled out before; for example, in the talk given in Amman by the Soviet Ambassador to Jordan, 5 March 1974, and carried by Moscow radio in Arabic, 23 March 1974. The Syrian radio version of the talk was vague on just this part. The January and April statements were the first occasions when the Soviet government officially linked the steps organically.

[27] *Pravda*, 15 November 1974; Moscow domestic radio, 19 October 1975; *Izvestia*, 2 December 1975; Tass, 12 November 1975.

[28] Saddam Hussein, Vice President of Iraq's Revolutionary Council, told the Rabat Conference: 'We believe the central objective of the Arab nation is the liberation of usurped Arab territory, including the whole territory of Palestine. We have our own views on the way this objective should be achieved, and we have reservations about any resolution that does not lead to its realization.' (*As-Siyasa*, 31 October 1974.) Problems with Iraq over SCR 242 and the whole 'Palestine problem', as Iraq called it, correcting the term 'Middle East question', were not a new phenomenon. See Saddam Hussein's comments, Baghdad radio, 5 June 1974.

[29] *Shu'un Filastiniya*, February 1974, in *Journal of Palestine Studies*, vol. III, no. 3, 1974, p. 202. (Emphasis added.)

[30] *Al-Nahar*, 10 March 1974.

[31] In his conversation with Abba Eban at the Geneva Conference, Gromyko cited the Soviet Union's 1947–8 support for the founding of Israel as a commitment for the future as well, but it is doubtful that such need be the case should Soviet priorities or estimates change; *Ha'aretz* (Tel Aviv), 4 October 1974.

[32] J. D. Zvyegelskaya and G. J. Starchenko, 'Israel: The Army and the State', *Narodii Azii i Afrikii*, no. 4, 1974, pp. 27–37. See also V. V. Grigoryev, 'International Zionism and Mandated Palestine Between the Two World Wars', *Ukrainski istorichni zhurnal*, no. 8, August 1974, or *Zaria vostoka*, 11 December 1974.

[33] *Izvestia*, 26 September 1974, 22 December 1974, 12 April 1975. See also Alexandr Ignatov, 'The Palestinian Tragedy', *New Times*, no. 32, 1974, pp. 26–31.

[34] *Izvestia*, 30 July 1974; Lev Tolkunov, 'The Middle East Crisis and The Ways of Solving It', *Kommunist*, no. 13, 1974, p. 99.

[35] UN General Assembly, 1st Special Session, 77th Plenary Meeting, vol. I, 1947, pp. 127–35.

[36] Kudryavtsev's articles, then and since, tended to leave room, however, for a second stage, for in 1975 he said that in order for a Palestinian state to be formed 'it is *above all* necessary for the Israeli occupiers to leave all the Arab lands they seized in 1967' (*Izvestia*, 12 April 1975; emphasis added). And in 1976 'It is known, and it is mentioned in the Soviet government statement, that the Near Eastern crisis cannot be settled without the withdrawal of all the Israeli armed forces from all the Arab territories occupied by them in 1967. And these are precisely the territories that as far back as 1948 were supposed to enter the composition of the Arab State of Palestine.' (*Izvestia*, 20 May 1976.)

[37] Tolkunov also criticized the failure of some in the PLO to agree to the very existence of the State of Israel (those who advocated a Palestinian state instead of Israel), though he claimed that 'most' PLO organizations agreed to a more 'realistic' position (*Izvestia*, 30 July 1974).

[38] Igor Belyaev, 'Middle East Crisis and Washington's Manoeuvres', *International Affairs*, no. 4, 1970, pp. 31, 35 (Russian version in no. 3, 1970). He also mentioned demilitarization, on both sides of the borders.

[39] According to Lawrence Whetten, *The Canal War* (Cambridge, Mass.: MIT Press, 1974), p. 115, this was the plan presented to the United States on 23 July 1970.

[40] *Pravda*, 15 October 1970.

[41] Victor Laptev, 'Middle East Divide', *New Times*, 10 February 1970, p. 5.

[42] Tass, 21 December 1973.

[43] *Pravda*, 23 December 1973.

[44] *Al-Hadaf*, 17 May 1975; *Journal of Palestine Studies*, vol. IV, no. 4, 1975, p. 145. At the time of the 1973 memo the Palestinian radio (30 October 1973) said that a Soviet–American peace plan including a Palestinian state on the West Bank and Gaza and 'occupied Jerusalem' had been proposed 'not unlike other plans to liquidate the cause of our Palestinian people. . . . The Palestinian Revolution has already rejected the setting up of a Palestinian state in any part of the Arab land with the exception of a democratic Palestine state in the entire occupied Palestine soil'.

[45] Moscow domestic radio, 27 April 1975.

[46] *Le Monde*, 12 April 1975.

[47] V. Vladimirov, 'A Peaceful Settlement for the Middle East', *Mezhdunarodnaya zhizn*, no. 10, 1974, p. 109.

[48] English version, V. Vladimirsky, 'The Doomed Policy of Israeli Expansionists', *International Affairs*, no. 3, 1975, p. 49.

[49] English version, E. Dimitriyev, 'The Struggle for Peace in the Middle East', *International Affairs*, no. 4, 1975, p. 38.

[50] Yuri Potomov, 'Middle East: Aggressors Self-Exposed', *New Times*, no. 6, 1976, p. 12.

[51] Tass, 28 April 1976. It will be noted that the implication in the clause regarding the Palestinians is that the refugees will live in the new Palestinian state, not necessarily return to their pre-1948 homes, while nothing is said of the Israeli Arabs (i.e., the $1\frac{1}{2}$ million Palestinians inside Israel). The Soviet Union occasionally refers to the right of the refugees to return to their homes, or receive compensation (and she does put the total of Palestinians at 3 million – presumably including those in Israel). But since she began advocating a separate state alongside Israel, she has been vague on this issue, the implication always being that the creation of the state will answer the Palestinians' right to self-determination (as distinct from the 1971 position of the Syrian Communist Party wherein self-determination was conceived, probably in Soviet terms, as a cultural-educational phenomenon, within Israel).

In the Syrian version (SANA, 6 March 1973) of his 5 March 1973 talks in Jordan, the Soviet Ambassador said that the first stage of achieving Palestinian legitimate rights was liberation of the occupied territories and bringing about the possibility of the Palestinians returning to their land, or suitable compensation. Together with this they were to be given the right to determine their own fate – which right was to be obtained from Israel. He added that the Arabs and Palestinians must find a proper solution to obtain these rights, but that 'a just solution, from our point of view, does not begin with the destruction of Israel but in finding basic points to be agreed upon to achieve a sound and just solution'. In the Soviet version (Moscow radio in Arabic, 23 March 1974), the territories occupied in 1967 were to be liberated 'so as' to give the Palestinians the opportunity to return to their land *and* receive compensation *and* self-determination.

A 27 July 1976 *Pravda* editorial repeated the 28 April formulation exactly.

[52] Moscow domestic radio, 19 October 1975, on policies in 'the territories occupied eight years ago' and policies in 'Israel proper'. *Pravda*, 6 April 1976, on strikes in 'occupied territories' and in 'Israel proper'; *Izvestia*, 9 May 1976, on Arabs living in the 'territories occupied in 1967'

and 'Arabs living in Israel proper'; *Pravda* and *Krasnaya zvezda*, 1 April 1976, on the Galilee, 'a region of Israel with an Arab majority' and the 'Arab population of the West Bank' *Pravda*, 1 April 1976, quoting Syrian Communist Party support for the Arabs in the 'occupied West Bank and Gaza Strip as well as in Israel proper'.
[53] The flexibility *vis-à-vis* the Palestinians was suggested by a Kuwaiti report on Arafat's November 1975 visit to Moscow, claiming that when the Soviet Union urged the Palestinians to recognize Israel she stipulated that this could be within the 1967 or 1947 borders, insisting only that a state occupying all of Palestine was out of the question. (*As-Siyasah*, 12 January 1976.)
[54] See Dimant (*op. cit.* in note 8) or Galia Golan, 'Internal Pressures and Soviet Policy', unpublished paper, Jerusalem, 1973, 45 pp.
[55] *Al-Nahar*, 10 May 1974.
[56] Tass, 28, 29 November 1973 and 24 February 1974. An exception to this was *Trud*, 30 November 1973, which did contain the Algiers Conference reference to Jerusalem.
[57] Moscow radio in Arabic, 14 March 1974; *Izvestia*, 21 March 1974; *Pravda, Krasnaya zvezda, Trud, Sovetskaya Rosiya*, 27 August 1975.
[58] Ashhab (*op. cit.* in note 20). The same article went on to demand that Jordan declare invalid its 1950 annexation of the West Bank.
[59] Moscow radio in Arabic, 23 March 1974.

[60] *Za rubezhom*, no. 36, 30 August–5 September 1974; Moscow radio in Arabic, 2, 24 September 1974.
[61] Tass, 28 October 1974, explained that, while the PLO wanted strict observance of the Algiers Conference resolution recognizing the PLO as the sole legitimate representative of the Palestinians, Jordan wanted a referendum on the West Bank, so that the population could express its view as to whom it wanted.
[62] *Pravda*, 31 October 1974; Moscow radio in Arabic, 29 October 1974; Radio Peace and Progress in Arabic, 31 October 1974.
[63] See Abu Ayyad in *Al-Nahar*, 20 November 1974.
[64] Independently of the PLO–Jordanian issue, the Soviet Union was not, apparently, sufficiently interested in the Jordanian connection to make an offer Hussein couldn't refuse (her offer carried with it certain demands and conditions unacceptable to Hussein, regarding personnel and payment). This may have been due to the Soviet estimate of the chances of actually eliminating American influence there or, perhaps, to the relative decline of Soviet interests in the Middle East states as other areas rise in importance and as the cost of maintaining the Soviet presence and influence in the Arab confrontation states rises as well.
[65] Indeed the PLO office in Moscow was finally opened just before Hussein's visit of 17–28 June 1976. (*Pravda*, 12 June 1976 on the arrival of the PLO office chief.)

III. Geneva Peace Conference

[1] As one Arab Liberation Front representative said in 1970, 'This resolution . . . consecrates the Zionist presence on Arab land'. (*Al-Anwar*, 8 March 1970.)
[2] They said, for example, that Arafat opposed attempts of 'some forces' to harm a political solution. (*Al-Safir*, 26 March 1974.) Further examples cited below.
[3] Moscow radio in Arabic, 22 October 1973.
[4] Verging on double-think, the Soviet Union said, for example: 'Concerning the refugee question, Security Council Resolution 242 mentions this point, namely the guaranteeing of the legitimate rights of the Palestinian Arab people'. (Moscow radio in Arabic, 28 April 1974.)
[5] INA, 2 June 1974.
[6] Voice of Palestine, 8 June 1974.
[7] For Chabash, see *Al-Hadaf*, 28 September 1974, in *Journal of Palestine Studies*, vol. IV, no. 2, 1975, p. 167. On 19 July 1974 Chabash, Jibril, and the Arab Liberation Front issued a statement protesting the decision by 'some officials' to participate in Geneva, and on this basis (as well as objections to Moscow's support for a 'mini-state') Chabash refused to join the PLO delegation to Moscow in July 1974. (INA, 20 July 1974; *Journal of Palestine Studies, op. cit.*, pp. 165–70.) Baghdad radio, 6 July 1974, had reported a joint Iraqi Ba'ath–Jibril statement rejecting the Geneva Conference, SCR 242 and 338 and Hussein's federation plan.
[8] *Izvestia*, 30 July 1974; Bukharov (*op. cit.* in chapter II, note 21), p. 13.
[9] *Le Monde*, 4 June 1974, 25 March, 3 April 1975. According to the last, Zuhair Mohsen, following a meeting with the Chinese Ambassador to Lebanon, said that a reconvening of Geneva was impossible because the PLO would go only if SCR 242 were amended, and the United States opposed any such move.

[10] *Le Monde*, 4 June 1974, referring to *Al-Nahar*.
[11] Tass, 3 August 1974.
[12] *Althliad*, September 1974; *Izvestia*, 30 July 1974; *Literaturnaya gazeta*, 14 August 1974. Another source of attack on such participation was Iraq. Saddam Hussein told the Rabat Conference that 'if the Palestine Liberation Organization goes to Geneva, our commitment to the draft resolution [supporting the PLO] will be cancelled' (*As-Siyasa*, 31 October 1974). The Soviet communiqué with a visiting Iraqi Communist Party delegation, however, called for the reconvening of Geneva (Tass, 29 October 1974).
[13] *Le Monde*, 11 December 1974; *Al-Nahar*, 7 December 1974.
[14] Tass, 30 November 1974.
[15] See commentary in *Journal of Palestine Studies*, vol. IV, no. 4, 1975, p. 146 on the importance of this. Chabash also saw this as Arafat's agreement to participate, labelling it 'treason' (*Al-Hadaf*, 10 May 1975).
[16] *Le Monde*, 6, 10, 11–12 May 1975. See also Arafat's comments on the significance of the invitation (*Le Monde*, 5 April 1975); also Kuwait radio, 11 May 1975 (PLO sources). Sadat also claimed that the PLO position was still unclear and that the idea of a joint Jordanian–PLO delegation was still being examined.
[17] There had been an unofficial linkage earlier (E. Dmitriev, 'For a Peace Settlement in the Middle East', *Aziia i Afrika Sevodnia*, no. 6, June 1975, pp. 7–8), but this was an isolated case. A possible hint of such a concession to the PLO may have been Ponomarev's comment to visiting American Congressmen that Geneva should be reconvened 'of course with due preparation and in full compliance with the well-known decisions of the UN Security Council and the General

Assembly' (*Pravda*, 12 July 1975). This was, however, quite vague and not an entirely new formulation (indeed in the past such a formulation was usually seen as a reference to the 1947 partition decision!).

[18] Tass, 9 November 1975. For example, *Izvestia*, 13 November 1975 mentioned GAR 3236 but *Pravda* omitted it, as did *Sovetskaya Rosiya*, 19 November 1975, Moscow domestic radio, 11 November 1975, and Moscow radio in Polish, 11 November 1975.

[19] Independently of the Geneva link, this resolution and those of the following year on Zionism are referred to generally as the recent decisions, or simply decisions, of the UN. In some cases the wording has become so vague (where it once was clearly a reference to the Security Council, i.e., SCR 242, or when referring to the General Assembly meaning the partition plan and/or subsequent decisions on the Palestinian refugees) that one can no longer be sure what decisions are meant. For the Israelis as well as the Palestinians this is of great importance: the broader term might well mean the 1947 decision, rather than SCR 242 plus the 1974–5 decisions regarding the Palestinians, though from another point of view the new resolutions provide the possibility, via the general wording, of justifying Palestinian statehood *without* referring to the 1947 decision.

[20] *Le Monde*, 20 December 1973.

[21] Moscow domestic radio, 7 December 1973, reported without comment Jordanian efforts to work out a common position for Geneva with the PLO; Tass, 9 December 1973, reported, also without comment, the PLO's refusal of a Jordanian proposal for a joint delegation. Moscow did not report a later PLO refusal carried by *Al-Nahar*, 5 May 1974.

[22] Moscow radio in Arabic, 25, 27, 28, 29 April 1974.

[23] Moscow radio in Arabic, 29 May 1974. A specific demand for Palestinian participation in Geneva was not, however, included in the call for Geneva contained in Brezhnev's note to Assad upon the conclusion of the Syrian–Israeli disengagement agreement (*Pravda*, 31 May 1974).

[24] Tass, 3 July 1974.

[25] With the exception of a Moscow radio broadcast to Poland, 19 July 1974.

[26] Moscow radio in Arabic, 20 July 1974.

[27] With the PLO criticism of the Sadat–Hussein communiqué, the Soviet Union ceased her embarrassingly warm response, limiting herself thereafter to descriptions and reports provided by the Arabs, all of which were negative (e.g., Tass, 22, 25 July 1974).

[28] Tass, 3 August 1974.

[29] Criticism of Hussein: *Za rubezhom*, no. 36, 30 August–5 September 1974; Moscow radio in Arabic, 2, 24 September 1974. Criticism of Egypt for her communiqué with

Hussein: Moscow radio in Arabic, 3, 24 September 1974; Radio Peace and Progress, 13, 19 September 1974, and *Za rubezhom*, *op. cit.*

[30] Moscow radio in Arabic, 12 October 1974.

[31] Tass, 18 October 1974.

[32] See *Pravda*, 31 October 1974; Moscow radio in English to Africa, 29 October 1974, even said that Rabat had agreed to PLO representation at Geneva as members of the Jordanian delegation. Tass, 26 October 1974 had the message.

[33] Chabash and Jibril refused at the last minute to participate and called on Iraq, Libya, Algeria, and the People's Democratic Republic of Yemen to reject any programme aimed at a settlement, while Saddam Hussein, as we have seen, opposed the Geneva Peace Conference itself. *Le Monde*, 27–8 October 1974; *Al-Hadaf*, 2 November 1974 (Chabash 25 October press conference); *As-Siyasa*, 31 October 1974.

[34] Gromyko, 6 November; Podgorny, 18 November; and Brezhnev, 26 November 1974.

[35] Tass, 30 November 1974.

[36] Tass, 14 February 1975 (Brezhnev speech). Several Soviet reports at this time claimed that the PLO had agreed to participate: Tass, 24 February 1975 (which cited Khaddumi, though later it ignored a Khaddumi statement to the contrary); *Pravda*, 26 February 1975; Tass, 13 February 1975; *Za rubezhom*, no. 4, 17–22 January 1975, and others.

[37] This might explain Brezhnev's omitting to mention Palestinian participation in his 18 March 1975 speech, despite his earlier (February) reference. (Moscow domestic radio, 18 March 1975.)

[38] *Izvestia* and Radio Peace and Progress in Arabic, 11 March 1975.

[39] *Le Monde*, 22 March 1975. Jibril said he would approve it if Syria renounced SCRS 242 and 338.

[40] Radio Moscow, 2 February 1975; *Pravda*, 4 February 1975.

[41] *Le Monde*, 12 March; *New York Times*, 16 March 1975.

[42] *Le Monde*, 21 March 1975 (reported meeting of Soviet Ambassador with Hawatmeh).

[43] *Pravda*, 5 January 1975 and 14 February 1975; *Izvestia*, 7 January 1975; *Za rubezhom*, no. 10, 28 February–6 March 1975.

[44] *Le Monde*, 12 April 1975; 10 May 1975; *Ha'aretz*, 11 April 1975.

[45] The change began to appear gradually in October 1975.

[46] Presumably Vinogradov's visit to Jordan early December 1975, just after Arafat's Moscow visit, was related to Soviet efforts to reconvene Geneva, possibly still with the idea of some Jordanian–PLO link.

[47] Moscow radio in Arabic, 4 September 1974 (report of Arafat's denial of Chabash charges).

IV. INTERNAL DIFFERENCES IN THE PLO

[1] For example, a Jordanian Communist Party official comment that a reasonable attitude to SCRS 242 and 338 had finally gained ground among the Palestinians – Ashab (*op. cit.* in chapter II, note 20), p. 29 – the treatment in *Izvestia*, 20 July 1974, of the abandonment of the 'all or nothing' principle, and a comment on the PLO's growing maturity – *Aziia i Afrika Sevodnia*, *op. cit.* in chapter III, note 17), p. 7.

[2] Bukharov (*op. cit.* in chapter II, note 21), pp. 12–13.

[3] Vladimirov (*op. cit.* in chapter II, note 41), p. 109. (In what may have reflected a difference of Soviet opinions, an *Izvestia* commentator said on Moscow domestic radio, 17 November 1974, that the PLO had 'a precise, constructive programme'.)

[4] Ignatov (*op. cit.* in chapter II, note 33), pp. 26–31.

[5] Moscow radio in Arabic, 28 November 1974. The last

part did not appear in the Tass version of the interview.
⁶ See, for example, Kudryavtsev articles in *Izvestia*, 12, 15 April 1975.
⁷ See John Cooley, 'The Shifting Sands of Arab Communism', *Problems of Communism*, vol. XXIV, no. 2, 1975, pp. 22–42.
⁸ In 1971 the Soviet Union chastized them for concentrating on the Palestinian problem and thereby risking the sin of 'national tendencies'. ('Special Document', *Journal of Palestine Studies*, vol. II, no. 1, 1972, pp. 187–212.)
⁹ INA, 24 November 1973. For Soviet claim regarding Hawatmeh's 1973 position see Moscow radio in Arabic, 26 February 1975.
¹⁰ *Izvestia*, 30 July 1974.
¹¹ Moscow domestic radio, 28 March 1974. For Soviet response to this action, see section V of this paper.
¹² *Le Monde*, 6 November 1974. For differing analyses of relations between Hawatmeh and the Soviet Union, see 'Correspondence' in *Problems of Communism*, vol. XXIV, no. 5, 1975, p. 87.
¹³ See chapter II, note 16, for the issue of a government-in-exile.
¹⁴ *Izvestia*, 12 April 1975.
¹⁵ Moscow radio in Arabic 19 December 1975.
¹⁶ *Ibid.*
¹⁷ *Pravda*, 2 March 1976 (text of Arafat cable); *Pravda*, 6 March 1976 (text of Hawatmeh cable); *Pravda*, 9 March 1976 (mention of PFLP cable and others). Arafat found himself opposed to a front of Chabash, Jibril *and* Hawatmeh regarding the Syrian plan of July 1976 for Lebanon, although they were all united, with the Soviet Union,

against the Syrian intervention in June 1976.
¹⁸ Moscow radio in Arabic, 3 September 1975; Moscow radio in Arabic, 23 November 1974; *Le Monde*, 22 May 1975.
¹⁹ Bukharov (*op. cit.* in chapter II, note 21), p. 13. Moscow radio in Arabic, 3 September 1975.
²⁰ *Pravda*, 13 April 1974; *Izvestia*, 14 April 1974.
²¹ See also praise for PNF's work in occupied territories, *Izvestia*, 15 April 1975.
²² Regarding elections: *Pravda, Izvestia, Krasnaya zvezda, Trud*, 15 April 1976. *Pravda*, 15 April 1976, and *Izvestia*, 16 April 1974, claimed victory for 'leftist elements who stand for the establishment of an independent state on the West Bank'. This position is that of the PNF (and the Soviet Union) but not, officially, of the PLO as such.
²³ The Refusal Front consists of Chabash's Popular Front for the Liberation of Palestine (PFLP), Jibril's PFLP General Command and the Iraqi-sponsored Arab Liberation Front (ALF) under Ahmad Abd-Avrahim.
²⁴ See, for example, *Al-Hadaf*, 3 August 1974.
²⁵ INA, 20 July 1974.
²⁶ *Al-Nahar*, 18 August 1974. See also *Al-Hadaf*, 3 August 1974 and 28 September 1974.
²⁷ Moscow radio in Arabic, 27 September 1974. *Al-Safir*, a somewhat dubious (Libyan-sponsored) source, claimed on 4 October 1974 that the Soviet Embassy in Beirut was ordered to cease all contact with the PFLP, in support of Arafat.
²⁸ Moscow radio in Arabic, 24 October 1974.
²⁹ Tass, 29 October 1974.
³⁰ *Pravda* and *Krasnaya zvezda*, 7 April 1976.

VI. Terrorism

¹ See, for example, G. Mirski, 'The Arab Peoples Continue the Struggle', *Mirovaya ekonomika a mezhdunarodnye otnoshenie*, no. 3, 1968, pp. 120–25; G. Mirski, 'Israel: Illusions and Miscalculations', *New Times*, no. 39, 1968, pp. 6–8; *Za rubezhom*, no. 26, 6–12 June 1969.
² Moscow radio in English to North America, 25 February 1973; Moscow domestic radio, 11 March 1973; *Pravda*, 4 March 1973; Tass, 7 March 1973; Moscow television, 24 March 1973.
³ Moscow radio in Arabic, 28 November 1972; Tass, 27 November 1972; *Pravda*, 7 January 1973; *Sovetskaya Rosiya*, 18, 25 October 1972; 7 August 1973 (some of these in response to the Munich murders).
⁴ See Golan, 'Internal Differences', 1972.
⁵ *Pravda, Trud, Krasnaya zvezda, Sovetskaya Rosiya, Komsomolskaya Pravda* and others, 19 December 1973.
⁶ Vladimir Terekhov, 'International Terrorism and the Fight Against It', *New Times*, no. 11, 1974, pp. 20–21.
⁷ Moscow radio in Arabic, 23 March 1973.
⁸ Ashhab (*op. cit.* in chapter II, note 20), p. 29.
⁹ Tass, 15 April 1974, said Israeli Arabs were responsible; Moscow radio in Arabic and domestic radio, 15 April 1974, spoke of Palestinian partisans operating from the occupied territories. Radio Peace and Progress in Arabic, 12 April 1974, said fedayeen from the occupied territories were responsible.
¹⁰ Moscow radio in Arabic, 27 April 1974; *Smena* (Czechoslovakia), 4 May 1974 talk with Arafat; Hungarian television interview with Arafat, MENA,

14 May 1974.
¹¹ *Pravda*, 19 May 1974; unsigned, 'The Aggressor's Crimes', *New Times*, no. 21, 1974, p. 17; *Pravda*, 17, 19, 22 May 1974; Tass, 16 May 1974.
¹² Unsigned, *New Times* (*op. cit.* in note 41). Moscow radio in English to North America, 20 May 1974, said: 'The USSR condemns terrorism, believing it can solve no political problem including the problem of the Middle East'.
¹³ *Praca* (Czechoslovakia), 31 May 1974.
¹⁴ Bukharov (*op. cit.* in chapter II, note 21), p. 12. *Izvestia*, 30 July 1974; Tolkunov (*op. cit.* in chapter II, note 34); *Izvestia*, 12, 15 April 1975.
¹⁵ *Izvestia*, 30 July 1974.
¹⁶ Ignatov (*op. cit.* in chapter II, note 33), pp. 26–31.
¹⁷ *Al-Nahar*, 4 November 1974 (interview with Belyaev). The Soviet Union was later to report the PLO's decision to try the terrorists who had hijacked a British plane from Dubai, praising this decision for 'demonstrating the maturity of the Palestine Resistance Movement and its leadership's comprehension of the treacherous role that the extremist elements can play against the just struggle of the Palestinian Arab people'. (Moscow radio in Arabic, 17 December 1974.)
¹⁸ *Al-Nahar*, 7 December 1974. Criticism of Palestinian use of terror also in R. Landa *Aziia i Afrika Sevodnia*, no. 3, 1976, p. 8.
¹⁹ *Pravda*, 5, 10 July 1975; *Izvestia*, 13 July 1976; *Krasnaya zvezda*, 10 July 1976.

168

[1] Tass, 19 September 1972; *Pravda*, 17 October 1972.
[2] Tass, 28 July 1973.
[3] Published in *Pravda* only on 19 October 1973.
[4] *Pravda*, 11, 13 September 1973.
[5] *Le Monde*, 6 November 1973.
[6] Tass, 28, 29 November 1973; *Pravda*, 30 November 1973; Moscow radio in Arabic, 29 November 1973. A Tass report from Algiers, 27 November 1973, had reported the full draft for the resolutions, but a 15 November 1973 broadcast in English (to Africa) even referred to the PLO as one of various Palestinian organizations. The only other resolution ignored by Moscow was the one referring to Jerusalem.
[7] *Trud*, 30 November 1973. Shelepin made the same point the following week in 'The Arab Summit', *New Times*, no. 49, 1973, p. 8.
[8] Belyaev said: 'When the interested parties begin to discuss possible variants of a solution to the problem of the Palestinians during the forthcoming political settlement, they will have to deal with the Palestine Liberation Organization'.
[9] *Pravda*, 29 December 1973. Moscow radio in Arabic on 27 December 1973 did include this point.
[10] Ashhab (*op. cit.* in chapter II, note 20), p. 74.
[11] As well as the one on Jerusalem, Tass, 24 February 1974.
[12] Moscow radio in Arabic, 25, 27 February 1974.
[13] *Al-Ahram*, 6 March 1974; *Al-Nahar*, 8 March 1974.
[14] Moscow radio in Arabic, 6 March 1974.
[15] *Al-Nahar*, 19 March 1974 (Arafat interview); Moscow radio in Arabic, 9 March 1974. Arafat was to make this claim again after a 6 May 1974 meeting with Gromyko in the Middle East, just as he had after the November 1973 visit to Moscow and this March meeting (Voice of Palestine, 8 May 1974).
[16] Moscow radio in Arabic, 23 March 1974; *Novosti*, 28 March 1974; Moscow domestic radio, 29 March 1974; *Pravda*, 23 March 1974; *Izvestia*, 21 March 1974. There was an interesting break in such reporting from 24–27 March – the three days Kissinger was visiting Moscow.
[17] Tass, 3 August 1974.
[18] Arafat later told an interviewer that Ponomarev had told him at this time that the Soviet Union usually opens such offices 'so that they may be turned into embassies' (*Al-Ahram*, 8 November 1974). In fact the Soviet Union did not permit the actual opening of this office until two years later, in June 1976, when they finally approved a PLO official, Mohammed Shayer, to run it (*Pravda*, 12 June 1976).
[19] Voice of Palestine, 24 August 1974.
[20] The Soviet Union praised the statement as a sign of possible Jordanian–PLO co-operation, when in fact it was bitterly rejected by the PLO because it gave Hussein responsibility for a large number of Palestinians.
[21] Moscow domestic radio, 11 October 1974.
[22] *Pravda*, 31 October 1974; Moscow radio in Arabic, 29 October 1974; Radio Peace and Progress in Arabic, 31 October 1974. As we have seen, one Soviet report on this resolution even said that the Palestinians would now be accommodated in a Jordanian delegation for participation in Geneva.
[23] Tass, 30 November 1974.
[24] Tass, 9 November 1975.
[25] Tass, 28 April 1976. One isolated exception was the Soviet–Kuwaiti communiqué (Tass, 5 December 1975), which did give the PLO exclusive rights.

APPENDIXES

Appendix 1: Component Groups of the PLO mentioned in the text

Group	Leader
Al-Fatah	Yassir Arafat
Sai'qa	Zuhair Mohsen
Popular Democratic Front for the Liberation of Palestine (PDFLP)	Nayif Hawatmeh
Palestine National Front	Kerim Halaf
Refusal Front Groups	
Popular Front for the Liberation of Palestine (PFLP)	George Chabash
PFLP General Command	Ahmed Jibril
Arab Liberation Front	Ahmad Abd-Avrahim

Appendix 2: United Nations Resolutions mentioned in the text

SECURITY COUNCIL RESOLUTION 242 (adopted 22 November 1967)

The Security Council,

Expressing its continued concern with the grave situation in the Middle East,

Emphasizing the inadmissibility of the acquisition of territory by war and the need to work for a just and lasting peace in which every state in the area can live in security,

Emphasizing further that all member states in their acceptance of the Charter of the United Nations, have undertaken a commitment to act in accordance with Article 2 of the Charter.

1. Affirms that the fulfilment of charter principles requires the establishment of a just and lasting peace in the Middle East which should include the application of both the following principles:

   (i) Withdrawal of Israeli armed forces from territories occupied in the recent conflict;
   (ii) Termination of all claims of states of belligerency and respect for an acknowledgment of the sovereignty, territorial integrity, and political independence of every state in the area and their right to live in peace within secure and recognized boundaries free from threats of acts of force.

2. Affirms further the necessity
   (a) For guaranteeing freedom of navigation through international waterways in the area;
   (b) For achieving a just settlement of the refugee problem;
   (c) For guaranteeing the territorial inviolability and political independence of every state in the area, through measures including the establishment of demilitarized zones.

3. Requests the Secretary-General to designate a Special Representative to proceed to the Middle East to establish and maintain contacts with the States concerned in order to promote agreement and assist efforts to achieve a peaceful and accepted settlement in accordance with the provisions and principles in this resolution.

4. Requests the Secretary-General to report to the Security Council on the progress of the efforts of the Special Representative as soon as possible.

SECURITY COUNCIL RESOLUTION 338 (adopted 22 October 1973)

The Security Council

1. Calls upon all parties to the present fighting to cease all firing and terminate all military activity immediately, no later than 12 hours after the moment of the adoption of this decision, in the positions they now occupy;

2. Calls upon the parties concerned to start immediately after the cease-fire the implementation of Security Council resolution 242 (1967) in all of its parts;

3. Decides that immediately and concurrently with the cease-fire, negotiations start between the parties concerned under appropriate auspices aimed at establishing a just and durable peace in the Middle East.

GENERAL ASSEMBLY RESOLUTION 3236 (adopted 22 November 1974)

The General Assembly, having considered the question of Palestine, having heard the statement of the Palestine Liberation Organization, the representative of the people of Palestine,

Having also heard other statements made during the debate,

Deeply concerned that no just solution to the problem of Palestine has yet been achieved and recognizing that the problem of Palestine continues to endanger international peace and security,

Recognizing that the Palestinian people is entitled to self-determination in accordance with the Charter of the United Nations,

Expressing its grave concern that the Palestinian people has been prevented from enjoying its inalienable rights, and in particular its right to self-determination,

Guided by the purposes and principles of the Charter,

Recalling its relevant resolutions which affirm the right of the Palestinian people to self-determination,

1. Reaffirms the inalienable right of the Palestinian people in Palestine, including:

   (a) The right to self-determination without external interference;
   (b) The right to national independence and sovereignty;

2. Reaffirms also the inalienable right of the Palestinians to return to their homes and property from which they have been displaced and uprooted, and calls for their return;

3. Emphasizes that full respect for and the realization of these inalienable rights of the Palestinian people are indispensable for the solution of the question of Palestine;

4. Recognizes that the Palestinian people is a principal party in the establishment of a just and durable peace in the Middle East;

5. Further recognizes the right of the Palestinian people to regain its rights by all means in accordance with the purposes and principles of the charter of the United Nations;

6. Appeals to all states and international organizations to extend their support to the Palestinian people in its struggle to restore its rights, in accordance with the charter;

7. Requests the Secretary-General to establish contacts with the Palestine Liberation Organization on all matters concerning the question of Palestine;

8. Requests the Secretary-General to report to the General Assembly at its thirtieth session on the implementation of the present resolution;

9. Decides to include the item entitled 'Question of Palestine' in the provisional agenda of its thirtieth session.

INDEX

Islam:
  revival in Iran, 97
  stability in Middle East, 102
Ismail, Hafiz, 67, 68
Israel:
  air force baits Syrian air force September
    1973, 70
  alliance with Lebanese Christians, 117
  American peace proposals 1978, 128-9
  arms purchase by, 20, 34
  besieged Egyptian troops after October
    war, 76
  blockade of Straits of Tiran, 47, 49-51
  Camp David talks, 121-23, 125-7
  canal war, 56-67, 93
  challenge to Soviet Union, 65
  dependence on Iranian oil, 110
  dependence on US, 13, 18, 30, 39
  disillusioned with UN, 46
  effect of 1973 war on, 13-4, 18-9
  Egyptian peace moves of 1978, 120
  extent of military superiority, 13
  IAF superiority 1969, 58
  IDF attack on Es Samu, 46
  IDF casualties October 1968, 57
  IDF success December 1969, 59
  and Israeli Arabs, 127
  invades Lebanon, 117, 125
  on Jarring, 64
  and Jordan, 134
  in June war, 52-4
  and Kissinger negotiations, 73-82
  and Lebanon civil war, 117
  lessons of October war, 86-7
  loss of forces in October war, 29
  misinterpretation of events prior to
    October war, 68-9
  and Nasser's moves of 1967, 51
  negotiations of 1978, 120-1
  negotiating strategy of, 63
  nuclear attack vulnerability of, 31
  and nuclear weapons, 31
  oil from US, 85, 87
  on PLO, 131, 133
  on Palestine, 120, 122, 128, 131, 133-6,
    136-7
  on Palestinian rights, 122, 145
  population of, 127
  rebuilding of military forces, 20

relations with US, 77, 122-123
Second Rogers Peace Plan, 63
settlements in Sinai, 126
settlements in West Bank, 122-123, 125,
  133
significance of Arab oil embargo for, 87
and Sinai oil fields, 123
Soviet Union breaks off diplomatic relations with, 52
Soviet Union on boundaries of, 142-5
state of economy in 1978 in, 127
support for Ethiopia, 116
Syrian disengagement talks, 149-50
Syrian water diversion programme destroyed by, 45
and Third Rogers Peace Plan, 64-5
on UN, 46, 80n
US pressure on, 17, 62, 80-1, 83, 122,
  123
and US sponsored peace initiative, 17-20,
  130-1
US support for, 4, 13, 16, 20, 21, 30, 34,
  39, 50, 90, 134, 135
water diversion programme of, 45
see also Arab-Israeli wars

Jadid, General Salah, 46
Japan: and control of Gulf, 40
Jarring, Gunnar, UN Special Representa-
  tive, 60
Jarring Mission, 21, 60, 67
Jerusalem:
  Begin's plans for development of, 126
  Camp David omitted discussion of, 122
  future of, 9
  Israeli refusal to talk about, 18
  Saudi Arabia's support of Camp David
    talks threatened by Israeli jurisdiction
    over, 115
  Soviet Union on, 146
  UNESCO denounces Israeli jurisdiction
    of, 78
Johnson, President Lyndon: n
  blockade of Straits of Tiran, 50
  canal war, 56
  June war, 54
Joint Soviet-American Declaration on the
  Middle East, 1 October 1977, 93

government of saved by combined action of US and Soviet Union, 55
and Iraq reconciled, 113, 115
Israeli disengagement talks, 149-50
and Israeli invasion of Lebanon, 117
and Israeli right to exist, 56, 140, 142
and Jordan, 117
and Kissinger's peace proposals, 149
and Lebanese civil war, 117
Left-Ba'athist coup February 1966, 45
military delegation to Moscow 1967, 46
military forces rebuilt, 20
note to UN Security Council April 1967, 47
and October war, 69
split with PLO, 152
support for PLO, 117, 149, 152
on Palestine, 15, 129, 140
Soviet aid to, 5, 20, 45, 80, 89, 90, 94, 117, 149
Soviet influence in, 5, 9, 17, 90, 140
Soviet refusal to supply missiles to 1967, 46
in Soviet view of Palestinian state, 146
US influence in, 5
and use of terrorism, 46, 70
water diversion programme of, 45

terrorism, use of:
Al-Fatah on, 46
and Arab unity, 46
by Arabs, 45, 46, 47
by Israel, 45
by PLO, 125, 139, 153, 155. 156-9
by Palestinians, 128
Soviet Union on, 139, 153, 155, 156-9, 162
Thant, U., see U Thant
Third World:
Arab economic aid to, 26
and price of oil, 26
Soviet Union and, 45
Tiran Straits:
blockade 1967, 47, 49-51
strategic value of, 30-1
Tripartite Declaration 1950: 37, 38
Turkey:
dispute with Greece, 35
implications of revolution in Iran for, 105

and Soviet Union, 5

UAC (United Arab Command):
formation of, 46
Jordan joins, 47
and October war, 69
UN (United Nations):
and blockade of Straits of Tiran, 50, 51
and Canal war, 56
and defence of Israel's interests, 46
Egypt and forces of in 1966-67, 46
and June war, 52-54
peacekeeping force to supervise ceasefire after October war, 76
note to Security Council April 1967 from Syria, 47
withdrawal of UNEF from Egypt, 47
UNEF (United Nations Emergency Force):
in 1975 disengagement agreement, 84
dismantled, 55
mandate for in Golan Heights, 78, 84
withdrawal from Egypt, 46, 47
UNESCO (United Nations Educational, Scientific and Cultural Organization):
denounces Israel for ruling Jerusalem, 78
UNIFIL (United Nations Interim Force in Lebanon), 117, 125
U Thant:
blockade of Straits of Tiran, 50
withdrawal of UNEF from Egypt, 47
United States:
acceptability of as mediator, 8-9, 16-7
and Arab countries relationships. 16-7, 79-80, 86, 121
reaction to Arab-Israeli conflict, 6-8, 44-88
arms to Israel, 20, 34, 66
arms sales to Middle East, 34, 35
blockade of Straits of Tiran, 49-51
Canal war, 56-67, 90
diplomacy in Middle East, 8-9, 17, 93
and Egypt, 64-5, 89
fighters to Egypt, 121
Geneva Peace Conference, 86
history as superpower, 4
and Iran, 27, 100-1, 107-9, 111
guarantees to Israel threatened by Arab action, 48, 49, 50, 66
pressure on Israel, 17, 62, 80-1, 121, 123

reaction to Israeli violations of ceasefire, 75

relations with Israel, 80, 112-3

support for Israel, 4, 13, 16, 20, 21, 30, 39, 50, 90, 134, 135

and June war, 53-4

military intervention possible in 1967, 48-9

military lessons of October war for, 31

nuclear power plant sales to Middle East, 35

and October war, 76-85, 85-6

oil for Israel, 85, 87, 200

and PLO, 93

and Palestine, 15, 18, 128, 135-6

and control of Persian Gulf, 40

policy in Middle East, 5, 16-7

fighters to Saudi-Arabia, 121

support for Saudi-Arabia, 5, 114-5

and Soviet support for Egypt in Canal war, 59, 60-1, 63-4

and Soviet warning of impending hostilities, 70-1

special relationship with Soviet Union, 4-12

and Syria, 55

and Tripartite Declaration 1950, 37

and UN troops in Syria, 78, 79

see also Kissinger, Henry; Rogers Peace Plans

'War of Attrition', 30, 56-67, 90

water diversion:
  by Israel, 48
  by Syria, 48

West Bank:
  Begin on settlement of, 125-6
  economic development of, 132
  Israel on Palestinian state in, 18

West Germany: arms to Syria, 117

YAR (Yemen Arab Republic)
  see North Yemen

zionism: questioned after 1973 war, 17